Sexual
Stratification

Sexual Stratification

A CROSS-CULTURAL VIEW

ALICE SCHLEGEL, EDITOR

Columbia University Press—New York—1977

Columbia University Press
New York and Guildford, Surrey

Printed in the United States of America

Library of Congress Cataloging in Publication Data
Main entry under title:

Sexual stratification.

    Includes bibliographies and index.
    1. Sex role.   2. Women—Social conditions.
I. Schlegel, Alice.
GN479.7.S48   301.41   77-2742
ISBN 0–231–04214–0
ISBN 0–231–04215–9 pbk.

To My Son

Preface

THIS BOOK REPRESENTS an attempt to pull together many threads in the discussions about sexual status. The contributors, anthropologists and scholars from other disciplines, were invited to write papers representing points of view and illustrative cases that I believed needed expression and elaboration. In the process of working with the empirical data, I found my own ideas sharpening and shifting, away from the evolutionary paradigm that encompasses so much anthropological thinking toward a more precise perspective of social and historical forces contributing to the status location of females and males. A collection such as this owes as much to its contributors as to its originator, and I am happy to acknowledge the debt. Each contribution has left its mark on my own thinking—but only I am responsible for any errors of interpretation.

I owe special thanks to several people, and I take this opportunity to make that public. Constance Sutton and Leonard Pearlin graciously gave of their time and knowledge to the writing of the first paper, and their thinking has left its mark on my own. Amy Masters prepared the index with care and good humor. My colleague John M. Roberts listened patiently. And finally, I owe thanks to my son, James Biery. As a companion in much of my field research, he provided me with insights into the ideas and activities of Hopi men and boys, insights which take on broader meaning in cross-cultural contexts. By watching him grow into young adulthood, I have learned much about the development and assumption of male roles and attitudes in our society, and now we talk together about them. It is for these reasons that I dedicate this book to him.

Introduction

THIS BOOK DEALS with one aspect of the relation between the sexes, equality and inequality. It is an attempt to move toward a theory of sexual stratification, the need for which is increasingly felt as the wave of studies on sex status and roles grows, and as these studies become increasingly sophisticated in theory and method. The papers in this collection were selected to illustrate social settings of sexual equality or inequality and the conditions under which they arise.

The first chapter treats the problem of sexual stratification analytically: it asks about the meaning and assessment of sexual stratification, and it suggests lines of investigation into the determinants of sexual status. The papers that follow deal with women's roles in domestic and public relations, in economic, political, and ceremonial spheres of activities, and in affective and symbolic systems of meaning. They have been arranged in a rather loose sequence, with the more male-dominant societies presented first and the more egalitarian societies presented last. Between these identifiable types are placed those papers dealing with societies that are neither strongly male-dominant nor notably egalitarian, societies in which changing conditions have either enhanced or undermined the decision-making powers of women in their domestic or public relations.

This ordering is not to be construed as a typology: in most of the societies discussed here, the interplay of spheres in which one sex or the other is dominant is complex and does not permit us to make simple ascriptions. What we find is that even in the more male-dominant societies, women do not simply accept or adjust to a subordinate status, but may strive to check male dominance in some way, thereby achieving a measure of autonomy for themselves. And in the more egalitarian societies, the relation between males and females is not characterized by the independence of one sex or the other but rather by a necessary interdependence of equals.

Few would argue that the three societies examined first—Morocco, Sicily, and India—are sexually stratified in ideology and in practice. In each case, the authors discuss the stragegies that women employ to circumvent the effects of male dominance or the existential conditions that ameliorate it. Neither in Sicily (Cronin) nor among the lower-caste Indians (Ullrich) are men fully able to implement the ideal of male authority; and in Morocco (Dwyer), the 'arifa acts as a broker between the male and female domains, often to women's advantage. In sexually stratified southern Bantu societies (O'Brien), the superordinate status of royalty or chief and the subordinate status of wife are incompatible, so that queens must be husbands rather than wives.

The next three papers deal with African societies in which male dominance is qualified. In Sudan (Fluehr-Lobban), traditional male dominance is increasingly called into question by the activities of the Women's Union. Although most Yoruba political leaders are male (Awe), the women do have representation at the highest level, the king's council, through their leader the Iyalode. Men in Ivory Coast (Lewis) have greater access to resources than do women, but women use the economic opportunities they do have to advance their positions in the home, among their kin, and in their social networks.

In contrast to Sudan, where changes away from traditional patterns are raising the status of women, much of Africa has experienced a lowering of women's status and autonomy because of changes in modes of production introduced by participation in the colonial market system and continued since the end of co-lonialism. Smock discusses this process in Ghana.

Denich's paper on Yugoslavia deals with a society in which women are fully engaged in industrial production. Since World War II, industrialization and a new ideology of female equality have broken down the ideal of the patriarchal family and the domestic wife. New opportunities have opened, but social arrangements do not always permit women to take full advantage of them.

In the remaining societies discussed in this book, an ideology of sexual stratification is absent and women have the means to activate their equal status. Complementarity of sex-role characterizes the Hopi (Schlegel) where, if anything, women are more highly valued than men. Cooperation and a lack of separation of the sexes is given by Bacdayan as the basis for sexual equality among the Bontoc. Within the plantation system of slavery that operated on Barbados (Sutton and Makiesky-Barrow), there was no basis for sexual stratification, nor has one arisen since that system was abolished. Finally, the ideology and movement toward sexual equality in the Israeli kibbutz is examined by Datan and is contrasted with stratification in the Arab village that exists within the same ecologicial setting.

These societies, then, illustrate the range of sexual stratification, from male dominance to sexual equality. The concluding chapter of this book discusses the papers in light of the theoretical issues they illuminate, and attempts to summarize their findings and the questions they raise.

Contents

Introduction   ix

Contributors   xv

1—Toward a Theory of Sexual Stratification
    ALICE SCHLEGEL   1

2—Bridging the Gap between the Sexes in Moroccan Legal
    Practice
    DAISY HILSE DWYER   41

3—Illusion and Reality in Sicily
    CONSTANCE CRONIN   67

4—Caste Differences between Brahmin and Non-Brahmin
    Women in a South Indian Village
    HELEN E. ULLRICH   94

5—Female Husbands in Southern Bantu Societies
    DENISE O'BRIEN   109

6—Agitation for Change in the Sudan
    CAROLYN FLUEHR-LOBBAN   127

7—The Iyalode in the Traditional Yoruba Political System
    BOLANLE AWE   144

8—Economic Activity and Marriage among Ivoirian Urban
    Women
    BARBARA C. LEWIS   161
9—The Impact of Modernization on Women's Position in the
    Family in Ghana
    AUDREY CHAPMAN SMOCK   192
10—Women, Work, and Power in Modern Yugoslavia
    BETTE DENICH   215
11—Male and Female in Hopi Thought and Action
    ALICE SCHLEGEL   245
12—Mechanistic Cooperation and Sexual Equality among the
    Western Bontoc
    ALBERT S. BACDAYAN   270
13—Social Inequality and Sexual Status in Barbados
    CONSTANCE SUTTON AND
    SUSAN MAKIESKY-BARROW   292
14—Ecological Antecedents and Sex-Role Consequences in
    Traditional and Modern Israeli Subcultures
    NANCY DATAN   326
15—An Overview
    ALICE SCHLEGEL   344

Index of Names   359
Subject Index   364

Contributors

Bolanle Awe was trained as an historian at University of St. Andrews, Scotland, and Somerville College, Oxford University, where she received her D. Phil. Oxon. She has taught history at the University of Ibadan and the University of Lagos. Until recently, she was a Senior Research Fellow in African Oral History with special reference to the Yoruba at the Institute of African Studies, University of Ibadan. As commissioner of Education for Oyo State, Nigeria, she is a member of that state cabinet.

Albert Somebang Bacdayan is a native of Bangaan, Sagada, Mountain Province, the Philippines. He received his Ph. D. in Anthropology from Cornell University, and has been an Andrew W. Mellon Postdoctoral Fellow at the University of Pittsburgh and Visiting Fellow in the Southeast Asia Program at Cornell University. Currently an Associate Professor of Anthropology at the University of Kentucky, his areas of interest include social and political anthropology, social change, and Southeast Asian ethnology and history.

Constance Cronin, Associate Professor of Anthropology at the University of Arizona, received her Ph. D. in Anthropology from the University of Chicago. She has worked with Italians in Italy, and subsequently with Sicilian immigrants in Australia, in an effort to probe new ways of studying social change. She is currently analyzing data, collected in Iran during a field stay of one and a half years, pertaining to social mobility during the nineteenth and twentieth centuries.

Nancy Datan received her graduate degrees from the Committee on Human Development at the University of Chicago and is now Associate Professor of Psychology at West Virginia University. She spent ten years as a permanent resident of the State of Israel and has done extensive field research in that country. Her research interests lie in comparative studies of personality and socialization, and the focus of her research in Israel was the cultural determination of the responses of women in five ethnic groups to the transitions of middle age.

Bette Denich is an anthropologist whose interests include feminist theory and the trends of contemporary American culture. Her field research has been on economic development in Yugoslavia, and she is moving into the study of the local-level politics of regional planning in the United States. She received her Ph. D. in Anthropology from the University of California at Berkeley, spent several years on the faculty of Barnard College and Columbia University, and is presently Adjunct Associate Professor at the State University of New York at Albany.

Daisy Hilse Dwyer received her Ph. D. in Anthropology from Yale University and is at present an Assistant Professor of Anthropology at Columbia University. Her field area is the Middle East, in particular Morocco, where she did her fieldwork. Her theoretical interests concern law, politics, and belief; a current interest is in ideology as a mechanism of social control in male-female relations.

Caroline Fluehr-Lobban, an Assistant Professor of Anthropology at Rhode Island College, received her Ph. D. in Anthropology from Northwestern University. During her fieldwork in Khartoum, Sudan, she concentrated on cultural interpretations of male and female homicide and the participation of women in the Islamic courts in Khartoum and Omdurman.

Barbara C. Lewis received her Ph. D. in Political Science from Northwestern University and is an Associate Professor of Political Science at Rutgers University. Her dissertation research was done on the Transporters' Association of Ivory Coast, and she subsequently studied rotating credit associations and political organization among Abidjan market women. She maintains a continuing interest in political responses to economic and employment conditions among social strata and the effects of governmental planning and policy upon these strata.

Susan Makiesky-Barrow received her Ph. D. in Anthropology from Brandeis University. She has taught at New York University and at the University of the West Indies, and is presently Senior Research Scientist in the Biometrics Research Unit, New York State Psychiatric Institute. Her field research was on social and political change in Antigua and Barbados, and her research interests include the Caribbean, social inequality and culture, and sex roles.

Denise O'Brien, Chairman of the Department of Anthropology at Temple University, received her Ph. D. in Anthropology from Yale University, She did fieldwork among the Konda Valley Dani of Highland Irian Jaya (West New

Guinea) in 1961–63 and returned for a brief restudy in 1976. She is currently working on a life history of George Peter Murdock.

Alice Schlegel, an Associate Professor at the University of Pittsburgh, received her Ph. D. in Anthropology from Northwestern University. She conducts continuing field research among the Hopi Indians. She is presently engaged in a cross-cultural survey of adolescent socialization, one of its goals being to learn about socialization for adult sex roles.

Audrey C. Smock is currently Visiting Senior Research Fellow at the Institute for Development Studies of the University of Nairobi. Since receiving her Ph. D. in Political Science from Columbia University, she has held a variety of academic and foundation appointments in the United States, Ghana, Lebanon, and Kenya. She is now completing a five-country study of the relationship between women's opportunities for education and employment in Kenya.

Constance R. Sutton received her Ph. D. in Anthropology from Columbia University and is an Associate Professor of Anthropology at New York University. Her fieldwork has been primarily in the Afro-Caribbean region, where she has conducted several studies of plantation workers. She is currently conducting research on male and female models of power and inequality among the Yoruba of Nigeria. Her research interests include sexual stratification and ideology, migration, and ethnicity.

Helen E. Ullrich, at present a Research Scientist in the Department of Oriental and African Languages and Literatures at the University of Texas at Austin, earned her Ph. D. in

Linguistics at the University of Michigan. Her field research has been conducted principally in Karnataka State, India. Her most recent work has been on changing marriage patterns in a South Indian caste.

ALICE SCHLEGEL

Toward a Theory
1 of Sexual
Stratification

A S THE NUMBER of studies on sex roles and sexual status
increases, it is becoming increasingly apparent that a theory
of sexual stratification is needed to give coherence and meaning
to the kinds of problems that are being posed and the questions
that are being asked.

Those of us concerned with developing theory in this field
have little to guide us. Unlike so many areas of anthropological
concern, there is no single body of theory to draw on. The field of
culture and personality was an extension of research in analytic
psychology that was theoretically well developed before it entered
the anthropological mainstream. Similarly, theoretical outlines for
research into social organization, including social stratification,
had been established by eighteenth- and nineteenth-century investigators into the social and economic structure of the family,
the community, and the state. In contrast to these areas of work,
we find ourselves facing the task of creating a theoretical framework for our research. We are able to draw upon a multitude of
findings in the fields of social structure, economic organization,
cognitive psychology, symbolic analysis, and primate behavior.
But at present we are far from a unified theory of sexual inequality.

There is a reason for this. The recent surge of anthropological
writings on women began in the 1960s, not as a logical outgrowth
of theory developed within anthropology or related disciplines but

rather as a response to social and ideological factors that questioned the moral defensibility of systematic inequality, that is, inequality built into social relations. For most of us working in this field, our studies are two-pronged: we ask not only how equality and inequality came to be, but also how the identification of the critical determinants can provide the knowledge needed for initiating change.

This is not to say that anthropologists have only recently shown an interest in sex roles. However, leaving aside the turn-of-the-century speculations about primordial matriarchy, the majority of the earlier accounts of female roles and behavior have been incidental to a predominant concern with economic, political, social, or religious activities generally directed by men. One gets the impression from many ethnographies that culture is created by and for men between the ages of puberty and late middle age, with children, women, and the aged as residual categories; women are frequently portrayed, at best, as providing support for the activities of men. Noteworthy early exceptions are Mason's *Women's Share in Primitive Culture* (1894) and Parsons' *The Old Fashioned Woman; Primitive Fancies About the Sex* (1913). Among rather more recent authors, Mead's work is perhaps the most significant: in *Sex and Temperament* (1935), she demonstrated the variability among cultures in the ascription of personality features by sex, and in *Male and Female* (1949), she dealt with the biological and psychological bases of sex roles. The works by Landes on Ojibwa women (1938) and Kaberry on Australian Aboriginal women (1939) have also become classics in the documentation of women's activities and behavior.

Although none of these writings deals directly with sexual stratification, they do provide some useful insights into the problem. An early statement on this question was made by Engels (first edition 1891), whose theory had been largely ignored by anthropologists until very recently. We shall examine Engels' theory and its contemporary formulations in a later section of this paper.

The discussion that follows will deal with the problem of sexual equality and inequality. I shall look at the dimensions of sexual stratification, discuss contemporary theories of sexual inequality, and ask how sexual rank can be assessed and determined.

What Is Sexual Stratification?

Debates on the definition of social stratification have generally focused on three dimensions of social relations: relations of rewards, relations of prestige, and relations of power. Hierarchical arrangements exist within each of these dimensions when access to rewards, prestige, or power is differentiated in a systematic way. That is, when there are sets of statuses and roles that are characteristically accompanied by greater rewards, prestige, or power than others, and when movement between one set into another is restricted, inequality exists. By this definition, I exclude from inequality differential prestige awarded to different age categories, because in a normal lifetime everyone passes through each stage. I also exclude the greater material rewards of the successful versus the unsuccessful peasant or hunter, for example, and whatever difference in power within the community may accrue to each, if success depends upon vagaries of intelligence, persistence, luck, and so on. If, however, certain categories of peasants always receive fewer rewards (serfs versus freeholders, for instance), or one category of men in an agricultural society has greater access to material goods or power than do others, I consider this to be systematic inequality. When such systematic social inequality differentiates men and women, the condition is one of sexual inequality.

The distinction is generally made in studies of social organization between inegalitarian and stratified societies, the latter, like ranked societies, being one type of the former. This distinction will not be made in this volume, although as the theory of sexual inequality becomes more refined, it may prove useful to initiate it. For example, we might want to call societies in which women are by law or custom excluded from major decision-making positions sexually *stratified* societies, reserving the term sexually *inegali-*

tarian for those societies in which women are not automatically excluded from major decision-making positions but in which organizational features such as family or community organization, or patterns of socialization for sex roles, effectively exclude women from recruitment to these roles to the same degree as men. An example of the former in this volume would be Morocco; an example of the latter would be contemporary Yugoslavia.

Systematic social inequality can exist even when the movement of individuals between ranked categories is possible; that is, there is a difference between movement of individuals between categories and the durability of the categories themselves. This is obvious in the case of the class system, where social mobility is one of the defining features of this type of hierarchical societal arrangement. More to the point of this discussion, movement between gender categories is also possible in some societies, a good example being the berdache (Jacobs 1968) and the "manly hearted women" (Lewis 1941) of North American Indians, among whom sexual inequality is generally somewhat muted when it does exist (see Schlegel 1972). Even markedly sexually inegalitarian societies may allow for gender status transfer: speaking of medieval Muslim female prophets, Levy (1962, p. 132) quotes one authority who states that "a woman on the path of God becomes a man." More dramatically, the Abkhaz woman who renounced her conventional female role and took on the clothing and behavior of men was considered a man, albeit inferior to men who were born male (Dzhanashvili 1894). A rather more limited instance of cross-sex role assumption is the case of the African female husband, discussed by O'Brien in this volume. For none of these peoples do role transfers appear to involve homosexuality (with some exceptions in the case of the berdache); rather, they are movements into social categories distinguished by gender. It is important to recognize the difference between movement into the opposite gender category, on the one hand, and access to roles open to both sexes even when one sex predominates, on the other.

In recent years there has been considerable discussion about the relationship between social stratification, that is, a social class system, and sexual inequality. While it is true that most classless foraging societies appear to be more sexually egalitarian than many other more complex societies, and socially stratified societies as we know them tend to be sexually inegalitarian, the data do not support a simple or direct correlation. Classless societies at the "middle range" of complexity—horticultural, herding, or fishing societies—can go in either direction. (For a discussion of male dominance and sexual equality in domestic arrangements, see Schlegel 1972.) And in looking at European stratified societies over the past 100 years, we see real gains, however slowly and painfully made, in avenues of participation and achievement open to women.

Rewards, Prestige, and Power:
The Dimensions of
Sexual Stratification

One of the major difficulties in defining sexual stratification has been to disentangle the three dimensions of sexual rank. It is not unusual, for example, to read in ethnographic accounts that women who are confined to domestic activities having little bearing on community economic or political life may nevertheless be highly valued and have great influence on their sons. Or that women can sometimes amass more property than their male kin, yet they are expected to defer to them. Or again, that the relations between the sexes are open and unmarked by unidirectional deference, yet women have no voice in community decision making. Let us look at each of the three dimensions.

Rewards

Inequality in material rewards for labor characterizes complex societies, in which the division of labor encompasses more than age and sex differentiation. Simple societies, in which the division of labor beyond age and sex is minimal, generally reward highly valued social roles with prestige rather than material goods. In rather more complex traditional societies, those with some occupational specialization, inequality in reward is possible but is usually mitigated by leveling devices, such as redistribution of goods through the political or religious system. Systematic and persistent differences of reward, where classes of people receive rewards of differential value, is found in complex societies that produce for the market; and it is here that wealth, or the accumulation of property, may insure long-term distributions in reward. Even in such societies, leveling devices may exist within classes, as in the cargo system in Latin American peasant communities. This, however, does not mitigate differences between classes, such as between these Latin American peasants and the occupational elite or large landowners, whose economic power at the national level far exceeds that of the peasants.

When men and women work together as a corporate unit of production, as does the family in so many societies, there is little or no differentiation in reward between the sexes: whatever comes in is pooled within the unit, although control over the use of goods may lie with one sex rather than the other. The question of differential reward between the sexes arises when individuals rather than composite units control marketable skills or property; and it is here that the distinction between male skills or property, on the one hand, and female skills and property, on the other, can become critical in determining which sex, if either, receives greater rewards. The same problem arises when men and women are permitted to practice the same skills or own the same kind of property, but access to training or to means of production is differentiated by sex. Among the Tuareg, for example, women can own camels and can even build up sizable herds in their own name; but since inheritance rules favor sons, men are more likely to be materially rewarded than are women (Nicolaisen 1963). In industrial societies today, there are pressures to give more highly rewarded tasks to men, and women are socialized to accept this, even in societies ideologically opposed to female subordination (for the case of Israel, see Kanter 1976).

The issue of differential reward is muddied by that fact that most people live in mixed-sex families, so that whatever one sex brings in is generally shared with the other, although the degree to which sharing occurs may vary from society to society. Lewis, in this volume, describes a case in which there is relatively little sharing of rewards. In considering the differences between social classes, reward and property ownership per se is important because income determines features of life-style that distinguish one class from another. This is not so between the sexes: rather, reward only becomes important to the degree to which it can be translated into prestige or power.

Prestige

Prestige can be measured behaviorally by the amount of deference granted an individual, a role, or a category. Here the concern is not with individual prestige: I assume that in any society there will be persons of both sexes who are deferred to, generally or within specific settings, by others. The concern is rather with systematic prestige—whether prestige is granted to social roles, either generally or within specific settings, and the degree to which men or women occupy these roles; and whether prestige is granted generally to one sex by the other.

When we consider evaluation, we cannot assume that a highly valued role will necessarily grant prestige to one who holds it. Motherhood, open only to women, may be highly valued by both men and women without women necessarily receiving prestige as mothers. In patriarchal societies, for example, women may be valued as mothers because they are the channels through which men reproduce themselves; women become objects of genetic and social transmission. (Slaves may also be valued as objects of economic production.) If one takes the Lévi-Straussian position that women are the means by which social bonds are created through marital exchange, then women are indeed necessary and valued objects, but objects nevertheless. An object may be valued, but one does not grant it prestige; prestige goes only to those who own or control valued objects. Thus, when assessing the status of women in a society, it is not enough to know that women are valued; rather, we must ask whether they are valued in their own right, and therefore are in a position to receive prestige, or whether they are valued as objects in the social, political, or economic affairs of men.

Power

In discussions about the relative position of the sexes, two terms that frequently arise are *dominance* and *subordination.* Thus, there is already a precedent for framing the problem of inequality in terms of differential control of one sex by the other. The concern here is with the differential power objectively present in social relations; we are not concerned with beliefs about the latent or feared power of women, which are often expressed in ritual, myths, or notions about female witchcraft or other covert antisocial behavior in male-dominant societies (Murphy and Murphy 1974; Harper 1969), even though such beliefs will feed into the relations between the sexes.

From my point of view, the status of men and women within the dimension of power derives from their ability to control their own persons and activities and the persons and activities of others. Thus, if men control the persons and activities of women to a greater degree than women control the persons and activities of men, men are dominant. Where neither sex controls the other—a situation one is likely to find in societies where male and females either have equal control in all spheres, or where spheres of control are different but balanced—we can speak of sexually egalitarian societies.

Sexual inequality or equality in the power dimension are not simple univariate phenomena but rather composite phenomena of power, authority, and autonomy, operating within social spheres. By power, I mean the ability to exert control, whatever the means to this control may be within the domestic, political, economic, or religious spheres. Authority is one form of power; it is the socially recognized and legitimated right to make decisions concerning others. (The interplay of authority and power achieved by other means, which may modify or override authority, is the subject of much discussion about social or sexual politics.) By autonomy, I mean freedom from control by others. These variables must be taken into account in assessing equality or inequality: indeed, they are the means by which this dimension is measured. For each of these measures of control we must ask several questions. First, in what spheres and under what conditions are women or men in control of their own persons, activities, and products of their labor, and the persons, activities, and products of labor of the other sex? Women may have considerable control over their own lives without necessarily having much control over the lives of men; that is, both sexes may have a large measure of autonomy. Second, how do areas of female control compare with areas of male control—is one subsumed by the other, or do they exist in balance? The paper on the Hopi in this volume discusses a society in which spheres of decision making are different for men and women, but neither is subordinate to the other. Third, do areas controlled by women include institutions that are central to social organization? For example, women may control household decisions, but this will give them little voice in societal decisions if the household is peripheral to the greater arena within which major political decisions are made. On the other hand, if women fill important decision-making roles in the economic, political, or religious systems, or if the household is a central institution, their impact on major societal decisions may be very great.

We have examined the three dimensions along which the relative status of men and women can be measured. I see the power dimension as the critical one, although the other two cannot be left out of consideration. What we might expect to find in most societies is that power and authority are highly correlated as either causal or consequential features with reward and prestige, although we must be careful to note and analyze the exceptions.

I turn now to a consideration of current theories of sexual inequality. This discussion goes beyond a review of thinking in this critical area; it sets the background for my own views of what a coherent and useful theory of sexual stratification involves.

ask is not "who produces for what?" but rather "who controls the product of labor and how is the product used in forming social relationships?" Social power, as expressed in relations of dominance and submission, is not a relation of person to goods but rather a relation of person to person, for which goods may provide the material basis.

Sacks (1974), in a more recent reinterpretation of Engels, does not agree that private property in class societies is the determining factor in sexual stratification. She looks, rather, at political power that results from the ability to give and receive goods in exchange. This theoretical perspective has the advantage of allowing for sexual stratification in nonclass societies. She ties her argument to the concept of social labor: "any work done (singly or as part of a group) for use or appropriation by someone of another household" (p. 212). Where women are equally involved in social labor, they have adult social status and can participate in decision making and dispute settlement. The more removed women are from involvement in social labor, the less they are considered to be social adults and the less power they exert. The most extreme forms of female subordination, therefore, are found in class societies, where male labor is expropriated by the ruling class and women are relegated to domestic production. This theory also fails to distinguish between participation in production and control over labor and goods.

Sanday (1974) achieves something that neither Leacock nor Sacks do: she measures female status by devising a scale of female participation and control within different areas. Her theory of female status is encapsulated in a flow chart (p. 197) in which she relates variations in status to the degree to which men and women participate in activities of reproduction, warfare, and subsistence. The critical factor determining equality, according to her theory, is a balanced division of labor in production (p. 205). Thus she finds that both in societies in which women make a low contribution to subsistence and in those in which they make a high contribution, women are subordinate. There is some confusion here between contribution to subsistence and contribution to production, which includes production for exchange as well. Nevertheless, this theory has the distinct advantage of considering other activities related to societal maintenance and expansion—reproduction and warfare—thereby putting the division of labor and social function of the sexes into a broader perspective. Furthermore, by defining her terms, she lays the basis for a systematic cross-cultural examination of female status.

Friedl (1975) also considers sex roles and status within the broad perspective of social tasks and requirements. She argues that not rights and control over production, but rather rights of distribution and control over the channels of distribution are critical economic factors in sexual stratification (p. 61). This emerges even in foraging societies, she claims, when there is a surplus of goods (meat) that is exchanged by men, thus providing the material basis for social power.[1] In horticultural societies, men monopolize the distribution of land. Friedl ties this monopoly to the relationship between the acquisition of land and endemic warfare among horticultural peoples: "Among horticulturalists men rather than women clear land for cultivation because new lands are frequently on the border of the territories of other peoples, with whom warfare is a potential threat" (p. 135). Therefore, male control over warfare leads to male control over property, which in these societies is the material basis for power of men over women. However, as Friedl is careful to point out, women may have opportunities through trade or through inheritance of high-status positions to counteract this power.

In this brief description it is impossible to do justice to these theories. (Friedl's study, in particular, contains many insights and much data.) They have in common the assumption that sexual stratification is primarily a response to relations of production or distribution, or both, although Sanday's, commendably, takes a broader view. Since these relations vary at different historical periods or within different ethnographic settings, sexual stratification cannot be seen as universal, though all agree it is widespread. As theoretical positions, they have the distinct advantage of being predictive; that is, one can construct hypotheses about relationships between economic factors of sexual status and test them against the ethnographic data. Since they all hold the assumption that sexual stratification is not universal, they can provide a basis for theoretical discussions about variations in sexual status that can be observed among and within societies. Their explanatory value lies in the concept that economic power can be translated into social power, a viewpoint that has received wide support from many kinds of anthropological studies.

A major weakness in these theories is that they ignore the role of ideology—or sets of beliefs about the natural, social, and supernatural worlds—in motivating action and initiating change. People produce and exchange ideas as well as goods, and ideological axioms can play an important role in the perception of reality and the forms that new adaptive processes take. This point will be brought up later.

Inherent Conditions:
Sexual Status and Femaleness

Unlike those I have considered above, the theories under discussion in this section are all based in one way or another on the nature of femaleness, with universal social roles and the way these are expressed psychologically or symbolically intervening between biological differences and sexual stratification. They all assert the universal subordination of women.

Collins (1971), a sociologist, asserts a position of blatant biological reductionism. He sees raw physical power as the basis for social power: the ultimate basis for power, in his view, is that men can physically coerce women. This theory merits little discussion: from all evidence, we know that social power derives from control over resources of various kinds and from networks of loyalty and obligation, and has little to do with physical strength.

Tiger (1969) asserts that male dominance arises out of the social bonding that characterizes males in distinction to females. This bonding has its basis in biological difference, for men learned to bond in order to hunt large game, an activity from

which women were restricted. Bonding, therefore, was an adaptive feature in early human society. This theory has been widely
discussed, and several points have been raised which call it into
question: (1) What evidence is there that all human societies
derive from a big-game hunting system of production? (2) Even if
they do, why should an adaptive feature persist under conditions
(i.e., when there is no big-game hunting) where it is no longer
required? (This is the old argument about cultural survivals in new
guise.) (3) Why does this theory overlook the widespread female
bonding, going beyond the household, that characterizes so many
societies? [2]

Chodorow (1974) and Ortner (1974) present much more sophisticated arguments. Chodorow looks to women's universal and
biologically determined role as mothers to account for universal
female subordination. Since females rear boys, boys must break
away from a feminine identification in order to establish masculine
identity. So far, so good. However, in order to do so, Chodorow
believes, they must devalue any femininity in themselves, and
femaleness in general. I fail to see why identification depends
upon devaluation, except in societies in which women are already
considered inferior and devaluation is part of the masculine identity package that a small boy must learn. Furthermore, we must be
cautious about using devaluation as a measure of subordination:
as discussed above, evaluation is not the major criterion for mea-
suring social power.

Ortner looks to the symbolization of femaleness as the cause
for universal subordination of women. Through their reproductive
and child socialization functions, women are perceived as closer
to nature than men, mediating between nature and culture,
whereas men take instrumental roles in creating technology and
symbols. This ignores female contributions to technology—for example, the strong possibility that women first domesticated plants
and thus "invented" agriculture—and to the rich store of symbols
around which female rituals are focused. Furthermore, through
their involvement with death in the killing of animals and enemies,
men also perform social tasks that result in biological transforma-

tions. By presenting her theory as she does, Ortner implies that it is ideology, the set of beliefs as expressed overtly through explicit statements or covertly through symbols, that accounts for female subordination. While most materialist explanations of social behavior tend to ignore ideology as a justification and motivation for social action, it would seem that Ortner errs in the other direction, overlooking the interplay of ideology and the constraints and opportunities provided by the social and natural world to which societies respond.

All of these theories are grounded in the indisputable fact that there are significant biological differences between men and women that everywhere lead to differences in social task performance. Women bear and nurse children, and are thereby restricted to some degree in the energy they can devote to other activities, and men everywhere engage in any tasks that require long absence from home and strength—hand-to-hand combat, big-game hunting, and long-distance trading expeditions, for example. But none of these theories explains satisfactorily why one set of activities should be more highly valued, or should necessarily lead to greater social power, than the other. By ignoring the social bases of social power, these theorists blind themselves to the range of variability of sex status that exists among and within societies. By asserting universal subordination, and thereby of necessity having to fit all ethnographic data, no matter how recalcitrant, into this schema, they lay themselves open to the charge of uncritical deductivism.

The Requirements of a Theory of Sexual Stratification

The foregoing theories all attempt, with more or less success, to pinpoint factors related to the widespread subordination of women. We need to bring together those factors that have value in predicting and explaining the variability in sexual status into a broad, comprehensive framework.

A theory of sexual stratification must deal with two major problems: how to assess the relative status of the sexes within a given society; and how relative sexual status is determined.

The first problem is one of definition. I have already mentioned the need to discover for a society areas in which men and women exert power and authority, and how these areas of control stand in relation to one another. Whyte's cross-cultural study of the status of women (in press) is an important contribution to the definition and assessment of sexual status.[3]

The second problem is the major question that a theory of sexual status is designed to answer. To deal with this, we must consider the factors that shape equality or inequality, and the determining or conditioning force these factors have on one another and on the allocation of power and authority between the sexes. In the following sections, we shall examine these two problems.

The Assessment of Sexual Status

The Contexts of Sexual Status

One widely applied way of looking at male and female spheres of action has been to divide the context of action into the domestic and public, or extradomestic, domains. The domestic domain, the household or similar small corporate mixed-sex group, is the locus for a large portion of female activity, as it is indeed for male activity in many societies. The public domain includes those institutions and systems of activity that bring together members of different domestic groups into corporate groups or networks of relationship. While a division into women-domestic/men-public may fit the facts of sexually segregated societies that exclude women from almost any decision making beyond the household, it is inadequate to describe most social action in many societies. In place of the gross domestic-public distinction, it would seem more fruitful to consider the domestic institution as only one kind in which women participate and in which they can have important decision-making roles. An overview of any society reveals a broad range of institutional contexts; what is needed is a transinstitutional perspective that permits us to assess the roles and positions of women within these separate contexts. Furthermore, we must look at the larger systems within which these institutions operate.

It is commonplace in anthropology to analyze societal organization by breaking it down into interrelated systems. Generally included are the subsistence system directed toward the production of food; the economic system directed toward the production, distribution, and consumption of goods and services; the political system directed toward the maintenance of order within the community and polity; the military system directed toward offense and defense outside the polity; the legal system directed toward the settlement of disputes; the social system directed toward the formation and maintenance of social bonds through kinship and association; and the religious system directed toward relations between the human and supernatural worlds. This list can be expanded to include other systems of action, such as educational, socialization, or communication systems, as required for analysis.

Institutions as defined here are those structures of roles designed to fulfill certain social functions. The court of law, for example, is a restricted institution, existing in some but not all societies, as one means of settling disputes. The family, on the other hand, is a generalized institution existing in some form in all societies. The debate about the function it fulfills has been a lively one; it performs activities that lie within the domains of several systems. However one may wish to subdivide the organization of society into systems and institutions, the questions to ask are how and to what degree the two sexes participate in them, and how power and authority within them are allocated to men and women.

Furthermore, it is necessary to assess the centrality of each of these systems and institutions to the power structure of the society as a whole. It has been widely observed that different systems and institutions may play a compelling role in influencing the structure and values of other institutions. Levy (1952) speaks of "crucial" and "strategic" institutions; Turner (1972) refers to "dominant institutions" (although he uses *institutions* to refer to what anthropologists generally call *systems*); Herskovits discusses "cultural focus" as "the tendency of every culture to exhibit greater complexity, greater variation in the institutions of some of its aspects than in others" and, gives the example of the Toda buffalo dairy (1952, p. 542 ff). The point of view taken here is closest to Feibleman's definition of a "leading institution" as one that "governs the others; it dictates the theory of reality for the entire culture; and it sets the standards of value accordingly" (1968; p. 228). (Rawles' [1971] definition of "major institutions" is similar to this.)

To recast this into my framework, I define a central institution as one that establishes priorities in the allocation of time, goods, and personnel, and legitimizes motivation and justification for action. For example, the clan is a central institution in many societies, for decisions regarding the clan affect a spectrum of actions outside the clan. In patrilineal clans, women are unlikely to have much decision-making power. In matrilineal clans, on the other hand, they may or may not—Hopi society is an example of one in which they do. Or take the military institution as another example: is it a central one, as it is likely to be in societies participating in endemic warfare? Women are likely to have little decision-making power in military action. Does the religious system provide the main channels through which social action is mobilized? For any of these, we will want to know how men and women participate in them, and, more importantly, to what degree the allocation of positions of power and authority is divided between men and women. Is only one sex recruited to these positions? If recruitment is open to both sexes, does it operate equally or is one sex favored?

But central institutions do not operate in isolation from one another; the same people are likely to be actively involved in more than one, so that there may be conflicts within the individual over priorities. And even where different social groups have a greater involvement in one central institution than another, some resolution must be attained when central institutions come into competition for social resources or power. To illustrate this last condition, we need only look at the competition between feudal aristocracy, Church, and state in medieval Europe. Where differential investment in central institutions follows sex lines, it could be expected that competition between the sexes would arise when priorities come into conflict. Among the Iroquois, for example, men controlled the military institution and women controlled the domestic institution, both of them central. In such a situation, questions to ask are: under what conditions do these institutions come into competition for social resources? How is competition controlled, and how is it resolved? How is authority in one institution counteracted or balanced by authority in the other? Such questions lead to an examination of the process of sexual interaction, not only within institutions, but also across institutions to the organization of the society *in toto.*

The Dynamics of Sexual Status

I have treated sexual status as a single element, but in fact it is crosscut by other elements of social structure. The division of society into males and females is only one way in which any society isolates social groups. I shall consider two others—age and social status.

While we are concerned only with the sexual status of adults, we find across cultures that position in the life cycle may have important consequences for the relative status of men versus women. It is not uncommon for gender distinctions to become muted or even disappear as people age, particularly as women reach menopause. Both the Comanche (Jones 1972) and the Mundurucu (Murphy and Murphy 1974) can be described as male-dominant societies; yet in both cases old women fill important decision-making roles otherwise restricted to men. In an assessment of sexual status, it must be clear whether one is speaking of women of all ages or women in particular age categories.

With regard to the interplay of sex and social status, in socially ranked or stratified societies the location of a woman in the status hierarchy may affect the access she has to positions of authority or the means to power, within her home or within other social institutions. Friedl (1975) points out that in nonegalitarian societies, women of high rank may have access to important decision-making positions, their location in the social hierarchy overriding their location in the sexual hierarchy. In such cases, it is particularly important to assess whether recruitment to leadership is equal for men and women or whether one sex is favored, and to weigh the relative power and authority of female-specific roles (e.g., queen) to male-specific roles (e.g., king).

When we examine societies in which women can rise to positions of importance, we will also want to know the means by which these positions were attained. Is it by ascription—does a woman's status depend on inheritance, does it depend on her relationship, as for example a wife, to a male leader? Is it by achievement—and if so, what kind of achievement? Is it through the display of instrumental skills, such as the Iyalode described in this volume? Or is it through expressive skills, by which she gains the patronage of a powerful person? The favorite wife, concubine, or mistress of the king was often a person of great power in the European or Oriental court. It is easy to dismiss this as a case of sexual intrigue; but in settings in which the power of any individual, male or female, depends upon the patronage of an important leader, the status of a favored woman may differ little in its practical effects from the status of a favored man. Both can exercise power through the dispensation of benefits to kin and clients.

As the foregoing discussion has demonstrated, the assessment of sexual status can be a problem of great complexity. As we examine the contexts within which power and authority are exercised, and the ways in which these contexts are crosscut by other elements of social organization, it becomes increasingly difficult to speak of *the* status of women in a society, let alone any type of society. It is understandable that the problem requires analytic refinement, for we are dealing with what is, after all, a fundamental division into social categories that is universal across societies. We must next identify the forces that shape sexual status.

The Determinants of Sexual Status

The position taken here is that sexual status is a response to a number of factors that operate on the economic, social, political, and ideological systems of a society. It is not invariate, as one group of theorists would have us believe; rather it is variable within and among societies and changes along with other changes in the manner in which goods, social groups, and ideas are produced. It would be going too far to say that sexual status is merely an epiphenomenon of social arrangements; for sexual status, like other social facts, becomes embedded in the beliefs and symbols that express the axioms about the nature of mankind, and, as such, it can itself become one of the determinants of the form that changes in social arrangements take. One would expect, for example, that a society that holds the sexes to be equal would respond differently to changes in production or social structure than would a society that holds the sexes to be unequal. The tensions between cultural axioms and new conditions would differ, and the resulting synthesis would be likely to take on different forms. This is a problem that requires empirical, comparative examination across cultures.

I have deliberately avoided using the term *adaptive* to characterize sexual status for two reasons. First, as Alland (1975) and others have pointed out, it becomes teleological unless one can measure the degree to which the adaptation contributes to homeostasis or change. Second, *adaptive,* like *functional,* carries a connotation of the good, "the best of all possible worlds" given the conditions under which a society operates. There is no reason to assume that a society that denies opportunities to half of its population is making the best use of its potential talents. *Response* is a morally and analytically neutral term that allows us to consider maladaptation as well as adaptation, if we are indeed in a position to consider the question of adaptation at all with a given body of ethnographic data.

In the discussion that follows, I shall isolate some of the features of social arrangements and beliefs that shape the roles and statuses of men and women in society.

Biological Foundations

The fact that humanity is divided biologically into two sexes is the foundation for the universal social division into men and women. The different social roles that men and women fill in every society are obviously based to some degree on their differences in reproductive activity and the consequences of this activity in offering opportunities for, and imposing limits on, social behavior. We are only beginning to examine the meaning that morphological, hormonal, and possibly neurological or cognitive differences between the sexes have for perception and action; this discussion cannot even attempt to consider the debates that have arisen on these questions. I begin with the consideration that if a society is to maintain its population, some proportion of women must spend some of their adult years bearing and nursing children, and if a society is involved in activities that require freedom from the constraints of childbearing, these activities are likely to be conducted by men (Brown 1970; Murdock 1949). How these biologically based differences affect social action, and how they are perceived, varies greatly across societies. It is the examination of this variability and the forces that determine it that characterize an anthropological view of sexual stratification.

Economic Forces

To undertake a sensitive analysis of male and female economic roles, we must break away from a technological and evolutionary paradigm based on subsistence systems—sex roles in foraging societies, sex roles in horticultural societies, and so on. We should follow the elementary anthropological maxim that economic systems are social systems, systems of relations among people in the production and exchange of goods and services, and look rather at sex roles in modes of production, systems of production, and relations of production.

Sahlins speaks of a mode of production as comprising "an appropriate technology and division of labor, a characteristic economic objective or finality, specific forms of property, definite social and exchange relations between producing units—and contradictions all its own" (1972, p. 76). The mode of production he discusses, one that operates in many of the societies anthropologists deal with, is the domestic mode, in which productive activity is primarily directed toward use and the household is the major unit of production. Such a mode is characterized by domestic relations of production: relations between men and women as producers are embedded in their relations as wife and husband, parent and child, kinsman and kinswoman.

Because productive relations in the domestic mode of production are embedded in other kinds of relations, the division of labor within the economic system must complement the division of tasks in noneconomic social systems, as these are played out within the domestic institution. Here, I believe, the procreative system is of overriding importance in determining which tasks are best suited to men and women, considering procreation to be those activities that bring the offspring to reproductive age and status.[4] It would clearly not be to the advantage of the household, as a productive unit, to operate to the detriment of the household as a procreative unit. Therefore, the division of labor that obtains within the domestic mode of production must attempt to ensure both productive and procreative success to the fullest possible extent. In some societies this may be an impossible task: Nerlove (1974) discusses the conflict between subsistence activities and the requirements of nursing infants, and the attempt to ameliorate this through supplementary feeding. The consequences are not necessarily beneficial to the infant.

The feudal manor, another unit of production often discussed by economic theoreticians, is also a unit that had to maintain itself through both productive and procreative activities, although its procreative bonds were clearly quite different from those that characterize the household. Here, also, the productive activities cannot operate in isolation from procreative ones if the unit of production is to survive through time. It is in the advanced modes of production, where the industrial bureaucracy is the unit of production, that this isolation appears; for the bureaucracy maintains itself without itself being a unit of procreation. Since it need not concern itself with procreative activities, there is no functional requirement within industrialization for sexual division of labor, as there is likely to be within those units that have both productive and procreative ends. (This leads us to ask whether the kibbutz, or any other communal form of both production and procreation, will not inevitably be led to division of labor by sex in spite of ideological strictures against it. That certainly seems to have been the case for the Israeli kibbutzim discussed in Tiger and Shepher [1975]).

The division of labor by sex, I believe, is fundamental to the process by which sexual stratification arises. If economic and social tasks within the central institutions, or the central institutions themselves, are not sexually specific, there exists no basis to oppose men against women as a socially predominant class, nor does there arise a material basis, through control over resources or social ties, for concentration of power in one sex at the expense of the other. Symbolic opposition, in the sense of male and female cosmic or social principles, may well occur without any or much division of labor by sex: the basis for symbolic opposition lies in the fundamental bifurcation between the biological categories of male and female, ever separate, ever joining in the attempt to create social unity out of biological diversity. But symbolic opposition by itself does not lead to inequality: inequality arises out of social relationships operating within the context of social axioms.

Is division of labor by sex, then, a cause for sexual inequality? Only if it is regarded in the sense of a necessary but not sufficient cause can it so be considered. Without it there is no material basis for stratification; but even where it exists, as among the Hopi discussed in this volume, it does not lead to sexual stratification because the central institutions controlled by men and women respectively or jointly are in balance. (Interestingly, it is also true that the only major subsistence tasks in this society that are absolutely sex specific are those linked to the cosmic definitions of masculine and feminine—male hunting and corn planting as predatory and fructifying acts, and female corn grinding as a nurturant act in the feeding of mankind and spirit. In comparison with many other horticultural societies, division of labor among the Hopi appears to be relatively flexible.)

We conclude from this, then, that sexual stratification does not follow a simple evolutionary line, although the factors leading to inequality may be more abundant in some modes or systems of production than others. There has been a recent tendency to consider foragers as more sexually egalitarian than societies following other modes of subsistence; yet, Friedl makes a case for stratification among the Eskimo, and it is clear that among the Yavapai, Yuman-speaking foragers of the upper Colorado River, women were subordinate. In both cases, this may have been due to male control of central institutions beyond the household: for the Eskimo, an extra-domestic unit of production (see note 1 to paper 15); for the Yavapai, the military activity that was constant in this region of endemic warfare. Nevertheless, sexual equality does appear to characterize foraging societies in contrast to those utilizing the more complex subsistence systems (Whyte, in press). Perhaps one reason for this is the greater flexibility in the division of labor among foragers than among most other primitive or traditional peoples—hunting by women and gathering by men as secondary activities. Among foragers, the pull between production and procreation is not so strong as in the more technologically advanced societies. Fecundity is not highly valued, and children are frequently spaced so as not to overburden the woman as she makes her foraging rounds: in these societies, procreative success does not demand large numbers of children. Therefore, even within a domestic mode of production that contains division of labor by sex, women are freer from the constraints of childbearing and rearing than they are in societies where economic and social success may depend upon the labor and loyalty of the social group one has created—one's children and the affinal kin linked through them. This is generally the case in horticultural, herding, and agricultural societies.

The industrial mode of production poses its own problem. We

have historical evidence of sexual stratification rampant during the transformation into this mode in the West and continuing into the present, and we see the effects of this transformation undercutting the traditional positions of women in the Third World countries, first under colonial rule and more recently under independence. Nevertheless, taking the long view, the industrial mode of production in itself can be a positive factor in sexual equality, for the reason stated above—that it entails no requirement within itself for procreative activities, which are left to the domestic and educational institutions, and therefore no requirement for the division of labor by sex. The sexual inequality that persists in industrial societies does so for reasons having nothing to do with the requirements of production. Procreative decisions occur within the privacy of the home, influenced by decisions made in the public sector concerning tax allowances, child welfare, educational benefits, and the like. Productive decisions are to a large degree isolated from these, although the isolation is not complete in the modern state where maternity benefits for workers, industry-related child care centers, and other features of labor regulations directly affect women's ability to be both productive and procreative. (For a discussion of a tendency toward sexual equality in industrial societies, see Whyte [in press], who cites empirical evidence from Goode [1963].) In the industrial society, the status of the woman is increasingly dependent upon her roles in the public sector and depends very little on her procreative activities in the domestic. For the first time in history, productive and procreative goals for large numbers of women come into conflict, as promises of success and personal gratification in one area threaten those of the other. We shall return to this problem at the end of this paper.

We have seen, then, that while the division of labor by sex, as other forms of division of labor, fits into an evolutionary paradigm, division of labor by sex per se is not enough to account for presence or absence of sexual stratification. Within the domestic mode of production, or any mode in which the unit of production is both a productive and a procreative unit, we must ascertain not only the division of labor but also the relations of production—

those relations, in this case between men and women, that come into play as a result of productive and exchange activities. We must examine those relations that arise from differential control over the means to production. In which sex do rights of ownership and use of resources reside, and which resources? Who directs or controls production of goods for use? Who directs or controls production of goods for exchange? We want to know the kinds of social networks that are established through the exchange of goods, and the role of each sex in establishing or activating these networks.

A complicating feature of some societies is the existence of more than one system of production, or sets of tasks involving closely related activities and resources. Of interest here is the relative involvement of each sex in each system of production. In the Japanese fishing village, for example, men are active in the fishing economy (primarily for market exchange) while women take charge of agricultural tasks (primarily for use), although they may help in fishing when necessary (Norbeck 1954). Among the traditional Hopi, who operated within a domestic mode of production, the participation of each sex in the coexisting systems of production was not so cleanly divided. Men had the major responsibility for horticulture, but both men and women participated in foraging activities, the men hunting and the women gathering wild plants. In this case the two systems of production were given symbolic significance that persists into the present in the conceptualization of sex roles: the major men's ceremonies focus around cultivated plants, principally corn and beans, while the women's ceremonies focus around foraged goods through objects and symbols that refer to wild plants—particularly grass baskets—and animals, in the symbolic equation of women and game animals.

In sum, I do not believe that division of labor by sex necessarily leads to sexual stratification, nor has the absence of a functional requirement for the division of labor within the unit of production necessarily led to sexual equality. Within the unit of production itself, one must look to relations of production as contributing to sexual stratification or equality, and one must consider features of social organization and ideology extending beyond strictly economic relations as conditioning variables.

Social Organization

If power and authority are by definition features of social relations, then it behooves us to look to social principles that determine the kinds of bonds people establish. In preliterate societies, these will generally follow channels of kinship and association. The former of necessity requires both sexes, while the latter is frequently restricted to one sex only (and by no means necessarily males). As Fox (1967) points out, rules of residence determine which sex forms the nucleus of the household as a corporate group. Ties of loyalty and obligation, then, tend to be the strongest among those members who form this nucleus, and, other things being equal, power or authority would reside with the sex that brings in husbands or wives, as the case may be. Unfortunately, other things never are equal, so there is no simple equation between matrilocality and female domestic power, on the one hand, and patrilocality or avunculocality and male power, on the other.

The structure of the kin group is another possible determinant of the status of men and women. In the societies that many anthropologists describe, the kin group provides the major channels beyond the household through which loyalty is activated and social action is mobilized. Control over corporately held property, principles of inheritance of goods and positions, rights to form alliances through marriage—all of these are kinship features that can support or modify the power and authority of men and women gained through other means.

Bonding through association crosscuts ties of household and kinship in many societies. But it is not merely the presence of associations that need concern us—women's societies are of little importance to women's status if they operate as "ladies' auxiliaries" or are peripheral to major social concerns. Rather, we must ask what roles these associations play in mobilizing loyalties and action. Are they central institutions within the economic, political, or religious systems? If their membership consists of both men and women, is access to decision-making roles equally open to both sexes?

Goal-directed social groups form to deal with relations internal to the society, but they also form to deal with external relations, particularly relations of exchange, as trading institutions, relations of aggression and defense, as military institutions, and relations of alliance, as interpolity councils. Where these activities involve danger or long absence from home, they are usually conducted by men and decisions made for them are made by men. Where these are central institutions, I expect the status of women to be depressed in comparison to societies in which they are not unless it is brought into balance by women's roles in other central institutions.

There has not been much examination of the effects on sexual status of long-distance trade or extrapolity alliance formation. Warfare, however, has received some attention. Langness (1967) has suggested a relationship between warfare and low female status in the New Guinea highlands. Harris (1974) has discussed this question more generally: using Chagnon's data on the Yanomamo, he derives a preference for males and the power of men over women from the necessity to produce aggressive and dominant males as hunters and fighters under conditions of a scarce protein supply. This can be countered with the example of the Iroquois, well known for both their bellicosity and the domestic and political power of women. Indeed, Wallace implies that it was the organization for warfare, necessitating long absences of men from the home community, that required that the women have important voices in economic and political decisions (1972, pp. 28–30). To his explanation I can add the important roles women played in the central institutions of household and clan.

One form of relationship between societies that can have profound effects upon social organization is colonialism, a relationship of political or economic dominance and subordination. Transformations in traditional authority patterns or relations of production initiated by the dominant society, or transformations that are the by-products of such imposed conditions as the cessation of warfare, can alter the relative status of men and women in unforeseen ways. Boserup (1970) has documented the adverse effects of European colonialism on women in Africa, and Smock in this volume discusses this phenomenon in Ghana. After reading Bacdayan's paper in this volume, one wonders what effect—in this case perhaps positive—the imposed cessation of warfare may have had on the status of Bontoc women. Central institutions wither, new ones arise, and existing ones change in the opportunities they provide to men and women for participation and access to positions of authority.

Ideology

People act, but they also think: they perceive, they organize their perceptions into cognitive sets, and they plan. They are aware of self and other, and they explain this distinction in beliefs about the nature of mankind and express it through symbols and ritual. These explanations lead to predictions and justifications of behavior and become a powerful motivating force for social action. Materialist theories tend to ignore this to their peril. Yet all around us we see people responding to new ideas about the nature of the world and mankind and straining to bring about a correspondence between these ideas and social behavior. It has become commonplace to accept the communication of ideology in the modern world, yet there is a tendency to overlook the exchange of beliefs and ideological axioms among preliterate societies in favor of emphasis on the exchange of goods or technological innovations.

If we discard the notion that ideology is merely an epiphenomenon of productive relations à la Marx, or social relations à la Durkheim, we nevertheless expect to find a relationship between the ontological axioms of a society, to use Feibleman's (1954) term, the norms and symbols by which these axioms are conveyed, and social relations, considering social relations in the broadest sense of relations of production and exchange, affiliation, and conflict. In stable societies, those in which a dialectic between ideology and action is minimal, we expect to find that the norms for action and the expressive activities of ritual behavior represent an actualization of axioms, the principles by which conduct is perceived, guided, and justified. To the point of this discussion, in such societies there is a correspondence between the nature of male and female as developed through beliefs and the ritualized expression of these beliefs, on the one hand, and social action, on the other. Let me illustrate with a few examples concerning spatial arrangements of the sexes. Keesing (1976, pp. 398–401) shows that the male/female opposition of purity and pollution among the Kwaio is spatially represented in the village plan, just as partitioning of the Moalan (Fiji) house diagrams a distinction between male and female, superordinate and subordinate (Sahlins 1976, pp. 32–35). For the traditional Hopi, the "right-handed" nature of females, linked with the sacred Earth and life, is opposed to the "left-handed" nature of males, linked with the sacred world beyond, the realm of death, and the supernatural; and this opposition determines both the position of the "male" and "female" prayersticks that are bound together and the usual position that husband and wife take in their sleeping arrangement—in both cases, the female is on the left, so as not to pull the male out of balance. In these societies, the social roles of men and women—the rules for behavior and the constraints placed upon it, and the activities that properly belong to one sex as against the other—are at one with the principles which define the view of the world (see Schlegel, this volume). For the Kwaio, where pollution characterizes women, and in Moala, where the "femaleness" of Land People, the wife-givers on the "weak side," is opposed to the "maleness" of the Chiefs, the wife-takers on the "strong side," the male and female roles are hierarchical; for the Hopi, where this world and the world beyond exist in a state of balance, male and female are equal.

In more general terms, we can expect to find a cosmic dualism between female and male where the specialized activities of women and men become social imperatives. While most

societies conceive of their deities as male and female
—differentiation by sex is, after all, a fundamental differentiation
in all societies—it is in horticultural and agricultural societies
that gender difference is elevated into cosmic principles to which
a range of symbolic oppositions are attached. Where maximum
procreation of plants and people is a major concern, the symbolic
equation of females with Earth or its surface and of males with Sky
or the fructifying elements of sun and rain is widespread. Where
the natural world is placed in opposition to the social world, so
may the sexes be assigned to one or the other: Rivière (1969) tells
us that among the Trio, a Carib group in Surinam, women belong
to the inside, the village, the house, culture, and humanity, while
men belong to the outside, the mysterious world of the forest, the
spirits, nature, and the unknown—but also to the core of the village, its plaza. The Iroquois made a similar distinction between
female/village and male/forest, and actualized it in granting each
sex domination within its domain (Tooker, 1975, p. 109). If the
kingdom in heaven is modeled after the kingdom on earth, as
Swanson (1960) convincingly shows, so may the principles that
govern social action correspond to the principles by which the
universe is believed to be ordered.

Nor is this reciprocity between symbol and action limited to
the primitive world. While complex industrial societies do not ele-
vate gender differences into cosmic principles that are actualized
in marriage classes, ritual drama, or village plans, they do take
account of gender differences in ascribing masculinity and femininity to the objects that surround us, particularly in the expressive
realm of fashion and design (see Sahlins 1976). It may be that the
most abiding expression of gender differences lies in spatial arrangements. While the places of public performance, such as
houses of worship, have discarded seating arrangements that isolate men from women, in the modern home, the last refuge of ar-
chitectural gender distinction, we still find the "femininity" of the
master bedroom (the place of procreation?) in contrast to the
"masculinity" of the den. (I leave it to symbolic anthropologists to

explain this dichotomy, and to ponder on why the kitchen, the location of most female domestic labor, is rarely "feminine" in design.)

So it is that the dichotomy between female and male is deeply embedded in the way we view and express the world around us. The decisions we make, and the action we take, occur within the matrix of ideology. And how could it be otherwise? People do not form social groups and productive relations and then sit down to think and symbolize about them; rather, they act in accordance with both material and social advantage and the guiding principles that give the stamp of approval—or disapproval—to their actions. For this reason, ideology, to whatever degree it traces its origin to material or social relations, must be treated as an independent variable in the exploration of sexual status.

Conclusion

The position taken in the foregoing discussion is that sexual status is the consequence of the interplay of productive relations, social relations, and ideology. To explain sexual status in any society, and to predict the changes it may take, we must first free ourselves from deductions about the inherent and universal subordination of women. A critical examination of the problem requires that, for every case, we look to the responses a society makes to its own internal dynamics and to relations with other societies.

One place to look is the central institutions of the society—the part they play in the operation of other institutions and the cultural axioms and values that legitimize them. When we determine the roles men and women play in central institutions, we can assess the degree of sexual stratification or equality. When we discover the economic, social, and ideological forces that support these institutions, we can understand the bases for sexual status.

A major assumption of this paper, grounded in empirical evidence, is that sexual status is variable. Of all the social tasks that can exist in human society, only one is sexually invariate, the addition of new members through childbearing. Other tasks, even those concerned with childrearing, can be and are shared by men and women. There may be, of course, psychological ramifications of this childbearing female function that we do not even have the data yet to discuss critically. It may be that the biological capacity for motherhood is accompanied by a genetically determined or hormonally activated predisposition in women to form very close attachments to young children. Owing to the prolonged helplessness of the human infant, a propensity to close bonding between mother and child would seem favorable for human survival and thereby would be likely to be selected for in human evolution. Unlike the male bonding hypothesis proferred by Tiger and criticized earlier in this chapter, such bonding would be adaptive to human survival under all conditions of economic and social organization and is represented in all known human societies. Even in the Israeli kibbutz discussed by Datan in this volume, in which mother-child bonding has been attenuated, the primary child caretakers are female. This does not, of course, deny the strong bonds that men also form with children.

Given the constraints on women of childbearing and early childrearing, some tasks may be more efficiently performed by one sex than the other. Tasks that require long periods of concentration or great exposure to danger, or that take performers away from home for long periods of time, are incompatible with the demands of childrearing. This means not only that most women are not involved in such tasks, although some may be for some periods of their lives, but also that most women will not be socialized to expect to perform or excel in these tasks. So even when sexual division of task performance is not a functional requirement of the system, it may arise within that system as a by-product of constraints upon women's time, energies, and levels of expectation. Where success is measured through achievements in skills that require long periods of training and a high level of energy expenditure, most women who put their time and energy into childbearing and childrearing find it difficult to achieve success within institutions that are not geared to the rhythms of domestic activity.

What does this mean for women in modern societies? Technological changes have isolated the unit of production from the unit of reproduction, thus removing a functional requirement for the sexual division of labor within the unit of production. (In the United States, even such dangerous occupations as coal mining have their female participants, usually unmarried.) Ideological shifts toward freedom of opportunity and choice have raised women's levels of expectations of success in the occupational hierarchy; and as hopes are raised, women become increasingly dissatisfied with playing only supportive or unskilled occupational roles. But a system that continues to put primary responsibility on mothers for the long-term socialization of children inevitably restricts their attainment of the highly rewarded positions to which they may now aspire. Features of the social organization prevent women, except at great sacrifice and with sustained self-discipline, from moving more prominently into the central institutions of our society. The nuclear family as we know it may be an efficient unit for reproduction and for consumption of goods, and it may provide for mobility of the labor force deemed necessary to an industrial economy; but it militates against female success in the central institutions in our society. Women, of course, are able to enter the work force, as millions do for reasons of necessity or personal desire; but the time, energy, and freedom of movement required to attain positions of importance in an achievement-oriented society are simply not available to women with children to the degree they are to men.

Women's role as childbearer has no alternative in the foreseeable future. In women's understandable haste to move into the larger world, it is tempting to devalue this role. If we do this, we do ourselves, as individuals and as a society, the greatest disservice. The personal gratifications of parenthood, and the well-being of children, depend upon some sense of satisfaction with nurturant roles. The problem we face is to create social arrangements that allow for both care of children and greater freedom for mothers from childrearing responsibilities.

We see around us a variety of experiments in caring for young children, such as greater involvement of fathers, institutional arrangements like the nursery, and households made up of two or more nuclear families, with responsibilities for childcare dispersed among its members. The transformation of female roles we are undergoing requires the flexibility to experiment, and the wisdom to choose the experiments that best meet the needs of women, men, and children. The task ahead is not an easy one.

Notes

1. Friedl focuses on relations of exchange. I feel it is, rather, relations of production that account for any degree of centralization of economic and social power that may exist in foraging societies. Those foragers whom she depicts as male dominant, the inland and maritime Eskimo (Friedl 1975, pp. 39–45), have productive institutions with positions of authority. For a further discussion of this point, see note 1 to chapter 15.

2. It may be true that in many societies, bonding in adolescence is greater for boys than girls; that is, male peer groups may be larger and their activities more time-consuming than is true for female peer groups. This proposition, and the reasons for it, are part of a cross-cultural survey on adolescent socialization now in progress. We have enough data already, however, to know that a sex difference in peer bonding is not true for all societies, so we wish to know under what conditions it occurs. Whether or not strong same-sex peer bonding persists into adulthood is a matter for further study.

3. After this paper was written, I learned that a cross-cultural study of female status has just been conducted by Martin Whyte (in press). This is an important work in that it examines many of the assumptions that have been held by anthropologists and other social investigators without having been subjected to critical empirical assessment. Not surprisingly, a number of these assumptions, such as simple materialist explanations of sexual status, fail to stand up to investigation.

4. This view of the household was stimulated by a discussion with Nancy Devore on social organization and reproductive success among the !Kung Bushmen.

References

Alland, Alexander, Jr. 1975. "Adaptation." In B. J. Siegal, ed., *Annual Review of Anthropology*, pp. 59–73. Palo Alto: Annual Reviews.
Boserup, Ester. 1970. *Women's Role in Economic Development*. London: Allen and Unwin.

Brown, Judith K. 1970. "A Note on the Division of Labor by Sex." *American Anthropologist* 72:1073–78.

Chodorow, Nancy. 1974. "Family Structure and Feminine Personality." In M. Z. Rosaldo and L. Lamphere, eds., *Women, Culture, and Society,* pp. 43–66. Stanford: Stanford University Press.

Collins, Randall. 1971. "A Conflict Theory of Sexual Stratification." *Social Problems* 19:3–20.

Dzhanashvili, M. G. 1894. "Abkhaziya i Abkhaztsy." *Memoirs of the Caucasus Section of the Imperial Russian Geographical Society* 16:1–59. Tiflis. (Translation in Human Relations Area Files.)

Engels, Friedrich. 1891. *The Origin of the Family, Private Property, and the State; in the Light of Researches of Lewis H. Morgan.* New York: International Publishers.

Feibleman, James K. 1954. "Toward an Analysis of the Basic Value System." *American Anthropologist* 56:421–32.

—— 1968. *The Institutions of Society.* New York: Humanities Press.

Fox, Robin. 1967. *Kinship and Marriage: An Anthropological Perspective.* Baltimore: Penguin Books.

Friedl, Ernestine. 1975. *Women and Men: An Anthropologist's View.* New York: Holt, Rinehart and Winston.

Goode, William J. 1963. *World Revolution and Family Patterns.* New York: The Free Press.

Harper, Edward B. 1969. "Fear and the Status of Women." *Southwestern Journal of Anthropology* 35:81–95.

Harris, Marvin. 1974. *Cows, Pigs, Wars and Witches.* New York: Vintage Books.

Herskovits, Melville J. 1952. *Man and His Works.* New York: Knopf.

Jacobs, Sue-Ellen. 1968. "Berdache: A Brief Review of the Literature." *Colorado Anthropologist* 1:25–31.

Jones, David E. 1972. *Sanapia: Comanche Medicine Women.* New York: Holt, Rinehart and Winston.

Kaberry, Phyllis M. 1939. *Aboriginal Woman, Sacred and Profane.* London: Routledge.

Kanter, Rosabeth M. 1976. "Review of L. Tiger and J. Shepher, *Women in the Kibbutz.*" *Science* 192:662–63.

Keesing, Roger M. 1976. *Cultural Anthropology: A Contemporary Perspective.* New York: Holt, Rinehart and Winston.

Landes, Ruth. 1938. *The Ojibwa Woman.* New York: Columbia University Press.

Langness, L. L. 1967. "Sexual Antagonism in the New Guinea Highlands." *Oceania* 37:161–77.

Leacock, Eleanor B. 1972. Introduction to the 1972 edition of F. Engels,

Origin of the Family, Private Property, and the State. New York: International Publishers.

Levy, Marion J., Jr. 1952. *The Structure of Society.* Princeton, N.J.: Princeton University Press.

Levy, Reuben. 1962. *The Social Structure of Islam.* Cambridge: Cambridge University Press.

Lewis, Oscar. 1941. "Manly-Hearted Women amongst the North Piegan." *American Anthropologist* 61:965–90.

Mason, Otis T. 1894. *Women's Share in Primitive Culture.* New York: D. Appleton.

Mead, Margaret. 1935. *Sex and Temperament in Three Primitive Societies.* New York: W. Morrow.

—— 1949. *Male and Female.* New York. W. Morrow.

Murdock, George Peter. 1949. *Social Structure.* New York: Macmillan.

Murphy, Yolanda and Robert F. Murphy. 1974. *Women of the Forest.* New York: Columbia University Press.

Nerlove, Sara B. 1974. "Women's Workload and Infant Feeding Practices: A Relationship with Demographic Implications." *Ethnology* 13:207–14.

Nicolaisen, Johannes. 1963. *Ecology and Culture of the Pastoral Tuareg.* Copenhagen: Nationalmuseets Skrifter, Etnografisk Raekke 9.

Norbeck, Edward. 1954. *Takashima: A Japanese Fishing Community.* Salt Lake City: University of Utah Press.

Ortner, Sherry B. 1974. "Is Female to Male as Nature Is to Culture?" In M. Z. Rosaldo and L. Lamphere, eds., *Woman, Culture, and Society,* pp. 67–88. Stanford: Stanford University Press.

Parsons, Elsie Clews. 1913. *The Old-Fashioned Woman: Primitive Fancies About the Sex.* New York and London: Putnam.

Rawles, John. 1971. *A Theory of Justice.* Cambridge: The Belknap Press.

Rivière, Peter. 1969. *Marriage among the Trio: A Principle of Social Organization.* Oxford: Clarendon Press.

Sacks, Karen. 1974. "Engels Revisited: Women, the Organization of Production, and Private Property." In M. Z. Rosaldo and L. Lamphere, eds., *Woman, Culture, and Society,* pp. 207–22. Stanford: Stanford University Press.

Sahlins, Marshall. 1972. *Stone Age Economics.* Chicago and New York: Aldine-Atherton.

—— 1976. *Culture and Practical Reason.* Chicago: The University of Chicago Press.

Sanday, Peggy R. 1974. "Female Status in the Public Domain." In M. Z. Rosaldo and L. Lamphere, eds., *Woman, Culture, and Society,* pp. 189–206. Stanford: Stanford University Press.

Schlegel, Alice. 1972. *Male Dominance and Female Autonomy*. New Haven: Human Relations Area Files Press.

Swanson, Guy. 1960. *The Birth of the Gods: The Origin of Primitive Beliefs*. Ann Arbor: The University of Michigan Press.

Tiger, Lionel. 1969. *Men in Groups*. New York: Random House.

Tiger, Lionel and Joseph Shepher. 1975. *Women in the Kibbutz*. New York: Harcourt Brace Jovanovich.

Tooker, Elisabeth. 1975. "Ethnometaphysics of Iroquois Ritual." In Carole E. Hill, ed., *Symbols and Society,* pp. 103–16. Southern Anthropological Society Proceedings, no. 9. Athens, Georgia: University of Georgia Press.

Turner, Jonathan H. 1972. *Patterns of Social Organization: A Survey of Social Institutions*. New York: McGraw-Hill.

Wallace, Anthony F. C. 1972. *The Death and Rebirth of the Seneca*. New York: Vintage Books.

Whyte, Martin. In press. *The Status of Women in Pre-Industrial Societies*. Princeton: Princeton University Press.

DAISY HILSE DWYER

Bridging the Gap
between the Sexes
2 in Moroccan
Legal Practice

FOR THE ISLAMIC world, and for other societies in which a strong separation of male and female worlds exists and is coupled with expectations for passivity on the part of women, the question arises as to how women maneuver in those spheres of action that are male-run and male-oriented. What institutions allow men and women to interact in these settings? What points of ideology are used to determine whether interactions should be prohibited, regulated, or freely undertaken? How are necessary interactions conducted within the bounds of the propriety code?

The questions of how and where contact can properly occur between the sexes in Islamic society concerns any of a number of spheres of action in which sexual segregation is strict. Among these, in highly traditional Muslim areas, are the religious and the economic domains. Perhaps most interesting in terms of interaction of the sexes, however, are the areas of law and law enforcement. Both of these linked realms are exclusively male-staffed in traditional Moroccan society, apart from the exceptional institution that is recorded below. Expectations for reticence in relations be-

The fieldwork upon which this paper is based was undertaken with National Institute of Mental Health support in 1969–71. Subsequent fieldwork was carried out in the summers of 1973, 1975, and 1976. The last two research periods were funded by the Columbia University Councils for Research in the Humanities and Social Sciences.

tween the sexes in these two areas tend to be marked. Yet officials in both spheres not only must deal with women; in many instances, they must undertake detailed investigations under the law. Interactions thus, of necessity, tend to be much more intimate than in the economic and religious spheres. Women who should ideally be protected and kept separate, according to custom, must frequently come under intensive male scrutiny by law.

This paper focuses upon how these two contradictory tendencies—one for limited and one for intensive interaction—are coordinated and resolved within the judicial domain in Morocco. It is based upon fieldwork in the area of Taroudannt in the south of Morocco, and it deals with that individual traditionally charged with making interactions of the sexes proper and possible in legal situations in Taroudannt and in many other areas of Morocco as well. Occupying a structurally crucial position and affecting male-female relations in a multitude of ways, that individual is called the 'arifa (pronounced AH-ree-fah) or "woman who knows."

Social Setting

A primary characteristic of life in Morocco's traditional regions is the separation of social life into male and female domains. Women spend the bulk of their time with women, performing women's activities, while men spend the bulk of their time with men, occupied with tasks that in large part can be classified as men's work. When it occurs, interaction of the sexes is often sharply restricted and regulated.

The separation of the sexes is evident in many aspects of Moroccan life. It is immediately apparent, for example, in the public arena. In the streets, women walk alone or in the company of other women; men walk alone or in the company of other men. Men and women are rarely seen walking together. Similarly, cafés are frequented only by men, and stores are serviced only by male attendants. At a recent festivity in the South, male and female observers were placed into separate groups, divided by barriers, while the public ceremonies took place.

This separation of the sexes is apparent also in more private settings. At celebrations held for personal friends and family, women congregate separate from those men who are guests. A similar division occurs during moments of everyday socializing; women tend to gather with women friends and neighbors, while men friends and coworkers tend to congregate in male groups for relaxation and gossip. The locations for these gatherings are typically the home or the Turkish bath (during women's hours) for the women; for the men, they are generally stores, gardens, or cafés. It is only within the privacy of the nuclear family that men and women regularly exchange information and that they intensely and rather consistently interact.

The separation of the sexes is institutionalized in much of Moroccan culture in the traditional South. It is maintained most consistently and explained most explicitly within the religious setting. Women are prohibited from praying in the main Muslim worship areas located in the mosques, for example. Their devotions are limited to the home or to those few sparse cubicles that serve as women's worship areas in a limited number of mosques. The religious brotherhoods, important in traditional areas and in some westernized regions in Morocco, maintain a similar organizational separation. In almost all instances, brotherhoods limit their membership to men. In those few groups that permit women's participation, men and women form different groups, and a separation of the female units from the male groups is maintained. Such separation is believed to be sanctioned by Allah and established for the purpose of limiting sexual interest and thereby maintaining spiritual purity.

In the economic realm, separation of the sexes occurs, it is said, in order to maintain the purity of women and thereby also their families' honor. Few occupations, as a result, are performed by both men and women, and men's work areas are generally separate from women's. Women work at curing, midwifery, woolspinning, sewing, and laundering, tasks carried out in the home or in predominantly female settings. On those occasions when they engage in marketplace activities, women sell only certain produce, such as eggs, poultry, and ready-to-eat items, and work within rather discrete areas of the market. Similarly, when men and women harvest grains or olives, a degree of separation is maintained. Only in such modern occupations as nursing, teaching, and office work is a blurring of sexual boundaries typically found.

On those occasions when women seek help of a political sort, a separation of the sexes again is practiced and fostered. Women wait in areas separate from men when they consult the *qaid* or other regional political leaders. At election time, they go to the polls not with their menfolk, but generally as women of a neighborhood, in pairs or in small female groups. Positions within the political hierarchy are filled only by men.

Not only must women remain separate from men during many activities, but they are generally subordinated to men as well. Within the Moroccan family, men determine where their wives live, when those women go out, if they do wage labor, and whether or not they get divorced. (A woman rarely sues for divorce from her husband.) In the economic realm, a woman is similarly her husband's dependent, and the finances of the family are generally under the husband's ultimate control. In religious terms, a woman constitutes a force that not only must be kept separate but that is also felt to be dangerous. This religious notion is part of a more general ideology viewing women as less rational and less intelligent, more emotional and more sexually driven, than are men.

Kept separate and subordinate, the Moroccan woman has developed a world within limited boundaries that is insulated from men. In that world, many institutions and customs occur that are distinctive to women. Women's religion thus goes far beyond formal Islam or the brotherhood traditions: it relies heavily upon magic in practice and belief. Tied to the household, women have also developed economic emphases different from the emphases of the broader, male-dominated economic system. Extensive networks of borrowing and lending and an emphasis upon production within the household are patterns typically found among Taroudannt women. Socially, the Moroccan woman has elaborated certain relationships within her limited domain. The street neighborhood, for example, is a much more complex unit for women than for men, serving as a focus of a great variety of activities.

Segregation, subordination, and a degree of cultural autonomy are characteristic elements in the lives of traditional Moroccan women (Dwyer 1973, pp. 6–67). These elements also figure prominently in the judicial domain. Taken together, they provide broad guidelines for male-female relations in traditional Moroccan society. They define a social setting in which an official like the 'arifa of necessity must occupy a prominent place.

The Fields of Law and Law Enforcement

The interaction of the sexes within the judicial sphere is characterized by organizational divisions and underlying values similar to those found in the religious, economic, and political domains. A dichotomization of the sexes into separate spheres is maintained in court and court-related processes. Shame, modesty, and reticence—the qualities that women should exhibit in their relations with men—are important values throughout.

Both the judiciary and the system of law enforcement are male-run and male-dominated in Moroccan society. Men fill the positions of judge, notary, and scribe, the three major positions of importance in any regional court system in Morocco. They additionally staff the regular and court police. Moreover, the office of judge has been reserved as a male stronghold, being specifically restricted to male aspirants by statute. The basis for the restriction is Koranic decree.

Judicial behavior entails sharp sexual separation as well as female subordination. In Taroudannt, for example, court sessions are attended almost entirely by men. Male litigants sit in the courtroom awaiting their cases, while women litigants are kept outside of the court building by the court police. They huddle on the steps of the court building or in a garden nearby; only when their cases are considered are they allowed into the courtroom. Then, after their cases are heard, they are quickly ushered outside.

At those times when a woman's case reaches the judge, their

interaction is generally characterized by formality and reserve. "Proper" women generally exhibit reticence and modesty when dealing with men, and such behavior is additionally expected and fostered by the judge. As a result, judges and female litigants interact minimally. Judges solicit women's testimony less intensively, and they encourage short answers from them. When possible, male witnesses or male representatives are questioned in a woman's stead. Interaction, as a result, remains formal and terse.

Because judicial principles are often unclear to Moroccans, supplementary explanations of a judicial kind are often provided by a judge in the privacy of his chambers. Such counseling, however, provides enlightenment primarily for men. Women litigants are often absent from such sessions or are only cursorily advised during these periods. Again, on such occasions, coolness and distance characterize the interaction of woman and judge. It is only when professional counsel is employed that a fuller consideration of women's problems takes place.

Differences in the treatment of men and women extend to the area of substantive law. Men and women are treated differently by law with regard to a large variety of issues in Morocco: women inherit less; they can be freely divorced and yet can divorce their spouses only rarely; a curfew is imposed upon them, but not upon men; and their virginity is legally of interest and can be legally tested. Women are recognized as dependents by law, and their need for protection is legally maintained.

These substantive and procedural elements place women in a unique and difficult position vis-à-vis the law. On the one hand, face-to-face interaction is limited for women and male court officials. Communication between these men and women is generally difficult. This minimization of interaction is strengthened and legitimized by important Moroccan values. And yet the protection of women is legally sanctioned and controlled, which means that an increased level of communication is necessitated in many instances. To assure virginity legally, virginity must be testable under the law; to impose a curfew, women who venture out after dark must be detained; to maintain women as legal dependents, the support of women must be reviewable by the courts. In sum, women often fall within the jurisdiction of male court officials who are outsiders because they are to be protected from outsiders who are men.

The situation is a difficult one strategically for women as well as for the courts. Ideally, women, like other litigants, should try to reap the benefits of greater communication with court officials, and yet they also should try to limit their male-female interactions. They should remain legally protected within a male-dominated system, but they also should have minimal interactions with the men appointed to protect them. In the light of such dilemmas, an intermediary is necessary to minimize the contradictions and to make the system workable. The 'arifa performs this interstitial task.

The 'Arifa

The 'Arifa as Described in the Literature

The 'arifa is described only briefly in past ethnographic writings on Morocco. In his 1951 glossary, Brunot calls the 'arifa a "jailor," a woman "charged with the surveillance and care of prisoners," "most often prostitutes" (Brunot 1952, p. 515). The duties of the 'arifa apparently were similar in the Qcar El Kebir region which Michaux-Bellaire described in 1905: the 'arifa is credited with running the region's prison for women—there called the dar at-tqa— where prostitutes and other women were held until their relatives paid their fines (Michaux-Bellaire 1905, p. 120). In Rabat, at the turn of the century, the 'arifa's duties were similar in kind. She is described as the woman who held prostitutes in her home, called the dar el 'arifa in that city, until the women paid their fines (Mercier 1906, p. 362). The 'arifa is also variously described as a harem-keeper (Brunot 1952, p. 515), as a duègne (Brunot 1931, p. 195), and as a sage-femme or midwife, the latter description refer- ring specifically to her work in the region of Sefrou (Brunot 1952,

p. 515). These and other duties are still performed by *'arifat* in Taroudannt and in other regions, as will now be seen.

The Role of the *'Arifa*

The *'arifa* is the only woman employed by local Moroccan governments as a court official. She serves as an important liaison between the court and her district's women, and she operates in a variety of contexts in which contact between men and women must take place.

Basic to the *'arifa's* role as an intermediary is her work as a chaperone to the police. She accompanies the police into areas that women inhabit alone or jointly with men, which the police, as male outsiders, cannot properly enter alone. When women are present in the home of a man who is under litigation, for example, the police cannot undertake an investigation, make a property assessment, or accomplish an actual seizure, without the presence of the court's female representative. The *'arifa* must be there, it is morally and legally maintained, in order to protect the women of the house. She therefore becomes the first person admitted to the premises in question. Only after she has spoken to the women can entry by the police properly take place.

The importance of the *'arifa's* work as police chaperone is evident when cases of police entry without her are considered. Such cases are rare but entail severe legal complications when they take place. In the following incident, the court police were sued, in effect, for failing to be accompanied by the *'arifa*. The developments that ensued illustrate the importance of the *'arifa* in a police-entry case.

The case of Mohammad ben Omar versus the court police developed out of a routine police investigation. Mohammad ben Omar was being sued for nonpayment of debts. Unwilling to pay, Mohammad found that his property was being investigated by the court with an eye toward confiscation. One day, the court police were sent to a garden that Mohammad owned which surrounded his home, in order to undertake a property evaluation. Since the police had no intention of entering Mohammad's house, the 'arifa was not asked to accompany them.

Upon entering the garden, however, the police not only came into contact with the women of Mohammad's family but they directly clashed with them. From the roof of Mohammad's house and from the windows, Mohammad's wife, Aisha, and her daughters began to shout insults and threats. Then, as the police began to examine the garden, Aisha and her daughters hurled down pails, baskets, and bricks. Neighbors gathered as the barrage of words and objects continued. The police eventually had to retreat, unable to stop the attack.

The police later charged Aisha with assault, but Mohammad ben Omar also pressed his own charges. The police had entered his property unlawfully, he said, for the 'arifa had not been with them. They had upset his wife, leading her to abort. In addition, Mohammad said, the police had insulted and hit his wife. As a consequence of these alleged outrages, he charged the police with assault.

Local witnesses at first supported Aisha in her court battle. No objects had been thrown by her, they claimed, nor any threats made. As they said privately, they felt compelled to support their neighbors. In the end, however, the testimony of these witnesses was challenged and discounted. It was difficult for the judge to believe, for example, that the leather pail from the house's well had been lying in the garden at the time of the attack, along with the household baskets. Moreover, Aisha refused to seek medical confirmation that she actually had been pregnant and did actually abort.

In the end, Mohammad's charges were dismissed, and Aisha was given a one-month suspended sentence for her unlawful actions. The police, however, were severely criticized for shortsightedness. They had laid themselves open to criminal charges because the court's female representative had not been present with them. Said the judge in private counsel, the 'arifa should henceforth accompany the court police into any area in which women might possibly be found.

Through her interactions with women in her capacity as police chaperone, the 'arifa performs several functions. Her initial duty is to announce the presence of the police. The use of a woman in this capacity, untouchable by the men of the household, concomitantly helps temper male resistance and display. Her second duty is to gather the women of the house together, moving them all out of view and out of danger. As a result of her action, the police see little of the women and have minimal contact with them, and the modesty of the women is better preserved. The police, in turn, are also better protected from interference by onlookers. As a third task, the 'arifa, if requested, explains police procedure to the women of the house. The 'arifa often provides needed advice at these times and helps calm the women's fears.

The 'arifa's job as a chaperone to the police extends to all situations requiring police entry into an area in which "proper" women might reside. Women are worthy of this protection if and when they are legally uninvolved in the particular criminal or civil action under dispute. Because of their innocence, these women must have their respectability preserved. The 'arifa provides the necessary protection.

In addition to her job as a police chaperone, the 'arifa has also preserved certain of her prison-keeping functions. As in former times in certain areas, the 'arifa still remains the keeper of women who are troublesome in their homes. The 'arifa in certain cases of family conflict takes charge of the wife at the husband's insistence or offers her refuge at the woman's own request. The approval of the court is required, however, before the 'arifa's intercession.

Once approached by the court, the 'arifa provides the woman in question with a temporary home if the woman herself desires separation or with a place of enforced residence if separation is requested by the man of the house. In both instances, the site is the 'arifa's own home, which in this sense is called the dar d-deqqa (house of blows) or more generally the dar el 'arifa (the 'arifa's house). Since no man may enter the dar el 'arifa without court approval, and since a sequestered woman may not leave it without court permission, the reputation and modesty of each woman within the *dar el 'arifa* is assured. Nor can family fighting continue within the *'arifa*'s residence, for interaction is regulated strictly there.

The *'arifa* acts in yet a third capacity in legally important situations. When virginity needs to be determined, the *'arifa* is frequently called upon to perform the task. When pregnancy needs to be verified, the *'arifa* is often approached in order to provide a professional judgment.

The presence or absence of virginity has important consequences in a judicial sense within the Moroccan system. Most immediately, while a man may always divorce his wife, the lack of virginity in a presumed virgin is sufficient cause for publicly approved divorce. More importantly, whether or not the marriage is actually terminated, a lack of virginity can affect the nature of the payments made between the husband's family and the family of the bride.

When virginity is unexpectedly lacking in a young bride, the crisis, in effect, involves a breach of contract, for the presence or absence of virginity is recorded explicitly in the marriage contract of a bride. An unmarried girl, for example, is given the contract of a virgin (*bint*), while a *hajjala*—that is, a widow or divorcée—is given a contract that specifies nonvirginal status. If proof of virginity is not forthcoming on the wedding night of a presumed virgin, the provisions of the contract can be changed or the contract itself may be nullified.

The fact of virginity determines marital payments. It affects the amount of money that is provided to a bride's family for the wedding festivities. It also determines the *sdaq,* the amount of compensation given to a bride in case of widowhood or divorce. For a virgin, wedding expenses are large; for a nonvirgin, they are minimal. For a virgin, the *sdaq,* which provides for a woman financially during the difficult days after the termination of her marriage, ranges from about 4,000 to 100,000 *ryals* (40 to 1,000 dollars approximately in 1971), depending upon the wealth of the families in question. For a widow or divorcée, even less than

4,000 *ryals* is generally paid. With the discovery of a bride's previous sexual experience, the *sdaq* traditionally is halved; often it is never paid at all in such cases. In these instances, a repudiated bride returns shamed and penniless to her family or to the streets.

Because of the importance of virginity in social and judicial terms, the *'arifa* is called upon to verify virginity rather frequently. Seeking proof of their daughter's purity, a family might have their daughter certified by the *'arifa* before her marriage. Hoping to be assured that their bride-to-be is pure and well chosen, the groom's family might similarly request the prior verification of that fact. On the night of the consummation, moreover, the *'arifa*'s testimony is often crucial to the success of the marriage. If physical entry is impossible or if the consummation itself is bloodless, the *'arifa* is generally hired in order to determine why defloration has not occurred. If the girl is still a virgin, the *'arifa* attests to that fact. If the girl has previously been deflowered, the *'arifa* pronounces that she is not a virgin, but a sexually experienced woman. If the hymen of the girl is closed over, so that defloration by the groom is deemed impossible, the *'arifa* cuts the hymen, spreading the proof of the girl's virginity and permitting the groom's customary first entry.

One or both families insist upon learning the truth in these situations. If the girl is actually a virgin, her family is intent that any doubt about her purity be dispelled. If she is not a virgin, the family of the groom seeks to dispel doubts concerning his virility and is likely to deal harshly with their new bride. Should the bride's hymen be closed over, it is to the advantage of both the bride and the groom that the condition be rectified and that their sexual adequacy be publicly affirmed.

The confirmation of pregnancy similarly has important social and judicial consequences. Verfication of pregnancy is potentially important in those instances in which the mother-to-be is recently widowed or divorced. Support payments are reckoned differently, for example, if a divorced woman is pregnant. Moreover, in cases in which the legitimacy of the pregnancy is contested, the date of conception determines the child's right to inheritance or support. Since a mother generally becomes her child's guardian, she controls his inheritance and support allotments. The mother thus has a major stake in winning a legitimacy case.

According to Islamic law, a woman who is repudiated by her husband—that is, who has been divorced by him—or a woman who has been widowed, must submit to a period of sexual continence ('idda) immediately after the termination of her marriage. The period of sexual continence varies in length according to the woman's physical state. The nonpregnant but fertile divorcée or widow must remain continent until the completion of three menstrual periods. The menopausal woman must abstain for a period of four months and ten days. For the woman who is pregnant, however, the period of sexual continence embraces the totality of her pregnancy, one year being the maximum designated length of a pregnancy according to national law.

Observing the 'idda provides a woman with certain financial advantages, and the longer period associated with pregnancy has its own special advantages, in turn. Most importantly, it is only during the 'idda that a divorcée or a widow herself has the right to receive support payments from her husband or from her husband's estate. According to the legal code, food, clothing, and lodgings must be provided to a wife by the husband for the full term of the 'idda. Since pregnancy considerably lengthens the 'idda in most cases, it thus can also considerably lengthen the periods of a woman's postmarital support.

The question of support is even more important with respect to the child than with respect to the mother. If a child is conceived during the marital period, the wife's husband is presumed to be the genitor. He is legally required to support such offspring until its maturation is reached. Similarly, if paternity is presumed, the child is legally eligible to inherit from his father's estate, to the proper Islamic degree.

When the legitimacy of a child or fetus is challenged, however, rights to support and inheritance are challenged too. In such cases, the 'arifa may be called upon to determine whether or not conception occurred during the marriage—that is, whether the pregnancy is legitimate.

In such instances, the 'arifa undertakes a general physical examination of the woman in question. By examining the nipples of the woman and by carefully feeling her abdomen, the 'arifa determines if conception has occurred and how advanced the pregnancy is. This information is then communicated to the judge who renders his verdict in the inheritance or child-support case.

The duties of the 'arifa are several and diverse. She acts as a police chaperone, she serves as a prisonkeeper, and she works as a medical adviser for the regional courts. She becomes involved in court-related cases in which women figure, directly or tangentially, and often affects the outcome. Her particular impact, however, still has to be ascertained. The sections that follow deal with the meaning of the 'arifa's behavior and its societal importance.

The Judicial Importance of the 'Arifa

The 'arifa's overriding importance to the judiciary lies in her role in facilitating communication between the sexes. Through her physical presence, she legitimizes contact between court officials and women, and through her investigations, a freer exchange of information between them can ultimately take place.

In her role as a police chaperone, the 'arifa legitimizes contact between the police and local women. Men alone cannot properly establish such relations, as has been seen. Men who are strangers are normally barred from approaching reputable women at home or in the street. To initiate a conversation with such women is a breach of the Moroccan code of behavior; to see them in their household garb, unveiled and unhidden, constitutes an invasion of privacy; to enter their homes alone is to subject them to suspicion. The 'arifa is thus needed as a liaison so that proper contact can be maintained.

The 'arifa, as keeper of the dar el 'arifa, is also a liaison, facilitating communication between women and the courts. The *'arifa* acts as a chaperone for women imprisoned in the *dar el 'arifa,* stringently regulating relations with men involved in the case. She also hears women's testimony and records women's complaints, if and when they concern the quarrel in question. Whereas modesty, embarrassment, and reticence generally characterize judicial situations in which both women and court officials are involved, through the *'arifa* interaction is facilitated: a more open and honest exchange of judicial information can typically take place.

The *'arifa* undertakes important investigations of virginity and pregnancy, which men can carry out only infrequently. Most Moroccan women are too modest to consult male doctors in cases which concern the genital region. French doctors are frequently avoided, and Moroccan male doctors are all the more shunned. The *'arifa* evokes no comparable embarrassment; she thus is readily called upon to make the necessary judgments.

The Basis of the *'Arifa*'s Unique Status

The *'arifa* provides the link that permits proper interaction of men and women in a broad variety of court-related situations. She has open access to women and, uniquely for a woman, general access to the judiciary's men. As a woman who is respected and venerated, she can approach all women within her territory, openly and directly. Even more interestingly, she can also approach men in the administrative hierarchy. She can do this chiefly because of her heritage as a slave.

The *'arifat* who are described in the sparse literature on the subject hold one characteristic in common: each is a black woman (Mercier 1906, p. 362; Michaux-Bellaire and Salmon 1905, p. 120; Brunot 1931, p. 195; Salmon 1904, pp. 12–13), often having the status of slave (Brunot 1952, p. 515). Because slavery has long been abolished in Morocco, the present *'arifa* of Taroudannt is a free woman but continues to partake of and harken back to that same slave tradition. She is classified locally as a *haratiniyya,* a traditional term for a brown woman who is free but who works as a servant. However, she herself stresses her descent from a slave through the female line. That slave was designated 'arifa by her master, a powerful precolonial warrior who controlled the Taroudannt region. Although he was eventually overthrown, the prerogative to be 'arifa remained in that woman's family throughout the Protectorate and the postindependence periods. Six women in that family, including the present 'arifa of Taroudannt, became 'arifat by virtue of their descent from that slave founder.

The heritage of the Taroudannt 'arifa provides each woman in her family with a potential and immediately activatable tie to the regional administration. The government need not choose an 'arifa: an 'arifa is available to them by tradition. She works whenever she is called upon, both days and nights, and she adapts her behavior to situational demands as is fitting for a servant. From childhood onward, a potential 'arifa is taught to behave in these ways.

Although descended from a slave, the 'arifa is nonetheless highly regarded by Taroudannt's female population. She is generally characterized as logical and fair-minded beyond what are thought to be the capabilities of most women. Her selection by what is felt to be a more rational male establishment is often cited as proof of that fact.

The 'arifa has won the support of women through impartiality punctuated with sympathy and understanding. The present 'arifa has also won the respect of Taroudannt's women in yet other ways. Several years ago, for example, the woman who is now 'arifa volunteered to take charge of the grounds of the saintly shrine in which the women members of the Jilaliyya brotherhood congregate. She has also become socially indispensable as the leader of the respected shexat, a group of older women who perform traditional music at marriages and other festivities for female guests. The shexat are now hired for most women's celebrations, and thus the 'arifa has come to be the city's main female entertainer. The 'arifa also leads the yearly procession of the city's hujaj, the pilgrims from Mecca, upon their return to their homes.

Perhaps most important in terms of her nonjudicial functions is the 'arifa's work as a traditional midwife. The present 'arifa is the most successful midwife within the city's walls. Her work in this capacity is sympathetic, willing, and cheap. She does not ask a set fee; instead, she is given whatever the new mother can afford. Moreover, when a new mother is poor, the 'arifa is typically generous: her gifts often exceed the delivery fee.

Despite the success of her many ventures, the 'arifa of Taroudannt has steadfastly maintained an inconspicuous life-style. The nature of her relationships, in fact, aligns her more closely to the less powerful women that she supervises and serves. The present 'arifa of Taroudannt, like her predecessors, is a mother and a grandmother, and she makes much of that fact. Now a widow, she has lived through two successful marriages while serving in the 'arifa role.

The 'arifa's manner, like her relationships, tends to deemphasize her powers. To this day, her home, her dress, and her demeanor are modest. Constant small-scale entertaining for clients and guests is the only visible outlet for the large amount of money that she earns. In fact, she maintains an air of inferiority throughout. She calls even a poor woman lalla or lady, for example, thereby signaling that she is serving rather than assuming control.

The 'arifa, whether consciously or unconsciously, behaves in a way that obscures her wealth, her success, and her power. She stresses her womanliness with regard to her family, and she emphasizes her servant-slave origin through her general style. She staves off resentment and jealousy quite successfully in these ways.

The 'Arifa's Formal Functions:
Her Importance to Men

The institution of 'arifa has probably remained part of a male-dominated judicial system because in many respects it works in conjunction with the goals and the desires of men. Limitations upon the jurisdiction of the 'arifa demonstrate this explicitly. The *'arifa* does not protect Moroccan women in all situations; she serves chiefly in situations in which men desire their women to be protected. She protects women not with respect to their many personal assets, but instead with regard to those of their qualities that are valued in male-female relations: their modesty, their sexuality, and their childbearing powers.

The *'arifa* thus does not act as a police chaperone in all judicial situations in which women are involved. If a woman is charged with robbery or murder, for example, the police can seize her without the *'arifa*'s presence. If she is a prostitute, the police need not wait for the *'arifa* in order to enter that woman's home. Should a woman engage in litigation, the *'arifa* does not mediate with court officials on her behalf. In sum, the *'arifa* does not protect women in situations in which they are independently involved. Instead she protects the proper and traditional woman who continues to submit to her husband's protection.

Similarly, the *'arifa* does not serve as a jailkeeper in all situations in which women are incarcerated. In Taroudannt, prostitutes and other female criminals, for example, are sent to a separate women's prison. It is only in cases involving marital conflict that women may legally be sent to the *'arifa*'s home.

In that limited number of cases, it is the men, in the end, who determine whether or not their wives will be sent to the *dar el 'arifa*. In cases of marital difficulty, a husband might send his wife off to the *'arifa,* he might keep her at home, or he might sue for divorce. The latter two courses of action represent the most commonly used alternatives by far. A husband, in fact, sends his wife to the *dar el 'arifa* only when he is determined to keep his marriage intact. His wife's stay in the *dar el 'arifa,* he hopes, will temper her emotional responses and will break her intransigence. Even when a woman herself seeks out the *'arifa* because she feels that her family life is intolerable, her husband again dictates the *'arifa*'s use. A wife remains in the *dar el 'arifa* only through her husband's approval. If she herself goes to the *dar el 'arifa* and he no longer desires her, the husband simply tells his wife to return to her parents and he files for divorce.

In a similar manner, virginity testing most directly serves the Moroccan male's interests. Testing rarely originates at the woman's request. Instead a bride's husband or his family typically demand that a girl's virginity be tested when under dispute. Testing in this sense is undertaken in order to assure the husband, his family, and their guests that they have not been cheated in their choice of a bride. She has nothing to gain but reaffirmation of her modesty; but if she proves to be a "woman," much is in jeopardy. Her marriage, her *sdaq,* and certainly her respectability are endangered.

Pregnancy examinations are similarly undertaken only when a woman and her husband's family find themselves at odds. The initiative again is taken by the man's family in these instances, for the legitimacy of a married woman's pregnancy is otherwise presumed. If the expectant mother's fidelity is doubted, or if her former affines wish to discredit her, the question can be definitively settled only by examining her physically. In both cases, the *'arifa* steps in at the husband's or his family's request.

At issue in all of these cases are rights over a woman's sexuality and only those rights. As a police chaperone, the *'arifa* protects the women of the house from improper contact with the police, be it physical, verbal, or visual. Since illicit sexual relations are believed to occur only when the woman is willing, the *'arifa* protects the husbands of these women from their wives' weakness as well. When a woman is sequestered in the *dar el 'arifa,* her modesty and her fertility as still claimed by her husband are the assets that are protected. Escorted to and from the *dar el 'arifa* by the court police and guarded by the *'arifa* in the interim, a wife who is later reconciled with her husband assuredly has not violated his sexual rights. Examinations concerning virginity and pregnancy likewise help assure a woman's marital fidelity: they help show whether a woman's sexuality has been properly used.

In all of these duties, the *'arifa* deals with the sexual aspects of womanhood. She protects and regulates female sexuality, but always with respect to male interests and prerogatives.

In keeping with the *'arifa*'s importance from a male perspective, the *'arifa* in most instances is paid for her services by those men who benefit from her use. As keeper of the *dar el 'arifa,* the *'arifa* is paid by the husbands of the women who reside in her home. In addition to providing their wives' daily food, these husbands pay for each day of their wives' seclusion. Amounts are proportional to the husband's personal wealth. One or two hundred *ryal*s (about one or two dollars) are typical payments for a day's stay in the *dar el 'arifa.*

The *'arifa* is also paid for her services as police chaperone by the husbands of the women who she protects. In those instances, the man who requests entry initially pays the *'arifa*'s fee. She is paid 200 *ryal*s for each visit if a number of different visits are made in one day, or 400 *ryal*s if the case constitutes the *'arifa*'s only entry. However, liability for the fee is afterward transferred to the husband's account. It is added to the list of debts for which his property may be seized.

Similarly, brides and pregnant women generally do not pay the price of the *'arifa*'s virginity and pregnancy examinations. It is only when these examinations are requested by the woman's family that such payment is made. By contrast, in cases involving possible court action, a woman's opponents generally pay the *'arifa*'s salary. Thus when a bride's virginity comes into question, 100 *ryal*s or a garment of some kind is paid by the groom's family to the *'arifa* for her professional aid.

The *'arifa* receives no salary from the regional government to which she renders service. Instead, she is supported by those individuals whom she most actively serves. In most cases, these individuals are men or the members of a man's family. They are the husbands who wish to have their wives' reputations preserved; they are the men who want their brides' fidelity assured. In these situations, women come under the *'arifa*'s scrutiny.

The *'Arifa*'s Informal Functions: Her Importance to Women

The institution of *'arifa,* as defined through its formal functions, provides important safeguards for the Moroccan man's marital rights. The functions of the *'arifa* as they are actually carried out, however, provide legal and moral support to Moroccan women. In large part, this support arises because the *'arifa* herself is a woman: she spends her time largely with women and she understands women's problems. Her sympathy for women is frequently evoked.

Because the *'arifa* is privileged in terms of her access to people and information, however, her aid to women can go beyond emotional support. The *'arifa* not only consoles; she can also mediate and advise. She thus can serve as an informal counselor and ally to women in the judicial domain.

The *'arifa*'s informal dispensation of judicial information is extremely important in Morocco's traditionally sex-segregated society, for most women have little or no direct access to legal information and aid. They interact predominantly with other women who also tend to be legally inexperienced. In the vast majority of cases, women additionally lack the resources necessary to seek out professional advice. Judges and other court officials generally discriminate against them. Moreover, women sometimes feel psychologically unable to contact legally knowledgeable men because of feelings of modesty. In the face of these social disabilities, the *'arifa,* as a knowledgeable and approachable woman, provides an important source of legal advice.

The Moroccan woman, in sum, is badly in need of a counselor and a liaison. The *'arifa* frequently provides these services for those women with whom she becomes involved in a case. In cases of police entry, she repeats the court's charges to women as she removes them to the side. She sometimes advises them concerning advantageous courses of action. On occasion, she estimates the duration and effect of a suit.

The *'arifa* is even more of an adviser and aide to the women of the *dar el 'arifa.* During the days and weeks in which she is secluded there, a woman has the opportunity to plead her case in detail before the *'arifa.* Support for the woman's story can be obtained from neighborhood and family women by the *'arifa,* in turn. The *'arifa,* moreover, takes special note of a husband's behavior while he visits his wife in the *dar el 'arifa.* She notes whether or not he has brought adequate food supplies, and whether or not he has treated her acceptably. When the woman is finally released, the 'arifa provides the judge with a combination of the woman's testimony, of corroboratory evidence as provided by witnesses, and of her own firsthand observations. She, in sum, submits a report in which the woman's point of view is more fully provided.

The 'arifa, in fact, often takes an active role on behalf of women in dar el 'arifa cases. She defends women before their husbands, and arbitrates in their favor. When a husband brings his wife's daily food ration to the dar el 'arifa, for example, the 'arifa generally tells him to treat the mother of his children or the keeper of his household with greater respect. She stresses those qualities that are important to the man in his wife. She might also counsel him to mend his ways if he is difficult, or to be patient if justice appears to rest with him. If support payments are inadequate or if they do not arrive promptly, the 'arifa might chide a husband or shame him. It is even rumored that some 'arifat falsely report that dar el 'arifa women are pregnant by their husbands. In that way, a temporary advantage is gained by the women, for the husbands become less likely to file for divorce.

The 'arifa can approach husbands freely in these ways because she is a duly constituted representative of the local government. A husband cannot fire the 'arifa, for her position is not dependent upon him, nor can he directly remove his wife from her care without the court's aid.

The 'arifa can also successfully shame many men in her interactions with them. She is old and venerated, and as a woman she must be treated with a general reserve. Moreover, many 'arifat also work as midwives (Brunot 1952, p. 515), and as such must be accorded additional respect. The 'arifa of Taroudannt, for example, is said to have delivered half the city's population, and she is by far the city's most important traditional midwife. Those men who were delivered by her must treat her reverentially and listen to her counsel, for she is their jidda (deliverer, grandmother). So, too, should respect be accorded to her by those men whose children were delivered through the 'arifa's aid.

In cases involving pregnancy and virginity testing, the 'arifa is said to make her assertions with women's futures in mind. Thus in one region in the south of Morocco, the 'arifa was credited with falsifying reports of virginity on several occasions. This option is always available to the 'arifa, it should be noted, for she traditionally has the right to slit the unperforated hymen of a young bride if consummation is difficult. With a judicious cut of the razor, the 'arifa thus can simulate virginal blood in a nonvirginal bride. Similarly, with a judicious guess at the advancement of a pregnancy, the legitimacy of an illegitimate child can be legally established.

The 'arifa, of course, also aids women through her formal functions. She helps to preserve the reputations of respectable Moroccan women, reputations that, in turn, are the women's key to success. Because of such protection, the dar el 'arifa is viewed favorably by women, whereas the women's prison, in which women are left unprotected and unchaperoned, is viewed with unmitigated dread. In fact, the 'arifa's intervention in cases concerning virginity, her presence during police entry, and her guardianship at the dar el 'arifa generally are viewed with favor by women. Through the 'arifa's intervention, a respectable woman's reputation is better maintained.

The 'arifa is important to women both formally and informally. She protects those assets that make a woman valuable to outsiders, and that a woman therefore values highly. This is the aid that the 'arifa provides to women through her formally ascribed tasks. She also provides advice and support and acts as a sympathetic and willing accomplice on occasion. These informal functions provide an added dimension to the work that she performs in her professional role.

Conclusion

The 'arifa is unique in Morocco's male-dominated and male-oriented judicial system. As the Moroccan woman's judicial representative at the regional level, she is the only legal professional who deals exclusively with women's problems. Moreover, she is the only woman engaged professionally within the judiciary and the only woman who has a functioning legal institution under her control.

That institution itself is structurally crucial in Moroccan society. As a bridge between the sexes, it is unusual in Morocco's sharply sex-segregated world. Paradoxically, however, the need for the institution arises precisely because segregation is so pervasive along sexual lines. The institution of 'arifa comes to be of vital importance if the sexes are to be kept separate and yet contact is to be maintained.

The sexual segregation that makes the institution of 'arifa necessary also makes possible the assistance to women that the 'arifa provides. The 'arifa, in essence, segregates women from men. By performing that task, however, she also bars male onlookers and has unchallenged access to women who come under her control. Abundant opportunities exist in these situations for counsel and support. Moreover, having become the only politically approved, professional link between the sexes within the judicial domain, the 'arifa tends to become an unchallengeable intermediary. Her testimony must be accepted on such questions as virginity, for no man is permitted to verify the 'arifa's claims.

The institution of 'arifa is interesting because it is representative of a number of institutions that occur in sex-segregated societies. These institutions are interstitial institutions in a social sense, for they bridge the gaps between the sexes that sexual segregation maps out. The 'arifa of Morocco, the dueña in Spanish culture, and the barber's wife among Swat Pathans (Barth 1959, p. 33) are three institutions of this kind.

These interstitial institutions define one aspect of male-female relations that has remained inadequately described in the anthropological literature—what in Baily's terms (1969, pp. 167–75) would be called middlemen or brokers acting between male and female groups. The 'arifa is a broker, a mediator, and an interpreter, according to situational demands. She exhibits a complex set of behaviors that facilitates communication between a dominant male and a subordinate female group.

'Arifa-like middlemen are interesting not only because they facilitate communication, however; for when communication is otherwise blocked between two populations, middlemen are generally found. The striking element is how structural realities and ideological demands mold the form of the middleman institution. The 'arifa of Taroudannt has a background that permits her to act easily as a liaison: her value as an intermediary in part revolves around the structural position in Morocco of servants and slaves. The actual form of her work similarly is a function of the presence of co-occurring and yet differentially empowered male and female groups. Moreover, her informal aid to women arises because an ideology of separation maps out an autonomous sphere of activity, however small, for women in Morocco. This has arisen because restraints exist upon men as well as upon women in Moroccan society. Men are limited in their supervision of women by an ideology decreeing that the purity and hence the separation of women must be maintained.

The existence of institutions like the 'arifa points to a need to investigate the structural space that exists between male and female worlds in sexually segregated societies. Sexual segregation creates numerous social and political difficulties: limited communication, limited access, and limited control are among them. Interstitial institutions, varying in form according to their structural and ideological correlates, are an expression, if not always a resolution, of these problems.

References

Bailey, F. G. 1969. *Stratagems and Spoils—A Social Anthropology of Politics.* Oxford: Blackwell.

Barth, Fredrick. 1959. *Political Leadership among Swat Pathans.* London: Athlone.

Brunot, Louis. 1931. *Textes Arabes de Rabat.* I: *Textes, Transcriptions et Traduction Annotée.* Paris: Librarie Orientaliste Paul Geuthner.

Brunot, Louis. 1952. *Textes Arabes de Rabat*. 2: *Glossaire*. Paris: Librairie Orientaliste Paul Geuthner.

Dwyer, Daisy Hilse. 1973. "Women's Conflict Behavior in a Traditional Moroccan Setting—An Interactional Analysis." Ph.D. dissertation, Yale University.

Mercier, L. 1906. "L'Administration Marocaine à Rabat." *Archives Marocaines* 7: 350–401.

Michaux-Bellaire, E., and G. Salmon. 1905. "El Qcar el Kebir." *Archives Marocaines* 2: 3–240.

Salmon, G. 1904. "L'Administration Marocaine à Tanger." *Archives Marocaines* I: 1–37.

CONSTANCE CRONIN

3 Illusion and Reality in Sicily

S EX-ROLE PATTERNING as reported in some of the papers in
this volume reveals the formation of two generally separate,
and sometimes equal, major groups that we might call the world
of women and the world of men. It has been assumed in the past
that when this extreme form of sex segregation occurred, men
were the free and liberated leaders with all the authority and
power, while women were relegated to subservient and lonely
places in the household as onlookers to the world of men. Some of
the material presented in this volume reveals instead a very different constellation of support, authority, and power, showing the
complexity of the women's groups and the importance of women
for other women.

In our own society and in many other complex and industrialized societies, the sexes may be socialized differently and
there may be differences in the opportunities open to men and
women, but there is a cultural belief to the effect that all people
are created equal. Western Europeans and Americans live in a

The material used in this paper was obtained during two fieldwork periods: 12
months in a western Sicilian town of 25,000, and 14 months in Sydney, Australia
with Sicilian immigrants from all parts of the island. Although I cannot speak
definitely for all Sicilians, I feel, from literature and interviews in Australia, that the
pattern described here is generally valid for Sicily as a cultural and social entity.
The time period under consideration is the early 1960s.

world that includes both sexes, and it seems fair to assume that men and women perceive that they need each other. Like-sex persons are not the sole referent for either men or women, and both play out their culturally conditioned role constellations with and often for each other.

It is extremely popular in and out of the academic literature to view Sicily as one of those magical crossroads between east and west, which has somehow taken diverse cultural elements from the Middle East and Europe and blended them. The island of Sicily, lying as it does between continental Europe and the coast of North Africa, may have appropriated cultural, social, and material items from these two powerful and vast areas, but it would be a serious error to view contemporary Sicily as a part-this-part-that society. One cannot deny that there are cultural and social elements in Sicilian society that are generally characteristic of Western Europe on the one hand and of the Middle East on the other. European factors such as bilateral kinship and neolocal residence, combined with Middle Eastern elements such as the honor and shame complex, almost total isolation of women from the public sector, and the key role played by the eldest son, are all characteristic of Sicily.

Sicily

Sicily, which has been occupied since at least late prehistoric times by 14 recorded governments, is today part of the national state of Italy. It receives special status as a semiautonomous province; but it must comply with Italian laws, rules, and regulations while representing itself in the national parliament. The island is hot and dry in the summer, cold and wet in the winter, and is plagued with a serious shortage of water, except along the east coast. Families tend to be large and birth-control techniques are largely unknown (and are illegal in any case); overpopulation is serious, but massive emigration for the past 100 years has staved off a crisis.

Most of the people are directly or indirectly involved in agriculture. Industrialization, although highly developed in the north of Italy, has not yet made a notable impact in the South (*il mezzogiorno*). (For a fuller understanding of this problem see Chapman 1971; Cronin 1970; Banfield 1958; Barzini 1964; Moss and Thompson 1959.) However, Sicily, in common with the rest of southern Italy and Spain, Greece, and Yugoslavia, has never fit very well into peasant theory for a number of reasons. Almost all Sicilians live in densely settled towns and cities of some considerable size. There are almost no communities of a few hundred people; rather, a town such as Poggioreale, with a population of about 5,000, is considered small and lacking in amenities.

A Sicilian town is almost totally devoid of greenery. The center of every town is a piazza where men gather to talk, surrounded by stores, coffee bars, and the main church. Off the piazza runs the main street, the Corso. The wealthy and higher-status families live on or near the Corso. The rest of the streets are narrow and roughly cobbled with small one- and two-room houses directly adjacent to each other. Most towns are divided into named quarters that have no administrative recognition; but aside from vague beliefs that the people in each quarter share some characteristics, these are not viable entities.

Towns are heterogeneous for occupation and class. They contain not only persons with typical urban occupations such as doctors, lawyers, and white-collar employees, but also farmers and agricultural day laborers. Sicilians prefer to live in urban environments that have entertainment, action, life, and a never-ending flow of people and activities. Most of the farmers are poor and along with shepherds rank at the bottom of the social stratification scale; professionals and shop and office workers are middle-class; some towns have a resident upperclass, usually aristocratic, but most do not. Therefore, while the variation in the class system is limited, the gulf between the majority of farmers and all the rest is vast.

There is no positive view of peasantry. On the contrary, a number of proverbs completely devalue farming as a way of life: it is said that "a man who farms the land is his own slave." Until World War II there were few opportunities for upward social mobility; today, however, while mobility between classes is still difficult, it is possible to move upward within a class. Young men are rapidly abandoning their fathers' farms to become coffee-bar attendants, construction helpers, and auto mechanics, and always with their parents' approval. Girls and their parents prefer marriage with a nonfarmer because of the possibilities for more money and greater prestige.

Since agricultural plots lie outside the town, farmers must travel to their land. However, this is not a simple round trip. Italian law, which in this case mirrors customary law, stipulates equal inheritance for all children, so that shares of the family patrimony must be given at the marriage of each child or divided equally at the death of the father. Since this system has been in effect for over 100 years, limited land resources plus large families have today resulted in extremely small fields. Each person or nuclear family, if fortunate, will own several of these plots, but they are usually widely dispersed. Therefore, the farmer spends inordinate amounts of time traveling first to the countryside and then to the various sections he must work. Many spend up to half their time slowly moving on mules or carts. To complicate matters, most of the land is rocky and impoverished, water must be brought in by cart, and modern fertilization techniques are generally unknown. Many families are even worse off since they have no land at all. The father must hire out as a day laborer and work an average of fewer than 100 days a year, or he may sharecrop under conditions disadvantageous to him. Women may not and do not work; in most areas of Sicily they may not even help out in the fields during busy periods.

Most towns, because of their size, have a number of government offices. A few of these are for agricultural-assistance programs, but most reflect the complexities of a highly bureaucratic government. There are schools that, depending upon the size of the town, extend from first grade through the classical high school. School attendance is mandatory until the age of fourteen, and books and other supplies are given without charge. There are other national agencies that regulate electricity, taxes, customs, police, paramilitary police (the Carabinieri), courts, and identity papers. The local government, composed of elected officials, manages streets, water, vital statistics, and yet another police force.

Political parties are active primarily through clubs where men can meet nightly to talk and see friends. All of the many major parties are represented in most towns by at least a few activists, but only the governing Christian Democrats have any real power and most of the people vote for them. They do not like the government's perceived neglect of Sicily, but the other parties are either too "right" or too "left"; and besides, "We are Christians."

The Roman Catholic church is represented everywhere. Attendance by both men and women is low, but adherence to the values of the church is almost universal. Very few Sicilians know Catholic rules for daily observances such as abstinence from meat on Friday and obligatory attendance at mass on Sunday (this was before the recent reforms in the church), but they love the Pope, revere Jesus Christ, adore the Blessed Mother, and maintain devotions to many special saints. Anyone not a Catholic is a "Turk."

Even though there are national, regional, communal, and subcommunal institutions, these do not serve as a focus for groups. Sicilians have no sense of belonging in reference to the country or the town and do not share with others any beliefs or actions based on shared membership. The town is there, it picks up the garbage and supplies water erratically, but it is not an entity to which one owes anything. People do not perform services voluntarily, and community-action programs have proven to be totally unworkable. People from other towns are foreigners and therefore highly suspect, but there is not a reciprocal respect or concern for those of one's own town. The only grouping in the society that has any real validity is the nuclear family. Banfield (1958), Covello (1944),

Chapman (1971), and Pitkin (1954) have all noted this phenomenon for southern Italy, which is often called "amoral familism," a term coined by Banfield.

Sicilian kinship is bilateral. "The relatives" (*i parenti*) is a category comprising all affinal and consanguineal kin outside one's nuclear family. Relatives are supposed to be good to each other, to render aid when necessary, and always to show *rispetto* (respect) for one another. But relatives are not a corporate group; they do not hold property together, they do not live together, and they do not meet as a group to make decisions, work, or socialize. The nuclear family does all these things.

This family unit is the hub of the society to which each individual owes his complete loyalty and from which he derives his greatest rewards. The members of the nuclear family should live together, love each other, obey those in positions of authority, contribute all earnings to the family coffers, make decisions together, and demonstrate total undivided loyalty. The demands of this family group militate against the development of strong friendships outside it, for these would tend to weaken family loyalty and are therefore discouraged for both children and adults. In the same fashion and for the same reasons, closeness to other relatives, strangers, priests, the city, the country, and even oneself is a potential threat to the unity and integrity of the nuclear family. A well-known proverb states that "the real relatives are those inside the house" (*lu veru parenti sunnu chiddi dintra la casa*). This exclusivity extends to all others who are not "real relatives."

Within this family there is a complex but clear set of rules for relationships. The husband-father should command his wife and children and oversee the activities of the family both inside and outside the house. The wife should obey her husband and direct activities inside the house, while the mother should guide the children in carrying out the commands of the father. Sons should obey their father, help their mother, and oversee their sisters, while daughters should obey father, mother, and brothers. Brothers should respect one another and sisters should care for and help each other.

As males and females, always within a family setting, the rules are even more vivid. The *onore* (honor) of the family and the relatives depends ultimately upon the purity of the women. Women are weak and easily led astray; therefore, it is the responsibility of men and of other women to maintain the virginity of unmarried women and the constancy of married women. The best way to maintain *onore* is to ensure the protection of all women, and seclusion from others is believed to be the most effective method. Thus women must obey men who are stronger and remain in the house guarded by the men and other women in the family. On the rare occasions when women leave the house they should always be accompanied by others.

The culture does recognize the fallibility of men also, for God and His mother alone are perfect. Therefore, men too must be controlled. This control comes somewhat from other men, but the most important agent of control is the family—not the individual members, who are controlled themselves, but rather the family as a collective and single unit. Members of the community help in this regard and so do the rules and beliefs of the Church. Thus we now have stated the ideal by which Sicilian society functions. But ideals or norms are only rules for behavior and in practice are often not observed. To get a complete picture of the life of a society, it is necessary to observe both norms and behaviors, noting the congruencies and the inconsistencies.

Problems and Solutions

The major problem, from which all others derive, stems from the culture's demand that men do everything—make all decisions, carry out most of them themselves, and delegate the rest of the tasks to others while still remaining responsible for them. To do all this requires not only a considerable amount of time, but, more important, skill—intelligence, farsightedness, craftiness, and the ability to manipulate situations and people. Unfortunately, very few men have all the requisite skills. They desperately desire them and they feel unworthy and inferior because they are not as capable as the culture demands. One hears constant references by men to themselves as "poor things" or as having "hard heads": they do not understand everything they hear about and grow angry and hostile; they apologize for their stupidity and lack of sophistication. This does not mean that they can do nothing but rather that they cannot do everything. The cultural demands are so great and the societal opportunities so meager that failure is almost preordained. Men never really have a chance to be successful in their own world. However, so long as they appear to be in control, they and they alone receive public rewards.

One of the key words in understanding the complexity that is Sicily is the local meaning of the Italian word *rispetto*. The English definition of respect is "to feel or show honor or esteem for," and the Italian is almost identical. But when used in Sicily the word means "to keep up the appearances." One hears constant references to "having respect for the relatives," "I respect my brother," and "that is a man of respect." All this means is that the cultural front is kept in place; it does not necessarily imply love, loyalty, help, or admiration. The man who maintains the proper public stance has *rispetto* and his family has *onore*. In this he is aided by members of his family.

In contrast to a man, the only obligation for a woman is to maintain her honor, which she does by keeping shame intact. The concept "honor and shame" has for years been a key concept in Mediterranean studies, but for Sicily at least the meaning is at variance with other societies. One of the reasons we have not understood this critical difference is that little work has been done in Sicily, and another reason is that the Italian terms translate so easily into exact English equivalents. Thus *shame* in English means "a painful emotion arising from a consciousness of something dishonoring, ridiculous, or indecorous in one's own conduct or circumstances." We use the term with the verbs *to be* or *to feel*. It is a transitory state that induces slight or serious reactions in the individual, reactions that must be resolved. However, in Sicily the term *vergogna* is used with the verb *to have* (*avere*) and indicates a quality with which persons, especially women, are born. A good woman, a proper woman of *rispetto,* has *vergogna.* One is born with it and keeps it by decorous actions such as using a low voice or sitting correctly in a chair, behaving submissively to authority figures, and cherishing one's own purity. The more proper translation from the Italian would appear to be "an enduring sense of modesty and decorum." A woman loses her *vergogna* by violations of these cultural codes and is then called a *svergognata* (indicating the opposite of the original word).

The almost total emphasis in the literature on the fact that honor and shame equal virginity is highly exaggerated. For while the easiest and surest way for a woman to lose her *vergogna* is to have sexual relations with a man not her spouse, there are other ways as well. But all that the culture demands of women is that they maintain *vergogna* by remaining pure and modest and obeying figures of authority such as father and husband. Very few women violate these rules, for punishment is swift and awful. The majority have *vergogna* and with it do not need intelligence, wit, ability, or any of the other impressive qualities that men must exhibit. This very insistence upon one factor, or cluster of factors, leaves the woman free to choose what else she will be. She can sit back and spin out her life in total physical and mental laziness, relying on father, husband, son, and daughter to carry the demands of culture and society. But she can also choose to operate in the system of adjustment and use the many skills and talents she feels are hers. (This, of course, leaves out the important question of whether she really has any ability; but since even women who are incapable attempt to work through the system, we will not be concerned here with actual ability.)

Thus the prison of culture restricts a man from being and doing what he wants, whereas the fetters placed on the woman, although seemingly more rigid, actually allow her much greater personal freedom if she will but publicly maintain her *vergogna.*

Problems and solutions for both women and men come from the operation of the social system. There are a number of critical problem areas. One of these is the relation between the systems of education and social stratification. While schooling is available to all, it is, with very few exceptions, only the middle class who can take advantage of it. The two main reasons for this are home environment and finances. Working-class parents in their one- or two-room houses cannot provide quiet study areas for their children, nor do they see the need for such a luxury. It is assumed by most that learning is done in school and that homework is an exercise in obedience rather than in learning. Therefore children are told they should study in school and help out at home or in the fields after school. As a result, peasant children begin leaving school either voluntarily or by failing repeatedly—usually after two or three years. There are other families who for financial gain must take children, especially boys, out of school and put them to work as early as possible. Almost none of these parents think that education is a waste of time, again especially for boys, but they simply do not understand what is necessary for success in a modern school system.

Children from middle-class families do continue in school with varying rates of success, although their social-class standing ensures that no teacher will fail even the dullest pupil. Teachers, middle class themselves, frequently draw public comparisons between middle-class and working-class children to the children. So a growing feeling of inadequacy in a seven-year-old peasant is reinforced by teachers, middle-class success, and his parents' characterization of him as a *cretino* or a *testa dura* (hardhead). In a very short time this results in his first real failure when he drops out of school at nine or ten. This process is directed specifically at boys.

Girls are not expected to do well in school nor is it necessary for them to do so. The skills they will need to manage a house and family are learned at home; education beyond the ability to read, write, and work simple arithmetic is not only superfluous but damaging, because it will eventually make girls dissatisfied with their homebound role. Exceptionally bright little boys are praised, but little girls who display high intelligence are a constant source of worry to their parents, whose most frequent comment is *che peccato* (what a pity).

By the age of ten, boys have already experienced their first major setback, and whatever native intelligence and capacity they have has been effectively covered over by feelings of ignorance and inability. With girls it is different. They too may fail in school, but there is little if any public censure. They can reassure themselves that they are intelligent but left school, as many do, because they didn't like it. It is their decision, and they emerge with ego and self-esteem intact.

The boys then go to work with their fathers or in the town while girls remain at home helping mothers, learning housekeeping tasks, and beginning the embroidery of linens which will form part of their dowry at marriage. Engagements are early; marriages are late. During this rather long period, boys work and are, for the most part, isolated from social contact. If they go to the fields then the isolation is all but complete. If they work in town there is more contact with others, but employers expect a lot from their workers and there is very little time or opportunity for socializing or discussion. Workdays, six or seven days a week, are long, and there is only time for an hour or so after work to stand in the piazza with other men.

Girls remain home and the limits of their physical world are narrow—the house and the street extending for the block on which the house is located. But this street, the living room of all working-class families, is filled with people. Most are women of all ages, but usually there are a few men as well: artisans who repair shoes, carts, and implements or make barrels or bridles at home. Here, among the women, age differences have a tendency to blur and girls learn early to take an equal place in these women's groups. They take on the gestures, postures, speech patterns, and ideas of the older women and have an opportunity to learn not only the necessary housewifely skills but also the techniques of influencing decisions and controlling others without seeming to. Not just gossip but, more importantly, strategies are communicated. For example, in chatting about a husband and wife who have recently fought, an older woman will digress and enlarge to make a more general case: "Now see, a type like this Signor Tizio who is so brutal is not common but you might just marry one. The problem here is his wife who doesn't know how to handle him. She does so-and-so but what she should do is this. . . ." The girls listening learn a valuable lesson.

By the time marriage takes place personalities are developing and the scene is set. The prime task of the couple is to establish and even increase the prestige of this new nuclear family. This is accomplished in a variety of ways, such as eating and dressing well, keeping a neat house, bringing up properly behaved children, owning a house, later owning more houses as rental property, and generally maintaining everything and everyone in order. When a person marries he and she say they are going to *sistemarsi* (to settle, arrange oneself). This, properly and consistently done, will bring praise and prestige to the family itself and to the husband in particular, since he is in total command.

The culture dictates that the husband-father must direct all activities, make all decisions, ensure they are carried out, and represent the family and its members to the public. In addition, men should perform all the tasks outside the house, such as paying bills, visiting experts and professionals, buying groceries, and conferring with relatives and outsiders if advice is needed. This plus a full-time job proves impossible. The man is at work six to seven days a week from at least sunup to sundown (and farmers normally work much longer hours than this), and thus he is not available to perform all his obligations in the public arena. There are no other adult males in the house, and only the members of the nuclear family would even be considered for these tasks. Boys work also, unmarried girls never leave the block, and so most of these activities fall to the wife. It is she who visits the doctor and lawyer and goes from one government office to another paying bills, arranging accounts, and keeping up with identity papers. It is also she who makes rounds of visits to relatives, friends, advisers, and others for counsel on legal problems or financial affairs, and to determine whether a son in another family is a likely spouse for their daughter.

It is rare that the casual visitor will see her doing all this, because she leaves the house early in the morning with the long mourning veil pulled low across her face, tracing a path around and about the back streets where she will be seen only by other women. Quite a bit of impromptu visiting and chatting occurs on these travels and much information is exchanged. She will never admit that she was across town. If you visit her house when she is out, family members tell you that she is next door or across the street, and if you ask a neighbor she gives the same reply. Women do feel that their *vergogna* is liable to harm in these forays because these trips are potentially dangerous, but they also derive a great deal of satisfaction from them.

When the husband at last returns home, they confer together on their day's activities. Women are said to be much more verbal in these exchanges and in general, but information received is weighed and judged by both and decisions are reached together. Even though the woman gathers most of the information, the man can still make the decisions by himself. Very few do because they realize that their wives are intelligent, concerned, and often more skillful than they themselves. Women are frequently said to be *furbe* (crafty, cunning, sly), which is generally considered to be a female attribute. Note that no claim is being made for Sicilian women taking over male roles; it is simply that the social system places the woman, in practice, on the same level with the man. Each has his or her own skills and specialties and these together help the couple to maintain an orderly family that enjoys the respect and prestige of the entire community. While women are skilled at conversation, manipulation, and intrigue, men have greater seriousness, farsightedness, and sophistication in other aspects of the public sector of life. Together they are a good pair.

All of this is carried out in secret, but everyone else knows that it happens and works to keep it in the private sector—the house. It is extremely important that the cultural rules concerning male and female roles be maintained; if it appears that they have been broken, disaster will result. The man who does not command is not a man, while the woman who does command has lost her *vergogna;* and the family will become the laughing-stock of the community, the public butt of jokes, ridicule, and scorn. Therefore, the fewer who know the better.

It is impossible to hide the truth from children in the house, but they will not talk. Neighbors also know what really happens, but so long as appearances are maintained the neighbors will aid in the public deception, partly to protect an honest situation and partly because they are doing precisely the same thing. Others may guess and gossip but they need never know. It is not a fiction that is being maintained because there is an earnest and sincere desire to conform as closely as possible to the cultural ideal. It is interesting to note that Mafia families are constantly being held up as examples of how things should be. They, with their special resources and ultrarigid code, are said to be the only families who can maintain themselves in the proper way. The term *mafioso* can be used for one who is involved in underworld activities, but it can also be applied as a compliment, a term of respect, to any man who is scrupulous in carrying out the cultural dictates to command, to be proud, to keep silent. While most families cannot measure up, they do try. It is said that a poor wife is one who lets everyone know she is important; a good wife is one who lets only her husband know; and a perfect wife is one who lets no one know.

Another serious chink in the cultural armor is caused by the child socialization practices. Children are taught from the earliest age possible that the world outside the house is dangerous and that the streets are peopled with individuals who will "do bad things to you." The only safety and protection lie with family members inside the house. It is also emphasized that all people are weak and imperfect and not capable either of making decisions by themselves or of assuming responsibility for decisions once made. Therefore, all decisions are made by the group of capable adults in the family: father, mother, and adult children. Decisions are considered in the light of what is best for the family prestige, not for the wishes of the individual involved. If a child wishes to continue in school but the interests of the family will be better served by putting him to work and using his earnings to buy a house, then his desire and possibilities for the future are sacrificed. Parents are assumed to know more than even adult children and to have their best interests at heart; therefore, they will not put the child on the wrong road. There is little rebellion against the strongly stated decisions of the group, because one person alone does not feel capable of making decisions and probably is not. Decision making is a learned skill, and if one learns it in a group it will be extremely difficult later to stand alone, particularly against group pressure.

But this is another area in which both adult men and women feel inadequate, and it is reassuring for the man who is not, or at least does not feel, up to culturally imposed standards to have an intelligent spouse who can help shoulder these responsibilities. Men say and probably feel that most women are not as whole in their humanness as men, with the exception of one's own wife who has been tested in the trials that marriage brings.

This cooperation between husband and wife and among family members does not imply emotional closeness and intimacy. The entire social system of interpersonal relations fosters at best affective distance and at worst outright hostility. Here is another of the discrepancies between culture and the social system. The total effect of the socialization practices is to isolate individuals each from all others. Women feel the brunt of this more than men, but women also have ways of using the system to lessen the felt isolation.

Young adults do not date; they have no contact whatsoever with members of the opposite sex who are not close relatives or neighbors. Engagements are long but the contact pattern is one of seeing each other every few days in a living room with others in the family always present. Not only is conversation difficult and strained, but isolation from all boys tends to make girls very shy and embarrassed in front of their fiancés. After marriage, affection and love do develop in a few cases. For most couples a working relationship of mutual dependence develops; intimacy, companionship, and frank disclosure of feelings is impossible.

Men, in order to show command and maintain authority,

should be distant, silent, and brusque. From their sons they demand extreme respect, and a real battle for supremacy develops as the sons mature. Daughters are loved, coddled, and petted until puberty when this must cease. The father may still love and take pride in her, but he may not display this in front of her. After her marriage he remains her protector and a warmer relationship sometimes develops, but generally feelings of *vergogna* and distance prevail. Two brothers can have a decent working relationship, but it is said that personality differences loom large. Also, elder brothers have authority over the younger, and since they frequently wield this with a heavy hand little possibility for closeness remains. A man and his sister have an extremely difficult and hostile relationship. The brother is always in a position of authority and power over the girl, and if he is the eldest brother this is officially delegated by the father. The boy tends to be very strict and often cruel with his sisters who, impotent to strike back, come to hate. This relationship is considered by Sicilians to be the most stressful and most hostile within the family.

For the women the situation is not much better. Mothers and daughters who are in the house together for up to 25 years argue, nag, and bicker over work, and any real intimacy that might be fostered by their joint seclusion is prevented by *vergogna*. In this case *vergogna* means embarrassment in discussing "intimate" subjects with anyone but especially with those who are theoretically close. The most extreme *vergogna* is between mother and daughter. The mother cannot confide in her daughter and discuss problems she may be having in her marriage; the daughter is prevented from asking advice from her mother about sex, love, and marriage. Two sisters may be friends and often are, but differing personalities and competition for the attention of others often lead to fights and ultimate estrangement. The mother and her sons have one of the strongest, most affectionate relationships in Sicily. While *vergogna* intrudes here too, they still can move closer to each other, display more affection, and demand more help from one another than is possible in any other relationship.

However, the son must marry, and then a process of what the

mother sees as rejection begins. It is the mother's cultural responsibility to see that her son marries. But when she does this, given the primacy of the nuclear family of procreation, the son's wife begins to pull him toward her and away from his mother. There is usually a period of intense rivalry, jealousy, and even fighting between mother-in-law and daughter-in-law, but eventually the son-husband must step in and choose one. That one is always the wife. The mother then is totally bereft. She still maintains a close relationship with her son, but she is not first with him as before, and she feels totally alone.

After their marriages the children visit their parents; but the close nuclear family ties have been broken as the culture says they must be, and each is now enclosed in a new family unit. The strains in the various sibling dyads now surface, and, exacerbated by the introduction of the "outside sex," the spouse, relationships break down almost completely.

Friendship, which in many other societies is a viable alternative to kin-based relationships, is weakly developed in Sicily. Here women have an advantage over men. Men must be the cultural models, and while they may be friendly with a number of men they rarely have friends who can provide support, affection, and an outlet for feelings. While women too have very few friendships and have far fewer opportunities to be friendly with outsiders, they nonetheless usually do become friends with at least one neighbor. This is as true of young girls as it is of older women, and most of these friendships are between two people of widely divergent ages. The friend is the person to whom one can talk, cry, pour out confidences, and ask advice with the expectation of support, affection, and discretion. Many of these women call each other *co-mare*. This godparent relationship, which is formally reserved for certain church ceremonies, is used informally as a means of cementing a relationship that is frowned upon by the culture. To say "this is my friend" implies an empty relationship, but "this is my *comare*" means much. When asked if they have been sponsors for a baptism or marriage, women say they have not but add that they are *"comare* in San Giovanni," the patron saint of godparenthood.

Given the Sicilian culture, social system, physical environment, and an adaptive system to integrate the three, what are the rewards offered and what are the costs to the individual? For a man the rewards are great while the costs, although painful, are not staggering. If a man is able to follow the cultural dictates to appear strong, independent, self-reliant, commanding, serious, and silent the society will heap its greatest rewards and acclaim upon him. He is said by all to be a true Sicilian and is constantly praised for his demeanor, his family, his house, his daughter's marriage, and everything else commendable that he and his family members do. He is a man of honor and prestige, and if he also has money and social position better still, although these are not prime ingredients. He is deserving of deference and respect even from those who avoid him socially. If he is poor and of the working class they will not live with him or marry into his family, but they will admire him and hold him up as an example of what a Sicilian of his class should be. There are actually very few men who do not perform this part well.

Privately, he may know that he is not all that he projects in public. He is not very capable, he can't figure things out easily or well, he must have help, which he receives primarily from his wife. Deep feelings of inferiority, insecurity, and fear result; he worries that his public face may be lifted to expose the poor fallible man underneath. He has the satisfaction of knowing that he is trying as hard as he knows how to meet cultural demands that are too great. Still, the public reinforcement seems enough to enable most men to cope with their self-professed incapacity.

The pattern for women is very different because there is very little public reward and the costs to the individual are enormous. A woman is culturally rewarded only for maintaining her *vergogna,* which she can do very simply by remaining pure, modest, and circumspect with outsiders. This is not a difficult task and almost no women fail. Therefore, no one individual can feel that she has accomplished something unusual or difficult.

Women can be rewarded and praised by a small circle of people for other more specialized skills. Women of at least middle age can appear in a variety of contexts that call for an expert. There are four major roles of this sort, all of which demand a person with highly developed social sensitivity and an ability to talk well—two attributes women are felt to possess.

The first of these roles is the marriage matchmaker (*ruffiana*). These individuals serve as representatives of families when engagements are in the beginning stages. They may or may not be the friend or neighbor who first suggested the match, but they know all the intricacies of bargaining and dowry settlement, and the histories of the two families. This is considered an extremely difficult job and calls for a person who is not only skilled but trusted implicitly. The *ruffiana* is usually not paid for this work but may be given a present later.

The second job for which women are suited is the peacemaker. When arguments develop between branches of a family or between two families and there is a possibility that control may be lost and outright fighting or a *vendetta* may develop, then one or several people are called in as arbitrators in a collective-bargaining session in which the litigants have agreed to abide by the decision of the judges.

Both of these roles may be carried out by men and women, but a third is almost exclusively the province of women—the social expert. These are generally older women who know everything about everyone going very far back into the past. If, for instance, an engagement is contemplated by a family who want to know everything about the other family, they will send someone, usually a woman, informally to a social expert known to them and ask for a rundown on the family and all its members. These experts can usually go back long before their own lifetimes because they have, as younger women, learned from social experts now dead.

The fourth area of expertise, ribaldry, is one known only among women. There are women who function in the role of comedians or social satirists, always in an explicitly sexual context. They can make any subject and any person a figure of such hilarity, ridicule, and grotesqueness that the person will never again appear to be the same. The joking can be teasing and affectionate when applied to a person who is present, but it usually concerns someone who is not there and is strong, biting, and, underneath all the laughter, bitter. The women's groups that sit outside in good weather and indoors in the winter sewing and embroidering usually contain one woman who is such an expert. Her quips, jokes, and impersonations are circulated among other groups of women and her fame spreads. Men know who these women are but to my knowledge are never permitted to participate. The young girls and women who have such *vergogna* that no one can mention giving birth in their presence are privy to these shows, which often appear intended for their edification and education. This is not always rough humor, for most such women are also virtuosas at puns, word plays, and bits of drama. Humor at this level is usually sophisticated and smooth and would be the envy of any professional comedian.

Although some of this is humor for humor's sake, much is an effective form of social control. For instance, three teen-age girls were sewing with a group of women inside the house one afternoon. The satirist mentioned the marriage soon to take place between an aged widower and a forty-year-old spinster. She assembled her props and began to act out what it would be like to be married to an old man, to a spinster, and then to a young man. The skit was screamingly funny and quite explicit, but when this woman left the young girls began to talk seriously about the problems portrayed. The point of the older woman's acts was that girls who are too romantic and wait for the knight in shining armor end up with nothing but an old man; it was a point these three girls understood and believed. This entire complex of sexual joking and satire is a powerful covert strategy used only by women to give notice publicly that they are not always the innocent, ignorant, and put-upon creatures demanded by the culture. For while men do not participate in these sessions, they know of them, acknowledge the experts, and fear the day when they will be the subjects of these female dramas.

But the price to be paid for being a woman in Sicily is high.

Women, who do develop excessively romantic notions about love and marriage, are doomed to spend their lives without love and companionship with their husbands. In addition, they must never admit their skill at decision making and manipulation, and neither must anyone else, because to do so would ruin the husband and thereby the family. Thus no one ever alludes to these abilities nor do they ever praise or commend a woman for a job well done. She knows how good she is and so do her children, but for the rest she must remain the little submissive wife sitting quietly in the corner.

There are a number of ways in which dissatisfaction and hunger for affection and attention show themselves. Three have been most noted by observers of the Sicilian scene. The first is what the Sicilians call *neurasthenia,* considered to be a nervous debility and manifested in constant physical complaints. Women, and even young girls, are always ill or ailing. A casual greeting elicits from almost everyone a long detailed description of her aching feet, a headache from ironing, a backache from laundry, a cold because she stepped outside the door yesterday, or a more generalized feeling of ailing all over. Sicilians today are generally in good health, and when these same women are really sick they bear it stoically and without comment. This constant and maddening complaint is a bid for attention, a cry to "see me, listen to me, talk to me, me, me."

A second and more serious but more effective method is the social use of culturally defined mourning patterns. The etiquette of mourning is rather complex but generally follows the rule that the closer the kinsman, the longer the mourning period. For women, mourning apparel always includes black dress, hose, and shoes, but it can and often is elaborated far beyond this with the addition of black gloves, a black scarf hiding all hair, and a long black shawl pulled around the body and over the face in public. Women who go into perpetual mourning or those who wear the full garb (often the same women) demand and receive a great deal of respect and attention. They are deferred to and they are talked about, always in complimentary terms. In other words, they get attention. But there is a price to pay here too, for persons in severe mourning may not attend social events—movies, parties, baptisms, wedding receptions, or *fiestas*. When the official mourning period is over—it rarely lasts more than a year—the rest of the family goes to these, the only social gatherings the society offers, while the mourning woman remains home alone.

The third way in which women, and men too, reveal their hunger is by affection heavily laden with eroticism. Homosexuality is a controversial subject for many societies, especially in the Mediterranean and the farther reaches of the Middle East, and expert opinions differ on its prevalence. I feel that while there may not be actual sexual activity between Sicilian women, there are overt expressions of love, tenderness, and affection. This is much more noticeable among, although not limited to, younger unmarried women. They kiss each other, run their hands over each others' bodies, fondle each others' hands, hair, and faces, and sit in corners touching and feeling. In addition, especially among girls with more schooling, there is much writing of love letters. These are in flowery mid-Victorian style, filled with poetry, and express the writer's desolation at being from her "beloved" and her dreams of "your burning lips, your white skin." None of this means sexual activity, and I feel there is very little sexual experimentation or preference for women (although it is certainly known), but it does indicate that the total ban on affective relationships with men is finding an outlet with other women.

Conclusion

Sicily is one example of a society in which the cultural ideals and the social system are out of balance and where a system of adjustment has developed to deal with this problem. This adjustment permits the culture and the society to continue, but it also forces individual men and women to play roles that are far more complex than is usually believed. This paper does not imply that women have assumed all the power and left men with empty authority. Rather, we argue that while both sexes try to act out culturally determined roles, they must act in ways in the private sector of life which have differential advantages and disadvantages for men and for women.

One of the crucial factors in the Sicilian pattern is the distinction between formal cultural values and actual behavior that may or may not be culturally sanctioned. For too many years social anthropology focused almost exclusively on values and normative systems in an attempt to construct models of culture. When behavior was considered, it generally assumed that actions followed prescribed rules, and behavior patterns that diverged were labeled "deviant." We are now coming around to the idea that values and norms may set general guidelines for behavior while permitting wide latitude for individuals to differ from each other, to manipulate people and ideas, and, in general, to follow personal adaptive strategies. Thus in our own society there is a generally held cultural rule to "honor thy father and mother," reinforced in law and religion. But the working definition of the term "honor" may vary tremendously depending upon socioeconomic factors such as age, social class, religion, and ethnicity.

Even though we may never know first causes, we do know that societies vary in the amount of behavioral latitude allowed individuals. Those systems in which there is wide variance between values and behavior may be responding to historical or other outside forces such as colonial occupation, ecological shifts, or rapid social change, so that a total system that was once tightly knit may today be one in which the subunits do not have that "fit" that anthropology once expected of every human community. It may be that when the functional interrelations of the parts of the culture become attenuated, then opportunities for individuals to maximize their personal adaptive strategies become greater. In other words, when the value system demands one kind of behavior but the requirements of contemporary agricultural practices force another, the person may use this disjunctive situation for gain.

Such a condition may lead to serious problems regarding the relative importance of authority and power. Authority is the culturally legitimized "right to" while power is the "ability to," which may or may not be culturally recognized. While authority is always rightfully in the hands of the holder, power may often be seized and held illegally or covertly, thereby allowing the holder to present a surface of helplessness while underneath manipulating and bringing about desired results.

A good illustration of this important and far-reaching duality is in the area of sex roles. Anthropologists have frequently made explicit statements to the effect that in societies around the world men are the holders of both formal authority and the power to back up their legitimate demands, while women have possessed neither of these attributes. It is easy enough for students to see that in patrilineal societies descent, authority, and power all pass through the men, but most anthropologists have been meticulous in explaining matrilineality so that while descent may be traced through women, authority and power are still viewed as resting in men (but see Schlegel 1972).

Granted that in most societies men are generally the legitimate bearers of authority supported by the power necessary to enforce compliance. What then of the women? Can we continue to assume that women have no wishes, desires, or needs of their own, and if they do that the socialization procedures are so perfect that women never attempt to gratify needs or satisfy desires? This view, so common in the social sciences, today appears to be discriminatory on an ethical level and distorting or falsifying on the empirical level. If women do have strategies, even socially approved and institutionalized strategies, for getting what they want, then we must know these systems too. Without them we will continue to see societies through the man's eye, and we cannot then understand how whole societies, systems, or processes are structured and function. I am not referring to the occasional woman who defies everyone to satisfy her needs and probably is a deviant, but rather to socially and culturally defined subsystems available to all the women in a group and known to all the men.

Using Sicily as one example, it seems clear that if all the values, environmental needs, and institutions of a society or a class within it become unbalanced, the overt culture may remain the same but subsystems may develop to handle the resulting discontinuities. This in turn may permit individuals or groups without authority to maximize their perceived advantages by employing adaptive strategies within the context of a subsystem, thereby gaining power and importance that is socially but not culturally recognized. This paper refers only to those groups based on sex differences, but the hypothesis could also be applied to other groups or subgroups that lack broad authority bases—the young, religious minorities, racial and ethnic groups, the lower classes, and criminals.

Sicily, a small island with a homogeneous population of about 4 million, has a very clear set of rules for how life should be lived. The culture is uniform across the island and there are few who seriously disagree with the value system, but most find it difficult and sometimes impossible to put those values into practice. So another system has grown up that allows the society to adjust to these conflicts and permits the orderly continuance of life. Both men and women participate, but it is women who have been able to maximize the opportunities inherent in this system of adjustment to take and use power formally denied them by the culture. In a seeming paradox, cultural powerlessness and low status have become the bases for a freedom not available to men that permits women to move, operate, and manipulate the daily exigencies of life so that they become not only skilled and crafty but absolutely indispensable to the normal maintenance of affairs. This idea may come as a surprise to many social scientists but is not a surprise to the Sicilians, who were almost universally in agreement that this is how things are. Very few think that this is how things should be; they would much prefer abiding by all the rules, but it is simply not possible in their world.

This total system is likely to run into an increasing number of problems in the future as the society and culture change. Sicily is beginning, albeit slowly, to be pulled into the modern industrial complex that today characterizes the north of Italy. As more change occurs on the island and as more opportunities open for individuals, it will, I think, become increasingly difficult for the women especially to take advantage of these openings. There is no one to support a woman in her bid for change. Margaret and Lloyd Fallers' (personal communication) comments on women in western Turkey, where female groups support and encourage individual women to break through centuries-old barriers, are extremely interesting and to the point here, because such groups do not exist in Sicily. There are women's groups that talk, sew, gossip, and render aid, but they too conform to the cultural system, and it would be unthinkable for such a group to solidify to the point where it would encourage deviance from the norms. On the other hand, a system that discourages independence and self-sufficiency will not permit single individuals to go it alone. Independence, which is fostered generally in Western Europe and North America, is little known in Italy. Sicily may be extreme, but the Sicilian system is an Italian system and the ideas outlined in this paper are probably operative in an attenuated way in the rest of Italy; they may help to account for the exceedingly small percentage of women in higher-level professional and executive positions—one of the lowest in all Europe.

Whatever may occur in the future, the current Sicilian system presents the social scientist with one example of the rewards of looking beyond the culture to the interrelations of norms, behavior, and systems of adjustment. The reality that is Sicily is so full and rich that one wonders why we have for so long settled for a static, dull, and essentially untrue picture.

References

Banifield, Edward. 1958. *The Moral Basis of a Backward Society*. Glencoe, Ill.: Free Press.

Barzini, Luigi. 1964. *The Italians*. London: Hamish Hamilton.

Chapman, Charlotte Gower. 1971. *Milocca: A Sicilian Villiage*. Cambridge, Mass.: Schenkman.

Covello, Leonard. 1944. "Social Background of the Italo-American School Child." Ph.D. dissertation, New York University.

Cronin, Constance. 1970. *The Sting of Change: Sicilians in Sicily and Australia*. Chicago: University of Chicago Press.

Moss, Leonard and Walter H. Thompson. 1959. "The South Italian Family: Literature and Observation." *Human Organization* 18:35–47.

Pitkin, Donald. 1954. "Land Tenure and Family Organization in an Italian Village." Ph.D. dissertation, Harvard University.

Schlegel, Alice. 1972. *Male Dominance and Female Autonomy: Domestic Authority in Matrilineal Societies.* New Haven: Human Relations Area Files Press.

HELEN E. ULLRICH

Caste Differences

4

between

Brahmin

and Non-Brahmin Women

in a South Indian Village

IN SOUTH INDIA there appears to be a relationship between the importance of women's economic contribution and their power. A comparison of the Divaru caste, a peasant group in Karnataka State, with their Havik Brahmin neighbors provides an example of this phenomenon. The Divaru women work in the fields. In other arenas such as decision making and ritual they play a proportionately more independent role than their Havik Brahmin counterparts. This paper will examine the contrast.

The Divarus and Havik Brahmins discussed in this paper are from Totagadde, a village in the Malnad region of Karnataka State, formerly Mysore State. The pseudonym Totagadde refers to the two principal crops of the village. *Tota* or areca (betel) nut, is a cash crop grown on about 42 acres of land owned by Havik Brahmins, or 4 percent of the total village area. The members of the caste owning this valuable land are the economically dominant group in the village. Havik Brahmins also dominate Totagadde politically and ritually. *Gadde,* or rice paddy, land is owned by a nearby temple, Havik Brahmins, and some non-Brahmins of the

The fieldwork upon which this paper is based was done between October 1964 and May 1966, and was made possible by an American Institute of Indian Studies Junior Fellowship.

Sudra castes. Over three-fourths of the cultivated land is rice paddy. The temple-owned and much of the Brahmin-owned paddy is leased to the Divarus, numerically the largest Sudra caste in Totagadde (see Harper 1959).

Totagadde consists of nine different hamlets, each located at some distance, beyond visibility, from the others. In general, they are organized on a caste basis. Only one, the peasant-potter hamlet, contains more than one caste. The location of the different hamlets allows a certain measure of autonomy for each group. Even among the numerically dominant Havik Brahmins who occupy three hamlets, there is a tendency to interact primarily with people in one's own hamlet. This is less true of the men than of the women: Brahmin men go out, but the women rarely visit the other Brahmin hamlets, let alone non-Brahmin ones. In many cases they have never seen the non-Brahmin hamlets.

The low degree of communication among the various hamlets has resulted in the development of dialects. Although a detailed analysis would illustrate that each caste and each hamlet has its own linguistic characteristics, the major dialects in the village serve to demarcate the major social groupings—Havik Brahmin, Divaru or peasant, and Untouchable. The three-way division of social dialects reflects the situation common to Karnataka State and South India in general (Ullrich 1968).

Both Brahmins and Divarus occupy areas of the village close to their land. The Brahmins hire labor to assist in working the land, while Divarus do the work themselves. Some Divarus lease rice paddy; others own land. Members of the Untouchable hamlets work for Brahmins on a daily basis or as indentured laborers. Since there is insufficient resident labor for the areca-nut plantations, immigrant or contracted laborers have entered the area and founded two hamlets. The residents of these hamlets regard their presence as temporary, but in fact they may remain in Totagadde for several decades. To a large extent, then, the hamlets represent caste occupational groups. One can rank the hamlets, as well as the castes, on the basis of which groups will accept cooked food from which other groups.

I have chosen to contrast the Havik Brahmin and Divaru castes because of their numerical significance and independence from one another. The Divaru is the largest group not primarily employed by Havik Brahmins. In the ensuing discussion Havik Brahmin and Divaru women will be contrasted as to their roles and statuses in the occupational, authority, and ritual systems.

Occupational Roles

Both Havik and Divaru women take charge of the housekeeping. They are responsible for child rearing, cooking, and housework. The Divaru woman's responsibilities are not limited to housekeeping, however; she also works in the fields.

The work a Havik woman does confines her to her own household. She takes care of the livestock, prepares the meals, and cleans the house. Many a Havik woman feels that she is primarily a cook. Her job is to serve her husband: even though she may have likes and dislikes, her husband's wishes or suggestions are theoretically law. The shopping is done by the men, while the women stay at home. Even though men may not dictate every meal, they exert some control over menus by doing all of the marketing. Curiously, a widow may dominate the decisions about meals by deciding how many and which food taboos need to be followed. The ritually pure state required for a Havik widow may result in certain foods being avoided.

Independence among the Havik women is discouraged by the men.[1] They are rarely unchaperoned, nor do they have frequent need to leave the house. Like children under the age of twelve, they are thought to fear being alone, so are never left by themselves in the house. When women travel, their children or a servant accompany them. There is a stated reason for this precaution: approximately 20 years ago a Havik woman paid dearly for her independence. She dared to venture forth to other villages alone.[2] Several Havik youths decided to punish her for her boldness, so they mass-raped her on one of her excursions. Her husband filed a case in court against the rapists, which he certainly seemed likely to win; however, when asked who removed the cloth Havik women wear covering their pudenda, the woman replied that she had. As a result of this statement, the case was lost. Reluctance to decide in favor of a woman believed to be transgressing accepted behavioral practices resulted in attempts to find reasons why she could be designated the one at fault.

Divaru women, like most non-Brahmin women in Totagadde, engage in agricultural work. A typical day for a Divaru woman would be to rise at dawn, milk the cattle, wash the previous night's dishes, prepare food, feed the men, comb the children's hair, eat her meal, and then go off to the fields at about ten or eleven in the morning. Old people, sick people, and new mothers do not go to the fields. Those who stay home take care of the children. Usually, in situations where a person would not ordinarily remain at home, women may make cooperative arrangements so that they take turns staying home to watch the children. In nuclear-family households where only one adult woman is present, the woman may stay home or arrange for somebody in the neighborhood to care for the children. In the Divaru hamlet, as in the Brahmin hamlets, women are the primary caretakers of children. However, the emphasis on the mother's caring for all the needs of her child is less pronounced among the Divarus than among the Brahmins. In spite of the prevalence of the joint family among the Brahmins, its members do not engage in much cooperative childminding. Whenever a mother leaves the house to go visiting, the child comes along. The child may go visiting on its own, but the mother may wait several hours before leaving for the child to accompany her: the child is allowed an independence denied the mother. It is almost unheard of for a mother to leave a four-old-year child for the day. The need for Divaru women to work in the fields forces them to be more independent of their children.

The major occupation of the Havik Brahmin hamlet is arecanut cultivation; that of the Divaru hamlet, the growing of rice. Havik Brahmin women participate minimally in cultivation. Women may husk the areca nut, but their work even in this is nonessential, as others can be hired to do this job. As this is the one way a Havik woman can earn money[3] in Totagadde, many do gather at various houses for husking bees. Money so earned is for their own use and is not handed over to a husband or household head; a Havik Brahmin woman's contribution to the family income is generally nil. Women like to have this money so they can buy bangles, sweets, and other small items for themselves and for their children without asking their husbands. A Divaru woman, in contrast, is an essential member of the work force. When her husband ploughs the fields, she sows the rice. She transplants seedlings and weeds the paddy. It would be unlikely for a Havik woman to know much about the growing of areca and improbable that a Divaru woman would not know about rice cultivation. The skills that one group has and the other group lacks may be related to the relative economic position of the two groups. After all, Haviks can afford to hire others to work on the areca plantations; Divarus must do the work themselves. Divaru women, while constituting an essential part of the work force, develop skills and acquire the knowledge necessary to manage the land. It is not surprising that Divaru women are independent, while Havik women are reared to be ab-solutely dependent upon their fathers and husbands. Divaru women in the course of their work require greater freedom of movement, and restrictions would be impracticable. Dress and jewelry designate caste identity, which may serve as a form of protection. Divaru women are expected to be able to take care of themselves; Havik women are expected to be helpless. Freedom of movement does not challenge Divaru male authority, but for Havik women it implies an independence from a woman's per-sonal god, her husband.

Authority: Women in the Decision-Making Process

Positions of authority may be viewed as internal and external to the family, the caste, and the village. The recognition given a per-son's power may be formal (i.e., legal) or informal. The Havik

Brahmin woman, who lacks authority, is forced to operate through channels of informal power; the Divaru may achieve some degree of formal authority in the family unit. Havik women who try to act as decision makers, even if their decisions are wise ones, are regarded as embarrassments to their husbands, while Divaru women are allowed to act as decision makers when they are qualified. This discussion of authority will be restricted to the family unit.

Authority among Havik Women

The Havik Brahmin woman normally has no formal authority, except over her daughter-in-law. As a child she is under the jurisdiction of her father; as a wife, under the jurisdiction of her husband and mother-in-law; and as a widow, under the jurisdiction of her son. A Brahmin woman cannot represent her household in legal disputes. Whatever power she exerts is acquired through men. When her husband is the eldest male in the household, she is regarded as the female head of household. Should her husband die, she loses the position ascribed to her on the basis of her husband's position. I will present three case studies: one of a married woman whose husband is technically head of the household; the second of a widow who exerts informal power; the third of a woman who tries to follow the ideal pattern. All the case histories are composite ones and the names are pseudonyms.

Case 1: Kusuma Kusuma is an intelligent woman whose husband was likely to gamble all of his property away. In order to prevent this, she decided to take some action to obtain management of the land. No one doubted her ability to manage areca-nut land better than her husband. However, since she is a woman, she had to rely on her brother to arrange for the management of the land. Since Kusuma's husband is such a profligate, there was no difficulty in getting a settlement of land management for her. Technically, the management is in her brother's hands, but actually Kusuma manages the land herself.

Kusuma's position in the village is marginal. Her behavior, in spite of her husband's irresponsibility, is criticized harshly. She has caused him to lose all self-respect. When he sells the portion that was left to his management and leaves the area, nobody is surprised. Kusuma has gotten what she deserved by assuming the role of a man.

Case 2: Devkamma, the widow Devkamma was widowed when her daughters were young. She does not have any sons nor is she part of a joint family. She has no husband's brothers nor brothers of her own upon whom to rely. Her husband had gone into debt and had mortgaged his property to repay the debts. After her husband's death, Devkamma decided to manage the property herself. The first act of her management was to sell a portion of the land to repay her husband's debts.

When a neighbor moves boundary stones so that he can encroach on Devkamma's land, she is well aware of what is occurring. A meeting is called to censure the action of the neighbor. All Brahmin households are represented at the meeting, except Devkamma's. Devkamma initiated the meeting but cannot attend, for Brahmin women are not able to participate in caste *panchayats*.

Devkamma manages the land well. In spite of the difficulties a woman faces in the management of property, she makes a profit on the land she has retained. A good match is arranged for Devkamma's daughter. Since Devkamma has no sons, her daughter's husband is naturally expected to manage the land. One of his first actions is to bring a court case against the person to whom Devkamma had sold some of her land, contending that, as a woman, Devkamma should not have been allowed to sell any property. Although he loses the case to get the land back, his very attempt illustrates the limits of a woman's power even when she assumes the authority.

Case 3: Savitri Savitri's world revolves around her husband and children. If her husband would agree to sit still long enough, she would do a formal *pūja* (*pāda pūja*)[4] or worship to him. Since he is impatient with such an idea, Savitri has to be content with praising her husband. She does make a point of eating off his plate after he has finished his meal, the scraps on his plate being to her gifts blessed by god. There is no area where Savitri's husband does not excel. When guests come Savitri does not enter the conversation unless directly addressed. If Savitri is asked a general point of information, she will refer the question to her husband. The husband's role is to deal with outsiders, do the shopping, buy the clothes for the household, manage the land. On market day Savitri's husband always goes to town. Savitri awaits him in the evening. If he is late, her worry may manifest itself in tears. Savitri is unassertive and accepts her low status. She has learned to play the role of the ideal woman very well.

Savitri's position, although low, does allow for circumventing her husband. Sometimes her schemes are successful, sometimes not. Two children in Savitri's opinion provided a large enough family. Consequently, the third pregnancy was most unwelcome. Her husband allowed her to see a doctor for medicine to abort, but this was unsuccessful. When the child was born, Savitri wished to have her tubes tied. Although her husband consented, he thought the permission of Savitri's father was necessary. Savitri's father did not give his approval; hence Savitri did not have her tubes tied. When Savitri's father died, he left her some money. Savitri wanted jewelry but knew her husband would object. She went to the goldsmith covertly, ordered the jewelry, and then wore it. Her husband was upset, but faced with a *fait accompli* he could only scold her. Havik women are usually the complainers, as this and suicide are the only recourse when they have no formal power. In private Savitri does not hesitate to tell her husband his mistakes. One day he put in an order for new clothes for the children; however, he neglected to give the tailor recent measurements. Savitri's practical knowledge would have avoided a disastrous error, and she did not hesitate to tease her husband. However, it is doubtful that her advice would ever be taken seriously by him. Savitri's husband is intelligent, a good provider, and treats her well. She has no cause for complaint.

Savitri and her husband have had the same amount of formal

education. He was more than double her age when she married him at the age of twelve. His worldly knowledge put him automatically in a superior position. He is expected to make all of the decisions for the family. Savitri has no need for her education. When she and her husband studied English, she found the lessons difficult. Her mother-in-law told the teacher not to be hard on Savitri. The son's knowledge was sufficient; after all, he was supposed to be responsible for Savitri.

Rule-abiding Savitri may really be envious of her husband's independence. She enjoys traveling. When they go, she adapts to new situations; her husband no longer receives godlike treatment, and she does not ask his opinions before deciding what she wants. The tears she sheds when he is late returning home are no doubt related to the realization that he might be visiting relatives or attending the cinema. She would enjoy such freedom and urges others in a position to use freedom to do so. But the Havik woman has little authority or control over her destiny. By trying to adjust to the society's ideal, Savitri may be achieving the maximum that her position allows.

Authority among Divaru Women

Divaru women, like Havik women, have limited formal authority; however, the Divaru woman does have greater potential for exercising power. As a child, she is under the jurisdiction of both parents, rather than primarily her father. As a wife, she may be more under the jurisdiction of her mother-in-law than of her husband. As a widow, a Divaru woman may be in charge of the household. The Havik household is run by the eldest qualified person. However, in Divaru households there is an organizational division between the eldest living male and his wife or the widow of a former seniormost male. Not only is she responsible for the organization of all the work in and around the house but she also keeps the key to the household money chest. Thus, anyone in the house who wants money should consult with her (see Harper 1971).

A Havik widow has low status within her household. Under no circumstances would a Havik woman be in charge of family financial matters nor would she be allowed to borrow money. As the head of a household, a Divaru widow can borrow money, arrange for ceremonies when necessary, and assume responsibility for the household in general. Some of the considerations a Divaru woman has when borrowing money are illustrated by a conversation between an elderly Havik man and a widowed Divaru woman who had only a very small plot of leased land:

Ryot Woman: I have a favour to ask of you. I have been wanting to talk to _____ but he never comes to my hamlet. If you see him would you tell him that I want to talk to him? I am very anxious to have my son married this year and for this I need three or four hundred rupees. I want to borrow it from a single person.

Horticulturalist: I will tell him that you want to borrow from him. I will tell him that you are poor and old and have only one son and that he should help you out. I will be glad to do this for you.

Ryot Woman: I want to borrow from only one person because it is better that way. . . . If you start borrowing from several people and then pay one back the others begin to clamour for you to pay them. . . . Tell him that after all I shall not run away. . . . We will pay him back. And tell him that this is my only son and that I shall not put other claims on him. (Harper 1961, p. 175).

This woman clearly understands some of the ramifications of borrowing. There is no doubt of her being in a responsible position.

In disputes Divaru women may defend the family, and their arguments are listened to. If they represent the case more effectively than the men, the women will do all of the talking. Yet a woman speaking on behalf of her family in the settlement of a dispute would be without precedent among the Havik Brahmins. Divaru women are not obliged to play a dominant role; however, the independence they achieve through their economic contribution to the family may be a factor in their freedom to express opinions and their qualification for formal leadership roles.

Ritual Status

To a large extent ritual life as followed in each hamlet is known only to the residents of the hamlet. In the case of the Brahmins who occupy two hamlets, there is a common ritual life followed by the caste as a whole. The Divarus, because of their lower ritual status, are not allowed to enter Brahmin households, nor would they have reason to attend a Brahmin ceremony. Divarus do try to emulate the Brahmin ritual, but such emulation is based on their imagination of it and not on direct knowledge. The Brahmins and the Divarus have separate temples. The Brahmin temple is located in one of the Brahmin hamlets; the Divaru temple, in the Divaru hamlet. Just as in their occupations and internal authority relationships, there is also sharp separation between the Brahmins and Divarus in their ritual life. Two aspects of ritual will be reviewed, everyday ritual and life-crisis ceremonies.

Everyday Brahmin life is governed by ritual. Totagadde Brahmins recognize three ritual states: *maḍi* or ritual purity, *mailige* or ordinary purity, and *muṭṭuciṭṭu* or ritual pollution. The one who cooks the food to be offered to the household gods and the one who worships the household gods on behalf of the family must be in a state of ritual purity. After eating, excreting, touching a person who is not *maḍi,* or sleeping, the person goes from a state of ritual purity to ordinary purity. The state of ritual pollution is rare for men but a monthly occurrence for women, serving as a reminder of women's lower status. By touching a menstruating woman, a man will be ritually polluted, and a priest must be summoned for the purification ceremony.

Menstrual taboos are strict among the Haviks. The first menstruation is often traumatic for the Havik girls, for in spite of the strictness and importance of the taboo, she often had no idea of the cause of her mother's monthly period of untouchability. The stock reason given children is that their mother or a woman "sitting outside" (the euphemism for the ritually polluting state of menstruation) has touched a dog. The rigidity of the psychological isolation is great. Although there has been a noticeable relaxation

of the rules, women take the responsibility for preventing trans-
gressions. When a person seems likely to come closer than three
feet, the woman will warn him or her loudly as if she would be the
culprit responsible for the ensuing contamination. If two
menstruating women touch, they pollute each other. If a menstruating woman touches any of a number of substances, her pollution
is conducted to somebody else simultaneously touching that substance. Wood, rope, cloth, metal all conduct; earth and cement do
not. Conductors of pollution, however, with the exception of cloth,
do not retain pollution. Once a woman has finished crossing a
wooden bridge, others may cross without being polluted. However, should she still be on the bridge when another person steps
on the wood, he is in need of purification. Her cup similarly is a
conductor of pollution. If her cup is on a table, anyone touching
the table is polluted. In earlier times literate women would not be
allowed to read, as the written word is a manifestation of the
goddess of wisdom, Sarasvati. Now younger women read; older
women still observe this taboo.

The number of ritual ceremonies associated with an individual's life cycle may serve to indicate the relative importance of
that individual to society. Havik boys undergo more ceremonies
than Havik girls. The two ceremonies boys have which girls do not
are the *caula* or first hair-cutting ceremony and the *upinayana* or
sacred-thread ceremony. Under no circumstances would either
ceremony be performed for a Havik girl. Among the Divaru, the
only ceremony girls do not generally have in common with boys is
the first haircutting ceremony; and even here, Divaru girls do go
through this ceremony occasionally. The flexibility in the ritual and
the possibility of performing the same ceremonies for members of
either sex suggests a greater equality between the sexes among
the Divaru than among the Havik Brahmins.

Divaru women seem to know as much as Divaru men about ritual and religious worship. Havik Brahmin women may be a necessary part of ritual ceremonies, but their role is more complementary to that of the husband than of any independent value. Brahmin women are excluded from learning sacred *mantras* or sacred formulae. The daily *pūja* or worship must be conducted by a man in the family who has undergone the *upinayana* ceremony. Men worship on behalf of the entire family. Women then worship the high gods by proxy, through their husbands. They do not have the knowledge to instruct husbands in how to worship. I have observed Divaru women, however, reminding their husbands of the proper procedure in the *pūja*. The admittance of one group of women to religious life, in contrast to the exclusion of the other, serves to illustrate a greater equality between the sexes among the Divaru. Within the household and the community Divaru women hold a higher status than their Brahmin counterparts.

Conclusion

This paper has served to provide examples of areas where the status of women of two different castes varies within a society. The Havik Brahmin caste is a priestly caste. Although all the Havik Brahmins in Totagadde own areca-nut plantations, their hereditary occupation is a religious one. Their economic position further enables them to follow orthodox practices. They can afford to keep their women in the home and to restrict the woman's role to that of housekeeper. The Divarus, while not poverty-stricken, do not hire outside labor. Divaru women are needed to work in the fields. The independence and experience gained from being a part of the work force extends to the recognition of their competence in positions of authority and a more nearly equal role in ritual. There appears to be a correlation between the economic contributions of the women and the freedom of the rights they enjoy.

Both groups are patrilineal and patrilocal. However, among the Haviks the decision-making authority rests primarily with the eldest man in the family. Younger brothers and sons have no formal say. The only way to obtain formal decision-making power is to partition the land. Havik women are in a position similar to the subordinate men in the family, but there is no way they can ascend to a position of formal power. They legally may own land, but are not allowed to have any voice in its management. A Havik woman only inherits land if she has no brothers, and then the land is turned over to her husband upon her marriage. Before her marriage, male relatives manage the land. Divaru women, in contrast, may own land. They may be engaged in decision-making roles. They may borrow money, arrange for their children's marriages, and manage land themselves, and they often become competent in management. The Divaru women are more assertive than are Havik women. As a group they have gained more economic power than have the Havik women. The position taken here is that a major factor in the difference in status between the two groups is the difference in economic contribution to the households. A Divaru woman may regard herself as essential to the agricultural production of a family; a Havik woman may regard herself as just a cook. It is not surprising that Divaru women display an independence in thought and action as well as self-reliance, whereas Brahmin women approach the following ideal:

The ideal feminine behavior is characterized by submissiveness and deference. Women are believed to be shy, weak, and retiring, are expected to orient their activities toward the pleasing of males. But at the same time they are not only economically but also religiously and intellectually dependent upon them. A woman in the role of wife is subordinate to all desires, the whims, and the angers of her husband. (Harper 1969, p. 89).

Notes

1. With increasing education and a later marriage age this is beginning to change. In a sense the Havik woman is emerging from her dependence. Girls who marry after graduation from high school, in contrast to marriage at age eleven or twelve, already have established their identity. They are surer of themselves and are not afraid to express opinions. Extended and joint families are on the decline.

Women freely indicate their preference for their own household. Men praise those who partition the joint family before conflict has forcibly divided the family. But this trend is just beginning. The bitterness of some of the wives at having their education interrupted at age eleven or twelve, the opportunity for a high school and even a college education while living at home, and greater education for the men cannot help but produce a change in independence among the women. However, only one woman in the village had a high school education at the time that I was in the village. The effects of these trends remain to be felt.

2. With the advent of the bicycle age and its acceptance for women in Totagadde, Havik women now state that it is safe for them to cycle unaccompanied to other villages. The very expression of this sentiment, even though to my knowledge women have not in fact traveled alone by bicycle, indicates a movement toward independence.

3. If a woman has a special skill such as tailoring and if her family is poor, her earning skills may be used to supplement the family income.

4. Savitri states that her husband must be in the ritually pure state known as *maḍi* for her to perform *pūja* to him. Savitri's husband stated that he need not be in *maḍi* for his wife to perform a *pūja* to him. The implication of the husband's statement is that his normal ritual status is so much purer than his wife's that relative to her he is, always in a state of ritual purity.

References

Harper, Edward B. 1959. "Two Systems of Economic Exchange in Village India." *American Anthropologist* 61:5.

—— 1961. "Moneylending in the Village Economy of the Malnad." *Economic Weekly*, February 4.

—— 1969. "Fear and the Status of Women." *Southwestern Journal of Anthropology* 25:81–95.

Harper, Judy Wiltse. 1971. "The Divarus of the Malnad: A Study of Kinship and Land Tenure in a Paddy Cultivating Caste in South India." Ph.D. dissertation, University of Washington.

Ullrich, Helen E. 1968. "What's His Pigeonhole or the Role of Dialectal Diversity in Mysore State." Paper delivered at the Summer Lecture Series, Michigan State University.

DENISE O'BRIEN

5 Female Husbands in Southern Bantu Societies

T HE TERM *FEMALE HUSBAND* seems inherently contradictory; and in fact it refers to a woman who takes on the legal and social roles of husband and father by marrying another woman according to the approved rules and ceremonies of her society. She may belong to any one of over 30 African populations, and she may have lived at any time from at least the eighteenth century to the present. A female husband does not engage in sexual interaction with her wife; indeed, nowhere do the African data suggest any homosexual connotations in such marriages.[1] Rather, the wife of a female husband chooses or is assigned one or more males who become her sexual partners and the biological fathers of her children. The role of female husband, which seems anomalous to many observers, is not regarded as deviant or abnormal in those societies where it exists and may, in some Southern Bantu societies, be enjoined on and required of certain women. They always occupy a special status within their society, usually as a political leader or as a member of the royal family (two categories that only

Some of the material in this paper is taken from a paper presented at the annual meetings of the American Anthropological Association, Toronto, 1972. I am indebted to the Ford Foundation and to Temple University for support for further research on female husbands; to June Okal and Sharon Weinberg for bibliographic assistance; and to Regina Oboler, June Okal, Jay Ruby, Harold Scheffler, and Barbara Voorhies for their comments on earlier drafts. However, the conclusions are those of the author.

partially overlap), or sometimes as a curer or diviner with special skills and links to the supernatural realm.

This paper examines the significance of female husbands for sex-role studies in general, and more particularly, for our understanding of the nature of political leadership, the status of women, and the definition of marriage. I shall review briefly previous anthropological work on female husbands, summarize the relevant ethnographic data, and analyze in some detail the role of female husband among the Southern Bantu.

This form of marriage, unknown outside of Africa, has variously been labeled *woman marriage* or marriage involving a *female husband*. The latter term seems far preferable, since *woman marriage* is inherently ambiguous and does not immediately identify the unique component in this type of marriage. We find this marital role in population units within four distinct geographic areas: (1) West Africa (mainly Nigeria)—Yoruba, Ekiti, Bunu, Akoko, Yagba, Nupe, Ibo, Ijaw, and Fon (or Dahomeans); (2) South Africa (especially the Transvaal)—Venda, Lovedu, Pedi, Hurutshe, Zulu, Sotho, Phalaborwa, Narene, Koni, and Tawana; (3) East Africa—Kuria, Iregi, Kenye, Suba, Simbiti, Ngoreme, Gusii, Kipsigis, Nandi, Kikuyu, and Luo; and (4) Sudan—Nuer, Dinka, and Shilluk. (I have primarily relied on Murdock [1959] in attempting to distinguish cultural and linguistic relationships among these population units.)

Although instances of women marrying women have been noted in African societies for many years, anthropologists have paid scant attention to the phenomenon and devoted little concentrated research to it. They are probably most familiar with female husbands from Evans-Pritchard's (1945, 1951) accounts of the institution among the Nuer, although female husbands in other societies were noted much earlier. In 1910 O'Sullivan reported "the case of a woman buying a 'wife widow' for her deceased husband or father" among the East African Dinka (1910, p. 181) ; and in West Africa a few years later, Thomas described the existence of a "woman husband" among the Ibo (1914, p. 59). Brief mentions of this "strange custom" (Barton 1923, p. 73) recur in ethnographic accounts from the 1920s on. Herskovits (1937) offered the first comparative survey of the data on female husbands, mentioning in addition to his own Dahomean material the Yoruba, Nupe, Ibo, and Ijaw of Nigeria; the Dinka and Nuer of the Sudan; and the Venda of the northern Transvaal. About the same time, the first of many publications by the Kriges on the Lovedu and other Bantu peoples of the Transvaal appeared (e.g., E. J. Krige 1937, 1938, 1964, 1974; J. D. Krige 1937; Krige and Krige 1943, 1954). These provided rich ethnographic details about female husbands, particularly with regard to the Lovedu Queen. A few years later, female husbands among the Nuer, known to exist from earlier accounts (Huffman 1931; Seligman and Seligman 1932), were described in some depth by Evans-Pritchard (1945). Yet, despite the potential significance of female husbands for theories of descent and marriage, these accounts generated little interest.

Anthropologists concerned with social organization mention female husbands in their writings only fleetingly. For example, Barnes suggests that the presence of female husbands is one indication of "highly developed agnatic systems" (1951, p. 2), and Gough (1959) notes their existence among the Nuer in her now classic reformulation of the definition of marriage. Recently, however, the anthropological attention paid to female husbands has increased, in large part because of the discipline's current recognition of women and sex roles as significant subjects of study. Female husbands are discussed briefly in general publications on sex roles (e.g., Rosaldo and Lamphere 1974; Friedl 1975), and are analyzed at greater length in articles by Huber (1969) and E. J. Krige (1974). Huber's article is restricted to a discussion of female husbands among the Kuria, Ngoreme, Simbiti, and other Suba groups, all populations classified by Murdock (1959, p. 348) under either the Gusii or Shashi division of the Interlascutrine Bantu. A major point of Huber's study is that so-called woman marriage among these East African peoples does not really involve a woman assuming the role of husband. Krige, on the other hand, argues that women do take on the husband role in some African societies, as well as the roles of father and political leader. However, Krige (1974) interprets these data not as examples of women crossing sex role boundaries to assume male roles, but rather as an indication that some African populations, most notably the Lovedu, characterize the roles of husband and political leader as neuter in gender, instead of exclusively masculine or feminine.

The degree to which a female husband behaves as or is regarded as a male is crucial to our understanding of her role and can best be determined by surveying the relevant ethnographic data.

Two Types of Female Husband

A survey of all known populations in which female husbands occur indicates that two major types of female husband can be isolated: surrogate female husbands, and autonomous female husbands.

A surrogate female husband is a woman who acts as a substitute for a male kinsman in order to provide heirs for his agnatic lineage. In some cases such women are fully husbands in that they are regarded as the paters of their wives' children, while in others they merely act as deputies for a deceased or fictitious male who is regarded as pater to any resulting children. When the male for whom a woman is substituting is a deceased father or brother, the chances are that she will be regarded as his replacement and will assume the full husband and pater role. Such transference occurs among the Zulu where, according to Gluckman "If a man dies leaving only daughters and no son, the eldest daughter should take his cattle and marry wives for her father" (1950, p. 184). We also find it among the Pedi (Whitfield 1948) and Lovedu (Krige and Krige 1943), where a woman inherits her dead brother's wives and property if he has no male heirs.

When a woman takes on the role of a deceased husband or son, she is more likely to be regarded as a deputy than as a replacement. Such a situation prevails among the Simbiti (Huber 1969), where the female husband is a sonless widow who arranges a marriage for her deceased or fictitious son and is regarded by the bride as a mother-in-law rather than as a husband. Mayer (1950) also reports such unions among the Gusii, noting that the children produced are viewed as jural grandchildren of the widow (the female husband) and her dead husband.

An autonomous female husband is one who marries independently, without any reference to male kin, and who is always pater to children borne by her wife or wives. Barrenness is often cited as the reason why women among the Venda (Lestrade 1930), Nuer (Evans-Pritchard 1951), Ijaw (Talbot 1926) and Ibo (Meek 1937) take wives. ·The earliest known case of an autonomous female husband occurred among the Gusii, a Bantu population in the Lakes area of East Africa. According to oral tradition, during the middle or late eighteenth century a woman who was both a wife and a judicial chief had nine daughters and no sons. In order to become the father, if not the mother, of a son, she used some of the cattle from her daughters' bridewealth to become a female husband. The son who resulted became a powerful leader and founder of a Gusii clan that still exists today (Le Vine 1958).

Political and economic power are concomitants of the female husband role in many populations. In West African societies where women can amass wealth through trading, successful traders often marry several wives. Among the Southern Bantu populations where women can become political leaders, such female leaders are expected to become husbands as well.

The primary motivation of an autonomous female husband, in contrast to a surrogate female husband, appears to be a desire to improve or maintain her own status socially (by becoming a father), economically, or politically. Both surrogate and autonomous female husbands may be found within the same population, but the autonomous type is more likely to be conceptualized as male or as fulfilling a male role, while the surrogate type is seen as a female acting for a particular male.

Female Husbands among the Southern Bantu

Female husbands exist in at least ten Southern Bantu populations: Sotho, Koni, Tawana, Hurutshe, Pedi, Venda, Lovedu, Phalaborwa, Narene, and Zulu. Many of these people are geographically contiguous and most are closely related linguistically and culturally. Murdock (1959) classifies nine of these units as belonging to the Sotho division of the Bantu, while the tenth unit, the Zulu, is classed as part of the adjacent Nguni division. No attempt is made here to indicate the total range of cultural variation or the political and ecological separation among these various populations, and they are regarded as discrete units only to the degree that they have been labeled as such by one or more ethnographers. Both types of female husband, autonomous and surrogate, exist among the Southern Bantu, and in several populations both types coexist. The highest incidences and strongest examples of autonomous female husbands occur among the Koni, Venda, Lovedu, and Narene, where the female-husband role is correlated with roles of political leader or curer.

In four Southern Bantu populations no autonomous female husbands have been reported. Among the Tawana (Snell 1954) and the Phalaborwa (E. J. Krige 1937), female husbands are widows who are either childless or who have only daughters. Such a widow becomes a surrogate husband by marrying a woman as a substitute for her deceased or fictitious son. Female husbands are said to be rare among the Hurutshe, a Tswana population, and occur only in the case of women whose male kin die without male heirs (Whitfield 1948). The same type of female husband occurs among the Pedi (Harries 1929) as well as a somewhat more specific surrogate, the woman who marries her brother's daughter in lieu of her dead or neverborn son (Mönnig 1967).

Similar enactments of surrogate marriages occur among the Zulu (Vilakazi 1962), the Venda (Stayt 1931), the Lovedu (Krige and Krige 1943), and the Sotho (Ellenberger 1912). At the same time any rich and influential woman is said to be a potential female husband among the Sotho (Laydevant 1931), the Venda

(Stayt 1931), and the Zulu (Gluckman 1950). Such women act autonomously rather than as male surrogates.

Autonomous female husbands are most likely to appear in those Southern Bantu populations where women can become political leaders, as for example, among the Venda, Lovedu, and Koni. We cannot, however, assume that all female political leaders are female husbands. For example, the presence of autonomous female husbands among the Sotho has been noted and Ashton (1967, pp. 342–45) clearly indicates that "native authorities" in this tribe are often female. In 1949, out of 69 chiefs and headmen in one Sotho district, 7 were females, about 10 percent. Yet Ashton does not mention female husbands and there is no way to determine whether women who are "native authorities" are also female husbands. Similarly, the Thabina, another Sotho population closely related to the Lovedu, had at least one female chief during the nineteenth century (van Warmelo 1944b), but there is no indication that she ever became a female husband as did her Koni, Narene, Venda, and Lovedu counterparts.

Since the Lovedu have been so fully described by the Kriges, I shall concentrate here on a discussion of female husbands and their political status among the Venda, the Koni, and a population closely related to the Lovedu, the Narene. Certainly the Lovedu queen may be the model by which female political leaders were accepted by other Transvaal peoples, as E. J. Krige (1938) and van Warmelo (1944c) suggest. Ethnographers of the Venda agree that Venda women may exert considerable political influence and may become petty or district chiefs (Blacking 1959; Lestrade 1930; Stayt 1931). Lestrade notes that the position of *mukoma*, "the chief's right hand man," (1930, p. 314) is often held by a woman and in some localities must be held by a woman. A rationale for this prescription is available for only one place, Phephidi, where "It is said that only a woman can be *mukoma* there because 'the particular ancestral spirit associated with the place is a female spirit' . . ." (Rev. P. E. Schwellnus, quoted in Lestrade 1930, p. 315). A female *mukoma* is "regarded as a male person" (Lestrade 1930, p. 315) and must become a female husband, although she also usually becomes the wife of a male and may bear children.

The most extensive data on Venda female husbands are found in van Warmelo's *Venda Law* (1948), a massive compilation of cases and principles, most of which is devoted to domestic relations, especially marriage and inheritance. This source describes 23 cases of female husbands, but since each was included to illustrate a particular legal point, data on the cases are neither uniform nor fully comparable. Whether the female husband holds a political position is not noted, and the only indication of any special status is that 5 of the 23 women are doctors (van Warmelo 1948). Most of these 23 women were wealthy and were able to pay their wives' bridewealth through their own earnings (9 cases), through property inherited from a mother (3 cases) or father (2 cases), or through a combination of earned wealth and inherited wealth (1 case) (van Warmelo 1948, pp. 391–99, 645, 1005–13, 1021–23). Nearly all of these women were themselves married to males; in only 5 instances are there no data on the female husband's marital status as a wife.

The Koni are a small Sotho-speaking tribe in the Transvaal that had at least three female chiefs in the period from 1860 to 1940. The first of these was a chief's daughter named Maale who, apparently in the absence of male heirs, succeeded her father sometime in the 1860s (van Warmelo 1944c). Maale had several wives and at least three sons by her chief wife. Maale was succeeded by her younger sister, Mmakhodo, who together with her own son ruled until 1890, when Maale's eldest son became chief. Mmakhodo was already the wife of a male chief in another district when she succeeded Maale, and there is no indication that she became a female husband. But despite Mmakhodo's male husband, the Koni data provide some of the strongest indications that being a chief precludes being a wife. Speaking of the nineteenth century Maale, van Warmelo says "As a chieftainess she had no recognised husband" (1944c, p. 21). The case of the third Koni female chief, Maale's son's daughter, is even more striking. Maale's granddaughter, also called Maale, was acclaimed chief by her people in 1928 after the death of her elder brother. But Maale herself "protested, 'I am not the chieftainess. I do not want to be chieftainess . . . I have a husband already' " (van Warmelo 1944c, p. 24). Maale did become chief finally in 1931 and several years later she and all her relatives "strenuously denied that she had ever been married" (p. 24). There is no indication that this twentieth-century Maale became a female husband, but clearly being a wife is regarded as a serious impediment to being a political leader.

There are two examples of Koni women who were female husbands in the 1880s, although they did not hold political positions. These were sisters, daughters of a chief. They married a pair of sisters who were daughters of their brother, a chief (van Warmelo 1944f). It seems likely that these cases are examples of the Sotho norm that a woman is "born for" (i.e., should marry) her father's sister's son because the cattle given for her father's sister's bridewealth made her father's marriage and hence her own birth possible. If a woman's father's sister has no sons, then she may marry her father's sister, as did the younger pair of sisters in this example (E. J. Krige 1938). These two cases are therefore surrogate rather than autonomous female husbands.

The Narene are a small Sotho-speaking population who are closely related culturally to the Lovedu. From 1870 to 1940 there were four female chiefs of the Narene. No data are available about the marital status of one chief; but of the other three women, one was a female husband, one was the widow of a female husband, and one was the widow of a male husband (van Warmelo 1944a, 1944d, 1944e). Thus the Narene data support the hypothesis that the roles of chief and wife tend to be mutually exclusive among the Southern Bantu. The case of the female husband who was a chief is especially interesting in that it demonstrates the degree to which a woman would fight to become a political leader. Mmakaipea became chief about 1870 largely through her own efforts. According to oral tradition, she either murdered the ruling chief (van Warmelo 1944e) or encouraged the chief's son to murder his father (van Warmelo 1944a). In one version the previous chief was

Mmakaipea's elder brother, in another her elder brother's son. After she became chief, she took the name Mmakaipea, which means "Mrs-I-appointed-myself" (van Warmelo 1944a, p. 8).

Mmakaipea was succeeded by her brother's daughter, Mmamathola, who had also been her wife. Succession is determined or confirmed among the Narene by a ceremony in which the heirs to the deceased chief try to open the door of his or her hut.[2] After Mmakaipea's death none of the various male candidates for her position (her brothers' sons) was able to open the door, but Mmamathola did so easily. People decided that her success was a sign that the ancestral spirits wanted her to be chief (van Warmelo 1944a).

Few details are present in the ethnographic record concerning the day-to-day duties and activities of a chief, but some idea of the scope and nature of Mmamathola's role can be gleaned from a brief account of a tribal war against the Boers. After the Boers defeated the Africans in 1894, Mmamathola was jailed along with the other chiefs, who were male, while her people were resettled. When the British occupied Pretoria during the Anglo-Boer war, Mmamathola was released, whereupon "she returned home and reassembled the tribe in the present location" (van Warmelo 1944a, p. 9). Both the Boer response to Mmamathola's involvement in the war and her action after she was freed indicate that Mmamathola exercised executive power and authority. Mmamathola never married again after the death of Mmakaipea, the woman who was her father's sister, her husband, and her predecessor in office.

There is no indication that the other two Narene female chiefs ever became female husbands, but it is worth noting that the most recent one, MaaNtsana, successfully struggled to obtain her position. As one of several widows of the previous chief, MaaNtsana had no particular claim to the position and the recognized heir was a son of the late chief. MaaNtsana demanded recognition as chief on the grounds that the dying chief had entrusted her with the sacred rainmaking techniques and paraphernalia. The male heir was recognized as his father's successor by the government, but a large number of Narene preferred MaaNtsana, who is described as having "acted defiantly" (van Warmelo 1944d, p. 32). After inquiries in 1923 and 1924, the government agreed in 1928 to sanction MaaNtsana as petty chieftainess providing her followers would purchase the leased land on which they were living. Finally, in 1934, the division of the tribe into two sections, one headed by the late chief's son and the other by MaaNtsana, was officially recognized. There are no data as to whether other Narene women who were not chiefs ever became female husbands.

If we examine the Southern Bantu data on the marital status of female political leaders, we find that the four populations with female chiefs or queens can be arranged in a continuum of gradually increasing emphasis on the mutual exclusiveness of the roles of political leader and wife and on the necessity for a leader to be a husband. No normative statement can be made as to whether female chiefs among the Narene should be husbands, but at least one out of four such women was a female husband and there is every indication that a female chief was never simultaneously a wife. Among the Venda a female political leader had to be a husband but could also be a wife at the same time. The Koni emphasize more strongly the incompatibility between the roles of wife and leader by their expectation that a female chief should be a husband but must not be a wife. The strongest expression of the mutual incompatibility between leader and wife is found among the Lovedu, where the queen cannot be a wife but must herself be a husband. However, Lovedu female political leaders on a lower level, such as district chiefs or local headmen, may be wives as well as female husbands (E. J. Krige 1974).

Marriage and Female Political Authority

The linking of the assumption of political leadership by a female with the prohibition on her marriage to a male and the injunction to marry a female demonstrates that Southern Bantu females who assume power positions are expected to become "social males." The marriages that female leaders contract as husbands should be viewed as unions between individuals who occupy "the conceptual roles of male and female" (Rivière 1971, p. 68), rather than as marriages between two women. Such a statement may not seem novel since a similar conclusion has been reached by others (e.g., Gluckman 1969). However, it is strongly rejected by E. J. Krige, who argues that at least among the Lovedu, the roles of husband and political leader are as much feminine as they are masculine (1974). Other commentators on the Lovedu queens have viewed them as social males. Murdock, for example, explains, "We have spoken advisedly of the Lovedu monarchs as 'female kings' rather than as queens because they very consciously play a male role" (1959, p. 389). Similarly, Leach refers to the Lovedu queen as "an anomalous social person, for, though physiologically female, she is sociologically male" (1961, p. 97). Stayt, an ethnographer of the Venda, says in reference to female husbands and political leaders: "In actual practice there is a curious ambivalent attitude towards sex. Where a woman performs the functions of a man she is treated in every way as though she were a man, and is even called by the terms that would be used toward the man whose place she is taking" (1931, p. 179). The strongest counter to Krige's argument is the incompatibility among the Lovedu between the role of wife, on the one hand, and husband or leader, on the other.

Some of the Southern Bantu women who became political leaders did so by right of inheritance; theirs was an ascribed status. Others, such as Mmakaipea, the Narene chief, had to fight for their position; theirs was an achieved status. In at least two African societies outside the Southern Bantu area, the Shilluk and the Nyoro, women with a high ascribed political status are forbidden to become wives. Among the Shilluk of the Sudan the king's daughters cannot become wives and mothers. A Shilluk princess may become a husband (Farran 1963), or she may take lovers, but she should not give birth. Shilluk princesses not only symbolize royal power and status, but they also exercise political influence and authority at the local level (Seligman and Seligman 1932). The Nyoro are a Bantu-speaking people in Western Uganda in which princesses are treated like men, rule as chiefs, and are not allowed to become wives and mothers (Roscoe 1923; Beattie 1960, 1968). Yet the idea of a princess becoming a husband does not appear to have occurred to the Nyoro. Beattie attributes the ban on royal females' marriages to the low valuation of the role of wife, for "it would have been unthinkable for persons of such high status to assume the markedly subordinate status of wives" (1960, p. 30). It appears that Shilluk and Nyoro princesses are forbidden to marry males because they are both royal and female. Preserving the "purity" of royal blood lines by restricting marriages of royalty to persons of equal rank is deemed important by many cultures, European and Asian as well as African, but among the Shilluk and the Nyoro the degree of restriction is much more severe for females than for males. Shilluk and Nyoro princes are not banned from marrying women of inferior rank, for as Farran notes in speaking of the Shilluk "a woman is subject to her husband and so is brought down to his social level, but a prince may marry a commoner girl, for he raises her by the marriage sufficiently near to his own status for her to become the mother of princes" (1963, p. 80).[3]

At the beginning of this paper I noted that, in addition to women who became political leaders, women who were curers or diviners ("doctors") were expected to become female husbands. Although there are no indications in the Southern Bantu literature that these marriages are prescribed for women "doctors," it is very common for such women to contract them, particularly among the Lovedu (Krige 1974) and Venda (van Warmelo 1948). E. J. Krige's (1974) argument that Lovedu female husbands do not necessarily adopt a male role is not convincing, particularly for those female husbands who are also political leaders, but that is not to say that all female husbands adopt a male role. Clearly those who are surrogates do not become social males, and more data about the concept of the role of "diviner, curer, shaman, doctor" among the Southern Bantu are needed before we can determine the gender

attribution of that role.[4] Among the various examples of autonomous female husbands, Krige's hypothesis that female husbands are not social males seems most applicable to the West African market women. There is no implication that the Ibo women
who, as successful traders, become female husbands are
regarded as or behave as social males outside the domestic context (cf., Uchendu 1965).

Data on female husbands are not only relevant to our understanding of marriage and the family but are also highly significant
to anthropologists' recently intensified interest in the distinction
between sex and gender, and in the degree to which social statuses are biologically determined. Despite the many acculturation
pressures militating against the institution of female husbands, it
still exists and its incidence may even be increasing in some African societies. E. J. Krige (1974) notes the continued existence of
female husbands among the Lovedu, and they are also present
today among the Yoruba (Sandra Barnes, personal communication), Kuria, Kikuyu, Kipsigis, Nandi, and various Southern
Bantu populations such as the Venda. Field research in one or
more of these societies should go a long way toward resolving our
residual questions about female husbands.[5]

Conclusion

Given the data currently available, we can conclude that in at
least some societies, if women are expected either to exercise
power or to symbolize power, they must be conceptualized as
male, or at least must not take on the subordinate status of wife.
Women with a high ascribed status are already "royal," perhaps
"divine," but they may still need a male element to mark their
elevated roles. Women who achieve high political status may
have an even greater need for some dramatic marker to symbolize
their new role and set them apart from other women. What more effective symbol than a reversal from the expected roles of wife and
mother to those of husband and father? There are two widely rec-

ognized conditions relevant to sex roles and sex-differentiated spheres of action that appear to be widespread in human populations. First, men in a great many societies occupy the principal positions of dominance and power. Second, men act in the public sphere, while women are often restricted to the domestic sphere, the home. At first glance, Southern Bantu women who are political leaders appear to be exceptions to both generalizations. But are they? By their need to reject the roles of wife and mother normatively associated with women in the domestic sphere, and to assume the roles of husband and father, these female chiefs and queens are but one more demonstration that persons who occupy power positions in male-dominant societies must be males.

Notes

1. Out of all the ethnographic sources examined, only Herskovits (1937) states that "occasionally" homosexual women may become female husbands, but without reference to any actual cases. E. J. Krige (1974) strongly denies that "woman-marriage" has any homosexual overtones. Given the minimal data on female homosexuality present in most ethnographic literature, it is impossible to make other than inferential statements about a possible association. However, it seems obvious that if homosexual behavior were a regular component of female-husband marriages, the association would have been noted in the ethnographic record.

2. According to Krige, this ordeal is common among Lowveld Bantu populations of the Transvaal and the outcome is determined by someone inside the hut who bars "the door against the wrong claimants" (1938, p. 273).

3. The idea that a queen or a princess or a chief cannot be a wife is not limited to African societies. In the English terminology used to denote the spouses of monarchs the term queen has two basic meanings. Most often it denotes "the wife of a king," but it may also refer to a woman who is a ruler in her own right. Women who are ruler-queens may, in Great Britain, have husbands, but they may not have husbands who are kings. The male term king has a more restricted meaning than its female counterpart and preeminently denotes "a ruler." If a queen marries, her husband must be designated "prince" or "prince consort." The same distinction applies in other European cultures and languages as well.

4. There are suggestive but contradictory data from the Shilluk indicating that although both men and women may become shamans (ajuago, "good medicine-men"), only male shamans may marry. Female shamans may not marry but could have lovers. The same source also reports that both male and female shamans are expected to be celibate (Seligman and Seligman 1932). A significant correlate of

the curer-shaman role could be control of sexuality rather than marital status. As is the case in many cultures, it may well be that Southern Bantu women do not become doctors until they are post-menopausal and hence, in societies which value fertility very highly, regarded as sexually neutral.

5. During a survey trip to Kenya and South Africa in July, 1976 I was able to confirm the current existence of female husbands among the populations mentioned. Regina Oboler, a doctoral candidate in anthropology at Temple, is currently doing field work on female husbands among the Nandi.

References

Ashton, Hugh. 1967. *The Basuto.* (2d ed.) London: Oxford University Press.

Barnes, J. A. 1951. *Marriage in a Changing Society.* Rhodes-Livingstone Papers, No. 20. Cape Town: Oxford University Press.

Barton, J. 1923. "Notes on the Kipsikis or Lumbwa Tribe." *Journal of the Royal Anthropological Institute* 53:42–78.

Beattie, J. H. M. 1960. *Bunyoro: An African Kingdom.* New York: Holt, Rinehart & Winston.

—— 1968. "Aspects of Nyoro Symbolism." *Africa* 38:413–42.

Blacking, J. 1959. "Fictitious Kinship amongst Girls of the Venda of the Northern Transvaal." *Man* 59:155–58.

Ellenberger, D. F. 1912. *History of the Basuto, Ancient and Modern.* London: Caxton.

Evans-Pritchard, E. E. 1945. *Some Aspects of Marriage and the Family among the Nuer.* Rhodes-Livingstone Papers, No. 11. London: Oxford University Press.

—— 1951. *Kinship and Marriage among the Nuer.* London: Oxford University Press.

Farran, Charles. 1963. *Matrimonial Laws of the Sudan.* London: Buttersworth.

Friedl, Ernestine. 1975. *Women and Men: An Anthropologist's View.* New York: Holt, Rinehart and Winston.

Gluckman, M. 1950. "Kinship and Marriage among the Lozi of Northern Rhodesia and the Zulu of Natal." In A. R. Radcliffe-Brown and D. Forde, eds., *African Systems of Kinship and Marriage,* pp. 166–206. London: Oxford University Press.

——1969. *Ideas and Procedures in African Customary Law.* London: Oxford University Press.

Gough, E. K. 1959. "The Nayars and the Definition of Marriage." *Journal of the Royal Anthropological Institute* 89: 23–34.

Harries, C. L. 1929. *The Laws and Customs of the Bapedi and Cognate Tribes of the Transvaal.* Johannesburg: Hortors.

Herskovits, M. 1937. "A Note on 'Woman Marriage' in Dahomey." *Africa,* 10:335–41.

Huber, H. 1969. " 'Woman Marriage' in some East African Societies," *Anthropos* 63/64:745–52.

Huffman, Ray. 1931. *Nuer Customs and Folklore.* London: Oxford University Press.

Krige, E. J. 1937. "Note on the Phalaborwa and Their Morula Complex." *Bantu Studies* 11:357–66.

—— 1938. "The Place of the North-Eastern Sotho in the South Bantu Complex." *Africa* 11:265–93.

—— 1964. "Property, Cross-Cousin Marriage, and the Family Cycle among the Lovedu." In R. F. Gray and P. H. Gulliver, eds., *The Family Estate in Africa,* pp. 155–95. Boston: Boston University Press.

—— 1974. "Woman-Marriage, with Special Reference to the Lovedu—Its Significance for the Definition of Marriage." *Africa,* 44:11–36.

Krige, J. D. 1937. "Traditional Origins and Tribal Relationships of the Sotho of the Northern Transvaal." *Bantu Studies* 11:321–44.

Krige, J. D. & E. J. Krige. 1943. *The Realm of a Rain Queen.* London: Oxford University Press.

—— 1954. "The Lovedu of the Transvaal." In D. Forde, ed., *African Worlds,* pp. 55–83. London: Oxford University Press.

Laydevant, le R. P. J. 1931. "Étude sur la famille en Basutoland." *Journal de la Société des Africanistes* 1:207–57.

Leach, E. R. 1961. *Rethinking Anthropology.* London School of Economics Monographs on Social Anthropology, No. 22. London: Athlone Press.

Lestrade, G. P. 1930. "Some Notes on the Political Organization of the Vendu-Speaking Tribes." *Africa,* 3:306–22.

Le Vine, Robert A. 1958. "Social Control and Socialization among the Gusii." Ph.D. dissertation, Harvard University.

Mayer, P. 1950. *Gusii Bride-Wealth Law and Custom.* Rhodes-Livingstone Papers, No. 18. Cape Town: Oxford University Press.

Meek, C. K. 1937. *Law and Authority in a Nigerian Tribe.* London: Oxford University Press.

Mönnig, H. O. 1967. *The Pedi.* Pretoria: J. L. van Schaik.

Murdock, G. P. 1959. *Africa: Its Peoples and Their Culture History.* New York. McGraw-Hill.

O'Sullivan, H. 1910. "Dinka Laws and Customs." *Journal of the Royal Anthropological Institute* 40:171–91.

Rivière, P. G. 1971. "Marriage: A Reassessment." In R. Needham, ed., *Rethinking Kinship and Marriage,* pp. 57–74. London: Tavistock.

Rosaldo, Michelle Z. and Louise Lamphere. 1974. *Woman, Culture, and Society.* Stanford: Stanford University Press.

Roscoe, John. 1923. *The Bakitara, or Banyoro.* Cambridge: Cambridge University Press.

Seligman, C. G. and B. Seligman. 1932. *Pagan Tribes of the Nilotic Sudan.* London: Routledge & Kegan Paul.

Snell, G. S. 1954. *Nandi Customary Law.* London: Macmillan.

Stayt, H. A. 1931. *The Bavenda.* London: Cass.

Talbot, P. A. 1926. *The Peoples of Southern Nigeria.* London: H. Milford.

Thomas, Northcote. 1914. *Anthropological Report on Ibo-Speaking Peoples of Nigeria* Part IV: *Law and custom of the Ibo of Asaba District, S. Nigeria.* London: Harrison & Sons.

Uchendu, Victor. 1965. *The Igbo of Southeast Nigeria.* New York. Holt, Rinehart & Winston.

Valakazi, Absolam. 1962. *Zulu Transformations: A Study of the Dynamics of Social Change.* Pietermaritzburg: University of Natal Press.

Warmelo, N. J. van. 1944a. *The Batswalo or Nanarene.* Union of South Africa, Department of Native Affairs Ethnological Publications, No. 10. Pretoria.

—— 1944b. *The Bathlabine of Moxoboya.* Union of South Africa, Department of Native Affairs Ethnological Publications, No. 11. Pretoria.

—— 1944c. *The Bakoni ba Maake.* Union of South Africa, Department of Native Affairs Ethnological Publications, No. 12. Pretoria.

—— 1944d. *The Banarene of Sekororo.* Union of South Africa, Department of Native Affairs Ethnological Publications, No. 13. Pretoria.

—— 1944e. *The Banarene of Mmutlana.* Union of South Africa, Department of Native Affairs Ethnological Publications, No. 14. Pretoria.

—— 1944f. *The Bakoni of Mametsa.* Union of South Africa, Department of Native Affairs Ethnological Publications, No. 15. Pretoria.

—— 1948. *Venda Law.* Union of South Africa, Department of Native Affairs Ethnological Publications, No. 23. Pretoria.

Whitfield, G. M. B. 1948. *South African Native Law.* Cape Town: Juta & Co.

CAROLYN FLUEHR-LOBBAN

6
Agitation for
Change
in the
Sudan

S OCIAL CHANGE DOES not occur overnight, nor without some degree of dislocation and often painful rupture. Social change for the modern Muslim woman in Sudan has only begun to pick up momentum over the last generation; it is a dynamic process where the present can only be understood in terms of the past. One must examine Sudanese Islamic culture and the political history of the country to grasp fully the directions that current winds for change are taking. There is a woman's movement in the Sudan that has a quarter-century of history behind it already, which has emerged within a Sudanese cultural and historical context. This article is an effort to understand this movement for change on its own terms. Too often writers from the West view movements for emancipation of women in western terms, and this, I submit, does a great injustice to the indigenous character of these movements.

Field research was carried out in the Sudan, in Khartoum, from 1970 to 1972. Research grants were made available from the Program of African Studies and the Council for Intersocietal Studies, both of Northwestern University, Evanston, Illinois. Special thanks are given to the Faculties of Social Anthropology and Law at the University of Khartoum for their cooperation and hospitality.

Sudanese Cultural Diversity

Before independence in 1956, the Sudan was ruled by imperial Britain as the Anglo-Egyptian Sudan, although Egypt's role was never more than administrative. The boundaries of the Sudan, like other former colonies in Africa, were not drawn with any consideration of the peoples who lived within them, so that Sudan is an ethnically heterogeneous country. As Africa's largest country, its enormous expanse of land, roughly equal to the territory east of the Mississippi, touches in some way on nearly all that is Africa. Its vast borders are shared with eight other African countries and within its territory nearly every African type can be found: from Arab to Hamite to African Nilote; from nomad to sedentary cultivator and seasonally nomadic pastoralist; from Muslim to animist, with a smattering of Christians as a legacy of colonial rule. Arabic is the *lingua franca* in Sudan, but it is the first language of only a third of the population. Sudan's vastness and diversity are overwhelming. From the time of the first penetration from the outside, resulting in Turco-Egyptian rule from 1821–24, through the reign of the anticolonialist Sudanese Mahdiya (1884–98), through the long period of British colonialism (1898–1956), no one ruling group has effectively governed the Sudan.

From these diverse peoples it is the Nubians, living in the extreme north of the country along the Nile, and the central Sudanese, living farther south along the Nile and controlling its important centers, who history has favored and who exert a dominant influence on Sudanese culture today. These people had the most prolonged contact with the Egyptians, ancient and modern; moreover, they were the ones contacted by other outsiders eager to control the Nile and its headwaters and to exploit the land for the rich sources of gold, ivory, and slaves in *Bilad Es Sudan,* "the land of the blacks." These people were the settled Nile dwellers who adopted Islam with great vigor in the sixteenth century and who seriously took up learning and teaching the Koran, acquiring as a result a high regard for literacy. Under British colonialism this penchant for literacy gave the northern, riverine peoples an advantage, and they were educated in English and trained as lower-level bureaucrats and administrators. Economically, too, these people profited the most from the few crumbs that fell from the colonial table of the Queen; so in the postindependence period this group of northern and central Sudanese emerged as a dominant economic and political force. Today their culture is thought of as "Sudanese" culture.

Culture of the Northern Muslim Sudan

The main urban complex of the Sudan is the three towns generally referred to as Khartoum, comprising Khartoum, Omdurman, and Khartoum North. The total population of the three towns is about 800,000. The other major cities in the provinces are considerably smaller; and in a country of 15,000,000, the overwhelming majority of people live in rural areas. One might even speak of the ruralization of the cities, as does Abu-Lughod (1961).

The northern and central Sudanese are strict Muslims, and through Islam, a religion that emerged in Arab culture, certain values from the desert have been retained. There is a strong sense of honor, dignity, and well-being when one is in absolute control of one's property, any threat to which is a threat to survival in the harsh desert climate. In the north, control over the Nile's waters (and indeed any source of water), irrigation rights, and rights over plots of land are protected.

Woman, as perhaps another form of private property, is likewise protected from her own uncontrollable passions and from the licentious designs of men upon her. She is protected by men, first by her father and brothers, later by her husband, and possibly in later life by her sons, because women are believed to be weak. If they are not controlled and their behavior is not scrutinized, it is possible they will bring shame upon the family, shame felt most acutely by the men. In other ways she is protected by

being confined generally to the house, by wearing modest clothing when in public, and by pharaonic circumcision. These will be
discussed in more detail below.

Religion is the province of men, and they can be observed in
individual or communal public prayer in the streets or in the
mosque. Women observe Islam in a less demonstrative way—they
never pray publicly, and in the home praying is not regularly observed by women unless they are very old or passing through
some crisis such as sickness or pregnancy. Women observe the
40 days of fasting during Ramadan with men and hope, like all
Muslims, to make the pilgrimage to Mecca sometime before they
die, but if money is scarce, it is the men who make the *hajj* to
Mecca. Islamic law protects women from neglect and abuse, but
at the same time it favors men through its tenets and procedures.
Men have the unilateral right of divorce and need not come to
court to terminate a marriage. They simply pronounce *talag talata*
("I divorce you") three times in the presence of witnesses and the
marriage is dissolved; the divorce need only be registered with
the *maazun* (marital registrar). Women have no such right and
must appeal directly to the court, often using a brother or father as
legal adviser or guardian. The Islamic courts are generally sympathetic to women seeking support in personal matters, but the
law formally remains unequal in matters involving men and
women.

The patrilineal extended family is the primary unit of social
structure within which the most intensive and important social
relations take place. A young man expects and prefers to marry
his first cousin on the father's side, and 38 percent of marriages in
one sample are of this type (R. Lobban 1973, p. 96). Circum-
cisions, marriages, births, and deaths are the most significant cultural events around which the family unites. A traditional woman,
otherwise sheltered from contacts outside the home, has the most
intensive and intimate social life among her female kin and with
other women friends, while the only extended contact with men
she has is with her husband, sons, and male kin. Sexual segregation is a way of life, and women do not necessarily long for the

company of men; in fact it makes them generally uncomfortable, as it made me after several months of living in Khartoum. In short, it is a mistake to pity women this lack of association with unrelated men; life is pleasant and fulfilling with close relationships with one's family, friends, and children.

Northern Sudanese Women

Women's activities are circumscribed and controlled generally by men over women and secondarily by older women over younger women. Most of a woman's life will be concerned with work in the domestic sphere in the company of other women, where relations are far closer and warmer than in modern American life. A small number of modern, educated women work in jobs outside the home and are independent to a degree, and gradually the presence of these women in offices and as salespersons in stores is making it more respectable for a woman to work in public. However, even among this progressive sector of women and men, social life that mixes the sexes is still somewhat strained and uncomfortable.

There are differences between the life of rural women and that of urban women based on the degree to which the women participate in economic production. In the rural areas where women cultivate the land and carry water from long distances—generally where they are freer in their movements and where their work is needed—they are more respected and exert, relatively speaking, more influence. In the rural areas sexual segregation of work and social life is not practiced to the degree that it is in the cities, and women are not so closely confined to the home. The tōb or loose outer garment that conceals the woman's body is not required for public use in the rural areas as it is in the cities. Germaine Tillion (1964) points to a similar phenomenon in Algeria where, she observes, women put on the veil as their families move into the cities where more protection is required.

Within the domestic sphere, women exercise a great deal of

influence in the education of children and in the management of household affairs. While women influence the children in the informal, open, and warm atmosphere of the *hareem,* the women's section of the house, still they do not finally have control over the children in a formal, legal sense. Important decisions are made by fathers and husbands: under Islamic law[1] the father gains legal custody over a boy when he is seven years of age and he has custody of a daughter after the age of eleven or twelve. In the northern Sudanese household, the decision of a father or husband can easily override the wishes of his wife and daughter, in a conflict over the selection of a daughter's marriage partner, for instance.

In Sudan—as in many other parts of the world, including our own culture—there is one standard of behavior applied to males and a much more rigid standard for women. A man can be out often at night drinking or going to the prostitutes' quarters without losing much of his dignity, but a woman will be slandered if she goes out without permission from her husband or father or if she walks the streets alone. It is widely believed that women are easily tempted, and their weakness and passion must be controlled lest they bring shame and disgrace to the family. Like other parts of the Middle Eastern and Afro-Arab world, the honor of men is associated with the good sexual conduct of women (cf. Peristiany 1965).

Women are protected from bringing disgrace in a number of ways. The first and surest means is by female circumcision, of the pharaonic or *sunni* type. Pharaonic circumcision,[2] which involves the excision of the clitoris, labia majora, and labia minora, is still the most widespread form of female circumcision in the northern Sudan, but there is a gradual movement toward the practice of the *sunni* form, which is simply clitoridectomy.

A young girl is circumcised before she is ten years old, the operation being performed by a midwife or by an experienced female relative. This is meant to insure the chastity of the young woman until marriage, and in this respect it is effective. Some brides must have their circumcision scars cut open by a midwife before they are able to have sexual intercourse with their husbands.

The circumcision is associated with cleanliness and morality—the decency of a young woman cannot be insured without it. Even progressive younger people who want to stop or modify the practice of circumcising their small daughters are subjected to intense pressure from the family, with arguments suggesting that the girl will be "spoiled" without the operation. Even today one of the deepest insults that can be paid to a man is that he is a "son of an uncircumcised woman."

Women are further protected by being kept generally to the *hareem* section of the house, with visits permitted outside to friends and close relatives who are usually within close range. When women leave the house, they should not go out alone, but with other female companions. If a woman must travel alone, a brother or male relative should accompany her, usually by walking behind her. Men and women eat separately, sit or stand separately at public gatherings, and display totally different demeanors when in the company of the same sex than they do in the company of the opposite sex. Women who can be loud and even raucous together can barely be heard as they lower their eyes and drop their voices to greet a man formally. Men are nervous and uneasy in the company of women; once they have paid their respects they are eager to leave.

In public women must wear the *tōb* over their dresses. This consists of from six to nine meters of cloth draped modestly about the body. It is somewhat cumbersome to wear and always in need of adjustment, but to leave it off in the puritanical cities would be socially catastrophic. Women at the University of Khartoum who have attempted to raise the issue of female emancipation by removing the *tōb* symbolically have been beaten by more orthodox Muslim men, and one fight between male students over the matter resulted in the death of a student.

Marriage within families is another form of protection, with first-cousin marriage as the preferred and the dominant marriage pattern. Women are safeguarded and sheltered within the patrilineal extended family, and a woman who does not marry or who postpones marriage is likely to be socially ridiculed.

The behavior of men is reflected in what has been described

here for women. From the age of eight or ten years a boy has his primary social relationships with other males, and his close and regular relationships will be among men. If a man dares to gain some sexual experience before marriage, he must do it in the prostitutes' quarters or through temporary homosexual liaisons that are tolerated before marriage. Sometimes at an all-male gathering or party, some of the men will imitate the singing and dancing of women, as if to create what they cannot normally experience.

Life is further complicated for the young man by the high cost of marriage. At today's prices, perhaps 300 to 400 Sudanese pounds or about $1,000 in the cities, the average male is forced to postpone his wedding until he can afford it, often not until he is in his late twenties or early thirties. This postpones his achievement of the statuses of husband and father, without which he has not fulfilled his role as an adult male in the society.

The patterns of northern Sudanese culture became rigidified during the Mahdist Islamic reformation of the nineteenth century and are still relatively puritanical and conditioned by Islamic traditions. These traditions are a strong cultural force and a very real backdrop to any consideration of social change in the modern setting.

Movements toward Change
in the Last Quarter-Century

Within the cultural and historical context described above, there is a group of progressive Sudanese women and men who have actively sought to modify or transform altogether certain traditions that, they argue, are not compatible with modern life in the Sudan. For generations, no doubt, women have recognized inequities between men and women, and perhaps they sought to rectify them on an individual basis; but it was not until women organized themselves into specific associations to deal with their problems that any real change could be observed.

It often appears as a contradiction to western observers that Muslim women, who theoretically are subordinated by law and custom, are nonetheless individuals with strong and assertive personalities. There has been a long tradition of resistance by women, from the legendary nineteenth-century heroine Miheira Bint 'Abboud who led her people, the Shaygīya, into battle against the Turkish and Egyptian invaders, to contemporary open defiance by women of their husbands in court cases involving a woman's failure to obey. By tradition and law a Muslim wife owes absolute obedience to her husband; however, the Islamic courts are laden with obedience (ta'ah) cases where husbands have sought legal assistance in commanding the compliance of their wives on some matter (see Dwyer, this volume).

One of the most frequent reasons why a man comes to Shari'a court for an obedience ruling is to bring about the return of a wife who has fled the house of her husband, referred to as bāt eta'ah cases or literally "house obedience." In the main, ta'ah cases have dealt with bāt eta'ah rulings where a woman is ordered to return to her husband, with police assistance if necessary. The large number of obedience cases in the Shari'a courts suggest that on an individual basis women have offered resistance to certain of the unilateral privileges of men in the society. I have read cases that go back as far as 1922 where women have offered to refund dowries in order to be free of unwanted husbands; they have rejected the ruling altogether and fled from the husband time and again until the court gave up in despair of ever returning the woman to her spouse; and they have threatened to commit suicide or convert to Christianity in order to pressure their families into accepting their will. Over the years the Islamic courts have responded to certain of these messages from women, and they tend not to issue obedience rulings after two or three unsuccessful attempts to return a woman to her husband.

Incidents like the following are not uncommon in everyday life, and a number of such situations were reported to me. A friend's mother heard that her two adolescent sons had been caught sneaking into the cinema without paying admission and were being held in custody by the police. The mother went immediately to the police station to sign for the release of her sons, but she was turned away because only a man can legally carry out this procedure. The mother came home and complained bitterly to her daughter about the unfairness of the law, saying that she is full-grown, responsible, a person equal to her husband, and that she should be treated so. The daughter, who was a university student active in political affairs and in the struggle for women's rights, was pleased to hear this attitude expressed by her mother. This was the first time her mother had considered such matters. The next morning my friend overheard a heated argument between her parents over the affair.

Frequently I asked women friends and acquaintances if they believed men were better than women, and uniformly the response was negative. Rephrasing the question to "Are men more powerful than women?" produced the answer, "Yes, they can do more."

Set against a general background of this sort where there is a history of informal dissent by some women, the Sudanese women's movement found fertile ground within which to grow. Other issues were stirring the minds of educated and progressive-minded Sudanese: there was much talk of independence and anticolonialism in post-World War II Sudan, and the women's movement participated as an important force in this intellectual birth of the modern Sudan.

The Women's Movement: 1946–74

The first group of organized women emerged from the Communist Party, which was active in the aftermath of World War II in the drive for Sudanese independence. The party was formed in 1946 and was the first political party in the history of the Sudan to open its membership to both sexes and to establish the emancipation of women as one of its goals. In that same year the Sudanese Women's League was formed. The Women's League, like the party at large, began first with a group of educated women but spread throughout the northern Sudan to encompass working women and peasants. The original organizers had been students at Omdurman's Secondary School for Girls who had been expelled for their "outrageous" activities, such as participating in student strikes over the colonial issue. The women's movement did not begin or grow in isolation: it was in every way linked to the mass movement and the developing consciousness in the 1940s and 1950s of a country struggling for national independence.

In 1951, three communist women were among the founding members of the Sudanese Women's Union, the successor to the Women's League but with broader membership. Four years later the Union began to publish the progressive magazine, *The Woman's Voice.* The magazine took militant political stands in opposition to colonialism in Sudan and in Africa, and some years later after independence it stood opposed to neocolonialist designs of Britain and America. For example, it exposed U.S. Agency for International Development (AID) programs in Sudan as an effort to bolster the conservative rule of General Ibrahim Abboud (1958–64), which opposed the activities of the Women's Union. It also published articles that attempted to educate its female readership away from certain traditions it considered harmful to women: articles dealing with personal and child health care and hygiene, or articles questioning the utility of facial scarification, a traditional means of ethnic identification, appeared regularly in *The Woman's Voice.* A major campaign against the practice of female circumcision was never mounted by the magazine, perhaps because it was decided that the issue was too sensitive and might alienate potential supporters. Today it is still difficult to discuss female circumcision and no organized group is initiating such a discussion; on the other hand, the practice of facial scarification seems to be gradually disappearing.

In the early 1950s the Women's Union promoted equal pay for equal work for urban working women and fought to extend a seven-day maternity leave to forty days with pay. Trade-union organizing was spreading throughout the country at this time, and the climate generated by this first group of politically active women allowed the trade unions to penetrate professions where large numbers of women are employed. As a result the Union of Government Elementary School Teachers was established in 1949 and the Nurses' Trade Union was organized in 1950. The Women's Union also attacked the Islamic divorce and obedience laws that so heavily favor men, and it began to campaign against the marriage of a man to more than one wife at a time. Some referred to polygyny as "legalized prostitution."

It is difficult to express the impact, both positive and negative, these politically active women had on northern Sudanese society in the cities. They were outspoken, they were controversial, they were something entirely new; and to be sure many people opposed their actions as well as their words. Conservative forces in the society tried to discredit the Women's Union by saying their members were prostitutes—after all, who else would go out to public meetings and address gatherings of men to win their support? It takes great courage for women in an Islamic society to speak out on any issue, much less the issue of female emancipation. They suffer criticism from family and friends and reduce their attractiveness, from the point of view of traditional values, as marriage partners. In a small-scale society—even in Khartoum nearly everyone can establish some link with almost everyone else through relatives or friends—the pressures of public opinion are very great indeed.

Nevertheless, these women in the Union so stirred the Sudanese public that a rival group of reactionary women was hastily organized in the postindependence period after 1956, which functioned as the Sudanese equivalent of a ladies' tea association. Fatma Ahmed Ibrahim, one of the founders of the Women's Union, reacted to this rival organization by editorializing in *The Woman's Voice* that "independence is not women's teas or charity bazaars; independence is a free Sudanese society, both economically and politically, a socialist society, the society of the truly emancipated Sudanese woman."

The Women's Union and *The Woman's Voice* rose and fell in

accordance with political events in the country as a whole. During the conservative Abboud regime, the Union was officially banned; however, publication of *The Woman's Voice* continued and record sales were witnessed.

In October 1964, a popular revolution throughout the country overthrew the Abboud regime. For the first time in recent history Sudanese women came out in the streets and demonstrated and died along with men during the days of the revolution. Fatma Ibrahim led the first demonstration of several hundred. When the soldiers raised their guns to fire on the demonstrators, Fatma stepped forward, dropped her traditional outer garment (the *tōb*), and shouted to the soldiers: "I will be the first to die." The soldiers were so stunned by this dramatic event that they lowered their guns and no shots were fired that day. One woman, a member of the Women's Union, was killed during the October revolution, and five other women were injured seriously, three of whom were Union members. The participation of women in the October revolution began to break down some of the traditional ideas regarding the behavior of women. Women were shown not to be weak or timid; and with men and women working together to bring down the regime, absolute ideas about sexual segregation came to be questioned.

Officially the revolution brought women only the vote, but the right of universal suffrage had never been extended by any regime in the Sudan's history. In the first elections in which women participated, Fatma Ibrahim was elected to parliament, another political first; however, apart from this victory the voting patterns for women did not differ significantly from those of men.

In May 1969, a relatively progressive military regime came to power under the leadership of General Gaafar Mohammed Nimieri. The leaders of the coup enlisted support from large numbers of Sudanese progressives, including the Communist Party, the Women's Union, and other democratic organizations. Because of the years of political agitation and the efforts made by the Women's Union to educate the Sudanese public concerning women's rights, the new regime felt some pressures to consider the status of women in the country as part of its program. A woman, Nafisa Ahmed El-Amin, was appointed to a ministerial post, that of Deputy Minister of Youth and Social Affairs. More recently she has been appointed to the political bureau of the ruling party, the Sudanese Socialist Union, and another woman, Dr. Fatma Abdul Mahmoud, has replaced her at her previous post.

In the same period some reforms to raise the status of women were enacted. Equal pay for equal work was extended to working women, and government pensions were given to female employees as well as male employees. Maternity leave was extended from seven days to three months. It will be remembered that the Women's Union had campaigned for a maternity leave of forty days, which is the traditional amount of time a woman is afforded for delivery and recovery from childbirth.

Bāt eta'ah, or the right of a husband to bring back a wife by force, was abolished. This was the first time in Sudanese history that there was open rejection of a Shari'a law by the government. With the reform the element of force—the use of the police to return the woman—was eliminated. The new law was heralded by progressives, and women reported a slightly defensive and perhaps more respectful attitude on the part of men. Judges in the Shari'a courts complained that the reform was not fully understood and that women were taking it to mean that they did not have to obey at all, and they hastened to remind the community that first among a woman's duties is obedience to her husband!

The progressive Nimieri regime further amended the Shari'a law by increasing the amount of alimony and support that a woman has the right to receive, from one-quarter to one-half of a man's salary. During these early days of the regime the Women's Union reacted positively to the new government and organized demonstrations in support of the regime's reforms and declarations. It sent a list of demands, which in essence asked for equality for women in the political, economic, and social fields and for equitable treatment by the government and its laws.

As Nimieri moved to consolidate his own power in the country, opposition from the right and the left had to be eliminated. The

Communist Party became increasingly critical of many of Nimieri's domestic and international moves, and the Women's Union, having strong ties to the Communist Party of Sudan, fell out of favor with the regime along with the Party. Tensions between the regime and certain democratic organizations critical of Nimieri culminated in the official banning of these organizations by the government, the Women's Union included. When the Union was abolished in 1971, there were over 120 branches of the Union outside of Khartoum, comprising about 15,000 women. Several of these branches were in the southern Sudan where a civil war had been in existence intermittently since 1956, and it is significant that the Women's Union was attempting to ease relations between northerners and southerners long before it became official government policy to do so.

A coup and countercoup in July 1971 transformed Nimieri from a mild progressive into a militant anticommunist, and from this point all hope of friendly relations between the government and the Women's Union disappeared. A number of Women's Union leaders have been arrested or detained under house arrest and numerous others have been harassed by the government. Women from the families of jailed progressives demonstrated at the People's Palace in Khartoum for economic support from the government while their husbands and other male relatives were confined. The government has since provided this support.

The Women's Union has been "replaced" by the Women's Affairs Committee of the Sudanese Socialist Union, but it appears that this committee does little grass-roots organizing among women; it seems mainly to arrange teas and receptions for diplomatic wives. While the regime has retreated steadily from its early progressive stands, it does wish to retain a broadly socialist image; therefore, the long-range goal of female emancipation has not been abandoned.

The reforms regarding the status of women remain on the books, but it would be a mistake to suggest that the reforms are either fully understood by the people or that they are fully implemented by the government. Those reforms that touched upon areas where there had been long-standing resistance and a great deal of political agitation—the bāt eta'ah reform, equal pay for equal work, and maternity leave—are those that have been most easily accepted and implemented.

The Women's Union will no doubt reemerge as a strong social and political voice for women. The Union flourished for 25 years because it was integrated into Sudanese life. It introduced progressive ideas but was careful not to violate strongly held traditions. For this reason polygyny could be campaigned against because there is some measure of popular support for modification of the marriage and divorce laws; however, the continued practice of pharaonic circumcision, which is a sensitive topic, has not been a major area of concern for the Union.

The women's movement also succeeded because it never struggled around women's issues alone. It has had a strong tradition of involvement in Sudanese national politics, in the independence movement, in the October revolution, and in the early days of the Nimieri regime. The goal of an emancipated Sudanese society was concomitant with, and of equal importance to, the goal of the emancipation of women within the society.

Notes

1. Malikite Islamic legal traditions are followed in the Sudan.

2. Pharaonic circumcision or infibulation is known to have been practiced by the ancient Egyptians and by the Arabs in Arabia in pre-Islamic times. It is also found in Ethiopia and parts of non-Muslim East Africa. The practice is not traceable to Islam.

References

Abu-Lughod, Janet. 1961. "Migrant Adjustment of City Life." *American Journal of Sociology* 67:22–32.
Fatma Babiker Mahmoud. 1971. "The Role of the Sudanese Women's Union in Sudanese Politics." Honors' thesis, University of Khartoum.

Fluehr-Lobban, Carolyn. 1973. "An Anthropological Analysis of Homicide in the Afro-Arab Sudan." Ph.D. dissertation, Northwestern University.
—— 1974. "The Women's Movement in Sudan: Its Place among Arab Women's Struggles for National Liberation and Social Emancipation." Paper presented at the Middle East Studies Association meetings, Boston.
Lobban, Richard. 1973. "Social Networks in the Urban Sudan." Ph.D. dissertation, Northwestern University.
Peristiany, J. G., ed. 1965. *Honor and Shame; A Study of Values in Mediterranean Society.* Chicago: University of Chicago Press.
Tillion, Germaine. 1964. *Les Femmes et le Voile dans la Civilisation Mediterranéenne.* Paris: Etudes Maghrebines.

BOLANLE AWE

The Iyalode
in the Traditional
7 Yoruba
Political
System

THE PRINCIPLE THAT ensures that every major interest in the society is given some representation in the conduct of government is widespread in most West African societies and has probably been one of the underlying factors in the recognition given to women within their political systems. The institutions of the Queen Mother of the Ashanti (Ghana) and the Edo (Benin Nigeria), the female chieftains of the Mende (Sierra Leone), the Sagi and the Sonya of the Nupe (Nigeria), and the royal princesses of the Kanuri (Bornu Nigeria), to mention but a few, are examples of the efforts to associate women with the government of these various ethnic groups. Nor were the highly urbanized Yoruba—who now number several millions in southern Nigeria, Benin, and Togo—an exception. The component parts of their political structure were primarily the lineages and the council of chiefs whose titles were invested in the individual lineages, as well as the age grades and the titled societies. But the two basic institutions around which the intense competition for power, position, and material resources was fought were the ruler (Oba) and his hereditary title holders, his chiefs. Since Yoruba society is mainly patrilineal, women do not in normal circumstances become the head of a lineage or the representative of that lineage for a chieftaincy title. Oral traditions record the existence of a few female rulers in the remote past (see Abiola et al., 1932), but available evidence suggests that the practice has been discontinued for at least the past 200 years. But while the women were not associated with the political process on the same basis as the men, they did have channels of direct participation in it. The institution of the Iyalode,[1] the woman designated as their political leader and spokesman in government, therefore represented an attempt to give women a voice in government and was a recognition of their ability to participate meaningfully in the political process. Indeed, in the nineteenth century many women were given the Iyalode title for their contribution to the war efforts of their towns.

A study of the position of the Iyalode, or indeed of women generally, within the Yoruba traditional political structure is difficult for many reasons. The ubiquity and energy of the Yoruba market woman, like her sisters in many parts of West Africa, have caused scholars to focus primarily on her economic role in society to the neglect of her contribution in other spheres (see Mabogunje 1961). Thus her political participation has often been regarded as indirect and incidental to her economic interest. The tendency has therefore been to dismiss the Iyalode as politically insignificant and to misconstrue her role. Since the title, Iyalode (literally, "mother in charge of external affairs," i.e., in charge of dealings between members of the society and outsiders) is a generic term used for the female spokesman and leader of any society, her position is often confused with that of a club leader (Lebeuf 1963). Indeed, even now some Yoruba scholars (Fadipe 1970) still regard her as no more than the head of the market women.

A more crucial problem, however, is that of methodology and obtaining source materials. Although most evidence used in this paper is based on oral traditions collected from the various incumbents of the Iyalode and other offices, the investigation is still severely handicapped by some unavoidable factors. The colonial experience has in many ways disrupted the traditional political system and undermined the position and authority of the traditional rulers of the people. During this period of foreign domination, women seem to have been the most affected. With their Western preconceptions of female inferiority, colonial administrations tended to relegate women to the background in their governments. Consequently, many female titles disappeared while some of their functions became obsolete through lack of opportunity. In many instances, it is only the position of the Iyalode and her lieutenants that still exists within the political system and bears close examination; but even this institution of government has undergone many changes that have shorn it of its power and influence, so that what exists now is not necessarily a true reflection of the Iyalode's traditional position. For instance, with modern reorganization of local government administration in southwestern Nigeria, she is no longer a member of any of the important councils of government. Even the market, and therefore the market women, have been removed from her jurisdiction, and have been placed under the control of the new local government councils in each town. She has also lost a large part of the traditional means by which she maintained her position in the past. The customary tribute and gifts that were her due have disappeared and have been replaced with a salary that compares unfavorably with that of her male counterparts. Interest in attaining a position that in the past conferred great distinction has consequently declined. Modern changes have also given her position new accretions. In some towns where Christianity gained much ground, her position has been converted from a purely political to a religious one, and she is now known as the Iyalode of the Christians.[2] It would therefore be dangerous to assume that the position of the Iyalode now can be safely extrapolated back into the past.

In spite of such limitations, however, it is still possible to reconstruct the position of the Iyalode within the traditional political system from available evidence. Some of the traditional customs, practices, and functions—ritual, political, and administrative—associated with her position have survived. It has also been possible to supplement such information with some written evidence. European missionaries and other visitors to the Yoruba country in the nineteenth century who were impressed by the contribution of women to the general development of the towns they visited occasionally described the position of the Iyalode (Hinderer 1873). Even during the period of British administration, political officers commissioned to write intelligence reports[3] on the areas under their control often had to acknowledge the importance of the Iyalode in the traditional government. Local historians have also collected traditional accounts of the Iyalode in some Yoruba towns.[4]

The Iyalode was, like the male chiefs, a chief in her own right and had her own special insignia of office: the necklace of special beads (*ogbagbara* and *iyun*), the wide-brimmed straw hats (*ate*) of the Ondo and the Ijesa, the shawl (*itagbe*) of the Ijebu, her own personal servants, and her special drummers and bell ringers to call the women to attention. Her title was an all-embracing one that gave her jurisdiction over all women. This is why in some Yoruba towns she was given a more explicit title such as *Eiyelobinrin* ("mother of all women") at Akure and *Arise Ioran obinrin* ("she whose business is with the affairs of women") in Ilesa. And she was indeed the chosen representative of all women in her town. Unlike the Queen Mother among the Ashanti (Busia 1951) or the Sagi among the Nupe (Nadel 1951), she did not have to belong to a special social class to attain her office. Hers was an achieved rather than an inherited position: although in a few cases the post was hereditary, the office was generally elective and had to have the stamp of popular approval. Her most important qualifications were her proven ability as a leader able to articulate the feelings of the women, her control of vast economic resources to maintain her new status as chief, and her popularity.

Once she was appointed, the Iyalode became not only the voice of the women in government but also a kind of queen who coordinated all their activities. She settled their quarrels in her court and met with them to determine what should be the women's stand, for instance, on such questions as the declaration of war, the opening of new markets, or the administration of women at the local level. As a spokesman she was given access to all positions of power and authority within the state, exercising legislative, judicial, and executive powers with the chiefs in their council. To make her representation effective there was a clear-cut chain of authority through her by which the government knew the wishes of the people and vice versa. To coordinate all women's interests, she had her own council of subordinate chiefs who exercised jurisdiction over all women in those particular matters that pertained to women alone. Information about what these matters were is scanty. But in contrast to the council of male chiefs, which would be involved in the organization of war, the reception of foreign visitors, and so on, it is not unlikely that the women chiefs would be involved in the settlement of disputes between women, the cleanliness of the markets, and other female concerns. This council not only deliberated on women's affairs; their members also acted as area representatives through whom the Iyalode could feel the pulse of women in different parts of the town. Another means of keeping in touch with the women was through her control of the markets and therefore of the large majority of Yoruba women who were traders. In addition, she was a type of honorary president-general for all women's societies in the town.

But in spite of the right conferred on her to participate at all levels of government and the potentially massive support that could be mustered for her cause, the Iyalode's effectiveness in the political process was not necessarily guaranteed. In theory she was acknowledged as the representative of all women and in all cases was free to comment on all policy matters. In practice, however, she suffered from one big disadvantage: she was always outnumbered as the only female in the crucial decision-making body, the council of kingmakers which she had to attend. There was always therefore the danger that the social practice of government might not conform to the theoretical expectations that her position might imply (see Evans-Pritchard 1965). A great deal of what she could achieve would depend on at least two important factors: (1) the qualities of the Iyalode—her personality, her dynamism, and her political astuteness; and (2) the political milieu within which she operated. This second factor is particularly important, because the Iyalode throughout Yoruba country did not operate within a uniform political system. Although the various Yoruba governments often shared the same set of titles, their political constitutions were different (Lloyd 1954). In most Yoruba communities one of the main features of politics was usually intense competition for power, authority, and influence between the Oba on the one hand and his senior, hereditary chiefs on the other.

A brief examination of a Yoruba kingdom will illustrate the nature of their politics and provide a background for an understanding of the Iyalode's position. The Oyo kingdom before the nineteenth century provides a good example (Law 1972). The ruler, the Alaafin, had among his powers the right to approve succession to all titles in Oyo. He was the highest judicial authority in the land and he alone could order an execution of a convicted person. He also had control of Sango, the chief religious cult in the kingdom. His council of senior hereditary chiefs, the Oyomesi, on the other hand, had the final voice in his selection, served as an advisory body to him, and could engineer his removal from the throne if he proved unsatisfactory. In the eighteenth century this kingdom was the scene of a series of conflicts in which power alternated between the Alaafin and his chiefs. The issues that sparked these conflicts have been differently interpreted by different historians. Some see them as centering around the matter of Oyo's foreign policy—whether it should take a military form or whether the kingdom should concern itself with commercial expansion. Others believe a struggle to command the resources of the expanding kingdom was taking place. Whatever the issues were, they certainly represented the factors that engaged the attention of the ruler and his chiefs.

Each Yoruba constitution was in effect often an indication of the stage arrived at in that struggle between the ruler and his chiefs. At least three different constitutional stages are discernible. In some towns an even balance was maintained. In others the balance had been tilted in favor of the king, and in consequence there was a high degree of centralization of government under him. There were also instances where he had lost the initiative and power had passed into the hands of his chiefs and the powerful secret cults.

A clearer picture of the Iyalode's role and effectiveness, particularly in this struggle between the conflicting tendencies and divergent interests of the Oba and his chiefs (including the Iyalode), can only be gleaned by examining her position under different constitutional arrangements within the Yoruba country before the colonial period.[5]

The Oyo Yoruba

After the constitutional conflicts of the eighteenth century, centralization of power around the monarchy and the consequent decline in the power of the chiefs in the nineteenth century was very apparent among the Oyo-Yoruba of the Oyo kingdom. Under the constitution that then operated in their new modern settlement at Oyo (Babayemi 1974), the Alaafin had successfully whittled down the power of his chiefs and transferred most of their political, military, and economic functions to the palace officials who were his personal servants. Inasmuch as the Iyalode was outside this palace organization, her position was of little significance within the political system. Indeed, the pattern at Oyo as regards the participation of women in the political process was one of indirect influence, through the appointment of women to positions in which they could influence the ruler who had the authority.

Among the Alaafin's palace officials were the royal mothers and the royal priestesses. These were very powerful women. They were in charge of the different compounds in the large palace of Oyo; some of them were also priestesses of the most important cults, such as that of Sango, the god of thunder, which was the official religious cult of the kingdom. They were also in a position to wield great influence because they had the most direct access to the king. Even the Iwarefa, his highest and closest officials, had to go through them to arrange rituals, festivals, and communal labor. Tributaries of the Oyo kingdom could only approach the Alaafin through them, and they made it possible for the Alaafin to have effective control on different communities in his kingdom (Babayemi 1974). Far from being representatives of the women in Oyo, they constituted part of the system used by the Alaafin to strengthen his position vis-à-vis his chiefs. But insofar as they were female functionaries in the government to whom the Alaafin could always refer when issues affecting women were to be discussed or when he wished to have the view of the women, they undermined the effectiveness and influence of the Iyalode and made her political role an insignificant one. It is not surprising, therefore, that even when she attended the meeting of the council of chiefs, she deferred to the judgement of the males (Fadipe 1970).

Other Oyo-Yoruba constitutions reflect a similar weakness in the Iyalode's position, with a few minor differences depending on the degree of centralization of government that had already been achieved or the antecedents of the Iyalode's title. In Iwo, where by the end of the nineteenth century the balance of power had been greatly tilted in favor of the Oba, the fact of the first Iyalode's being the sister of the reigning Oba and the mother of another made her position less subservient; but her powers were still circumscribed by a number of female functionaries whose duties had political undertones and who were directly responsible to the ruler.

One aberration within this Oyo-Yoruba system is to be found in the comparatively new settlement of Ibadan, which in the nineteenth century threw overboard the idea of hereditary government and chose chiefs on merit. This same system of appointment was extended to the Iyalode's title.[6] A candidate would have to prove her mettle, which was often based on her contribution to the military success of the town. The first Iyalode, Iyaola, was said to have made generous contributions to Ibadan war efforts both by giving liberal credit facilities to the war chiefs, enabling them to acquire guns and ammunition, and by making her own direct contribution. In this regard she established a tradition that her successors as Iyalode followed. Like the male chiefs she contributed her own quota of soldiers to Ibadan's *ad hoc* army whenever there was warfare, out of a corps of domestic slaves trained to fight. She gave them equipment and food, and put them under the leadership of one of her more experienced soldiers, who led them to war as a unit of Ibadan's national army. In recognition of such services to the state, the ruler of Ibadan in the 1850s, Bale Olugbode, made Iyaola the Iyalode. Within a short time she so established her presence as the representative of the Ibadan women that Anna Hinderer could describe her as "the mother of the town to whom all the women's palavers (disputes) are brought before they are taken to the king. She is in fact a sort of queen, a person of much influence, and looked up to with much respect" (1854, p. 110). Her peculiar position in this society where a man's following, his popularity, and his economic resources virtually determined the amount of influence he could wield in the body politic, gave her de facto power in defiance of what was customary and traditional among the Oyo-Yoruba.

For no other Iyalode in Ibadan was this better borne out than in the famous Iyalode Efunsetan, a very successful trader who had acquired extensive riches through her business activities. Like other distinguished chiefs in Ibadan, she had three very large farms and more than 500 domestic slaves working for her, and had built around herself a large following of kinsmen and hangers-on. Her compound in consequence became one of the focal points of power and influence in the town. It is not surprising that she became a factor to be reckoned with in Ibadan politics, and that she provided a rallying point of opposition to the ruler of Ibadan, Are Latosa. She challenged his foreign policy that alienated Ibadan from its neighbors, and resisted his domestic policy that tended toward the establishment of sole rule, contrary to Ibadan's tradition of oligarchic government. In the struggle that ensued between Are Latosa and his chiefs, Efunsetan was deprived of her title and was eventually assassinated on what appear to be political grounds. The official reasons given for her elimination are of interest because they highlight the obligations and responsibilities of an Iyalode in wartime: (1) she did not accompany the head of state to war; (2) she never sent him supplies during the campaign; (3) she did not come in person to meet him outside the town wall to congratulate him on his safe return (Johnson 1937). These were also obligations expected of other members of the council of chiefs. Because of the precedents that Iyaola and her successor Efunsetan had set in Ibadan, the Iyalode had become so important in the council of chiefs in Ibadan that she was one of the signatories to the crucial agreement of 1893, which virtually handed Ibadan administration to the British; and in 1912 an Iyalode acted as regent in Ibadan for a few months after the death of a ruler.

Owu-Ijebu [7]

Among the Ijebu, where the initiative had passed from the Oba to the Osugbo secret cult, the age grades, and the chiefs, the position of the Iyalode was again different. She participated at all levels of policy making, including that of the Osugbo secret cult and the council of the Iwarefa chiefs. She also had an effective communication system with all women in the town. But in spite of such powers, her role, particularly in registering dissenting opinion, is not clear. There is no record of her opposition to the government. What seems to be obvious is that her role tended to be pacificatory, as a woman acting as peacemaker between the women and the other component parts of government, and diplomatic, looking for ways of arriving at a consensus by conciliation and negotiation. An interesting departure from this is the case of the successful trader Tinubu, who was made Iyalode in 1864 in appreciation of her contributions to the war efforts by the people of Abeokuta, where a system similar to that of the Ijebu operated. Her role in Abeokuta as Iyalode deserves further study. There is no doubt that it gave her, in addition to the influence that she wielded as a wealthy trader, a constitutional base from which she could play an effective role in the government and politics of the period. According to Biobaku (1960), she became involved in the succession struggle in Abeokuta and on a second attempt succeeded in installing her candidate on the throne.

Ijesa and Ondo[8]

Among the Ijesa and the Ondo, where the balance of power between the Oba and his chiefs was fairly evenly maintained, the position of the chief political representative of the women, the Arise in Ilesa and the Lobun in Ondo, presents another picture. This, in addition, is heightened by the fact that in both towns there had been a tradition of women rulers in the past, and women had been able to gain recognition as in Ibadan by their actual contributions to the welfare of the state. For instance, oral traditions (Abiola et al. 1932) in Ilesa relate that Arise helped to devise the strategy by which her countrymen defeated their Nupe invaders,[9] and thus she was invested with the title of Arise in recognition of her contribution to the war efforts. In both kingdoms these offices were endowed with a great deal of power, which was given ritual and symbolic recognition. In Ondo, the Lobun alone was responsible for the installation of the Oba, and in Ilesa, the Arise was one of the kingmakers. Indeed, their offices appeared to be coequal with those of the rulers in the two towns. They had under them the subordinate chiefs whose titles corresponded to the titles of the senior male chiefs of the ruler, and in rank order their own positions could be equated with that of the ruler.[10] In the Ondo polity the Oba and the Lobun were regarded as virtually equal rulers of the two societies which were distinct and separate; the Oba in charge of male society and the Lobun in charge of female society. Neither participated in the meetings of the other. The Lobun had meetings with her own chiefs on matters concerning women, such as the fixing of market days, the establishment of a new market, the organization of their traditional festivals, or of more general interest such as the declaration of war or the imposition of curfews during wartime. On such matters of common interest, the Oba acted as a link between her council and his own and she acted as a link between his council and her own. They would communicate their councils' decisions to each other, relay the same to their own councils, and bring back approval or disapproval of the measures contemplated. Either council was at liberty to initiate new measures under the leadership of the Oba or Lobun.

As if to emphasize their position within the political system, the rituals surrounding the installation of these two female chiefs were as elaborate as those for the rulers of both towns; and in both cases, their persons, like that of the Oba, became sacrosanct thereafter and they had to observe a number of taboos. The Arise in Ilesa must not leave her head uncovered, she must not be addressed by her real name but by title, and she must not kneel down as Yoruba do to show respect to elders of both sexes, and women do to honor males of their husbands' patrilineage. She had to move into an official residence specially built for her by the town, of the same opulence and grandeur as those of the more senior chiefs. The Lobun in Ondo must never again step on the bare floor, must not eat food that was not freshly prepared, and must put on new clothes every day.

But in spite of the tremendous power that their status thus conferred on them, they did not see themselves as competitors for influence and authority with the Oba and his chiefs. They regarded themselves primarily as part of an establishment that was essentially symmetrical in conception, where if the man was on the right hand, the woman must be on the left. Their position, however, was such that there was bound to be occasional conflict of authorities. Unfortunately, the evidence on this important element is very scanty. There is hardly any record of their leading the opposition to the government as in Ibadan. The present Lobun, however, indicated that any matter of disagreement, for instance on the opening of a new market, fixing market tolls, or arbitrary use of power by the male chiefs, would be one for negotiation between her council of chiefs and that of the Oba. If the Oba's council remained adamant there were forms of protest that could be adopted to show disapproval. The women under her leadership could boycott the markets or refuse to play their traditional role in the Oba's festival. The organization of all women under these female chiefs ensured their success in mobilizing female opinion.

The position of the Arise, who was part of the same decision-making process as the male chiefs, was more difficult. She often avoided direct confrontation, but if she were unable to carry all the women along with her, rather than discredit herself she would as a practical demonstration of disapproval lead a protest march of women to the Oba's palace. During this century there have been occasions when women in Ilesa rose up to protest in this manner. In the 1940s they did so over arbitrary and high taxation by the colonial government, and only recently they boycotted the king's market in protest against excessive stall fees and lack of security in the market.

There were in addition certain devices built into the position of both these women chiefs whereby pressure could be indirectly exerted on the Oba and his chiefs. The position of the Arise offers many examples. In her ritual role as the Oba's first wife, the Arise was his immediate confidante and had direct access to him at all times. She was indeed intimately involved in the affairs of his household. For instance, it was one of her duties to settle quarrels among his wives. She was also in close communication with all the important chiefs who held the balance of power with the Oba. The strategic position of her official residence near the palace ensured that all of them stopped to extend her their customary greetings in their movements to and from the palace. Some of them who were also obliged to render certain services to women usually did so through the Arise, their representative. The Arise herself had, like the Oba, certain important religious functions in the state, which helped to emphasize the importance and the indispensability of her position. This is best exemplified in the Obokun Festival, an annual festival in remembrance of Obokun, the legendary warrior founder of the Ijesa kingdom. As the Obokun's ritual daughter and his gift to the Ijesa people, the Arise had a major role to play at each stage of the festival activities. Moreover, unlike the Oyo-Yoruba where the priestesses were outside the

Iyalode's jurisdiction, the priestesses of the various religious cults acknowledged her leadership as they did that of the Oba and paid their respects and the traditional tribute to her.

Both the Arise and the Lobun also had practical but still indirect ways of demonstrating approval or disapproval. In Ilesa it was the Arise and her chiefs alone who participated with him when the Oba performed the ritual dances for certain religious ceremonies, and they alone escorted him back to his palace as an indication of their solidarity with and support for him. Their failure to do so was certainly a sign of disapproval. In Ondo when communications from the council of male chiefs were acceptable, the female chiefs led all the women in a dance, as it were of approval, from the market to the Oba's palace.

Conclusion

From the examples of the various female holders of the highest political office among the Yoruba that have been examined, it is clear that it is impossible to make sweeping generalizations about the position of the Iyalode or of women generally within the Yoruba political system. Nor can this paper claim to have covered all Yoruba country. It has not, for example, examined the position of the Iyalode among at least two important Yoruba subgroups, the Ekiti and the Owo, whose nearness and historical association with the Benin kingdom had modified their political systems and might have affected the position of the Iyalode within them. It has, rather, concentrated on those areas where there is a strong tradition as regards the institution of the Iyalode. Within these societies, it is clear that the institution represents an attempt to give women a chance to participate directly in the political process. It is an example of female power based on recognized authority. But the effectiveness of the Iyalode within the political system depended on her personality and the degree of power in the hands of the male ruler. Where power was concentrated in the hands of the ruler, she suffered as much loss in influence as did the male chiefs. Other variables affecting her position were her own personality and the historical tradition in the particular political system. But whatever the level of her achievement within the political process, she did not, on the whole, see herself as being in competition for power and influence with the Oba and his male chiefs, but rather as being in a complementary position. Hence she was often referred to as Otun Oba ("the ruler's right hand"). This pacificatory, complementary role is certainly the ideal that the present holders of the Iyalode title and their male colleagues like to stress. But this is a far cry from those instances where, by virtue of her wealth, ritual position, or her leadership of the female hierarchical order, the Iyalode was able to challenge male dominance. The cases of Iyalode Tinubu and Iyalode Efunsetan, and the potential power of the Arise and the Lobun, provide good examples of the contribution of the Iyalode to the political system. It is, however, important to point out that there are indications that such participation could only be tolerated within limits and did not often go unchallenged. The fate that befell Iyalode Efunsetan shows only too well that if at any time an Iyalode tried to lead opposition against the male chiefs, she was likely to be put down in a most brutal manner.

Finally, it should be noted that the participation of the Iyalode in the political process does not exhaust the forms of female political activity within the Yoruba country. It is only evidence of their direct participation. Female participation in government could and did take other less obvious forms. The evidence available at present, however, indicates that women did have political as well as economic interests, though their political power has often varied and has not always taken the same form. For a full appreciation of female contribution to the decision-making processes in traditional society, we need further investigation. The rapid changes that the Yoruba country has witnessed within the last 100 years make such an exercise an urgent one. There is no doubt that British colonialism has had an adverse effect on the role of women in the Yoruba society and that current development processes might sweep overboard whatever vestiges of her contribution remain.

Notes

1. For convenience I have used the title Iyalode for any woman designated as the political leader and charged with the responsibility for articulating the views of Yoruba women in government within any Yoruba society. In practice, such women have their own titles; for instance, in Ilesa she is called Arise, in Ondo she is known as the Lobun, and in Erin-Ijesa her title is Esemure.

2. This occurrence is not peculiar to the Iyalode among the Yoruba: see Onwue-jeogwu (1969).

3. Many intelligence reports were written in the 1930s when the British colonial government was contemplating changes in the local government administration.

4. There are many local histories of Yoruba towns written by the Yoruba themselves. Biobaku (1973) gives a fairly comprehensive list.

5. The nineteenth century is a fairly well-documented period in Yoruba history, and there is considerable information on the contribution of women in that period.

6. Information was obtained by interviews with Oluwo Folasade Labosinde, head of the Ogboni cult in Ibadan, who was about ninety years of age.

7. I am grateful to Professor Oyin Ogunba for introducing me to the present Iyalode of Owu-Ijebu, who granted me a long interview.

8. The following information comes from two interviews, with the present Arise of Ilesa, about sixty-five years old, and the Lisa Lobun, about ninety years old but very articulate and energetic. The Lisa Lobun is acting for the Lobun, since a new Lobun cannot take office while the old king whom the present one installed is still living.

9. The Nupe were horsemen and had an advantage over the Ijesa, who were mostly infantrymen and fell easy prey to Nupe spears and lances. Arise found a way of unmounting the Nupe horsemen and forcing them to engage in hand-to-hand combat.

10. Cf. Ondo titles:

Male Line	Female Line
Osemowe (ruler)	Lobun
Lisa	Lisa Lobun
Jomo	Jomo Lobun
Sasere	Sasere Lobun
Adaja	Adaja Lobun
Odunwe	Sama Lobun

References

Abiola, J. D. E., J. A. Babafemi, and S. O. S. Ataiyero. 1932. *Iwe Itan Ilesa* (The History of Ilesa). Ilesa: the authors.
Babayemi, S. O. 1974. "The Structure of Administration at Oyo Atiba." Paper read at the Twentieth Annual Congress of the Historical Society of Nigeria, University of Ife.
Biobaku, S. O. 1960. "Iyalode Tinubu." In K. O. Dike, ed., *Eminent Nigerians of the Nineteenth Century,* pp. 33–41. Cambridge: Cambridge University Press.
——1973. *Sources of Yoruba History.* Oxford: Oxford University Press.
Busia, K. A. 1951. *The Position of the Chief in the Modern Political System of the Ashanti.* London: Oxford University Press.
Evans-Pritchard, E. E. 1965. *The Position of Women in Primitive Societies and Other Essays in Social Anthropology.* London: Faber and Faber.
Fadipe, N. A. 1970. *The Sociology of the Yorubas.* Ibadan: Ibadan University Press.
Hinderer, Anna. 1873. *Seventeen Years in the Yoruba Country.* London: Seeley, Jackson, and Halliday.
Johnson, S. 1937. *The History of the Yorubas.* Lagos: C. M. S. Church Missionary Society.
Law, R. C. C. 1972. "The Constitutional Troubles of Oyo in the Eighteenth Century." *Journal of African History* 12: 25–44.
Lebeuf, Annie M. D. 1963. "The Role of Women in the Political Organization of African Societies." In D. Paulme, ed., *Women of Tropical Africa,* pp. 93–119. Berkeley: University of California Press.
Lloyd, P. C. 1954. "The Traditional Political System of the Yoruba." *Southwestern Journal of Anthropology* 10: 366–84.
Mabogunje, A. L. 1961. "The Market Woman." *Ibadan* 11: 14–17.
Nadel, S. F. 1951. *A Black Byzantium.* Oxford: Oxford University Press.
Onwuejeogwu, Michael. 1969. "The Cult of the Bori Spirits among the Hausa." In M. Douglas and P. Kaberry, eds., *Man in Africa,* pp. 279–305. London: Tavistock.

BARBARA C. LEWIS

8 Economic Activity and Marriage among Ivoirian Urban Women

OBSERVERS OF THE West African urban scene have emphasized the impressive role of townswomen in trade, characterizing them variously as formidable local economic powers, dominant forces in their households, or highly independent of men. Indeed, the West African woman trader is often an impressive entrepreneur, traveling across national boundaries to buy and sell, and holding her own against men in the extraordinarily competitive world of petty trading. Great admiration is due to these tough, hardheaded women who earn their living without benefit of education and often build up an impressive capital base.

But the big trader is the exception, the rare successful entrepreneur among those urban women who, largely without education and with little capital, compete with one another in the sale of inexpensive imports, craft products, foodstuffs, and prepared foods. The high visibility of the successful women suggests the possible, but not the probable, outcome for women in trade. And the extrapolation from this minority to a generalization that West African urban women are powerful, highly independent, and without need of a spouse, requires serious scrutiny. We must consider what proportion of townswomen are active in petty trade; how trade fits into, or replaces, married life and childbearing; and how such economic activity affects the status of women.

The world of petty trading must also be seen in the perspeclive of the larger, stratified, urban society. There is a substantial minority of women with varying degrees of education, some sufficient to assure them a secure and privileged status in the urban labor force. An educated and to some extent westernized woman is also disproportionately sought after in marriage. The presence of this new group of women inevitably affects societal views of occupational prestige and thus influences the aspirations of many women. In examining the relation between economic activity and the status of women, one cannot ignore the possible differentiation among women because of educational variation: how rates of economic activity of the more educated compare with those of the less educated and uneducated; how work is related to marriage and childbearing; and how economic activity affects a woman's status are important factors. It is not to be assumed that women of different strata have the same options and aspirations.

In addition to providing a profile of labor-force participation with regard to age, marital status, and fertility, we will pay particular attention to the meaning of status differences. While it is surely true that economic power somehow affects social power, how this occurs and relative to whom requires definition. The economic status of women may differ because of their own earning power or the economic means of their spouses. But our primary interest is how a woman utilizes her earning power to alter her status vis-à-vis her spouse. Her options in this regard will depend in part upon her income relative to that of her spouse; and in West Africa, as elsewhere, it is rare that women earn as much as or more than their husbands. The question cannot therefore be one of establishing female economic dominance, but of whether and how women utilize their earning power to ameliorate their condition relative to men.

Strategies selected, however, depend on cultural values as well as absolute economic resources. A woman may seek to increase her status in the household by establishing an economic partnership, as is the dominant pattern in the West. But she may also seek to maximize financial autonomy or independence rather than interdependence vis-à-vis her husband—a goal espoused by some women in the current American feminist movement. Alternatively she may use her earning power to establish personal networks outside the conjugal unit—the prevailing pattern among urban Ivoirian women. By investing their resources in ties with their own kin and with peers, these Ivoirians attain a truly social security (that is, greater social resources) of great psychological as well as material value. Thus, for them, the rewards of work are not autonomy in the sense of increased individualism but access to a fuller social being.

This discussion reveals the employment options available to Abidjan women, and the ways they utilize the income they earn. Keeping their incomes separate from their husbands' earnings, they both improve their status within the marriage and create extensive networks outside the conjugal unit. Employment does not remove the utility of marriage; rather, by building social obligations and resources outside the conjugal unit, it both improves a woman's bargaining power vis-à-vis her husband and provides a full social life in the larger community.

The following analysis of labor-force participation and relative earning power, and their consequences for women's status, is based on survey data, detailed interviews, and long observation conducted in Abidjan, the prosperous capital of the Ivory Coast. The context is important: Ivoirian economic growth is recent and has been unbroken for the past two decades. Therefore, social mobility has been high, aspirations of mobility higher still, and intergenerational change marked.

The survey of over 800 women, aged twenty to forty-four, was conducted in 1974 in three neighborhoods, selected in order to tap significant socioeconomic variation.[1] By sampling approximately equal numbers of respondents in the upper-class quarter of administrative cadres and businessmen, a middle-range housing estate, and a populous working-class quarter, I deliberately overrepresented the high-economic-status minority in the city. Thus, statistical distributions should not be considered to represent the city as a whole, but rather to indicate covariation in behavior and status variables. Motivational interpretation depends heavily on a far smaller number of detailed interviews and other research and observations in Abidjan during 1974, when the survey was complete, and three prior periods of fieldwork in the Ivory Coast in 1966, 1967–68, and 1970. The data presented in the tables that follow derive from the survey.

Economic Activity and Age, Education, and Occupational Status

While the majority of women in the sample (64 percent) engage in some form of economic activity, educational status clearly affects the probability that a woman will work. In addition, age and phase in reproductive cycle vary significantly relative to educational level. Two distinct patterns are perceptible among highly educated (high school or more) and little-educated or uneducated women. Few, if any, salaried positions for unskilled and uneducated women are available in Abidjan. After about ten years of education, a woman seems to have a reasonable chance to enter a professional program and gain specific training for work, whether as a salesperson in a large modern store, some type of secretarial or clerical employee, or a professional in education or medicine. While variably remunerative, all have the attractive feature of being "white-collar" positions and provide a steady income. There is a significant status difference between these modern-sector employees and the vast world of petty traders.

Commerce (self-employment) also yields varied income, and, to some extent, varied status.[2] Income differences are far more difficult to determine among the independent entrepreneurs: my coding scheme captures only some of this variation by distinguishing "big" traders (those owning a store or other major capital equipment such as a truck, or employing three or more persons) from other traders.

Very few (3.6 percent) of the independently employed qualify as "big" traders. Trading is not an attractive choice for women who possess the education permitting them to locate salaried

Table 8.1 Educational and Employment Status

	Educational Status				Total	
	None (N = 417)	Some primary (N = 124)	Some secondary (N = 111)	University or professional (N = 137)	No.	Pct.
	%	%	%	%		
Inactive	44	55	23	2	281	36
Trader	52	20	4	5	254	32
Salaried worker	2	21	57	71	195	25
Student, trainee	1	4	16	22	59	7
	100	100	100	100	789	100

Note: Kendall's Tau C = .44, signif. ⩾0.00.

employment (see Table 8.1). The high level of risk and the low prestige associated with trading contribute to the nearly exclusive recruitment of poorly educated women into trade. As will be seen, labor-force recruitment among traders and salaried employees also varies relative to age and phase in the reproductive cycle.[3]

The cross-tabulation of educational level and employment status shows that as education increases, economic activity increases. The more educated are far more likely to work, although, in the entire sample, the petty traders far outnumber the salaried and wage earners. Among the uneducated and those with some primary schooling (i.e., six years or less), the proportion of inactive is nearly one-half. This proportion increases slightly among the more educated. Nearly all of the most-educated women are economically active and employed in the salaried sector.

In Abidjan, education is not simply a social asset. It is an economic resource that, in the view of women and of the kin who educated them, is not to be left unutilized. In contrast to the norms of Victorian society, education here conveys the opportunity to join the labor force, and few pass up the opportunity.

The respondents with primary-school education and a portion of those with some secondary schooling are in an anomalous and difficult position. Caught between the paucity of salaried employment available for women of their educational level on the one hand, and their employment aspirations along with the expectations of kin who schooled them on the other, they are unwilling to accept less than salaried work. Yet their chances of gaining such employment grow ever slimmer as the labor force becomes even more educated and educational requirements for jobs increase. They are motivated in part by status consciousness and in part by economic realism: petty trade is associated with lack of education, but, more important, it is a poor alternative to steady work. The slightly educated tend to wait for their "golden opportunity"—the friend or boyfriend or kinsman who will, miraculously, get them "real work" for which they are either underqualified or face overwhelming competition.

To understand who joins the labor force, one must also examine the relationship between economic activity and marital status, age, and number of children. Some sources suggest that trading is a lifelong activity, with small girls working at their mothers' side and continuing without interruption through their childbearing years. Another possibility is that economic activity is higher among those whose husbands have rejected and divorced them or as the positive choice of women opting for independence and self-sufficiency rather than marriage[4] (Nadel 1952).

Among Yoruba women there is another pattern of commercial and reproductive activities (Sudarkasa 1973). Women view marriage and, above all, childbearing as the primary imperative. Trading follows as a cultural given and a financial necessity as the number of children increases and some reach school age. The husbands of Yoruba townswomen are frequently absent, farming in the countryside. But even the wife of a prosperous urbanite expects to resume trading after she has borne several children so that she can pay a share of the expenses. Thus, among this West African group with perhaps the oldest and most generalized tradition of female trading, women withdraw from trade at marriage. They reenter trade when they have proven their fecundity and, consequently, incurred economic responsibility for rearing their children.

The Abidjan survey permits the exploration of these differing hypotheses: (1) that married women are less active in the labor

Table 8.2 Marital Status and Employment Status

| | Marital Status | | | | |
	Married * (N = 575)	Engaged or free union (N = 126)	Unmarried, widowed, or divorced * (N = 88)	Total No.	Pct.
	%	%	%		
Inactive	36	39	25	281	36
Trader	34	21	39	254	32
Salaried worker	25	14	27	195	25
Student, trainee	5	19	9	59	7.5
	72.9†	16	11.2	789	100

* Column totals 100%.
† Marginals.

force, presumably because they are supported by their husbands; (2) that female economic activity increases as number of children increases, because women respond to the growing budgetary pressure. The data in Table 8.2 show the effect of marital status on economic activity as petty traders and as salaried employees.

For our purposes, a simplified, three-category summary of marital status is sufficient. The first includes all women currently married under the civil code, customary law, or religious law. Engaged women constitute a more diverse category, including those who are formally engaged, those who, with certain embellishment, so qualify a fairly casual bond not recognized by kin, and a smaller group who live in free union, sometimes of many years' duration. Single women are the unmarried or unengaged as well as widows or divorcées who state that they have no current fiancé or husband.

Married women may be expected to enjoy the more stable unions and possibly more reliable and greater economic assistance. Those not formally married, even those in relatively enduring free unions, should be less certain of spouses' support and thus more dependent on their own earnings. Single women, who all explicitly stated that they have "no man in their lives," are expected to be maximally self-sufficient.

A brief glance at the marginals shows that many married women are economically active: 64 percent of the sample are active, while 73 percent are married. And the distribution of inactives by marital status does not confirm the hypothesis that married women have markedly less need or desire to work. The percentage inactive among single women is significantly lower than that of married or engaged women who are inactive. However, an 11 percent difference is not powerful evidence that married women withdraw from the labor force. Also, the engaged women are not significantly more or less likely to be economically active than married women. Thus a woman without a man is slightly more likely to work, but marriage and engagement or free union are undifferentiated with regard to level of economic activity.

The trivariate table, presenting the percentage inactive for each age group and marital status, shows that when age is held constant, the slight increase in economic activity observed above persists. No matter what her age, a married woman is less likely to work than a single woman. But when marital status is held constant, the greater predictive power of age on labor-force participation is clear. The percentage change is twice as great between young and old women, whether single or married, as it is between married and single women within any age group. The even greater change between young and older "engaged" women does not alter this conclusion: the increase in economic activity reflects the absence of effective "fiancé" support among older women in free unions. They, like the older single women (largely divorced or widowed), are more likely to be compelled to work than married women of their age group.

That marital status is less powerful than age in explaining economic activity partially replicates the findings reported on the Yoruba. Mature women enter the work force in greater numbers than do young ones. But unlike the Yoruba, young unmarried women in Abidjan are only slightly more likely to work than young married women. Rather than withdrawal from the labor force and subsequent reentry as reported among the Yoruba, the trend here

Table 8.3 Inactive Women, by Marital Status and Age

	Marital Status				
Age	Married (N = 575)	Engaged (N = 126)	Single (N = 88)	Total No. Pct.	
	%	%	%		
20–24	49	47	37		
25–29	32	32	29		
30–44	29	19	17		
				789	100

is for inactivity to decline as age increases for all marital status groups. However, the finding on Yoruba women was based exclusively upon the uneducated women who have no option but petty trade, and Table 8.3 masks any effect that educational level, and thus employability, might have on the relationship between age and economic activity. The educational variable merits examination, for it is unlikely that persons with little or no education are similar to those with considerable education, both with regard to absolute levels of labor-force participation and trends across age groups. (Table 8.1 has shown the former to vary considerably, and the nature of employment available to the educated and uneducated is expected to result in very different motivations to work.) By grouping persons of like age and education, we can examine inactivity levels and the patterns of occupational type as both age and education increase. Table 8.4 presents these data.

The trivariate table of age, education, and occupation reveals that, in general, both increasing education and increasing age lead to higher levels of economic activity. Inactivity is highest among the twenty- to twenty-four-year-olds with no education or some primary education. Thus increasing age, which is doubtless accompanied by growing family burdens, leads to greater labor-force participation. The ability to find attractive salaried employment, which is largely a function of education, also affects inactivity levels.

Among the most educated, nearly all women work and nearly all actives have salaried employment. Inactives and the self-

Table 8.4 Wives' Employment Status by Their Age and Educational Status

Education	Occupation	Age 20–24	Age 25–29	Age 30–44	Number
		%	%	%	
	Inactive	58	41	38	
None	Trader	36	57	58	414
	Salaried or student	6	2	3	
		100	100	100	
Some	Inactive	71	50	15	
primary	Trader	14	29	30	124
	Salaried or student	15	21	56	
		100	100	100	
Some	Inactive	34	18	0	
secondary	Trader	2	6	9	111
	Salaried or student	64	76	91	
		100	100	100	
University	Inactive	4	2	0	
or professional	Trader	2	2	11	136
	Salaried or student	94	95	89	
		100	100	100	

employed are in the extreme minority. The category with "some secondary education" spans that ambiguous range in which women believe they should find salaried work but often do not succeed in getting it, particularly if they have only begun secondary school. Here inactivity decreases markedly as age increases, with the actives entering salaried jobs and, to a far lesser extent, petty trade. The slightly educated (with some primary school) form a similar pattern, although the change across ages is more dramatic. Inactivity declines from a high of 71 percent among the young to only 15 percent among the older women in this group. The actives are equally divided between trade and salaried employment among the young; but among the older little-educated women, salaried employment outweighs trading. Among the young women with no education, inactivity is lower than among those in the primary school category also twenty- to twenty-four-years-old, but the decline in inactivity is more moderate among the uneducated as age increases, dropping from 58 percent to 38 percent. This change is entirely due to entry into petty trade, as salaried employment at this educational level is insignificant. Indeed, the relative increase in petty trading across age groups is very similar between the uneducated and those with some primary-school training. The striking aspect of the table is the great difference in young and older primary- and secondary-school women who have obtained salaried employment: the older women are far more active in these coveted jobs than are the younger ones. The sharpness of this increase with age is not satisfactorily explained by the life-cycle factor. Personal observations lead me to believe that for these women with low levels of schooling who aspire to salaried employment, the probability of satisfying these aspirations has declined in recent years.

Expanded educational facilities are producing an ever-greater number of women with primary, or primary and some secondary, education. Despite a growing economy, it appears that salaried employment for women with this low level of education is increasingly hard to obtain. Few of the younger women are able to find such jobs as orderlies, receptionists, or telephone operators—low-skilled salaried jobs that were easier to find ten years ago. My own experience in seeking interviewers yields strong evidence that women of this age and educational level face a tight job market. I could not find interviewers who had completed half of their secondary-school education, but I was inundated with less educated job-seekers. They recounted at length their numerous efforts to find a "real job," one with a regular salary. They emphatically stated that petty trade was not an acceptable option. As young women, often unmarried, both they and their families felt that street selling was improper, insufficiently profitable, and beneath their dignity. They seem then to be caught between their expectations and an increasingly tight labor market for those with their education. But they have not yet given up hope that they will be lucky. They know of older women with less education than themselves who have secure jobs in some branch of the administration that they obtained a decade ago. They hope that, with patience, they can do the same.

These less-educated and marginally employable women under twenty-five years of age have other motives for holding out for jobs that they have a slim chance of acquiring. Generally unmarried and with few children, they can, in a strict financial sense, afford to gamble that they will be lucky and get an acceptable job. They do not have the pressing financial responsibilities of women with several children, and their youth is a temporary asset that they utilize to the fullest extent. As young women, they hope to attract boyfriends who will both pay them the customary flexible allowance, and better still, find them jobs. Some have boyfriends who, while employed, are unlikely to have such connections. Here the young woman's commitment to him is less than total: a better prospect may come along. Others have been befriended by more successful men. Here a particular combination of entrepreneurship and delusion often prevails. At the optimistic extreme is the hope that the liaison will lead to marriage; perhaps the boyfriend will divorce his current wife or will take the younger and more educated contender as his "civil law" wife, thus placing her above his other wives by customary marriage. Some hope for help in finding a job or funds to attend one of the many professional training courses available in Abidjan. Others settle for more immediate gains such as gifts of cash, clothing, or perhaps school fees for a younger brother. Because they are young and more desirable than uneducated women, they gamble for the long shot—a good job they find themselves, a good marriage, or a job opportunity through some male connection—rather than accepting the hard competitive business of petty trade. There will be time enough for that when they have expended the assets of youth and have no other means to meet the increasing burden of a growing family. They represent perhaps the most extreme form of the feminine struggle for social mobility in a society where rising expectations do indeed achieve remarkable proportions.

The distribution of employment and employment status by education displays two relatively stable extremes and a more unstable middle range. The uneducated have no option but petty trade, and they accept this alternative when they lose the assets of youth and acquire greater economic responsibilities. The well-educated women accept with alacrity the jobs to which they are fortunate to have access, for these jobs provide economic security, respectability, and prestige. Women of the intermediate educational level aspire to similar employment and social status, but they must ultimately accept what they can get. An ever-decreasing portion obtain the salaried jobs they all would like. The others remain jobless or take up petty trade, accepting the lower social status that goes with it.

The Effects of Economic Activities on the Status of Women

The large proportion of working women who are married shows that marriage is not perceived as an alternative to work in Abidjan. Nor, given the greater proportion of well-educated and well-married women who work, can labor-force participation be explained as the response to absolute economic necessity. The data show that many women work because they can obtain jobs that yield a more than marginal profit and also considerable social status.

But the effect of labor-force participation upon the status of a woman is a function not so much of her absolute earning power as of her earning power relative to that of her spouse. The greater her relative earning power, the lower her dependence on her husband and the greater her potential contribution to household costs. A substantial earning power renders independence and divorce a viable alternative, with a chance of making a good second marriage. A woman whose earnings are minimal has a far lower margin of independence; nonetheless, her ability to make some independent expenditures without asking her husband for the funds is not insignificant.

The examination of relative occupational status among couples where both spouses are working indicates the nature of options accruing to working wives in Abidjan. The data show that the vast majority of working wives have less earning power than their husbands. The italics in Table 8.5 mark all those cases in which spouses have equal occupational status. The cells to the right of the italics represent cases in which the wife's status exceeds that of her spouse, while those to the left represent cases in which the wife's occupational status is lower than that of her husband. Calculations made on this basis show that the occupational status of only 8 percent of the working wives (and 3.6 percent of all wives) is greater than their husbands'; 17 percent have approximately equal status; and 74 percent have occupational status inferior to their husbands.'

While few women have higher occupational status than their husbands, the margin of difference is in most cases unexpectedly small. Among husbands of higher occupational status (where the occupational categories are more reliable indicators of income than among petty traders), the pattern resembles the European middle class. The wife is educated and employed in respectable salaried work, but she is slightly inferior to her spouse in occupational status and earning power. Is this an accurate picture of an emergent bourgeoisie? Or is it distorted by the absence of less-educated, well-married wives from the female labor force? In other words, as women's earning power decreases relative to that of their husbands, are they increasingly unlikely to be economically active? To explore this proposition, all wives' employment status is presented in Table 8.6 by their educational level (as an indicator of their potential earning power) and the occupational status of their spouses.

The results must be seen from two perspectives. First, in descriptive terms, the level of activity among uneducated and slightly educated wives married to high-status husbands is notably high. Despite the presumably large gap in their earning power, the percentages active are 43 and 65, respectively. Second, the impact of husband's status upon the level of female activ-

Table 8.5 Occupational Status of Active Wives by Occupational Status of Husbands

	Husbands' Status												
	Upper cadre		Middle cadre		Skilled salaried		Independent business		Worker		Petty trader		Total	
Wives' Status	No.	Pct.	No.	Pct.	No.	Pct.	No.	Pct.	No.	Pct.	No.	Pct.	No.	Pct.
Upper cadre	9	10	5	7	1	2	0	0	0	0	0	0	15	3
Middle cadre	30	35	14	21	8	15	0	0	4	3	0	0	56	14
Skilled salaried	28	33	31	46	13	25	1	12	9	6	1	3	83	21
Independent business	4	5	2	3	2	4	0	0	1	1	0	0	9	2
Worker	4	5	2	3	5	10	0	0	3	2	0	0	14	4
Petty trader	11	13	13	19	23	44	7	88	138	89	29	97	221	56
	86	100	67	100	52	100	8	100	155	100	30	100	389	100

Note: The occupational code, based on the Ivoirian industrial code, is detailed and extensive. Some examples of the collapsed code I used are for men and women:

Upper cadre: liberal professions; university, educational, managerial, roles

Middle cadre: accountant, administrative assistant, teacher, nurse, midwife

Skilled salaried: gendarme, warehouse supervisor, typist, cashier, teller

Independent business: capital equipment or more than two employees

Worker: mechanic, mason, cook, carpenter, windowwasher, watchman, messenger (literate), hairdresser, salesgirl, domestic

Petty trader: distinguished from "Independent business" by smaller scale of business

Table 8.6 Wives' Employment Status by Their Educational Status and Spouses' Occupational Status

		Wives' Educational Status				
Husband	Wife	Uneducated (N = 384)	Primary school (N = 109)	Secondary school (N = 89)	University professional (N = 101)	Total
Upper status (high, middle cadre)	Inactive	% 57	% 35	% 20	% 0	
	Trader	34	29	5	5	
	Salaried, student, or trainee	8	35	75	95	
		99 (N = 47)	100 (N = 34)	100 (N = 60)	100 (N = 82)	223
Middle status (skilled salaried independent business)	Inactive	53	68			
	Trader	42	3			
	Salaried, student	5	29			
		100 (N = 66)	100 (N = 31)	(N = 19)*	(N = 12)*	128
Low status (worker, petty trader)	Inactive	40	57			
	Trader	58	29			
	Salaried, student	1.4	14			
		100 (N = 271)	100 (N = 44)	(N = 10)*	(N = 7)*	332
						683

*The number of wives with secondary-school education or more married to middle- or low-status men is so small that the percentages do not merit interpretation. Note also that I have collapsed husband's occupational status to simplify this trivariate table.

ity is strong among the uneducated and the slightly educated. The better married an uneducated woman, the less likely she is to work, although the drop in percentage active between those with high-status husbands and those with low-status husbands is only from 57 to 40. Among those with primary-school education, however, the relationship is reversed. The well-married at this educational level are more likely to work than those with middle- or low-status husbands. The percentage inactive changes from 35 to 68 to 57. Although this relationship is not linear, the direction of change is clear.

This unexpected finding recalls the divergence between employment aspirations and salaried labor-force demand for women at this education level. Note that the majority of those active among primary-school women with middle- or high-status husbands have salaried employment, which is highly atypical of women at this educational level. The link perceived by respondents between salaried employment and a good marriage does appear to have an empirical basis: this relationship (the causal link is unclear) may explain the unexpectedly high level of activity among the slightly educated and well-married, and is also a possible explanation of reversal of relationships between wives' educational level and husbands' occupational status among the uneducated and slightly educated. Thus, the conclusion is not clear-cut regarding the impact of men's relative earning power (actual or potential) on wives' economic activity. The hypothesis that the greater the earning-power gap, the less likely the wife is to work, cannot be rejected, but it is not confirmed by either a consistent, if slight, relationship or by a strong positive relationship at either educational level.

Most married working women earn less than their spouses. Their standard of living is therefore more dependent upon their husbands' income than their own, and with divorce their loss is greater. There is little question that in the translation of economic to social power, men play the dominant role. Should a marriage terminate or the bond become attenuated as the wife ages, her loss is greater than that of her spouse. Nor are there any cultural values that alter this fundamental female dependence.

Financial Autonomy between Spouses

Given this prevailing condition of feminine dependence upon men, the question is how the working woman uses her income to improve her status. Does she invest her earnings in her spouse's household, thus increasing her value to him? Or does she seek to retain all or part of her earnings to be spent at her discretion, investing in alternative social networks?

The Ivoirian Civil Code conflicts with social values rooted in rural traditional society. Over a decade ago, the Ivory Coast adopted the French Civil Code nearly *in toto*. The code defines the nuclear family as the primary economic unit. All goods acquired by either spouse following marriage become the *communauté de biens* (common property of both spouses). It thus excludes claims of the extended family on the earnings of either spouse in favor of the nuclear family. The Code is officially proclaimed as a force stabilizing marriage by insulating it from the competing demand of kin.

The Civil Code does indeed protect the legal wife from the competition of cowives and gives her prior claim to her spouse's earnings over mistresses or wives contracted in customary marriage. Most women recognize these advantages and seek the protection of a civil marriage. However, they are far less unambiguously in favor of the *communauté de biens*. They know that both law and prevailing norms grant the husband ultimate guardianship and responsibility for the couple's common property. Many say that an integrated family budget reduces them to supplicants for whatever expenditure they wish to make, while they have no effective veto over their husbands' expenditures. Faced with their legally and economically subordinate status, women must choose whether to conform to the Civil Code model of "junior partnership" in the nuclear family or to utilize the more traditional mode of separating both their income and responsibilities from those of their husbands.

While official pronouncements encourage marriage under the Civil Code, effective pressure to contract a civil marriage rather than a customary marriage has been largely restricted to the elite. The upper classes are thus expected to play an exemplary role and to become the model for future social development. The uneducated majority of the sample is married by customary law.

To determine how many and which couples practice the integrated budget prescribed by the administration and the new Civil Code, the occupational status of working women may be related to the type of budgetary arrangements between spouses (see Table 8.6). Because it was beyond the scope of my survey to detail household budget expenditures and their sources, all economically active wives were asked simply : "In general, what do you do with the money you earn?." The prestudy made it clear that women generally answered this question by naming the persons upon whom they spend their earnings. For example, many answered "on my own little needs and on my children" or added "and my family," or said "I help my husband to raise the children." Because my theoretical interest here is in the extent of budgetary autonomy and the extent to which women named persons outside the nuclear family, responses are coded on a continuum from (a) high budgetary autonomy to (b) total integration of earning to (c) explicit subordination of wife to husband. The responses are grouped into four categories. That representing the highest degree of autonomy includes all responses mentioning children, parents (i.e., respondents' own kin), and specific household costs (some upper-status women pay the domestic help or electric bills, while lower-status women frequently contribute to food costs). The next degree consists of respondents who mentioned all of the above and also stated that they sometimes give money to their husbands, indicating somewhat greater budgetary integration between spouses. The third practices *communauté de biens,* requiring the specific statement that "we put our earnings together" (as distinct from stating that "I sometimes help my husband"). This represents the greatest budgetary integration between spouses. Finally, a small number of women stated that they gave all their earnings to their husbands. Such women saw their economic activity as itself dependent upon the good will or financial support of their spouses. They regularly turned their earnings over to their husbands and disclaimed any right or desire to participate in decisions regarding expenditures; they asked their husbands to give them money for whatever needs they had.

The distribution of financial autonomy, integration, or subordination in relation to spouse is little related to female educational and occupational status. The positive correlation of .05 between increasing female occupational status and increasing household budgetary integration shows that the Civil Code's integrated model has not found a large following in the upper strata. The vast majority (73 percent) of all working wives fall in the category of maximal budgetary autonomy. In the three occupational categories where the number of cases merit confidence (middle cadres, skilled employees, and traders), the percentages show remarkably little variation: 71, 72, and 76 respectively. Only 8 percent practice the *communauté de biens;* while concentrated in the upper-status occupations, they constitute only 17 percent of all wives classified as high-level or middle-level cadres or skilled employees. Of the sample, 16 percent falls into the category of intermediate budgetary integration—those who occasionally give some of their earnings to their spouse. These are predominantly petty traders. And with one exception, the 12 women (3.6 percent of the entire sample of active women) who give all the earnings to their spouses are petty traders. At all status levels, the norm is to keep earnings separate.

No attempt was made in the survey to ascertain how much money women who kept their earnings separate from their spouses' actually spent on household maintenance and how much they used for discretionary or nonessential expenditures. My decision was based on the great difficulty of obtaining such information encountered during the detailed presurvey interviews. The problem is not just one of allocating sufficient time to chart all types of expenditures and their sources; it arises because such expenditures are not formally allocated and there is little general agreement on how essential household costs should be allocated between spouses. Husbands and wives both tend to claim that they contribute more than their share.

Table 8.7 Expenditure of Earnings by Occupational Status of Active Wives

	Occupational Status						Total	
	Upper cadre (N = 15)*	Middle cadre (N = 59)	Skilled salaried (N = 77)	Independent business (N = 7)*	Worker (N = 12)*	Petty trader (N = 203)	No.	Pct.
	%	%	%	%	%	%		
Separate budget, no mention of husband	67	72	73	57	50	76	276	73.5
Separate budget, occasionally gives to husband	7	7	16	29	42	17	56	15
Integrated budget, communauté de biens	27	20	12	14	8	1	29	8
Budgetary subordination; gives earnings to husband	0	2	0	0	0	6	13	3.5
	100	100	100	100	100	100	372	100

Note: Kendall's Tau C = .05; signif. > 0.001.
* Small numbers of cases render distributions unreliable.

The topic is a sensitive one within all strata. There is more explicit dissension in upper-status households, because the greater salaries of both partners result in a larger amount of discretionary income and thus traditional arrangements are less easily applied. Numerous high-status husbands claim that they support the entire household, while their wives spend their income on themselves and on trivia. And numerous wives make the counterassertion that they spend a great deal on household costs and the needs of their children, while their husbands spend their incomes in unknown but suspect ways. The "other woman," a constant threat, particularly to those in civil marriages where polygyny is illegal, is a primary source of conflict. A wife somewhat fatalistically accepts the probable existence of a mistress; the conflict concerns how much of the husband's income is being siphoned away from her household and her children.

Both sexes agree that husbands very rarely let their wives know their actual income. Men are willing to proclaim the virtues of the integrated household budget, but not to subject themselves to the inherent disadvantages of joint decision making, given their greater earning power. Thus systematic accountability is impossible. The "fair share" of each spouse is subjectively determined, and it is negotiated and renegotiated in each marriage. Sometimes a woman will pay for electricity, sometimes for food, sometimes for children's school uniforms. Her own wardrobe is nearly always her responsibility and the domain to which husbands are most likely to point as proof of the wife's "egotism."

Despite these tensions, the separation of earnings remains the optimal solution. The kin of both spouses constantly make demands upon them, and each partner is unwilling to contribute his or her own earnings to the other spouses' kin (see also Oppong 1974). Kinsmen inevitably make more extensive demands upon the upper class, both because they know the money is there and because they underline the obligation of the elite to recognize the sacrifices they made to educate them. Educating a child is an investment. Thus a woman finds ready allies or even unsolicited pressure from her family to maintain complete control over her own earnings. The link between education, income, and kin expectations remains the greatest obstacle to the application of the Civil Code, and, more broadly, to the nuclearization of the family and joint decision making between spouses.

An interesting analogue to the "investment in education—financial obligation to kin" argument among the upper strata is the source of capital funds among the petty traders. The hypothesis that women use their earnings to pay back the investments of kin or spouse can be examined among the petty traders: if the spouse is the source of initial trading capital, the wife should be more likely to integrate her earnings into the household. If the capital source is her kinsmen, they and not her husband should lay claim to the trader's earnings.

To examine this relationship, married women active in petty trade were asked who provided them with their initial business capital. Here too, responses are ranked along a continuum from spouse to kin (see Table 8.8). Response categories are: (1) my husband; (2) a friend or credit from a wholesaler or myself (usually meaning that she saved a very small portion out of her marketing allowance over a long time); and (3) my parents, my own kin (mother, brother, father, etc.). These sources of capital categories are cross-tabulated with household budgetary arrangement. (Only women residing with a fiancé or married and self-employed are included.)

The hypothesis that women whose business activities were made possible by their spouses would either pool their earning with their husbands' or give it directly to them, while those dependent upon kin for initial capital would keep segregated budgets finds only slight support in the data. The correlation coefficient is positive but very weak (.10). The majority of these self-employed women (57 percent) state that their husbands gave them the money to get started in their business or trade, but many more (76 percent) report that they spend their money on "themselves, their kin, and their children." Only 17 percent add that they occasionally help out their husbands. An insignificant 2 percent state that they practice the *communauté de biens,* and 6 percent

Table 8.8 Capital Source by Expenditure of Earnings among Wives in Petty Trade

Expenditure of Earnings	Capital Source			Total	
	Husband (N = 143)	Self, credit, friend (N = 38)	Wife's own kin (N = 32)	No.	Pct.
	%	%	%		
Separate budget, no mention of husband	70	84	87.5	161	76
Separate budget, occasionally gives to husband	20	10	12.5	36	17
Integrated budget, communauté de biens	2	3	0	4	2
Budgetary subordination; gives earnings to husband	8	3	0	12	6
	100	100	100	213	101

Note: Kendall's Tau C = .10; signif. ≥0.00.

give all their earnings to their husbands. The source of business capital does not greatly alter the prevailing norm: while women may contribute to household costs, they prefer segregated budgets.

Despite the preachments that have accompanied the Ivoirian Civil Code, few couples, even among the educated elite, pool their incomes to meet household costs together. Thus women enjoy economic autonomy, but their spouses enjoy the same autonomy. Because a husband typically earns far more than his wife, one may judge his to be the greater gain.

Given this prevailing type of budgetary arrangement, the question is how women utilize their earning to improve their status. At a minimum, a working woman gains self-esteem and reduces tension in her marriage: everyone agrees that it is best to avoid "holding out your hand to your husband for money." To the extent that she chooses, or is obliged, to spend her income on household necessities, she enhances her value to her husband. The greater her share of household costs, the greater her direct value to him.

However, the benefits to a woman of having her own income do not lie solely in the leverage gained by contributing to household costs or the pleasure of buying additional goods for herself or her children. A woman also uses her income to establish extrahousehold ties. These expenditures provide her with social networks that are a source of personal moral and emotional satisfaction and stabilize and improve her status within her marriage.

Economic Activity,
Social Being and Well-Being

An independent income permits married women to establish social networks of their own, on their own. A working woman can make contributions to kin that strengthen those ties, and she can join a variety of associations. Such a woman enjoys a reputation of substance and a public identity independent of her spouse. The reciprocal networks enrich her personal life and increase her bargaining power vis-à-vis her spouse.

Types of associational ties among Abidjan women vary by socioeconomic status, ethnic identity, and individual preference. However, all require some financial resources. For example, a woman may join a dance group, nearly always with women of her ethnic group, which performs on traditional and official holidays. On these occasions, each association dons uniform dress in a style selected by the group, and each member must pay for her outfit.

Moni are a form of rotating credit associations most common among the Dioula. In these groups, a fixed contribution (cash or cloth) is made to the kitty at every meeting and the proceeds are distributed regularly to each member in turn. The purpose of these *moni* vary: some are solely for the purpose of capital accumulation, while others are for the celebration of marriage or a baptism. The southerners (Bété and Baoulé) form ethnic or region-of-origin associations for mutual assistance: hospitalization, funerals, and so on. Some southern women join syncretic religious groups which also provide emergency funds for members. All of these memberships require regular payments. In addition, women belonging to associations frequently have to pay their carfare to and from meetings.

Some women join political or parapolitical groups such as neighborhood or ethnic sections affiliated with the national political party. Another type brings together persons from the same region of origin who are concerned with the development of that home region. The Students' Parents Association is an official group that permits parents to be informed about, and marginally to influence, the public educational system. Some employed women belong to professional clubs or unions. Contributions go to group maintenance and whatever projects the group undertakes.

The benefits of membership, beyond the explicit purpose of the group, are the identity a woman establishes as an independent and responsible member of the community and the friendships she makes with ethnic and political notables. She may find a source of emergency aid, as comembers occasionally lend or give money to one another. But more important, a member gains a reservoir of social support that can be brought to bear upon her spouse. These social resources are available only to those able to sustain the financial responsibilities of membership. Table 8.9 examines the relationship between employment status and associational ties.

The frequency of associational memberships is positively related to respondents' economic activity. Both salaried women and

Table 8.9 Number of Associational Memberships by Economic Activity

Associational Membership	Economic Activity				Total	
	Inactive (N = 281)	Trade (N = 254)	Salaried (N = 195)	Student, trainee (N = 59)	No.	Pct.
	%	%	%	%		
None	63	41	39	71	402	51
One	19	25	24	17	173	22
Two or more	18	36	37	12	214	27
	100	100	100	100	789	100

petty traders have far more associational ties than inactive women and students. The similarity in number of memberships of traders and salaried women shows that educational level and earning power have no effect on the density of networks: women join a group suitable to their means.

There is, however, an age factor affecting the frequency of associational ties. We have seen above that students are, on the average, much younger than the active women; inactive women, while more variable in age, are also more likely to be younger than the active women. Thus a busy associational life and a personal income are associated with maturity. They are not the exclusive domain of economically active women, for a woman may prevail upon her spouse to give her the money to join an association. But a woman's freedom to join one or more associations is far greater if she is not dependent upon handouts from her husband. Such peer-group associations are the principle source of nonkin social contacts and an important mode of social promotion: women of considerable means speak proudly of their numerous memberships and responsible posts within these associations. Thus, associational memberships are not an alternative to marriage; they are the desirable complement to marriage, and, like employment, gain importance as a woman passes her reproductive peak and loses her sexual attractiveness. Having satisfied her hopes and society's expectations with regard to childbearing, a woman elaborates a broader and highly satisfactory social life. Economic autonomy is both a part of this role and the means of extending social networks.

A personal income also enhances a woman's ability to lend support to her own kin. This ability is a major source of personal and social esteem. It also has a profoundly practical side: "A woman has a bad marriage unless her family is behind her." This does not mean that women bend to their parents' will in choosing a spouse: "A girl may marry for love, for her family may recognize the marriage when they see that it is good and has borne children." But if several years pass, children have been born, and the wife's family remains intransigent, she will do well to recognize that she has gambled and lost. Most women, including highly educated women, agree that such a woman had best leave that man and find a husband acceptable to her kin. Rarely is marriage free from serious disputes in which the wife finds herself the victim of financial irresponsibility or physical mistreatment. If she cannot call upon her kinsmen to bring pressure to bear upon her husband, both directly and through his kin, she has nowhere to turn.

A woman who has proved herself both productive and reproductive is likely to gain greater support from her kin. And because she has some income, they are more likely to demand a more favorable settlement for her. They will support her, if she insists that the marriage is impossible, rather than reprimand her and advise her to submit, because she will be less burdensome to them. If she remains with her husband, her kinsmen may also aid her by interceding with her spouse's kin on her behalf. Because her earning power increases her value to her husband, he will be more amenable to compromise and reconciliation. Thus her economic activity increases her leverage on two fronts, with her kin and her spouse. It affords her better treatment by her spouse, a wider social network, and greater dignity.

Conclusion

In Abidjan, the sources of feminine well-being are marriage and economic activity. Both provide a measure of material betterment and economic security. The material benefits of employment are compelling, and a greater income provides a measure of autonomy. But there is no evidence that women of greater means can forego marriage without considerable material loss. Marriage also facilitates a woman's personal fulfillment. Childbearing is an unquestioned source of community respect and self-esteem. Kinship ties and personal income notwithstanding, rearing children and ensuring their educational advancement without a spouse's assistance is not the optimal choice. The greater earning power of most husbands has been demonstrated. The vital importance to women of extramarital ties does not alter the reality that women can best enhance their well-being within the context of marriage.

The interrelationship of economic well-being, occupational status, and dependence upon men finds a somewhat different and less predictable and stable expression among young, slightly educated women. Their occupational aspirations exceed readily available employment. They, like other women, are subject to the laws of supply and demand. Thus they utilize their resources as best they can, seeking to maximize a range of goods through a variety of tactics. A secure respectable job can mean a good marriage, or a good marriage can mean a good job. If these are not forthcoming, their youthful attractiveness may gain them a liaison yielding, at the least, direct material benefits, and at best, the job they associate with success. But these alternatives are of limited duration. As they age, their options change. They come to express their dependence upon men through marriage. Yet, the importance of employment persists; an income of one's own and access to resources through relationships with men remain the essence of success.

In marriage, employment complements and improves a woman's well-being in two ways. The greater her potential contribution to household costs, the more satisfactory her marriage is likely to be, for her earning power lends her direct value to, and thus leverage upon, her spouse.

The second and, from a cross-cultural perspective, more interesting way a woman's earning power improves her status in her marriage is through social networks independent of her spouse. By controlling her own income, a woman does more than avoid "holding out her hand to her husband," although this is not unimportant. Nor does the value of budgetary autonomy reside in the right to make independent decisions, to express one's individual preferences. More importantly, it permits a woman to establish reciprocal social networks apart from her spouse. Associational memberships are a source of social support and personal gratification. Budgetary autonomy also permits a woman to invest in kinship support, which in turn betters her chances of preserving her marriage under favorable conditions.

Earning power, peer-group relationships, and strong kinship ties are not a substitute for marriage in this society. They are best utilized within the context of relative dependence on one's spouse. Although personal income and its resultant social networks permit single women to have a satisfactory and satisfying social existence, marriage remains a desirable asset. Capital resources available to a woman increase her well-being when they are translated into denser social ties—into a richer social being.

Notes

1. Three quarters were sampled: Cocody (the high-rent elite quarter of the city), Nouveau Koumassi (a moderate rent-level, semipublic housing estate of good-quality housing in great demand) and Treichville (the old traditional quarter of multihousehold courtyards and high population density). Note, however, that Treichville's central locale makes it more desirable than architecturally similar but more peripheral quarters, and far more desirable than the numerous "spontaneous" officially unrecognized quarters around the city. Cluster sampling units were randomly selected; eligible women were then selected on the basis of eligibility: age (twenty to forty-four years), and ethnicity (Bété, Baoulé, and Dioula). The strategy assured maximal representativeness of eligible women within each quarter. To the extent that the quarters selected represented larger distinctive socioeconomic strata, we may assume socioeconomic representation. Detailed interviews were conducted in analogous quarters. I have also drawn upon three prior research projects in the Ivory Coast, particularly a small-scale survey of 44 market women done in 1970 (see Lewis 1976).

2. Petty traders' income and status vary in terms of place of trade and goods traded. A place on the central market generally indicates more intense activity and greater income, as does a boutique on or off the market. Types of commerce requiring a greater capital outlay also convey greater status. I have not scaled these dimensions here.

3. Two factors must be borne in mind concerning the operationalization of economic activity. First, petty trade is broadly and exhaustively defined. Because women do not attribute the status of "work" to petty trade, we asked respondents whether they did "anything to earn money—either salaried work or petty commerce." Women selling single cigarettes or papaya as well as cloth merchants or seamstresses on the main market are all considered to be "active traders." Second, the overrepresentation of educated and thus salaried employees results from

the sampling strategy. Thus among the 65 percent active, there is a large portion of salaried women (26 percent) and of trainees or advanced students (7.5 percent). The numbers are large enough to permit confidence that results are not due to chance, but the distribution is highly misleading with regard to the proportion of women in such preferred occupations.

4. Nadel suggests that, while trade among the Nupe is reserved for childless women, fertile women may refuse to have children in order to become traders. I find no evidence that this is the case among any of the three ethnic groups studied here.

References

Lewis, Barbara C. 1976. "The Limitations of Group Action: The Abidjan Market Women." In Nancy Hafkin and Edna G. Bays, eds., *African Women in Changing Perspective,* pp. 135–56. Stanford: Stanford University Press.

Nadel, S. F. 1952. "Witchcraft in Four African Societies." *American Anthropologist* 54: 18–29.

Oppong, Christine. 1974. *Marriage among a Matrilineal Elite: A Family Study of Ghanian Senior Civil Servants.* Cambridge: Cambridge Studies in Social Anthropology, No. 8.

Sudarkasa, Niara. 1973. *Where Women Work: A Study of Yoruba Women in the Marketplace and in the Home.* Ann Arbor: University of Michigan. Anthropological Papers, No. 53.

AUDREY CHAPMAN SMOCK

The Impact of Modernization
9 on Women's Position
in the Family in Ghana

RECENTLY THERE HAS been a greater awareness that economic development may adversely affect the position of women in Third World countries by offering men disproportionately greater opportunities in the modern sector of the society (Boserup 1970; Economic Commission for Africa 1974). The tendency for modernization to reduce the scope or perceived value of women's roles has been the greatest in those areas of the world, like West Africa and Southeast Asia, where women traditionally assumed significant independent economic roles and were accorded considerable freedom. This tension between modernization and the traditional sex-role division results from the western model of development followed by colonial administrations and international development agencies alike, and not from any inherent dynamic in the process of economic development. Colonial administrators, who had been socialized to accept a Victorian ethos of women's fragility and dependence, came to their

Part of the research was collected during three years in Ghana (1969–72), during which time I was a fellow at the Institute for Statistical, Social, and Economic Research and a lecturer in the departments of Political Science and Sociology, University of Ghana. The other portion of the research, particularly the analysis of the unpublished census data that I employed extensively, was undertaken while I was a consultant to the Task Force on Women of the Ford Foundation, New York office, during 1974–75.

Portions of this chapter have been adapted from Smock (1977).

posts assuming that upper-class European sex-role patterns reflected a divinely ordained plan for the relation between the sexes. To the extent that the social organization of the territory they governed diverged from this European model, the thrust of colonial policies was to change the balance in the sex-role division: missionary and government schools focused on the education of men; extension services ignored the gender of the farmers and offered assistance only to men, irrespective of which sex actually performed most of the agricultural work; recruitment for paying jobs in the modern sector went to men; missionaries frequently sought to inculcate norms of European family life that increased men's authority; and colonial edicts recognizing and regularizing traditional institutions frequently misinterpreted safeguards for women and disregarded the existence of corporate embodiments of women's interests. Development advisers, despite their pretensions to enlightenment and universal standards, carry within themselves many of the same assumptions as their colonial predecessors, and many of the policies they recommend further widen the gap between men and women.

In countries like Ghana where women traditionally enjoyed relatively high status, the social changes accompanying modernization may in the long run undermine the position of women, and particularly their role in the family, even more than they reduce their economic options. In terms of affecting the quality of life and the future possibilities for redressing the present imbalance in the sex-role division, this social devaluation and weakening of women's roles may have even more profound repercussions than women's impaired access to opportunities in the modern sector. Ghana provides an interesting and relevant case to study this problem both because of the significant traditional roles of women and because of the length and intensity of exposure to western influence. Moreover, Ghana's relative affluence, deriving from the export of cocoa, provided a base for the expansion of the educational system, and the tropical climate and the prevalence of malaria predisposed the British colonial office and the European companies operating there toward training local personnel to fill all clerical and some middle-level posts. Thus, on the eve of independence, Ghana (then the Gold Coast) had a better developed system of schooling than any other black African territory (Foster 1965, p. 171). Furthermore, the Nkrumah regime, under which Ghana achieved its independence, was committed to the modernization and radical restructuring of society along socialist lines. With these objectives in mind, the government expanded the educational system and vaguely sought to mobilize women into a national development effort.

Nevertheless, despite some superficial efforts to redress the colonial legacy, Ghana's pattern of development is increasingly recasting women in a subordinate and dependent position. The postindependence equalization of access to education through the elimination of school fees at the lower levels of the educational ladder has increased girls' attendance, often at a slightly higher rate than boys, but it has failed to end the disparity (Census Office 1972, p. xxiv). However, at the upper reaches of the educational ladder, the percentage of women completing secondary school and enrolling at a university remains fairly constant. The 1968–69 educational statistics show that women constituted almost 26 percent of the students registered in secondary school, but at the sixth-form level (the final two years) only 16 percent of the students were women; and at Ghana's three universities only 8.5 percent of the student body was female (Ministry of Education 1971, pp. 50–51). Disparities in education as well as increasing competition for scarce jobs have restricted women's opportunities in the modern sector of the economy. Although a high proportion of women in Ghana remain economically active, the fields in which women participate the most heavily—trading, farming, farm management, domestic service—are those that do not require much education and in which they have always been engaged. Within the modern sector of the economy, women tend to be relegated to lower-level jobs that reflect the traditional European rather than an African sexual division of labor. A 1968 manpower survey indicates that women constituted only 9 percent of the high-level skilled professionals, 3.4 percent of the managers, and

25 percent of the middle-level subprofessional and technical workers (Manpower Division 1971, pp. 35, 37, 38).

The implications of this pattern of development for women's position in the family form the basis for the remainder of this paper. In order to understand the changed role of women within the family, it will first be necessary to discuss further the traditional sex-role division among Ghana's constituent ethnic groups and the nature of the colonial impact.

Sex Roles in Precolonial Ghana

As elsewhere in Africa, the contemporary boundaries of Ghana incorporate disparate ethnic groups that have varied significantly in their social organization and culture. The roles of women, as might be anticipated, have also differed among these groups. Women had the highest status, greatest independence, and held the most significant positions among the Akan and the Ga-Adangme peoples in southern Ghana, who today constitute slightly more than half of the total population of the country. Nevertheless, while the image of women's place in society varied, among all of the ethnic groups women performed key economic functions and enjoyed considerable autonomy. In all of these societies men and women had separate spheres of activity with their respective rights and duties deriving from them. The social separation of the sexes and the complementary sexual division of labor brought with them relative freedom for women to determine their own lives.

Although any efforts after the passing of precolonial society to measure female status cannot be conclusive, Sanday's model of the dimensions of female status in the public domain provides a starting point (1974, p. 172). She has suggested that four variables determine female status in the public domain in simple societies: female material control, demand for female produce, female political participation, and female solidarity groups devoted to female political or economic interests. When measured by these variables, southern Ghanaian women in the traditional context had fairly high traditional status in the public domain, and this status in turn reinforced their position within the family.

Without exception, females in all of the Ghanaian precolonial societies had substantial material control of produce and crafts beyond the domestic unit. Female produce also had a recognized value beyond the localized family unit, a value that in most cases did not differ substantially from male produce. The general pattern was for married women to be economically active in their own right and not merely as auxiliaries to their husbands, to have their own sources of income, and to assume part of the burden for the support of the household. Women commonly cultivated specific crops, engaged in petty trading, and sometimes produced handicrafts. The income from these economic activities was usually theirs to control (Fortes 1949, pp. 102–3; Manoukian 1950, p. 71; McCall 1961, p. 286; Nukunya 1969, p. 149; Tait 1961, pp. 197–98). Women usually farmed independently of their husbands on their own plots of land; men cleared the fields for women, but women did not have a reciprocal obligation to help their husbands cultivate their crops. With the exception of certain northern groups in which the men produced grains and yams and the women vegetables, women could grow the same crops as men. The presence of the tsetse fly in the southern part of the country also prevented men from raising livestock, which in some African societies is a male prerogative.

Control over their own income and property accumulated from their earnings conferred a considerable degree of independence on women. Among all of the groups, women engaged in petty trading, selling part of their own crops, the surplus of their husbands' (often for a fixed commission), and sometimes handicrafts or goods they had made. Among the Ga and Ewe, whose economy depended heavily on fishing, women handled the curing and selling of the fish (Manoukian 1950, p. 71; Nukunya 1969, p. 149). Women had control over their own property; even in the North where a man might beat his wife with relative impunity, he dared not utilize her property without her consent (Fortes 1949, p. 103).

The access of women to land for cultivation, which was owned jointly by the kinship group, and their ability to control their own earnings compensated to a considerable degree for the laws of inheritance that in both the patrilineal and matrilineal societies favored male members of the group. These laws of inheritance, as well as the instability of marriages among many of the groups, undoubtedly contributed to women's reluctance to work jointly with their husbands.

Only among the Akan did females have the ability to participate politically on a regular basis; but the consensual decision-making patterns commonly inhering within the lineage meant that among the Ga and Ewe, as women grew older, their views were often heard and taken into account as well. The matrilineal patterns of descent and inheritance of the Akan elevated women's importance and contributed to their sense of self-respect and dignity. The facts that women determined kinship connections and that all children belonged to the mother's family compensated somewhat for the male political predominance. Moreover, women held significant social and political roles among the Akan and came close to achieving equality in many respects (Fortes 1950, p. 256). Male lineage heads frequently had female counterparts to oversee female matters, adjudicate family quarrels, advise on matters of genealogy, and supervise key rituals. At higher levels of state organization, the queen mother, the most prominent female member of the royal lineage, had even greater power, for she nominated the new chief, advised him about his conduct, and was an expert on ritual and genealogy. Although the chief outranked the queen mother, a capable woman filling that office could command considerable authority in her own right. On occasion Akan women even served as chiefs (Rattray 1929; Busia 1951).

In the small, decentralized city-states of the coastal Ga, several key positions were also reserved for women, including ritual town offices and religious offices as the mouthpieces of the gods (Manoukian 1950; Field 1940). Since some anthropologists believe that the Ga originally had a theocratic form of government

(Field 1940, p. 3), women's religious roles must have accorded them even greater significance in the earlier part of the precolonial era. In the Ewe and northern systems women had more limited social roles than among either the Akan or the Ga.

The Ewe, Ga, and Akan women all had institutions embodying women's corporate sense of identity and in some limited ways pursuing their interests (Folson n.d., pp. 1, 5; Field 1940, pp. 6–8; Manoukian 1952, p. 26). Among many of the groups women lived apart from men, increasing the possibility for women to develop a corporate sense of identity and social networks. Thus, although males predominated in all groups politically and militarily, female status rested on a firm base. Akan women had the most power and could command the greatest respect, but even in the North, women were not devoid of the economic attributes of high status. The assessment of one woman anthropologist with regard to the place of women in African society—"whatever the system may be, the position of women within it is neither superior nor inferior to that of the men, but simply different and complementary" (Paulme 1971, p. 6)—applies fairly well to the Ghanaian precolonial social order.

A second major dimension of the precolonial social order that affected women's role within the family was the autonomy accorded to women. Whether the woman's place was considered to be substantially equal to that of the male members, as among the Akan, or subordinate, as among the Ewe or northern groups, men rarely interfered with or attempted to regulate directly women's conduct. The social segregation of the sexes into sexually distinct networks and the economic separation of the sexes did not give rise to limitations on women's freedom; quite the contrary, it provided them with considerable autonomy. The fact that these societies did not place a high premium on female chastity gave the male members of the lineage little incentive to attempt to control the lives of the female members. Ghanian traditional societies accorded women considerable premarital sexual freedom and did not punish women's adultery severely. The critical concern was for no woman to become pregnant before the celebration of the appropriate puberty rites, but this ceremony was usually held shortly after the onset of menstruation (Tettah 1967, pp. 203–4). In cases of proven adultery, the male offender paid the husband a fine, with the amount depending on the status of the aggrieved party (Vellenga 1971, pp. 132–33). The husband also accepted paternity of any child born of an adulterous union. Therefore, there was much less of a sexual double standard than inheres in most cultures.

This pattern of sex segregation and female autonomy made marriage into a kind of loose business partnership between equals. The payment of a bride price and the completion of the prescribed rituals established for both partners a series of rights and duties, some of which grew out of the sexual division of labor. The man received exclusive sexual rights, legal paternity of all children, and the right to essential domestic and economic services. In return, the woman had rights to sexual satisfaction, to maintenance for herself and her children, to care during illness, and, among many of the groups, to decide whether the husband could take another wife (Fortes 1950, p. 280).

The initiation of conjugal relationships did not necessarily result in the establishment of residentially or functionally discrete conjugal families (Oppong 1974, p. 34). Women frequently lived with their children apart from their husbands, sending food at meal times and going to sleep in the husband's home. Moreover, as mentioned above, the conjugal family rarely constituted an economic unit: the performance of economic activities and the ownership of property remained quite segregated even after marriage. Christine Oppong's description of the main functions of the traditional Akan conjugal family as the "regulation of the transient processes of sex, subsistence, and socialization" (Oppong 1974, p. 34) would apply as well to the other ethnic groups in precolonial Ghana. Moreover, training and rearing of children and providing for their material needs was easily assumed by the matrilineal or patrilineal kinship group if the conjugal tie was dissolved.

When either partner did not meet his or her respective obligations, the other, as in any business partnership, could withdraw from the union. Women had just as much right to initiate the divorce as men. As a consequence, the divorce rate apparently was fairly high among many of the groups.

Marriage also entailed a much looser relationship than in many other cultures because kinship bonds could and apparently often did conflict with marital ties; when this occurred, kinship obligations usually prevailed. In precolonial Ghana, the individual was also a member of other societal groups, and ties within the nuclear or conjugal family were often weak. Matrilineal societies were particularly liable to this type of instability; but even among the patrilineal groups, women were not assimilated into their husband's lineage but instead retained strong links with their own kin, and invariably returned to them in their old age (Fortes 1950, pp. 262–72; Fortes 1945, p. 251; Nukunya 1969, p. 57). Marriage represented an alliance between two kinship groups for the purpose of procreation. This mutuality of interest in the marriage established a connectedness between the conjugal pair and both kinship groups. As in other societies, the existence of a bilateral rather than a unilateral relationship of obligation tended to protect and strengthen the wife's position within the conjugal family (Liu, Hutchison, and Hong 1973). The readiness of the wife's kinship group to uphold her interests in the event of a conflict and to accept her back when the marital relation broke down enabled a woman to wield effectively the sanction of withdrawal from the union.

Thus, women's ability to withstand marital instability reflected two factors: the retention by women of a place in their own kinship group, and a low premium placed on female chastity. Marriage represented an ephemeral relation that involved a minimum of commitment and could be terminated without suffering a significant loss. The absence of a high valuation of female chastity meant that the previously married woman was not at a disadvantage in the marriage market. In fact, such a woman, whose first partner might have been selected by her kinship group, could usually play a greater role in determining whom she would marry and thus had a better chance of contracting a satisfactory alliance.

Furthermore, among the Ghanaian groups, and particularly in those that were matrilineal, women could employ the competing claims and obligations of their kinsmen and their husbands to their own advantage and neutralize the control of either over them. The relatively equal authority among the Akan groups of the husband and brother counterbalanced each other, and by so doing conferred autonomy on the woman; as is the case in other matrilineal societies in which neither the husband nor the brother is dominant, the total male authority over women was less and the independence of women greater than in most patrilineal systems (Schlegel 1972, p. 135). Even within the patrilineal groups, though, men probably exercised greater authority within kinship institutions than within the conjugal family.

The emotional bond between mother and child and not the sexual relation between a man and a woman was the strongest and often the most satisfying relationship in the social system. This enduring attachment between mother and child has, of course, characterized all human society, but in the case of the Ghanaian groups, it did not coexist with a hierarchical authority structure within the family that subordinated women to men. Among the Akan the father's position was further weakened by his lack of legal prerogatives over his children and by the precedence of kinship bonds over marital ones. Even in the patrilineal systems, though, the moral authority of the mother counterbalanced, to some extent, the influence of the father's lineage.

The Colonial Impact

Although small portions of the coastal area of Ghana came under Portuguese, Dutch, or British control much earlier, most of what constitutes contemporary Ghana became a British colony in 1902, some 400 years after the establishment of the first Portuguese forts. While some Ga and Akan villages had a heritage of sustained contacts with Europeans dating back to more than 100 years before the formal establishment of the colonial system, other Ghanaian groups in the North had little interaction with western culture until long after the territory became a British colony. This pattern of differential impact was further accentuated by the fact that in Ghana, as elsewhere, some groups had far greater access to schooling and to the new economic opportunities by virtue of their proximity to, and willingness to cooperate with, the colonial power. Largely by the accident of history and geographic location, the ethnic groups in which women held the highest status were the ones which benefited most. Some groups, particularly the Fanti (Akan) and the Ga, were producing university graduates to fill responsible positions by the second part of the nineteenth century, whereas the exclusion of Christian missionaries and the separate administration of the North meant that this area lagged behind the remainder of the country.

The spread of education, primarily under the aegis of the missionaries, adversely affected the position of women more than any other aspect of the colonial impact. Christian missionaries and colonial administrators, who brought with them Victorian conceptions concerning the place of women in society, accorded much higher priority to the education of men than of women. Women were never completely excluded from receiving a western education, but their opportunities were limited. Moreover, the education made available to women frequently taught them domestic skills appropriate for an English housewife rather than preparing them to go on to higher levels of the educational system. The expansion of the educational system on the eve of independence provided women with greater access to education, particularly at the lower levels, but it never redressed the previous imbalance between the sexes. The proportion of men increased at each succeeding level of the educational system, and the vast majority of the high-quality schools that served as the training ground for Ghana's elite remained exclusively male preserves (Graham 1971, pp. 71–93; Foster 1965). Thus, beginning in the colonial period, "education appears to have become the basis for a kind of social and economic sexual inequality from which Ghanaian society has previously been free" (Griffiths 1974, p. 13).

Women's restricted access to education limited their opportunities in the modern sector of the economy, particularly in white-collar, professional, and managerial positions, but, unlike else-where in Africa, women were not confined to subsistence farming. Ghana's pattern of economic development, which differed signifi-cantly from many other African territories, enabled women to par-ticipate in the cash economy in two respects, through cash crop-ping and marketing. The growth of the cocoa industry came through small-scale African farming and did not entail the open-ing of plantations or the involvement of government extension workers, both of which generally tend to exclude women (Boserup 1970). Nevertheless, men have predominated in the cocoa sector, possibly because cocoa farming has frequently involved emigra-tion from the village to find suitable land (Hill 1963; Addo 1971). Women's most significant economic advance during the colonial period came through the opening of the retail sector. Women found petty trading the most suitable economic activity to engage in because it did not demand much capital, education, or restric-tion on time. The greater law and order provided by the colonial administration enabled many women in the rural areas to expand their trade into more distant markets and gradually the limitations on the items women could deal in, which had been reserved for members of the chief's retinue, disappeared. The establishment of central markets in the towns enabled women to rent stalls and to regularize and enlarge their enterprises. Gradually women were able to monopolize the sectors of the wholesale and retail trade that were Ghanaianized (McCall 1961; see Lewis, this volume).

Colonial rule affected the status of women in subtle and less direct ways as well. European traders who established the small settlements along the coast, missionaries, and colonial adminis-trators all sought to deal with Ghanaian men, and over a period of several hundred years this both conferred advantages on the men involved and communicated the unsuitability of women for con-ducting affairs of substance. As Ghanaians became educated and aspired to be accepted by Europeans as their equals, they them-selves began to imitate western habits and practices. As one his-torian of the period has noted, "Often the imitation was unconscious, simply because the model was there. Europeans had, in fact, become a 'reference group' for patterns of behavior among those Africans who came in contact with them" (Kimble 1963, p. 133). Men among the elite encouraged their wives to dress in European style and to act like Victorian ladies (Kimble 1963, p. 134); and since Victorian ladies had more limited economic and social roles than Ghanaian women, such imitation could only have affected the status of Ghanaian women adversely.

Missionaries and educators consciously or unconsciously sought to cast relationships and mores in a European mold. Christian missionaries, usually unsuccessfully, sought to alter marriage patterns from the polygamous mode, in which the husband and wife or wives went their separate ways, to a European type of monogamous nuclear family in which the wife was subordinate to the husband and devoted herself primarily to him and their children. One of the by-products of Christian missionary activity during the colonial period was the creation of new forms of marriage. In order to set converts apart from the remainder of the community, missionaries petitioned the British government to introduce a pattern of binding monogamous marriage with inheritance rights for the wife and children comparable to those in western society. Marriage under the Marriage Ordinance provides the wife with greater security by discouraging divorce, by precluding polygamy, and by securing for the wife two-ninths of her husband's estate, but only a very small minority of the population has ever opted for this form of marriage. The very permanence of this form of marriage makes it less attractive, since most Ghanaians prefer to preserve the option of dissolving their marriages easily and inexpensively. Moreover, virtually all those who choose to marry under the Ordinance also go through the requirements for customary marriage (Tettah 1967, pp. 206–7; Vellenga 1971, p. 136). The major result of the introduction of the Marriage Ordinance seems to have been to devalue the worth of customary or traditional marriages by making them seem inferior and not completely legal.

The Family in Contemporary Ghana

Several trends in Ghanaian family structure and marriage relations are observable across the different forms of marriage. As with many other types of social change, many of these particularly characterize urban families in which the husband and wife are highly educated. Nevertheless, virtually no part of Ghana remains unexposed to modernizing influences, and it would be more accurate to describe rural communities as being at a different point along a continuum than to emphasize the contrasts between rural and urban Ghana. First, the nuclear household seems to be gaining greater autonomy from the extended family, with some concomitant independence in decision making. Second, although women retain considerable economic independence, an erosion in the sexual division of labor has brought greater involvement of husbands in household and family matters. Third, women's status in society depends to a considerable extent now on their husbands' success rather than on their own activities, and this has led to a greater subordination of the wife. Fourth, marital instability seems to be on the ascendance.

The nuclear or conjugal family remains intricately interwoven into the social fabric of the kinship group, but in its day-to-day living patterns it has greater autonomy. Several factors have promoted this trend in Ghana as elsewhere in the world: migration, education, changes in living patterns, spread of private prosperity, and economic development. The high rate of internal migration—in 1960, in two-thirds of the local authority areas at least half of the population originated elsewhere—means that Ghanaians frequently live apart from their kin groups in both rural and urban environments (Gil, Aryee, and Ghansah 1964, p. xliv). The important part that schools play in the socialization of the child, particularly in the South where school enrollment is very high, also decreases the influence of the extended family. Now the family no longer provides a total context for living and the individual is increasingly linked to the wider society. As a consequence, the act of marriage has become more an expression of personal preference than an alliance between two kin groups. With the current mobility, prospective mates are likely to come from outside the traditional locality that parents and elders surveyed to choose an appropriate partner, and may even be from a different ethnic group. While people rarely marry without the approval of their families, the initiative in the choice of a spouse now more frequently comes from the couple themselves. Potential for the autonomy of the conjugal family increases when the spouses come from different kin groups or when they live at a significant distance from the home community. Nevertheless, even in the rural villages the constituent units within the extended family now live apart in their own households and usually work separately.

The fact that husbands and wives more frequently live together now in the same household also contributes to strengthening the nuclear family. Formerly, women often remained with their own families or had a separate residence in the husband's community. According to census results, despite the high rate of internal migration, about two-thirds of the married women and men were living with their spouses. Joint households were more frequently the norm in rural than in urban areas (Gil, Degraft-Johnson, and Colecraft 1971, p. 254). As a corollary of these figures, one-third of all married Ghanaian women head their own households; while this may be a lower proportion than traditionally was the case among certain of the groups, it still means that a considerable number of women fend for themselves. Moreover, the women who head independent households probably have more responsibilities and less support from their own kin group.

It should be noted, though, that the conjugal family, even among members of the elite, tends to be an open unit linked to both the husband's and wife's kin groups. The residential and decision-making autonomy of the conjugal family has not been accompanied by a change in the inheritance laws or in a diminution of the sense of moral obligation for assisting members of one's wider kin group. Both spouses maintain strong ties with their own kin units, including providing relatives with financial aid and living accommodations. Fears that the property acquired during the time of the marriage will revert to other members of the husband's or wife's kin group (depending on the relevant traditional patterns of inheritance), or that the partner will use his or her earnings to support members of the kin group to the detriment of the life-style of the conjugal family, have motivated both men and women to refrain from acquiring joint property, from opening joint bank accounts, and from pooling their resources. Many of the financial and social arrangements within the conjugal family, therefore, continue to be role-segregated, particularly among the Akan (Oppong 1974, pp. 90–94). The inherent conflict between the demands of the husband's kin and his commitments to his conjugal family constitutes a fundamental source of domestic friction (Oppong 1974).

In those households in which the husband and wife coreside, the quality of the relationship has not changed significantly. In the conjugal family the relationship between the husband and wife still lacks intimacy, emotional bonds, and the shared interests and activities characterizing western family life. The emergence of the nuclear family as a more autonomous social unit has not transformed the attitudes of the members, and the convergence with the western family comes more in form than in substance. Even among the urban educated elite, husbands and wives go out together perhaps only once a month and rarely engage in recreation or socializing together as a family with husband, wife, and children (Caldwell 1968, p. 72). Although there may be an element of companionship involved in coresidence when both the husband and wife are well educated, the woman foremost in a man's affections, regardless of the living arrangements, is more likely to be his mother than his wife (Lloyd 1967, pp. 177–79).

In terms of their own security and well-being, therefore, women may, at least in the short run, be giving up more than they are gaining in the transition to the nuclear household pattern. They receive less protection and support from their own kin group and their independence is reduced, while they get back little in the form of greater marital stability or a more satisfying marital relationship.

Women's overall role within the family is changing from independence in the domestic sphere to subordination. Previously, women's autonomy within the domestic domain depended on the sexual division of labor, the social separation of the sexes, and their control of their own property. While contemporary women are not confined to serving as wives and mothers, their earning power is now proportionately lower in relation to their husband's income than it was formerly. This means that even though women regularly contribute to the family's maintenance, the husband usually provides a far greater portion. Among the elite, the husband's high salary and the modern house and amenities that frequently go along with his job enable the wife to have a comparatively luxurious life-style that neither she nor her kin group could otherwise afford; but in order to maintain this standard of living, the wife is dependent on the stability of the marriage and the willingness of the husband to accord priority to his conjugal family. The imbalance in the economic potential of the husband and wife very much alters the balance of power within the household, then, because the woman is less likely to resort to the traditional sanction of withdrawal to protect her own interests (Oppong 1974, 116–19).

The economic leverage of the husband, his higher status that reflects differential access of the sexes to schooling and to wage employment, and the emergence of the nuclear family all have brought about increasing involvement of men in the domestic sphere once reserved for the women. Men now make decisions on such matters as how the family income should be apportioned, where the children should be educated, and what style of life the family should have. For instance, a slight majority of students at two Ghanaian universities surveyed on an open-ended questionnaire by the author described the domestic power relationship between their parents as that of a superordinate father and a subordinate mother; only 17 percent considered their relationship to be one of equals. When asked to define the subjects on which their mothers made decisions for the family, 48 percent listed topics concerning the internal organization of the household, 19 percent said only on food, and only 10 percent mentioned matters relating to the upbringing of children; a small minority replied that their mothers did not make decisions on any subject. These responses cannot be considered representative of the Ghanaian population both because the university student bodies from which the samples were drawn and hence the samples themselves were disproportionately male, and because the families of the students tend to be elitist. Nevertheless, the breakdown of the traditional sexual division of labor has probably worked to the disadvantage of Ghanaian women in their efforts to uphold their domestic prerogatives. These trends should not be exaggerated, though. Ghanaian women at all levels of society still retain considerable economic independence and substantial control over their own income and property (Caldwell 1968, pp. 68–70; Field 1960, p. 30). While this pattern continues they will resist being cast fully in the mold of a subordinate inferior.

Another concomitant of the emphasis on the nuclear family and the intrusion of western concepts of marriage is the dependence of the wife on the husband for her status in society. The fact that elite women as a consequence of their marriage under the Ordinance carry their husband's name symbolizes other aspects of their relationship. Traditionally, spouses operated within such separate spheres that the activities of the one only indirectly affected the position of the other; but now among the elite the woman is seen more in the western perspective as an extension of her husband, and her status depends on his success (Little 1972, p. 276; Lloyd 1967, p. 171). This pattern of reflected status results as well from the differential access of men to higher education and prestigious occupations. Even in the most elite circles, few wives have attained an educational level equivalent to that of their husbands, and in many cases the disparities between them are quite considerable. Doubtlessly this new form of dependence has repercussions on the domestic relationship: it becomes more difficult for the woman to demand equality within the home when society accords a higher rank to her husband.

All available evidence points to greater marital instability. This instability manifests itself in two different forms: a higher rate of dissolution and a lower rate of acceptance of traditional obligations. No accurate figures exist on the proportion of marriages ending in divorce. Census questionnaires ascertain the number of divorced persons still unmarried at the time of the interview but fail to enumerate how many people have ever been divorced. The figure published in the census report of 5.2 percent of all adults does not accurately indicate the frequency of divorce, because most divorced men and women soon remarry (Gil, DeGraft-Johnson, and Colecraft 1971, p. 206). Ghanaians themselves acknowledge the prevalence of marital instability, and, at least among the elite, register disapproval of it (Caldwell 1968, p. 72). One study of the average percentage of time lived in conjugal unions showed that between the ages of twenty and forty-four, when according to social custom virtually all Ghanaians would expect to be married, rural males spend 23 percent of the time and urban males 36 percent of the time outside of conjugal unions, and that rural and urban women in the same age span are similarly without a partner for 16 and 18 percent of the period (Caldwell 1967, p. 73). When the respondents in that survey were asked about the number of conjugal partners they had ever possessed, in the age group of fifty and over, rural males averaged 3.5 mates and rural females 2.1, while the comparable rates for urban males and females were 2.5 and 1.4 respectively. All rural men over twenty-five averaged more than two different partners and all other males and females somewhat more than one (Caldwell 1967, p. 71). From this analysis of conjugal biographies, we can conclude that the unstable marriage patterns are more prevalent in rural than urban areas.

Women in customary marriages also seem to be having greater difficulty in asserting their traditional rights. Studies of two communities in southern Ghana show that whereas most cases in the customary courts dealing with marriage formerly were brought by husbands to claim damages from men who had committed adultery with their wives, the claimants now tend to be women suing their husbands for maintenance (Brokensha 1966, pp. 220–35; Vellenga 1971, p. 150). Moreover, when a prospective wife has already been married and divorced, a man often does not feel obliged to perform all of the customary rites to validate the marriage, which leaves the woman without legal recourse to traditional procedures of enforcing her rights. As the woman grows older, her bargaining position to insist on the performance of the customary procedures becomes weaker and she is forced to accept a common-consent union on the man's terms (Tetteh 1967, p. 209).

Conclusion

Elite and uneducated women confront different types of problems in marriage, but in both cases current trends render their position more difficult than in the past. Elite women tend to have greater legal security in marriage than their less-educated sisters because they more often contract Ordinance marriages and because their class frowns upon divorce. Nevertheless, their marital situation is not enviable; they have been thrust into a new pattern of relationships where the wife increasingly becomes an appendage of her husband and where her autonomy and independence have been reduced without affording her a more satisfying relationship with her husband in return. Although any efforts to draw subjective implications from the data must of course be highly speculative, it would seem that elite women, who had absorbed many European and Christian ideas concerning marriage, must find it difficult to accept a marriage in which the husband's loyalty to his mother and kin group still outweighs (or seriously competes with) his commitment to his wife and conjugal family and where monogamous marriage goes hand in hand with frequent male infidelity. Conversely, a woman socialized in Ghanaian cultural patterns probably balks at being subordinated to the husband within the household and being considered inferior by society. Rural and uneducated women are less influenced by changes in the relative status of men and women resulting from differential access to higher education and prestigious occupations and would seem to encounter fewer problems in maintaining their autonomy and independence within marriage. However, they must cope with the consequences of marital instability and insecure inheritance rights under customary law.

References

Addo, Nelson. 1971. "Some Aspects of the Employment Situation on Cocoa Farms in Brong Ahafo in the Pre- and Post-Aliens Compliance Era." Paper presented at African Population Conference, Accra.

Boserup, Ester. 1970. *Woman's Role in Economic Development*. London: Allen and Unwin.

Brokensha, David W. 1966. *Social Change at Larteh, Ghana*. Oxford: Clarendon.

Busia, K. A. 1951. *The Position of the Chief in the Modern Political System of Ashanti: A Study of the Influence of Contemporary Social Changes on Ashanti Political Institutions*. London: Oxford University Press.

Caldwell, John C. 1967. "Population: General Characteristics." In W. Birmingham, I. Neustadt, E. N. Omaboe, eds., *A Study of Contemporary Ghana, 2: Some Aspects of Social Structure*, pp. 17–77. Evanston: Northwestern University Press.

—— 1968. *Population Growth and Family Change in Africa: The New Urban Elite in Ghana*. Canberra: Australia National University Press.

Census Office. 1972. *1970 Population Census of Ghana, 2: Statistics of Localities and Enumeration Areas*. Accra.

Economic Commission for Africa. 1974. "The Changing and Contemporary Role of Women in African Development." Duplicated.

Field, M. J. 1940. *Social Organization of the Ga People*. London: Crown Agents.

—— 1960. *Search for Security: An Ethno-Psychiatric Study of Rural Ghana*. Evanston: Northwestern University Press.

Folson, B. D. G. n.d. "The Traditional Political System." Mimeo.

Fortes, Meyer. 1945. *The Dynamics of Clanship among the Talensi*. London: Oxford University Press.

—— 1949. *The Web of Kinship among the Talensi*. London: Oxford University Press.

—— 1950. "Kinship and Marriage among the Ashanti." In A. R. Radcliffe-Brown and D. Forde, eds., *African Systems of Kinship and Marriage*, pp. 252–83. London: Oxford University Press.

Foster, Philip. 1965. *Education and Social Change in Ghana*. London: Routledge and Kegan Paul.

Gil, B., A. F. Aryee, and D. K. Ghansah. 1964. *Population Census of Ghana, Special Report "E," Tribes in Ghana*. Accra: Census Office.

Gil, B., K. T. Degraft-Johnson, and E. A. Colecraft. 1971. *1960 Population Census of Ghana, 6: The Post Enumeration Survey*. Accra: Census Office.

Graham, C. K. 1971. *The History of Education in Ghana: From the Earliest Times to the Declaration of Independence*. London: Frank Cass.

Griffiths, John. 1974. "On Teaching Law in Ghana and Related Matters." *Law Center Bulletin* 21:4–28.

Hill, Polly. 1963. *Migrant Cocoa Farmers of Southern Ghana*. Cambridge: Cambridge University Press.

Kimble, David. 1963. *A Political History of Ghana: The Rise of Gold Coast Nationalism 1850–1928*. London: Oxford University Press.

Little, Kenneth. 1972. "Voluntary Associations and Social Mobility among West African Women." *Canadian Journal of African Studies* 6:275–88.

Liu, William T., Ira W. Hutchison, and Lawrence K. Hong. 1973. "Conjugal Power and Decision Making: A Methodological Note on Cross-Cultural Study of the Family." *American Journal of Sociology* 79:84–98.

Lloyd, P. C. 1967. *Africa in Social Change: Changing Traditional Societies in the Modern World*. Baltimore: Penguin.

McCall, D. 1961. "Tradition and the Role of a Wife in a Modern African Town." In A. Southall, ed., *Social Change in Modern Africa*, pp. 286–99. London: Oxford University Press.

Manoukian, Madeline. 1950. *Akan and Ga-Adangme Peoples*. London: International African Institute.

—— 1951. *Tribes of the Northern Territories of the Gold Coast*. London: International African Institute.

—— 1952. *The Ewe-Speaking People of Togoland and the Gold Coast*. London: International African Institute.

Manpower Division, Development Planning Secretariat. 1971. *High Level and Skilled Manpower Survey—1968*. Accra.

Ministry of Education. 1968. *Educational Report, 1963–1967*. Accra: Ghana Publishing Corp.

—— 1971. *Educational Statistics, 1968–1969*. Accra.

Nukunya, G. K. 1969. *Kinship and Marriage among the Anlo Ewe*. London: Athlone Press.

Oppong, Christine. 1974. *Marriage among a Matrilineal Elite: A Family Study of Ghanaian Civil Servants*. Cambridge: Cambridge University Press.

Paulme, Denise. 1971. "Introduction." In D. Paulme, ed., *Women of Tropi-*

cal Africa, pp. 1–16. Berkeley and Los Angeles: University of California Press.

Peil, Margaret. 1972. *The Ghanian Factory Worker: Industrial Man in Africa.* Cambridge: Cambridge University Press.

Rattray, R. S. 1929. *Ashanti Law and Constitution.* London: Oxford University Press.

Sanday, Peggy R. 1974. "Female Status in the Public Domain." In M. Z. Rosaldo and L. Lamphere, eds., *Woman, Culture, and Society,* pp. 189–206. Stanford: Stanford University Press.

Schlegel, Alice. 1972. *Male Dominance and Female Autonomy: Domestic Authority in Matrilineal Societies.* New Haven: Human Relations Area Files Press.

Smock, Audrey C. 1977. "Ghana: From Autonomy to Subordination." In J. Z. Giele and A. C. Smock, eds., *Women: Roles and Status in Eight Countries,* pp. 173–216. New York: Wiley-Interscience.

Tait, David. 1961. *The Konkomba of Northern Ghana.* London: Oxford University Press.

Tetteh, P. A. 1967. "Marriage, Family, and Household." In W. Birmingham, I. Neustadt, E. N. Omaboe, eds., *A Study of Contemporary Ghana,* 2: *Some Aspects of Social Structure,* pp. 206–16. Evanston: Northwestern University Press.

Vellenga, Dorothy Dee. 1971. "Attempts to Change the Marriage Laws in Ghana and the Ivory Coast." In P. Foster and A. Zolberg, eds., *Ghana and the Ivory Coast,* pp. 125–50. Chicago: University of Chicago Press.

BETTE DENICH

10 Women, Work, and Power in Modern Yugoslavia

R EVIVED INTEREST IN the condition of women in the United States and Western Europe has renewed the spirit of comparative inquiry as a source of insight into problems common to all cultures. The relation between sex and power is such a universal problem. This analysis of the economic and political status of women in contemporary Yugoslavia is written to contribute to a comparative understanding of widespread structures and processes, rather than simply to expose the contradictions within a particular society.

The relation between sex and power revolves around the issue of inequality. A pervasive source of inequality between males and females within a culture is the separation between a public sphere of societal power and a domestic sphere of household activity (see Rosaldo 1974). The degree to which public functions are elaborated apart from domestic ones varies among human cultures. The greater the wedge between the two spheres, the greater the probability that they will align on the basis of sex, linking males to public functions and females to domestic ones (see Leacock 1972). Sexual hierarchy results from the empirical superiority of the public sphere, as each domestic unit is subordi-

Research was carried out from January 1965 through April 1966 with the support of a National Institute of Mental Health predoctoral fellowship and supplementary research grant.

nated to larger structures: clans, villages, chiefdoms, bureau-cracies, national states. If these overarching structures are relegated to male control, then women are subordinated within the society as a whole, regardless of how much power they may wield within their own households. Sexual inequality accompanies segregation into unequal domains, just as in any situation involving unequal spheres, separate cannot be equal.

The coincidence of the public/domestic and male/female dichotomies is a crucial aspect of relations between the sexes in all highly complex societies, including contemporary industrial societies. For women to overcome the lesser status inherent in their confinement to the domestic sphere, it appears necessary that they win entry into the superior public sphere. Sexual equality was a goal of the revolution that brought the present socialist government to power in Yugoslavia. The revolution initiated rapid change in all areas of life, particularly through the far-reaching effects of economic development. This paper will focus on women in the transition from peasant to urban life and on the effects of women's employment in public economic institutions upon their participation in the power structures of both domestic and public life. The analysis will draw upon diverse sources, including recent studies by Yugoslav women social scientists and the author's own field research in an industrializing Serbian city. In ranging over a broad spectrum of material, we shall attempt to interpret a complex course of change that is fraught with contrary tendencies in the continuing dialectics between private and public, between female and male.

The Peasant Background and the Revolution

When the socialist government came to power in Yugoslavia, it recognized that women were especially disadvantaged in the agricultural economy that supported 75 percent of the population. Improvement in women's status was linked to the industrialization programs that were planned to develop a poor country. A new social order was to provide a basis for women to emerge from the subordinate position imposed upon them in rural environments.

Peasant social structures throughout Yugoslavia are based on varying forms of patricentric organization (see Goldschmidt and Kunkel 1971). Agricultural land in most regions was traditionally inherited only by males. Men represented their households in public affairs and were the chief authorities within the family. Males dominated in both public and private decision making, and sexual hierarchy was symbolically elaborated in values and rituals (see Denich 1974a; Erlich 1966). The condition of peasant women was defined by dependence on male-controlled resources. Exclusion from inheritance meant that each woman had to rely on a man for access to a means of subsistence. First as a daughter, then as a wife, a woman was a necessary member of a household labor force. In return, she was entitled to share in the produce of the land. Marriages were arranged, and a young bride left her natal home for that of her husband, where she was alone among his kinsmen and other in-married wives. Through bearing the sons to carry on her husband's family, she could eventually gain influence in that household. Marriage was a binding commitment for better or worse, and divorce was virtually impossible. An unsuccessful marriage was unpleasant for both spouses, but far more tragic for the wife. While the husband's life still centered on his kinsmen within the same household, the wife was alone among in-laws. Unhappy marriages underscored the lack of alternatives for women. Once married, a woman was no longer welcome to return to her natal household, which accrued to her brothers and nephews. If begrudgingly accepted back, her position would be difficult. A dissatisfied wife had no means of support without access to male property and usually found that her only recourse was to endure the unhappy marriage.[1]

The only occupation for which peasant girls were prepared was that of peasant wife. In the eastern regions of Yugoslavia, the four-year village elementary schools were attended almost entirely by boys. Girls grew up unschooled and illiterate, and, as adults, they were unprepared to cope effectively with the world outside the village, or to do anything but unskilled work when they did go elsewhere. Yugoslav illiteracy statistics still reflect the lack of female education in the past. In towns and cities, on the other hand, girls were educated and women held many kinds of jobs. Because the urban population was a very small part of the total, the impact of change has primarily involved the formerly rural population.

A sudden break from traditional women's roles occurred at the start of World War II in 1941, when women joined the communist-led Partisan resistance against German occupation forces. The first women guerrilla fighters were high school and university students, teachers, and factory workers from the urban areas. As the resistance shifted to the mountainous interior of Yugoslavia, it grew into a massive peasant-based movement and drew in rural women. The rifle-bearing "Partizanka" in military dress represented a radically new female image. At the war's end, women partisans became leaders in the revolutionary government on an egalitarian basis with their male comrades. A political woman in a tailored suit then came to represent still another new feminine image.

Wartime and postwar years were a period of great social upheaval that forever altered the peasant society of the past. Along with economic and political changes came programs aimed at improving the condition of women. In rural areas, a new women's organization (AFŽ) mobilized women to carry out social-action projects and brought them into literacy courses. Thus great numbers of rural women made their first contact with an institution representing the society beyond the village and learned the fundamentals of reading and writing. However, the chief mechanism for change arose not within the villages but in towns and cities, where industrialization opened new jobs at all skill levels and radically altered the economic possibilities for women.

Industrialization and
New Options for Women

In contrast to the peasant economy, urban employment provides each individual with direct access to a means of support, regardless of sex. An end to dependence on male-controlled resources means that women can support themselves, whatever their marital status. The most dramatic changes are experienced by single women and those who have found an escape route from unhappy marriages through the newfound ability to earn their "own piece of bread." Married women who make a financial contribution to the household are also in a different position from housewives dependent on their husbands' earnings. During my field research in 1965–66, I interviewed many women who had left villages and taken jobs in a rapidly industrializing Serbian city, Titovo Užice.[2] Because we gain insight into general patterns when we can see how they are reflected in individual lives, I shall quote from some of these interviews to illustrate the impact of employment upon women of rural origins. Each brief quotation will be followed by an explanation of its salient features.

We may begin with the experiences of a woman who was twenty-nine years old at the time of the interview, and had left her village five years earlier:

I was married for only a short time. I met my husband when workers from all over the country came to build a new railroad tunnel in our village. One of these workers, from Macedonia, wanted to marry me. I didn't want to accept, but my parents agreed to the marriage. When we arrived in his home village, I was dismayed to find that his family lived very poorly, with one room for sleeping and another for livestock, all in the same house. I escaped during the night and returned to my family. For some time afterward, my brother pressured me to return to my husband.

It was unusual for a girl to be married to a man from far away, but not unusual for a marriage to be arranged with little regard for her wishes. Girls usually acquiesced dutifully, if without enthusiasm, to their parents' choices. Many of these marriages actually turned out very well, but there was little room for failure.

Because I was on bad terms with my brother, I went to the city three years later. My brother didn't like me because I was not married.

Unmarried women were often resented by their brothers, who considered them a drain on resources to which they had no right.

I worked as a housekeeper for a year and then got my present job as a cleaning woman at the railroad station.

Uneducated women could qualify only for unskilled work, most often as cleaning women or textile and garment workers.

I now share a room with a woman friend. We rent the room from another railroad worker, and I have furnished it on credit. My problems are small pay and a lonely life. I would like to find a good man to have a good life with, but that is very difficult. I just want a husband who will know how to care about me, and I'll do the same in return.

A single woman with an unskilled job can survive on a modest level, but still has no doubt that married life could be better.

Some of the same themes can be recognized in the words of a twenty-seven-year-old unskilled textile worker:

My family was poor, and my parents gave me away when I was seven. My aunt and uncle needed another person to work on their farm and agreed to take me in, after agreeing with my father about the dowry they would provide for my marriage. When they arranged for me to marry the son of our nearest neighbor, I had to obey, although I did not love him.

Many peasants in Užice region lived at the survival margin and poor parents often sent their children to work for more affluent families for noncash payments. Because her marriage was arranged as part of such a contract, this girl saw no way to decline.

I only lived with my husband and his family for a short time. When I left my husband, I went first to my parents' home where I stayed for only a month before leaving for the city. My mother did not favor my leaving, but my father was angry because I had broken up my marriage and wanted me to go. Since I had no future in the village, I wanted to get a job.

We see again that peasant society had no place for unmarried women and offered no alternatives in unsuccessful marriages.

Now I am planning to start evening school so I can finish through eighth grade. My brother, who is here in the city, will help me. I would change my job if I could get a better one. We textile workers get little pay and we have to work the night shift.

During the earlier years of industrialization, unskilled workers were encouraged to improve their education and skill levels and could rapidly rise in job levels. The mutual aid provided by kinship and friendship networks has served as the fundamental adaptive device for people making such abrupt changes in their lives (see Denich 1970).

I have quite a number of friends in town, mostly manual workers from different enterprises. We visit each other after work and we often go out as a group to see a movie or walk on the *korzo* (promenade). But this way of life is somehow empty. I would like to marry again and have a good marriage. I would have a husband and, perhaps, children and would know why I'm alive. But men don't want to be serious about women.

Most rural-urban migrants have active social lives with relatives, neighbors, and friends. This vivacious young woman readily adapted to the circumstances of urban life and developed a circle of constant companions. However, in a society still based on family life, even a socially active single woman is not satisfied. But outside the bonds of arranged marriage, a divorcée finds marital prospects to be rare.

It was not always the woman who was dissatisfied with a marriage. A common plight was that of the childless wife, as illustrated by a woman who was thirty-six when she came to Užice:

My husband wanted children, but I couldn't have any and so we were divorced after many years of marriage. I set out for my brother's house in another village. Along the way, I stopped here in town to visit my sister and decided to stay here instead. I found work as a housekeeper, which I am still doing.

Infertility was tragic for peasant wives because their status required them to be mothers of children in their husbands' households. If driven out in the past, such women could only turn to their natal households where, as we have seen, they were unwanted. This woman took advantage of the new option to take a job in the city, where even the lowliest ranking domestic work was preferable to her village prospects.

All the women quoted thus far were severely limited in their job prospects by the lack of education that was the legacy of the traditional village society. An important effect of the revolutionary government was the enforcement of universal education for both sexes and the expansion of rural schools to eight grades. This has meant that girls growing up under present conditions have a great advantage over their mothers and older sisters. Many girls from peasant families now attend secondary schools in towns to prepare for working careers in the same way as their male schoolmates. We can trace this process in the story of a young woman, twenty years old at the time of the interview, who had recently graduated from the Užice technical high school and was employed as a machine technician in a large enterprise:

I am from a well-off village family, with five hectares of good land. My mother had plans to marry me to the son of the most respected, richest family in the village, but I couldn't stand the young man and did not want to get married at all. I saw how my mother and the other village women lived and did not want to lead that kind of life myself. I admired the young people from the village who had gone on to high school in town. I liked the way they looked and was attracted by what they said about life in the city.

In the past, a girl was unlikely to reject such a desirable marriage prospect. Now, however, she sees herself as making a choice between two distinctly different ways of life. The city has quickly come to represent a preferable life-style to young villagers and draws them like a magnet, regardless of their families' economic level (see Denich 1974b).

My father agreed with my decision to leave for town, and he helped me get there. One day he hitched up the horses and drove me here to town. After I left, my mother didn't speak to him for a whole month.

These parents were acting out opposing sides in the conflict exemplified in their daughter's choice between alternative ways of life.

My prospective bridegroom had promised me that I wouldn't have to work at his house, but could just relax and enjoy myself. When I walked by his farm some time later, I happened to see his wife hoeing in the fields. Then I realized that I too would be hoeing, if I were in her place.

To peasants and former peasants, hoeing typifies the drudgery of agricultural work. This self-confident, attractive career woman can't keep from gloating about the rightness of her choice to leave the village. However, even she has some complaints:

There is not enough entertainment for girls in our town. Boys and men can always find some way to amuse themselves, but it is much more difficult for us to go out in public. It is particularly unpleasant for a woman to enter a *kafana* (café) alone.

Separate rules continue to regulate male and female social activities. In all Yugoslav towns and cities, *kafanas* are social centers where groups of friends gather. While men freely circulate, women and girls are careful to appear in public only in the company of proper male escorts or enough other women (a minimum of two others) to appear "respectable."

These interviews illustrate the significant new ability of single women to be self-sufficient. Marriage does not alter the principle that women earn their own incomes. Given generally low wage levels, a single-income family finds it difficult to achieve the living standard associated with "modern" life that urban Yugoslavs now universally desire. The new circumstances have defined a woman's place in a factory or office, in order to bring home a paycheck. In the village, a woman's economic contribution includes both domestic work and the primary productive labor involved in agriculture. In the city, she continues both kinds of work: homemaking goes on as before, while primary productive work is removed from the household sphere to the public sphere of an economic enterprise. The change is not in going from housekeeping to productive labor, but in the locus of productive labor. If peasant women had become housewives after moving to town, their removal from productive labor would also have represented a change.[3] The prevailing view in Yugoslavia, that it is desirable for wives to have jobs, is expedient under the circumstances. Many uneducated women who cannot find jobs would like to, and there is little sentiment that wives should stay home.

Urban life has radically affected the comparative valuation and treatment of male and female children. The postwar rural-urban migrants have now reared a new generation of urban children, with a new set of expectations about the careers they are preparing for. While peasant families place a premium on sons to provide heavy labor and to inherit the land, neither of these considerations is relevant in an urban household. Although lingering sentiment fosters a desire for sons, the degree of preference seems to me no greater than it is in the United States. Large families are neither useful nor feasible in towns and the two-child family has become a norm. Most couples consider their families complete when the second child arrives and then devote themselves to providing both children, regardless of sex, with the best opportunities they can for education and careers. It is considered equally important for girls and boys to have occupations that assure reasonable incomes. The young woman machine technician, quoted earlier, represents the model that many parents set for their daughters. Considering the extremely different treatment of male and female children in the rural households where these parents were socialized, the change is quite remarkable. People joke that a girl's diploma is a substitute for a dowry, and the analogy is quite apt, as marriageability today is measured not by the gold coins on a girl's necklace, but according to the dinars in her paycheck.

The interviews with recent rural-urban migrants conducted in Užice in 1965 show that they had accepted the new standard of equivalent career aspirations for sons and daughters. Table 10.1 shows the conscious values that parents expressed with regard to their hopes for their children's occupations. Interviews indicate attitudes rather than behavior, but we can see that these attitudes are matched by performance in the one-third of university diplomas that are awarded to women throughout Yugoslavia (32.1 percent during 1965–69, cited by Burić 1972, p. 66). As Yugoslav universities have greatly expanded since the revolution, many students are the first members of their families to receive higher education. The high proportion of female graduates testifies to the rapid spread of egalitarian standards.

People from peasant backgrounds encountered a new set of conditions in industrializing towns. Rather than a gradual unfold-

Table 10.1 Career Aspirations of Yugoslavian Rural-Urban Migrants for Their Children (in percent)

	Sex of Child	
Career Aspiration	Female (N = 103)	Male (N = 110)
Professional careers (requiring university degrees)	40	40
Technicians (requiring secondary schools)	8	7
White-collar occupation (requiring secondary schools)	23	19
Skilled manual work (requiring secondary schools)	1	16
Teachers (requiring secondary schools)	10	4
Fine arts (usually requiring university degrees)	3	1
Marriage (actually married already)	2	—
"Let the child choose for him(her)self"	13	13
Total	100	100

ing of different behavior forms, the new circumstances induced immediate change in the possibilities for women's economic roles. The acceptance of women's employment led quickly to equivalent expectations about male and female careers, including those of husbands and wives.

Women at Work:
Occupations and Images

Because women's jobs are a regular part of their lives, occupations serve as a basis for their social identity, just as they do for men. People are often identified by occupation, and it is as usual to hear about "Marija the dentist" as about "Petar the electrician." Newspaper marriage notices specify the occupations of both bride and groom, reporting the wedding of "Jovan Marković, carpenter" and "Nada Andrić, office worker." The job is an important source of social relationships and friendships, and people in all occupations refer to their workmates as "colleagues," a term denoting the same respect and closeness that it does in elite professions in the United States. The work aspect of a person's identity is expressed even after death, when his or her enterprise publishes a commemorative newspaper notice. From work in the public sphere, a woman attains an important source of identity separate from that founded on familial, domestic relationships.

In Yugoslavia, many professions are considered equally appropriate for both men and women. Because there is less occupational sex typing than in the United States, an American visitor is impressed by the sight of men and women colleagues, side by side, doing the same work without the feeling that one sex is out of place in that particular role. Although medical fields are among the highest-status professions in Yugoslavia, there has been no effort to maintain male exclusiveness in them. Approximately half the physicians and dentists and about three-quarters of the pharmacists are women (Otto and Taylor 1973, p. 10, cited from Yugoslav Federal Institute of Public Health Yearbook). Typically male technical fields are also open to both sexes. When a new technical high school opened in Užice in 1960 to train electrical, machine, and other technicians, it admitted female and male students in equal numbers. In Yugoslav universities, one-fifth of the engineering and architecture students are women (Denitch 1976, p. 78). It is not considered odd for a young woman to choose a career like electrical or transport engineer, and it in no way detracts from her femininity. Because a Yugoslav woman's career is accepted as a practical necessity, it is considered logical that she seek the best possible, rather than being limited to the secondary occupations defined as female.

The performance of women at professional jobs has a sexual neutrality that surprises American observers. In a study of women physicians in Zagreb, two American women medical students remark, "One cannot help but be amazed at the high level of acceptance women receive by the medical community and the patient population. Also impressive is their own self-image as doctors, their ease and comfort in wearing white coats" (Otto and Taylor 1973, p. 27). I was similarly impressed by my contact with women doctors and dentists in Yugoslavia. I particularly recall one episode that occurred during a visit to a Dalmatian island when a slight injury sent me to the clinic. I took my place in a waiting room crowded with women, men, and children of all ages. In turn, each entered the door marked with a doctor's title. When my turn came to enter the doctor's office, I was surprised to find there, in a white coat, a stunningly attractive young woman. A few moments later, a seriously injured accident victim was brought into the clinic, and the doctor rushed off to attend the case. The only deviation from the American image of the efficient, authoritative physician was that the role was enacted by a women still, judging by appearance, in her twenties.

Although both sexes are included in high-status, well-paid fields like medicine and engineering, most Yugoslav jobs are still sex typed. Most highly skilled blue-collar occupations, such as electrician or machinist, are male. Where women break into such trades, they evoke some awe, but as curiosities more than as trendsetters. The Užice weekly newspaper, in 1951, reported on the town's first woman bus driver. In 1965, she was still its only woman bus driver. A story in the same weekly, in 1972, gave a sympathetic interview with two woman crane operators in a local factory, but featured them as exceptions. Burić (1972, p. 65) notes that, out of sixty-four fields of employment surveyed, the nine fields with female majorities are all in traditionally female lines of work: the textile, leather, and shoe industries; restaurants and hotels; social welfare and health; education and culture. Burić points out that these fields all have low profitability and low salaries. This information indicates that, despite the inclusion of women in high-salary professions, the overall work force still has a built-in wage differential between men and women.

Working Wives at Home

An American wife is a homemaker with a job on the side; a Yugoslav working wife is an employee who does housework on the side. Identical realities are given opposite cultural definitions, denying the opposing halves. The dual aspects of female economic performance continue as in the rural past, in that the wife works both in production and in the domestic services that provide for the personal needs of the men and children of her family. The job takes her outside of the domestic boundaries, but after work hours her life reverts to its traditional sphere at home.

Sexual equality was an important value in the Yugoslav revolution. However, government policy gave first priority to economic development as the necessary basis for solving other social problems, thereby tacitly reasserting a distinction between public issues and private concerns. The direct impact of new values on reorganizing social structures went only so far as the doorstep, beyond which the government did not meddle. Housekeeping and childcare were thereby left to the private area, where there was no inducement to change traditional concepts about sex roles. Although it is no longer considered inappropriate for women to have jobs that were formerly exclusively male, it is still regarded as unseemly for men to take on women's tasks at home. What may constitute a reasonable division of labor where the woman is a full-time housewife is obviously burdensome to wives with jobs. Although the unfairness of the employed wife's dual obligations is widely acknowledged, the threat of the unmanly image acts as a powerful deterrent to a more equal division of labor. The effect of this threat is illustrated by a conversation with two very modern Užice girl gymnasium graduates in 1972 who complained that, although their mothers have jobs, their fathers "won't even get themselves a glass of water." And yet, one girl mused, "When I get married, I would think it ridiculous for my husband to wash dishes."

Housework makes heavy demands on time and effort, keeping the employed woman busy both before and after job hours. Until electric appliances became widely available, within the last decade, all chores were done by hand. The washing by hand and ironing of all laundry, including sheets, is in itself a monumental task. With no refrigeration, daily marketing is necessary. The Yugoslav approach to solving these problems has been to introduce "labor-saving" devices in accord with the American and West European model. Washing machines, refrigerators, and supermarkets do lighten the drudgery of housework, but do not alter its structure. Instead of reducing the time necessary for housekeeping, mechanization often raises the standards and thereby maintains a constant time requirement. The boundary between public and private stays in place, with domestic chores still the woman's concern. Public services could provide alternatives for some forms of household labor, but amidst the enormous modernization of most facilities, laundries and childcare centers are still rare. It appears that once particular functions are defined as private and female, there is little pressure to redefine them as public.

Although community childcare centers exist in Yugoslavia, the care of preschool children has remained largely in the private sphere. At present, only one of twelve preschool children receives any kind of care outside the home (League of Communists 1974,

p. 52). Care for the children of working mothers depends on the continuing viability of kinship networks. The ability of people to reorganize their personal relationships to cope with new circumstances (see Denich 1970) has freed the government to concentrate on the larger areas of public economic policy. But the very adaptiveness of kinship structures has also permitted important social issues like childcare to be treated as private concerns. Enlightened social legislation provides working mothers with generous maternity leaves at full pay. But after that, private arrangements must take over. The childcare arrangements made by a sample of 25 Zagreb women doctors are typical: 84 percent relied on relatives, while smaller numbers used maids (16 percent), friends (8 percent) and day-care centers (only 1 percent) (Otto and Taylor 1973, p. 23). Three-generational households provide the most convenient baby-sitters and allow parents the greatest freedom, but most urban families do not include resident grandmothers, and the other solutions to the childcare probelm are left for mothers to arrange.

Social life in Yugoslav towns revolves around two distinct foci: the home and the *kafana*. While the social scene at home is predominately female, men are free to participate as they wish. But the *kafana* is a distinctly male domain, where women are always in a minority and only appear in suitable company. Social activities thus maintain considerable separation between the sexes and locate each in its customary sphere.[4] The same division carries over into political activity, leaving men freer after work to attend meetings and to hobnob informally in the *kafanas* with other male activists. While domestic responsibilities keep women at home, the continuing masculine atmosphere in public places reinforces traditions about the inappropriateness of women's presence there. (As a woman, I still feel quite uncomfortable about dining alone in most Yugoslav restaurants.) Yugoslav women recognize the inequity of the working wife's double burden; in fact, it was one of the first complaints I heard after my arrival there. However, discontent does not lead easily to change. Women often let off steam by complaining as they do their housework, but they usually address these grievances to a sympathetic female audience while the men are absent.

Marital conflicts involving working wives have been analyzed by two Belgrade women social scientists, as part of their study of family life in Kragujevac, a Serbian industrial city (Burić and Zečević 1969). The study found that the egalitarian ideal has most influenced relatively well-educated women with white-collar occupations, and that there was a high correlation between the wives' occupational status and their degree of marital dissatisfaction. The authors comment that "Our family law . . . . officially insists on a very egalitarian family ideology, but tends to leave family life to transform itself" (Burić and Zéčević 1969, p. 255, my translation). Norm and reality conflict when working women accept egalitarian ideas but do not succeed in achieving them at home. The strains caused by the discrepency between values and behavior then affect both spouses, as indicated by the finding that even more husbands of white-collar women are dissatisfied than are the wives themselves (see Table 10.2). Although more-educated women generally enjoy greater advantages than less-educated manual workers, they also feel more acutely their unfavorable position in comparison to their husbands. In socially stratified situations, it is often the best-off members of the subordinated group who compare themselves to the more privileged group and therefore feel the sting of deprivation most strongly.[5] Marital conflicts erupt when wives push for more egalitarian relationships, but their husbands resist. The authors of the Kragujevac study explain that "Change in every relation between exploiters and exploited only brings loss to the exploiter. . . . Thus, change in

Table 10.2 Wife's Employment and Marital Dissatisfaction

Wife's Employment Status	Percent of Dissatisfied Spouses	
	Husbands	Wives
Not employed	4.5	5.0
Manual worker	6.0	5.0
White-collar employee	26.0	19.0

Source: Burić and Zečević 1969, p. 244.

family roles means, for the husband, the loss of privilege obtained through birth as a male, while the wife can only gain what was not given her at birth in a society full of patriarchal vestiges" (Burić and Zečević 1969, p. 247).

One important area of change within the household is in the allocation of authority. In rural areas, women are not only excluded from public authority roles, but are often under male authority within their households as well. The extent of women's subordination within the household varies widely in different regions (see Denich 1974a), and women's authority is greatest where they contribute sizable dowries that are not turned over to their husbands (First-Dilić 1969). Urban women likewise have the most say in family decisions when they contribute a major share of the income. The Kragujevac study found that about half the couples interviewed shared the initiative in decision making, while the other half were dominated by the husband. There was not a single reverse case, in which the wife dominated, "probably not because it didn't exist, but because it would be considered insulting for both, under traditional models" (Burić and Zečević 1969, p. 236). Another study, which sampled all regions of the country, found that working wives shared equally in the household decisions of approximately three-quarters of couples (First-Dilić 1973).

For women to be closer to equality in the politics of everyday life represents an important change. However, there is a paradox in an increase of authority confined to the domestic sphere. Urban employment creates a physical division between work and household that is absent in the peasant economy. The husband's job removes him from the household, so that many responsibilities shift to the wife. She thereby gains authority, but also takes on added responsibilities that confine her even more firmly to the home. Burić and Zečević (1969, p. 241) point out that the more engaged a husband is in politics and career, the greater is his absence from home. While the wife gains authority within her traditional sphere, the husband gains more freedom to participate in the world outside. Because the domestic sphere is structurally inferior in power to the realm of public politics, gains in household authority that run contrary to women's increased participation in public arenas are pyrrhic victories.

Although the traditional sex typing of housework and child-care clearly dominates, variations in a pattern are significant as a basis for anticipating change. The Kragujevac study revealed a 10 percent minority of couples with egalitarian household relationships (Burić and Zečević 1969, p. 228), while slightly over half the Zagreb women doctors surveyed said that their husbands help with housework most of the time (Otto and Taylor 1973, p. 22). My own impression is that the youngest generation of husbands, socialized to expect women to have careers, are more flexible than their fathers about sharing in the tasks that have been traditionally associated with females. Trends toward a more flexible division of household labor would be important in lowering a major obstacle to women's participation in the traditionally male arenas outside the home.

Women's Place in Public Politics

The Yugoslav revolution established a legitimate place for women in public authority roles, as women partisans became civilian leaders along with their male comrades. The leadership today still includes many women from the revolutionary generation. However, while women in politics are not anomalous, they have never been more than a small minority of office holders. The dynamics of change have not been unidirectional, but involve continuing oppositions between public and domestic power centers. As a result of economic development, women have increased their proportion of the work force to nearly one-third (31.4 percent in 1971, cited by Burić 1972, p. 62). These economic roles in the public sphere have led to women's increased access to power within the domestic sphere. However, a concomitant increase in women's access to roles in the public power structure has not occurred. On the contrary, recent statistics reveal that the proportion of women economic and political leaders actually declined during the 1960s.

During the 1960s, the proportion of women in governmental posts at all levels declined from 15 percent in 1963 to only 7 percent in 1969. The proportion of female directors of large enterprises likewise declined from 1.3 percent to 0.6 percent between 1962 and 1968, while a fall from 2.1 percent to 1.5 percent occurred among directors of small enterprises (Burić 1972, pp. 65–67). Although women constituted 40 percent or more of employees in social institutions of all kinds, in 1970 they held less than 10 percent of the total directorships and held more than 10 percent of directorships in only three fields: health (12 percent), culture (14 percent), and social work (50 percent) (Burić 1972, p. 66). A lack of "qualified" candidates cannot be the reason for this low representation of women in executive positions, if education is the criterion, considering that from 1945–69 women received one-third of the university diplomas, 24 percent of the master's degrees, and 17 percent of the doctorates awarded (Burić 1972, p. 66).

Local-level politics in Užice replicate national patterns on a smaller scale. At the outbreak of World War II, the first anti-German resistance bands in the area included young women communists who were high school students, teachers, and textile workers. Many of these women were killed during the war, and are commemorated in various ways as part of the revolutionary tradition of the town. The textile mill, garment factory, and an elementary school in Užice are named after women partisan martyrs. A survey of Užice leaders conducted as part of my fieldwork shows that 17 percent of leadership during the early postwar years was composed of women, including offices at the highest regional levels (Denich 1976).[6] However, the proportion of women leaders had fallen to 8 percent in 1966, and none of these had high-level posts.

During my fieldwork in Užice, I frequently attended meetings of local political institutions, including the city council (*skupština opštine*), neighborhood assemblies (*zbor birača*), and Socialist Alliance local units. While women participated actively in all these organizations, they did so as a pronounced minority. Without an exact count, I would estimate retrospectively that the female presence at most meetings was about one-fifth. Women then in their mid- to late forties (judging by appearance), the age range of the partisan generation, often played a prominent part in the discussions. These women spoke with authority and received a respectful hearing. On some occasions, their remarks were the turning points in the course of debate. I particularly recall moments in very heated debates when such women made consensus-reaching statements that related the issues at hand to socialist principles. However, at no meeting that I attended did a woman preside.

Although women had been prominent earlier in Užice politics, the top offices in 1965–66 were all held by men, most of whom were then in their forties to mid-fifties. There were younger men in lower-level posts, but no younger women held offices and the young women delegates were generally silent at the meetings I attended. The partisan women held onto their beachhead in public politics, but it appeared that younger women were influenced by social conditions that retarded their advancement in public power arenas. These observations in Užice coincide with the national statistics showing that the gains made by women of the partisan generation were not perpetuated by younger women through the 1960s.

In addition to legislative and party positions similar, in their definition, to those in other parliamentary systems, the Yugoslav structure includes another level of unique institutions, the system of "workers' self-management," whereby the employees of each work organization are responsible for running it.[7] Elected councils of employees, headed by a "workers' council," are ultimately responsible for all decision making in the enterprise or institution. Individual employees vary greatly in their degree of involvement, from constant activity to total apathy. But even the most apolitical workers are drawn into some level of participation in periodic meetings of their work units, trade-union groups, and the collective as a whole. These meetings work out immediate problems of production, working conditions, and work relationships, in addition to implementing national policy changes. This structure of participatory democracy creates a direct link between job holding and decision making, and thereby provides one of the broadest bases of access into the sphere of public power to be found in contemporary industrial societies. Although women's participation in self-management councils is less than their part in the work force, it is significant that this most innovative aspect of the Yugoslav political system does include a higher female representation than do the traditional bodies. In industrial enterprises, where women are 26 percent of the work force, they make up 14 percent of workers' council members. In health, education, and welfare institutions, where women are 54 percent of the work force, they compose about one-third of the workers' councils in most fields, ranging from 22 percent in universities to 65 percent in social welfare. (All figures are cited by Burić 1972, pp. 68–69).

We may take a closer look at the impact of self-management in providing a link between work and politics in the public sphere through the experiences of women interviewed in Užice. Of the 32 women in my sample of rural-urban migrants with jobs, about one-third (11) had held at least one position in self-management bodies; five of these women were also members of the League of Communists. The others ranged from considerable interest in their work collectives to total apathy. The following illustrations will go from the least involved to the most active participants.

Of all my informants, uneducated women with unskilled jobs were the most alienated from politics. They tended to be poorly informed about the workings of the self-management system, and their participation was usually limited to attending compulsory meetings in the collective. In many cases, they professed too little knowledge to comment on the social problems in Užice or Yugoslavia, limiting themselves to comments about their own personal lives which, as we have seen, have not been easy. For example, in response to the question "Under what conditions would you permit the director alone to make a decision?," one unskilled woman answered: "I don't care what he does." Another, in a similar spirit, responded, "The director always decides alone. He doesn't ask anyone, especially me." Neither of these women volunteered an answer about the social problems of Užice or Yugoslavia, one of them explaining, "There are more literate people than me; let them answer." Neither of these women participated in discussions at self-management meetings. A third unskilled woman explained her lack of participation at meetings by saying, "I would have plenty to say, like every other worker, but I feel that I'm in no condition to do so." A fourth unskilled woman worker explained that she doesn't speak up because "When I begin to discuss, others criticize what I am trying to say."

However difficult it may be for uneducated women to gain sufficient self-confidence to participate in self-management politics, many with similar backgrounds did not show this kind of alienation from the system in which they found themselves. One cleaning woman, who is not active, still showed considerable awareness of the work place. In response to the question "What would you do if you became director of your enterprise?" she answered:

First I would settle affairs in the collective, because we have plenty of problems. Then I would do something to improve the pay of unskilled workers, so that it would be based on the amount of work we do, and not according to our skill level. However, I don't know what rights the director has, and can't say any more about this.

From her own experience, she described the electoral process, whereby members of the workers' council are chosen:

The workers' council and management board members are chosen by election. I know because there was recently a meeting of the collective called in which we nominated some colleagues to those bodies. Later they gave us ballots on which their names were listed, and we were supposed to vote for a particular number, less than the number nominated. I voted for those whom I know to be good workers and decision makers.

The answer has one inaccuracy, in that the management board is not elected directly by all employees, but indirectly by the workers' council. However, her statement gives us an otherwise accurate picture of the electoral process. It is important that she sees herself as voting for leaders she regards as "good workers and decision makers."

An unskilled textile worker, who is not active except for attending meetings of the collective or economic unit, did not hesitate to express her opinions in discussions:

I attend meetings of the collective because they deal mainly with questions important to us workers. I sometimes speak out when something isn't clear, or when something isn't all right. For example, we have to protest about our pay. At a recent meeting there was a discussion about a raise. We argued that all should get the same pay increase—the director and all workers—and that's what was decided.

This woman also had a ready answer for what she would do if she were director of her enterprise: "First I would settle the question of higher pay. In our enterprise, the norms are high and the hourly rates low, and we therefore earn little."

Other unskilled women workers had entered active participation in the self-management structure and been elected to positions in it. All of these women had completed fourth grade and were literate. One young garment worker explained how she became involved in enterprise political activity:

After struggling as a housemaid for a year after first coming to town, I saw that I should get a job in an enterprise and consider it like my own home. When I began work a year ago, I was immediately interested in activity. I began attending the youth organization meetings, as well as the regular meetings of the collective. I was also active on my job. The members of the workers' council nominated me for the union council in the enterprise, and I was elected. I participated in discussions. In the trade-union council, for example, I discussed the problem of how to increase work efficiency in changing to a seven-hour day, through more attention to the production norms. As long as I am single, I'll accept more responsibility, but I don't know whether I'll have enough time after I'm married.

An unskilled textile worker, who has held a number of positions in self-management and political organizations, explained how she became involved in activity: "I participate regularly in enterprise meetings and most often speak out on problems that concern the workers and the whole collective. That is how I distinguished my-self, and when it was seen that I gave an example in my job as well, I was nominated and elected to the workers' council."

A semiskilled garment worker, a member of the workers' council and president of the hygienic commission of her enterprise, commented:

I am generally interested in political and economic problems. From the time I started work, I have been interested in the enterprise. I am especially concerned about production. If the enterprise doesn't do well, then we workers can't do well. I would be interested in a position with greater responsibility, if elected. I might also want to become a Communist Party member—but I haven't yet given it much thought.

Another woman with aspirations for political involvement points out some of the difficulties; she was a white-collar worker with a secondary education, and was a member of the disciplinary court in her enterprise:

I am interested in the enterprise because it is mine, and it matters what happens. Sometimes I participate in the discussions. For example, I once spoke about work discipline. It seems to me that our workers are mistaken when they consider the directors alone to blame for failures. Very often, failure results from poor work discipline. The lack of time prevents me from planning any political activity; otherwise I would very gladly accept a position. I am a mother and can't do everything, because I need to get to work and get home and to study, and haven't time for anything more.

The interviews indicate that even many women workers with low education, recent migrants from peasant life, readily developed interest in the policy-making opportunities available in the self-management structures of their work organizations. A considerable number were interested in running for office and participating in the constant decision making entailed in running a socialist enterprise. However, political activism takes time beyond work hours for attending meetings and conferences. In opposition to the attraction of political activity are the family responsibilities that first claim their time and draw them back home after work.

The conflict between domestic and public spheres again looms large, and the discrepancy between male and female household obligations is manifested in the discrepancy between male and female participation in public politics.

Conclusion

Through employment, Yugoslavian women have gained a basis for autonomy as social persons. No longer dependent on men for physical survival, they have some measure of determination over their lives. In contrast to the peasant economy, industrialization has brought both sexes into the public sphere for productive work. But after work hours, the public/domestic dichotomy reappears in the allocation of the sexes into different spheres. Egalitarian trends in the households of working women indicate that, paradoxically, public economic roles have won women power within the domestic sphere, rather than in the public sphere. The importance of this change in familial relations cannot be disregarded. However, it does not alter the structural basis of inequality between the sexes inherent in public/domestic segregation, considering that each domestic module is necessarily subordinate to overarching public institutions. A gain in women's private authority that is matched by an actual decline in their public political participation—as documented in recent years in Yugoslavia—maintains inequality between the sexes.

In Yugoslavia, the definition of public issues reflects the small part played by women in setting policy. Important social problems involving the care of children and the maintenance of households are still relegated to the family, where women are bound to solve them. Thereby, women are also bound to the household and restrained from exercising their formal right to participate fully in public decision making. Revolutionary values emphasize the role of women in the public political sphere, but the exigencies of everyday life have maintained the cleavage between spheres and sexes. The division is reinforced by cultural definitions and psychological attitudes that enhance concepts of femininity and masculinity along lines that coincide with the public/domestic opposition. As long as a woman's evaluation as a person is based on performances that are antithetical to sharing in public decision making, she can ill afford to abandon the behaviors that give her a positive image. The price for being thus favorably evaluated is confinement to the sphere of lesser power and lesser privilege.

Some socialist revolutions have sought to reorganize family life as a necessary part of building a new society. In its early years, the Soviet revolutionary government legislated with a view to releasing women from the familial burdens that prevented their full entry into public life. However, these changes were later rescinded, and the sexes realigned within their traditional spheres (see Rowbotham 1972, pp. 134–69). Contemporary Chinese society has more consistently reorganized family life through such institutions as collectively organized childcare (see Rowbotham 1972, pp. 170–99; Sidel 1972). In Yugoslavia, there has been little direct intrusion by the state into family life. Amidst the extremely rapid changes involved in industrialization and urbanization, people have been free to reorganize their own personal lives and they have usually found very effective solutions to the problems involved. The resilience of family and kinship ties has been the major asset in enabling people to make drastic transitions with minimal personal disruption (see Denich 1970; Simic 1974). Insofar as these arrangements have developed around family relations, they have naturally tended to perpetuate traditional sex-role allocations. More direct governmental intervention into family life might have established a firmer basis for sexual equality, but there is no way of knowing what negative consequences might have resulted from undermining the vitality of self-generating interpersonal relations and social organization. It is tempting to speculate about paths not taken; but considering the unforeseeable effects of social engineering, it is questionable whether the directed reorganization of family life would have led to better overall results. It is more fruitful to speculate about the trends from this point on.

Because social changes are processes that unfold through conflict and discontinuity, there is no reason to assume that the present structural oppositions in Yugoslavia are permanently established. The discrepancies between women's status in the domestic and public spheres generate continual tensions. At present, these tensions are played out primarily in personal relations, but they create pressures for resolution of the sources of conflict that cannot be permanently contained within the household. The interest recently shown by Yugoslav women social scientists in the condition of women indicates a possible revival of an earlier revolutionary concern for sexual equality. As in the United States and Western Europe (see Mitchell 1971, pp. 19–66), conscious discontentment is greatest among the most-educated women with the highest professional status, to whom the discrepancies between the ideal and real loom largest. The potential exists for women to translate their private discontent into public issues, within the unique framework of the Yugoslav political structure. The degree of contradiction in the present situation of Yugoslav women may generate enough pressure to alter the structures that maintain the separate, unequal spheres of female and male power.

Notes

1. In the past, Chinese wives in a similar bind often resorted to suicide (Yang 1959).

2. There were 32 women among a sample of 200 rural-urban migrants. The original name of the town was Užice; Titovo (Tito's) was added in 1946 to honor the Yugoslav revolutionary leader. The town is still familiarly known as Užice, and the original name will be used in this paper as a matter of convenience.

3. This line of argument is developed from Boserup (1970) who gives a comparative view of women's role in traditional agriculture and the effects of urbanization upon their role in production.

4. Burić and Zečević (1969) found that recreation is the area of greatest marital discord among couples of all occupational categories, in that wives object to being left at home while their husbands go about town in the traditional manner.

5. A well-known example of this phenomenon is the tendency for peasant leaders to emerge from the most prosperous strata of the peasantry (see Wolf 1969).

6. This survey was based on the career biographies of 60 individuals then holding leading positions in Užice and 50 individuals who had moved from positions in Užice to functions in Belgrade. It was compiled from materials in the Historical Archive of Titovo Užice, with the assistance of Radoslav Poznanović.

7. For an overview of the self-management system, see Hunnius (1973). For a case study of self-management politics in two enterprises, see Adizes (1971).

References

Adizes, Ichak. 1971. *Industrial Democracy: Yugoslav Style.* New York: Free Press.

Boserup, Ester. 1970. *Woman's Role in Economic Development.* London: Allen and Unwin.

Burić, Olivera. 1972. "Položaj Žene u Sistemu Društvene Moći u Jugoslaviji" (Woman's Position in the System of Social Power in Yugoslavia). *Sociologija* 14:61–75.

——, and Zečević, Andjelka. 1969. *Porodični Život i Društveni Položaj Porodice* (Family Life and Social Position). Belgrade: Institut Društvenih Nauka.

Denich, Bette. 1970. "Migration and Network Manipulation in Yugoslavia." In R. Spencer, ed., *Migration and Anthropology,* pp. 133–48. Seattle: University of Washington Press.

—— 1974a. "Sex and Power in the Balkans." In M. Rosaldo and L. Lamphere, eds., *Woman, Culture, and Society,* pp. 243–62. Stanford: Stanford University Press.

—— 1974b. "Why Do Peasants Urbanize? A Yugoslavian Case Study." In A. LaRuffa et al., eds., *City and Peasant,* pp. 546–59. New York: Annals of the New York Academy of Sciences.

—— 1976. "Sources of Leadership in the Yugoslav Revolution: A Local-level Study." *Comparative Studies in Society and History* 18:64–84.

Denitch, Bogdan. 1976. *The Legitimation of a Revolution.* New Haven: Yale University Press.

Erlich, Vera. 1966. *Family in Transition: A Study of Three Hundred Yugoslav Villages.* Princeton, N.J.: Princeton University Press.

First-Dilić, Ruža. 1969. "Struktura Autoriteta u Seoskim Domaćinstvima" (The Authority Structure in Village Households). *Sociologija Sela* 23–24:53–60.

—— 1973. "Struktura Moći u Porodici Zaposlene Žene" (The Power Structure in the Employed Woman's Family). *Sociologija* 15:79–102.

Goldschmidt, Walter, and Evalyn J. Kunkel. 1971. "The Structure of the Peasant Family." *American Anthropologist* 73:1058–76.

Hunnius, Gerry. 1973. "Workers' Self-Management in Yugoslavia." In G. Hunnius et al., eds., *Workers' Control,* pp. 268–324. New York: Random House.

Leacock, Eleanor. 1972. Introduction to the 1972 edition of F. Engels, *Origin of the Family, Private Property, and the State.* New York: International Publishers.

League of Communists of Yugoslavia. 1974. *Ideological Foundations for Socialist Transformation of Education: Documents for the Tenth Congress.* Belgrade: Socialist Thought and Practice.

Mitchell, Juliet. 1971. *Woman's Estate.* New York: Random House.

Otto, Barbara, and Maida Taylor. 1973. "Profile of Women in Medicine in Yugoslavia." Mimeographed.

Rosaldo, Michelle Z. 1974. "Woman, Culture, and Society: A Theoretical Overview." In M. Rosaldo and L. Lamphere, eds., *Woman, Culture, and Society,* pp. 17–42. Stanford: Stanford University Press.

Rowbotham, Sheila. 1972. *Woman, Resistance, and Revolution.* New York: Random House.

Sidel, Ruth. 1972. *Women and Child Care in China.* Baltimore: Penguin.

Simic, Andrei. 1974. "Urbanization and Cultural Processes in Yugoslavia." *Anthropological Quarterly* 47:211–27.

Wolf, Eric. 1969. *Peasant Wars of the Twentieth Century.* New York: Harper and Row.

Yang, C. K. 1959. *The Chinese Family in the Communist Revolution.* Cambridge, Mass.: Harvard University Press.

ALICE SCHLEGEL

Male and Female

11

in Hopi
Thought
and Action

WHEN TRADITIONAL HOPI women are asked "Who are more important, women or men," a common reply is "We are, because we are the mothers," with the qualification that men are important, too, as the messengers to the gods.

This paper will examine some of the assumptions that have been made about female reproduction, separation of the sexes, and the position of women. In recently published literature on female status, the universally secondary position of women in society has been asserted, and it has been accounted for by women's role in bearing and rearing children (Chodorow 1974; Ortner 1974; Rosaldo 1974). It is furthermore implied that this secondary position becomes one of subordination when the sexes operate within separate domains, the public for men and the domestic for women (Rosaldo 1974, pp. 39–40). These assertions are contradicted by data from traditional Hopi society, where the sexes are divided into two domains of action, and women's role in

The data for this paper were collected on Third Mesa, primarily from older men and women. Unless otherwise indicated, the time period under examination is the late nineteenth and early twentieth centuries. Support for fieldwork came from the National Institute of Mental Health and is thankfully acknowledged. Statements are quoted as given by individual Hopi in English. I am grateful to Fred Eggan for commenting on this paper, although our positions on the predatory character of extramarital sex and the deference paid to the *mö'wi* differ.

the reproduction and maintenance of life is the conscious justification for the position of equality they enjoy.

We shall examine the separation of activity between the domestic organization of the lineage and household, under the control of a female head, and the religious and political organization
of the village, under the control of male community leaders. We
shall also note the level of the clan, midway between household
and community, in which authority is shared between a brother
and sister pair. We shall look at the Hopi concept of sexual interdependence—between male and female actors in the social
scene and between principles of maleness and femaleness in
ideology.

The key word here, I believe, is *balance*. Many societies
operate with underlying concepts of ideological dualism. A widespread form of dualism either focuses upon or includes male-
female relationships. Such notions are found both in tribal societies, such as Dogon (Griaule 1965), Trio (Rivière 1969), and Tewa
(Ortiz 1969), and in literate civilizations such as China, where *yin-
yang* is a core symbol for a range of binary oppositions. But dualism does not necessitate balance, or equality between the parts. It
would require a lengthy excursion into Hopi metaphysics and cos-
mology to treat adequately the concept of balance as applied to
man's nature and the universe, and that is beyond the scope of
this paper. But the Hopi relationship of equality between the
sexes, each with its own nature and social roles, will be examined
in this light.

Domestic Life

The Women in the Household

When a Hopi child is born, it is assured of a place within the
matrilocal household and the matrilineal clan. If it is a boy, he will
become a companion and helper to his father, who will teach him
to farm, hunt, and herd. He is a potential heir to any of the re-

ligious-political positions held by his "uncles," or mothers' brothers. If it is a girl, she is welcomed as a source of continuity of the household and the clan. When she grows up, she or one of her sisters will inherit her mother's house and be responsible for the maintenance of her aged parents. As a mother and sister, she will have responsibility for many of the ceremonial objects used by her sons and brothers. She will "feed" the sacred masks by sprinkling them with cornmeal, thus assuring continual life and power to these necessary features of certain ritual performances. When asked, the Hopi insist that they wish for sons and daughters equally; however, women state that "you raise up a daughter for yourself, but you raise up a son for somebody else." Daughters remain at home, whereas sons are sent out upon marriage to become the providers and progenitors in the households of other women.

When a girl marries, she brings her husband into her household to work under the direction of her father and the ultimate authority of her mother. If she is not the heiress to the house, her husband will build her a house of her own, adjacent to or near her mother's house. Although he builds the house, it belongs to her and she can request him to leave at any time. Furthermore, all household goods, except the personal property of men, belong to her. Her husband farms fields assigned to her through her clan, and when the produce is brought in and she has formally thanked him, it is hers to allocate or dispose of as she sees fit. Of course, her husband is free to leave and move in with another woman or return to the house of his mother or sister, but in any event he lives in a house controlled by a female head. He moves into his wife's house as a stranger, and it is only after he has proven his worth through providing for her family that he earns a position of respect within it. The Hopi recognize this by saying that "a man's place is outside the house." All the long hours of labor in this dry and uncertain climate go to benefit a household and clan over which he has no authority beyond the authority he exerts over his young children, and his domestic satisfaction lies in the love and respect he earns as a good father and provider.

As might be expected, young men are none too eager to marry. To a woman, however, marriage is essential, as she needs a provider for herself and her children. While illegitimate children are not looked down upon, they are at a disadvantage in that they have no father to provide for them. A man who never married the mother of his child, or who has left her, is expected to contribute to his child's support, but rarely does so to the extent of fathers living in the home. A woman can turn to her brothers for some help, but this is usually burdensome for these men who have enough to do just taking care of their own families.

As a girl matures, she is under parental pressure to bring a husband into the house, for her father is eager for the help a son-in-law can give. In addition, her marriage is necessary for her life in the Afterworld: the wedding robes that her husband's male relatives weave for her become her shroud and the vehicle by which her spirit is transported into the world of the dead.

The boy, however, is under no such pressures. He enjoys his relatively carefree life as a young bachelor and is somewhat reluctant to take on the heavy responsibilities of marriage. Marriages are normally not arranged, and the burden of finding a spouse falls mainly upon the girl. Girls initiate a marriage by making the proposal, which may or may not be accepted. The transfer of labor and loyalty to the wife's household is symbolized by a ceremonial prestation of cornmeal to the groom's household, conceptualized by the Hopi as "paying for him," and by the short period of groom service that the bride performs by grinding corn and cooking for her husband's household while her wedding robes are being woven.[1] Once the wedding rituals are completed, the groom moves into the bride's house and "goes over to her side." Few men beyond their mid-twenties remain bachelors in spite of reluctance to marry; for the good Hopi is one who accepts the heavy duties of community responsibility, and fatherhood, highly valued by the Hopi, is one of the ways a man can contribute to the village.

Unlike the woman, the Hopi man has his responsibilities divided between two social units. To the household of his wife he owes his labor and his protectiveness as a father and a husband. However, he also owes loyalty to his natal household and clan. When clan matters arise, such as the assignment of clan lands or clan participation in ceremonies, male clan members are expected to take part. If a man holds a religious-political position, inherited through the clan, he must train one of his young clan mates, usually his sister's son, to succeed him. To a man who holds such a position, life is doubly busy—not only must he fulfill his domestic duties but he must also spend a great deal of time involved in ceremonial activities. Most of these leaders are middle-aged and old men, who are likely to have one or more sons-in-law in the house to help with farming and herding.

Women have no such potential conflict of loyalties. Once they have succeeded in marrying and bearing children, particularly daughters, they are established as responsible adults in the eyes of the clan and the community. They have produced life, and their role lies in the maintenance of physical life through feeding their families and others, and spiritual life through feeding the sacred objects. Most of this activity goes to benefit their own house and clan. Toward their husbands' natal house and clan they owe little beyond some contributions of food during periods of ceremonial activity, and a relationship of respect exists between them. Their greatest duties to households other than their own revolve around their roles as grandmothers and "aunts," or father's sisters, to the children of their sons and brothers, with whom they have an amiable joking relationship.

Hopi women appear to be in an enviable position when compared to women in male-dominant societies. Indeed, when the system works as it is designed to, these women are self-assured and confident of their place in the world. However, their very strength is also the source of their vulnerability. While they can make the final household decisions, they are dependent upon those men who have married into the house. They must have a husband or a son-in-law to provide for them. Fathers grow old and unable to work, brothers are busy with their own families, and sons marry and move out. It is critical for a woman to get and keep a husband, while men always have the alternative of moving in with their mothers or sisters. If a woman and her husband separate, her relatives are likely to urge her to forget the quarrel and take him back, saying: "One of your own people might be willing to plant for you, but only a husband will give you meat and clothes" (Forde 1931, p. 382). The Hopi emphasize the need for tact in marital relations, for they believe that love and the willing acceptance of responsibility cement the marital bonds. Even infidelity, said to be the most common cause of marital trouble, should be overlooked if possible, or at least dealt with by appealing to the errant partner's sense of marital and parental responsibility.[2]

The Woman and Her Male Kin

A woman is not under the authority of her husband, nor is she under the authority of her brother or mother's brother, as is the case in some other matrilineal societies (Schlegel 1972). It is true that an uncle (mother's brother) must be listened to with respect, and children are expected to obey him; and if parents are having difficulty with a recalcitrant child, the uncle will be called in to remonstrate or ultimately to punish him or her. Nevertheless, upon reaching adulthood the individual becomes his own master, and the uncle can only advise and remonstrate. While uncles are treated respectfully, this respect is tempered with a good deal of humor, and there is considerable reciprocal teasing and mild joking. The lack of deference toward the uncle is illustrated by a joking situation I observed. At the wedding feast for her "son," actually a sister's son, a woman became annoyed at her uncle for talking about and praising another recent bride, when the focus of attention should have been the present bride. When he went outside, this woman ran after him with scissors in hand and snipped off some of his long hair, much to his chagrin and the amusement of the onlookers. I asked her why she did this, and she replied: "He talked about that other bride too much."

Brothers and sisters are equals; if the brother has the right to criticize or advise his sister, so has she the right to do the same to him. Furthermore, although it is acceptable for a man to move into his sister's house upon separation from his wife, she can always refuse his request if she feels justified in doing so. In one case, the sister refused because she did not approve of her brother's reasons for leaving his wife (Nagata 1970, pp. 280–81).

In general, women are thought of as more emotional and headstrong than men, and therefore women are believed to be in need of advising by men more than men are by women. The role of adviser to a woman generally falls upon her close male kin—father, mother's brother, and brother. Husbands are reluctant to advise wives, and they should do it tactfully, as wives are thought likely to take offense. However, women do not hesitate to speak out and criticize or advise their fathers, uncles, and brothers if they feel the need to do so. They may point out to the kinsman that he is not behaving in proper fashion and thereby is not setting a good example for their own conduct. (Men may say the same to their fathers and uncles.) Older people of both sexes should be listened to respectfully by younger men and women, but they must earn this respect through their own good behavior.

Unlike many matrilineal societies, the mother's brother is not the kinsman who receives the greatest respect in this society. Rather, it is the *mö'wi,* or female in-law, the wife of a son, brother, or mother's brother. She is both addressed and referred to by this term, which connotes respect and deference, and there is the belief that using her name might bring harm to the one who does so. At the very least, using her name would be disrespectful. For no other status, kinship or otherwise, is the use of the name prohibited. The *mö'wi* is always treated with special courtesy by all those who address her husband as "son," "brother," or "uncle." The explanation given for this respect is that "she cooks for us [while her wedding robes are being woven] and brings food when she comes to visit." This is but one example of the high value placed upon women as feeders.

Community Life

While most female authority is exerted within the sphere of household activities, women are not barred from participation in or influence over community activities. By withholding support they can informally exert the power of the veto (for an example, see below), although they rarely do so; for most of the community activities engaged in by men are for the benefit of women as much as for the benefit of men.

While household and community operate to a large degree as two separate areas of activity, they are not conceived of by the Hopi as two separate domains. The model of the house underlies the conception of the village; so to understand community authority and responsibility, one must understand the transformations of the concept of the house.

The house is, above all, the actual or symbolic structure that shelters the individual, that places and identifies him, and within which he is safe, whether in this life or the Afterworld. All creatures have houses, and to be without a house, as the spirit of the deceased is during his passage from the world of the living to the world of the dead, is to be in a state of danger to oneself and possibly others.

Each Hopi has a symbolic house, drawn for him when he is a newborn infant. One of the first actions of the Mudhead Clowns upon entrance into the plaza during ceremonial dances is to draw themselves a house upon the ground, for they are representing newly emerged beings.

The house of the family and matrilineage is the actual structure into which every Hopi is born and Hopi men marry. These are places for family privacy, and any adult caught spying into another house is believed to be up to no good, probably a witch looking at his or her victim. It is within these houses that women exert authority and men take a secondary place, as we have seen.

Each clan also has a house, one that is both actual and symbolic. It is actual in that it is the house belonging to the leading lineage of the clan, the lineage to which the Clan Mother and her brother the Clan "Big Uncle" belong. It is in this house that clan-owned ceremonial property is stored, and it is a duty of the Clan Mother to care for it. We can also think of the Clan House as symbolic, as the focal point of the entire clan under the joint leadership of a brother and sister pair. It is in the clan house in this sense that men and women share authority, in their roles as Mother and Big Uncle.

Finally, the entire village is conceived of metaphorically as a house: the term for village chief is *kikmongwi,* or leader of the house, the stem for house being *ki* and the word for leader being *mongwi.* The *kikmongwi* is addressed by all the villagers as "father," and his wife is addressed as "mother." It is at this level that authority over the "house" lies in male hands, the *kikmongwi* and his council. While an authority, the *kikmongwi* is by no means authoritarian; rather, like a father, his principal duty is to care for his children so that they may thrive. The father does this by providing food and clothing for them; the *kikmongwi* does this by acting as principal communicant with the rain-bringing, life-giving supernatural beings. It is through his prayers, coming from a pure heart and an untroubled mind, that the forces of blessing are released.

Women in Community Political Activity

While the political system can be studied as a structure of formal authority, it can also be examined as the process by which decisions are made that affect community life, and this must include noninstitutionalized power and influence as well as authority. This point of view is the more appropriate for the Hopi political system, in which authority over community action is dispersed rather than concentrated and decisions are appropriately arrived at by consensus rather than by decree. (For a discussion of the diffuseness of political leadership, see Titiev 1944, ch. 5.)

The Hopi do have a village chief, the *kikmongwi,* but his principal role is to maintain harmony between the village and the spiritual world. His council, composed of men who inherit their positions through their clans (having been selected and trained by the previous incumbent), serves more as an advisory group than as a legislative or judicial body. The focus of community life is the ceremonial system, and the individual ceremonies are under the control of *mongwi,* or leaders, who inherit their positions through their clans. (Some of these *mongwi* are on the council.) While some clans are more important than others, in that they "own" the more important ceremonies, there is no rigid hierarchy. As we have seen in the discussion of domestic life, authority is not a principle of social interaction of kin; similarly, it is not a principle of social interaction within the community. The principles that are discussed by the Hopi and observable in action are the acceptance of duty and cooperation toward common goals. Whatever authority is exerted by community leaders is directed at the coordination of effort, not at enforcement of unilateral decisions. Resolution of conflicts is essentially a private matter between the parties involved; and conflicts that cannot be handled privately either break the village apart, as happened when Oraibi split in 1906, or simply persist for years or even generations.

To say, therefore, that women have no positions in the formal authority structure is to say very little.[3] As the mothers, sisters, and wives of men who make community decisions, the influence of women cannot be overestimated. These women, after all, control the houses that the men live in; and the man's position in the home is to a large extent dependent upon his relationship to its female head. Women do not hesitate to speak their minds, whether in the privacy of the home to male kin and their visitors or in public meetings. One example illustrates what is in effect the veto power of women: in one village the chief and his sister were divided over a political issue concerning the village, and she refused to play her role in the Soyal ceremony, led by the chief, until he capitulated. As Hopi men readily admit, women usually get their way.

Each village is politically autonomous, and alliances with other Hopi villages or with communities from other tribes exist only on an *ad hoc* basis. Trade is conducted between individuals; women do not generally go on trading parties, but they participate actively in any exchanges that occur when outsiders come into the village for that purpose. They also control any proceeds gained from trade goods, such as corn products or pottery, that they have processed or manufactured.

The one community activity from which women were excluded in earlier times, before the *pax Americana,* was warfare. For both practical and ideological reasons, war was a male activity. However, if a raid occurred when men were away on long-distance hunts, the women of necessity helped defend the village and the nearby fields. One of the favorite legendary figures in Oraibi is Hehe'wuhti, or Warrior Woman, who was in the process of putting up her hair when the village was attacked. She led the women's defense with her hair up on one side, flowing down on the other, and thus is she portrayed.

Women in Community Ceremonial Activity

The Hopi have a complex ceremonial system, and it is the cycle of ceremonies that provides the rhythm of the yearly round. All children are initiated into the Kachina Society sometime between the ages of five and ten, after which they can take part in activities surrounding the kachina dances,[4] although only men actually dance as both male and female kachinas. In addition, some boys and girls are initiated at this time into the Powamu Society, which has the responsibility of caring for the kachinas.

In their late teens or early twenties, all men are initiated into one of the four men's fraternities: Wuwucim and Tao, which have a benevolent character concerned with reproduction and agriculture, and Al and Kwan, which have a fiercer character concerned with hunting (Al) and war (Kwan).

The ceremonial cycle contains four great ceremonies of village-wide involvement and some lesser ones put on by specific ceremonial groups. With the exception of the women's societies, control of all ceremonies is in the hands of male ceremonial leaders and most of the participants are men. Nevertheless, women play a vital role in ceremonial life. They grind the sacred cornmeal, the symbol of natural and spiritual life, that is a necessary ingredient in almost all ceremonies. When masked dances are held, the dancers are sprinkled with cornmeal by female members of the Powamu Society. Women provide the food that feeds the participants; in some of the ceremonies, this is distributed among onlookers, and this feeding is highly valued. Women as well as men may sponsor a kachina dance by providing, with the aid of their male and female relatives, the large quantity of food for the dancers to eat and to distribute to the audience. On such dance days the sponsor is said to "stand above the *kikmongwi.*"

Women's Ceremonies

While most of the ceremonial societies are controlled by men, although they may have women members, there are three women's societies—Marau, Lakon, and Oaqül. These are optional: a woman need not enter any, or she can join any or all of them, although most women who belong to any belong only to one. Initiation can occur at any age, but most join as children or young girls or are brought in as infants by their mothers or other female kin. Each women's society has several male members as well, who act as assistants to the head priestess and make the *pahos*, or prayer sticks, required by the ceremonies. Like other societies, each women's society is "owned" by a clan, and the chief priestess and her male assistants belong to the owning clan.

The women's societies hold their major public ceremonies in the fall, after the termination of the men's portion of the ceremonial cycle in late summer.[5] All of them last for nine days, although in Hopi thinking they are eight-day ceremonies, as the first day is considered to be the last day of the preceding time of preparation rather than part of the ceremony itself. The major public performances are held on the last day. Most of the ceremonial activity takes place in a *kiva,* or ceremonial building, borrowed from the men who use it daily.[6] The chief priestesses move in for the duration of the ceremony, with other members spending as much time there as they can spare from their household duties.

While each of the women's societies has its own ritual and

symbols, there are certain common elements. All include some representation of Muingwa, the god of germination and the protector of all wild and domestic plants. All use corn, actual or depicted, as the major ritual element. (It is a major ritual element in most other ceremonies as well.) All initiate new members by placing them inside a kind of hoop made of yucca, raising and lowering it four times to the accompaniment of prayers and blessings. The symbolism of birth is very clear.[7] In all the dances, the women form a semicircle with their backs to the spectators, while various activities occur within the circle. This is in contrast to the men's dances in which the dancers form straight lines. In the women's dances, unlike the men's dances, only the participants with special roles are dressed in costume, while the dancers in the semicircle wear traditional Hopi dress.

The most complex of these ceremonies is Marau, and it is the one with the most overtones of the male portion of the ceremonial cycle. Marau women are said to be "sisters" to the men of Wuwucim (and perhaps Tao), and there is much good-natured and bawdy bantering between these "siblings" at the time of the Marau dances. Three nights of burlesque plaza performances are included in the Marau ceremony, with women mocking the men's kachina dances and singing obscene or humorous songs about their "brothers."

The Marau ceremony itself contains elements that bring to mind elements of Wuwucim, the great winter ceremony of the four fraternities. (It takes its name from the Wuwucim Society, the largest of the fraternities.) As in Wuwucim, offerings are made to all the dead, and departed members of the society are called back to the ceremony. In the plaza performance on the last day, elements are included that seem to reflect some of the basic features of Wuwucim. After the dancers have formed their circle and begun dancing, two pairs of women in short men's kilts and headdresses come toward the circle. These are called *Marautaka,* or "Marau men." The first pair hold bows and arrows, and as they proceed they shoot the arrows into bundles of vines that they throw before them. These arrows are spoken of as "lightning arrows," and they symbolize fertilization, as lightning is thought to fertilize plants. Thus, they exhibit the benevolent, life-giving character of Wuwucim and Tao fraternities. However, by shooting arrows these women are also performing acts characteristic of hunting and warfare, related to the nature of the Al and Kwan fraternities. That this shooting has to do with more than germination is indicated by the fact that after the ceremony the arrows are deposited at the shrine of the war gods. The arrows, then, are a key symbol of two major, and contradictory, principles of Hopi relationship to their world—benevolence and predation. In the Wuwucim ceremony these principles are separated by allocating them differentially to two pairs of fraternities. In Marau, they are brought together.

The second pair of major performers carry long poles and rings wrapped in old buckskin, which is said to have come from the clothing of enemies slain long ago. As they proceed, they toss the rings to the ground and throw the poles at them. These poles bring to mind the lances carried by the Kwan society, and the association with enemies and the clothing of the dead parallel aspects of the Kwan society rituals. Thus, Marau seems to unite into a single set of rituals those rituals, and the principles underlying them, performed separately by men's groups during Wuwucim. It seems to be a condensation and transformation of the major symbolic elements of the men's ceremony.

Lakon and Oaqül are very much alike. They are both called basket dances because at the termination of each dance set in the major public performance, decorated baskets are thrown to the spectators. Men in the audience try to get them, shouting, pushing other men aside, and even grabbing them from each other's hands. Women and children, wisely, stand to the rear. At the end of the grabbing, both men and baskets are likely to emerge somewhat battered. It is said that all this aids men in their hunting, for the shouting attracts the curious deer and brings them close to the village.

There are symbolic and ritual features of Lakon that relate to hunting. Primary among these is the "sibling" relationship between Lakon woman and AI (and possibly Kwan) men. Here again, as in Marau, male and female elements are brought together. This is most vividly depicted in the headdress worn by the two central performers in the Lakon dance, which has a bunch of feathers attached to the right side and a horn protruding from the left. These elements have been interpreted by one Hopi as representing masculinity (the horn) and femininity (the feathers as a replacement for flowers) (Titiev 1972, pp. 99–100, 293). There is a subtle relationship between women and game animals, especially antelopes (the major type of hunted game), that crops up in various rituals and even in jokes about extramarital sexual adventures: men talk about "hunting for two-legged deer." Outside of marriage, males are believed to be the sexual aggressors, and the predatory nature of male sexuality is revealed in the notion that a woman should be "paid" with a gift if she acquiesces. This is not prostitution but rather reflects the idea that one should give something in return for whatever has been taken.

Lakon and Oaqül seem to be harvest festivals as well, for effigies or other representations of Muingwa form an important element in the private kiva rituals, and seeds are used as a part of the altars in the kivas. Decorated baskets, when not adorning the walls, are used for prestations of food at weddings and during Powamu, the spring festival of germination, so their use in these ceremonies seems to emphasize the feminine role of corn grinder and feeder. Oaqül, a recent introduction, is not so well integrated into the system as are the other two ceremonies.

The female portion of the ceremonial cycle, then, has a double role in the cycle. First, it emphasizes the distinctiveness of women by bringing in elements, such as baskets, that are specific to female activities. The birth-giving nature of the act of initiation is the most dramatic of these elements. Second, by incorporating, uniting, and transforming major elements that appear in male ceremonies, it transmits the message that women, like men, contribute to the Hopi community and universe. Men and women are separate and have distinctive functions and even characters, but they are both part of the total Hopi world and they work together for common goals. Through the women's ceremonies, the necessary interdependence of male and female is expressed.

Male and Female in Hopi Ideology

If we consider the women's ceremonies discussed above within the context of the total ceremonial cycle, particularly in relation to the men's ceremonies that immediately precede and follow them, we gain some insight into the way that male and female principles are conceptualized by the Hopi.

The major cycle, involving almost total village participation, ends in July with Niman, or the Home Dance. The kachinas, who made their first appearance shortly before Soyal in December, go after this dance to their home in the San Francisco Peaks, the sacred mountains to the southwest of the Hopi villages. In August, preceding the women's portion of the cycle, two men's ceremonies are held in alternate years. These are the Snake-Antelope Ceremony, conducted by the Snake and Antelope Societies, and the Flute Ceremony, conducted by the Flute Societies. They involve only the members of these societies and the clans that "own" them. These ceremonies can be thought of as complementary to one another, representing the two contradictory aspects of the masculine principle, benevolence and predation.[8]

The Flute Ceremony is replete with symbols of plant reproduction and the elements that foster it, such as water and the sun. This, I believe, is expressive of the male role as the germinator. As the farmer to his fields, the husband and father to his wife and children, the kikmongwi to his village, and the Great Spirit to his people, the male is needed to activate and care for life. In contrast, the Snake-Antelope Ceremony represents the predatory nature of males, who must also kill if life is to be maintained. Snake dancers wear war costume and refer to the snakes that they handle as "warriors." According to information given to Stephen (1936, p. 714) in 1843, the Snake Society members were the actual warriors in olden times, while the Antelopes were the old men who stayed home praying in the kivas for success. The duality of masculinity is represented in these two ceremonies, as it is represented in the two pairs of men's fraternities, Wuwucim and Tao, and Al and Kwan.

The Lakon ceremony, which is the first of the women's ceremonies, can be regarded as representing the different natures of male and female. Females are related to the elements that grow out of Mother Earth—edible plants in their natural form or as a medium of exchange, symbolized by baskets, and game animals. Males stand to females both as the farmer stands to his crops, a benevolent and protective relationship, and as the hunter stands to game animals. While this latter relationship is most obviously predatory, it contains an element of benevolence as well; for a hunter performs rituals that placate the dead animal by sending its spirit back to the animal world and thereby assuring the perpetuation of animal life. Men must activate the life force and they must protect it, but in protecting it they must also kill, both animals for food and enemies for safety. Women, however, do not partake of this dual role of life givers and life destroyers: their single nature is to give and keep life.

The Marau ceremony, which follows Lakon, can be regarded as the female counterpart to Wuwucim, as we have discussed above. The burlesque elements so prominent in this ceremony, which occur to a lesser degree in the Wuwucim ceremony, can be regarded as signifying the tension underlying the ambiguous relationship between men and women. On the one hand they are separate and have different characters; on the other they are the same, as members of the moral in contrast to the natural and supernatural worlds. That this joking is related to men and women as males and females is shown by the explicitly sexual nature of the songs and jokes exchanged and the vivid depictions of genitals used in the joking portions of the ceremonies. Wuwucim, the first ceremony in the male cycle, takes place in November.

The last of the women's ceremonies to be held is Oaqül, which is similar to Lakon. It seems to be the least important of the women's ceremonies and restates the message transmitted in Lakon.

The great cycle, involving four major community ceremonies plus a number of kachina dances, begins with Wuwucim and ends with Niman. This cycle expresses Hopi beliefs about the natural and social world and the progress of the Hopi people through time. The little cycle, which takes place between Niman and Wuwucim, consists of men's and women's society performances and transmits different messages. Taken all together, it is in part a symbolic statement about the nature of male and female and their roles in social life. It contrasts the double nature of men with the single nature of women. If I am correct in considering Marau to be a feminine transformation of Wuwucim, then this ceremony brings together the duality into an expression of unity.

The Female as the Source of Life

As the opening sentence of this paper indicates, Hopi women perceive their importance as lying in their reproductive role, and a good part of the role of men is to protect the women so that they can fulfill this role. When they act as guardians of the women and advisers to them, they are making it possible for women to have the physical and spiritual safety required if children, and the Hopi people, are to thrive. Health and life itself depend upon keeping harmony with other people and the spirit beings, and a troubled mind makes it impossible for a woman to care for herself and her children properly. If a woman is disturbed, she and her children are in danger.

Societal maintenance through the production and perpetuation of life is an important goal of any society, but it may become secondary if the immediate need of the society is focused around warfare or other specifically male activities. For the Hopi, who consider the taking of life in hunting and warfare a necessary evil, warfare is played down; productivity is the major social goal.[9] When the Hopi dance, they say that they are praying for rain; but this has to be understood not only realistically, as a desperate need in this dry climate, but also metaphorically. Rain, which the men induce through their harmonious relation with the spirit world, is a major symbol for the power that activates life. This power can also be dangerous—the lightning that fertilizes the fields can also kill, or torrential rains can wash away the young plants. The other major symbol of life activation, the sun, is potentially dangerous as well, for it can burn the delicate plants unless they receive the rain. So, the task of men is to control the life-activating force and permit it to operate beneficently through the bodies of women and within Mother Earth. Both sexes fulfill their necessary tasks within the natural and spiritual domains of promoting life.

The woman as the source of life itself is expressed by the feminine nature of corn, the dominant symbol of life and an ingredient in almost all ritual activity. Each newborn infant is given a perfect ear of corn, its Corn Mother, which will protect it as the symbolic house drawn for the infant protects it. It is not surprising that the god of plants, including corn, is a male, Muingwa, for it is a masculine duty to care for corn and all female life.

The life-giving nature of women is encapsulated in one of the Hopi witchcraft beliefs. In order to gain worldly power, a person bargains away his life, or "heart." In order to survive, he or she must magically steal the hearts of others, thus killing them. Children, being young and pure of heart, are the favored victims. It is said that the heart of a boy will give the witch four more years of life. The heart of a girl, however, will allow him or her to live eight more years.

Conclusion

We have examined some of the features of social organization and the ideological system that are related to the high evaluation of women among the Hopi and the equality they enjoy with men. In this integrated network of activities and beliefs, the social and subsistence roles of men and women form a model for the beliefs about masculinity and femininity. In turn, these beliefs provide the sense of "rightness" with which the Hopi perform their domestic and community activities. At every point along the path through life, traditional Hopi look to their beliefs to guide and justify their daily conduct, and the way in which they perform their daily activities influences their relationship with the spiritual world. When he tends his plants, or when he fulfills his marital and paternal duties, a Hopi man is not only performing subsistence and social activities but he is contributing to the maintenance of life as well; and his contribution takes on a sacred quality that permits him to stand in good relation to the spiritual world. When a Hopi woman grinds corn, she does so with the knowledge that she is providing food for her children and the people, and the very substance she handles is the sacred element of life. Corn grinding should not be regarded as the onerous and time-consuming task it would appear to be; rather, it is a sacred duty of women, to be done with a pure heart and untroubled mind. Women sing corn-grinding songs as they work to lighten the task and express its life-giving contribution.

Male and female are interdependent and equally important principles of Hopi social life and ideology. These principles are complementary rather than similar. The female sphere of activity is the household, and the male sphere of activity is the community. Men and women control different portions of the ceremonial cycle. Each sex has its own tasks—only men hunt, only women grind corn—although both may come together in caring for the fields or herds, even though this is primarily the duty of men. But the dichotomy of masculine and feminine that separates the sexes is bridged in their necessary interdependence at each point in the social and ideological systems. The separation of the sexes does not cause the subordination of one and superordination of the other; rather, it permits each sex to fulfill its necessary and equally valued role in the maintenance of the society. Where the ideological focus of a culture is life, and both sexes are believed to be equally necessary to the promotion of life, devaluation of either sex is unlikely.

The direction Hopi society is taking today with regard to female equality is not clear. There are three factors to consider here: the introduction of a cash economy, demographic change, and new attitudes toward fertility.

Around the turn of this century, when the Hopi economy began to make its transformation into a cash economy, money was handled just as other household goods were handled. Men were expected to turn over their earnings to their wives, and women controlled the family purse. In recent times, some men have become reluctant to follow this pattern. They are beginning to regard earned cash as their own property, just as they have traditionally regarded their sheep or cattle herds as their own property to allocate or dispose of as they wished.[10] As modern cinder-block housing, which is very expensive in Hopi terms, replaces the old hand-constructed stone houses, there is some reluctance on the part of the husbands who paid for these houses to leave them to their wives in cases of divorce. A former judge of the Hopi Tribal Court told me about litigation over this matter. The decision in this case was to give the house to the woman, the decision being justified by an appeal to tradition.

On the other hand, women are entering the cash economy in increasingly large numbers too, both as single women and as working wives. If they no longer spend the many hours grinding corn, using machine-ground meal instead, they still can contribute economically to the family by bringing in extra money.

The demographic change that could have an impact on the economic relation between men and women is the increase in females over males. From the cessation of warfare by 1870 to World War II, the sex ratio seems to have favored men, the probable cause being maternal mortality. Since World War II, owing to improved health care and the increasing death rate of men in car accidents, the sex ratio has begun to favor women (Stephen J. Kunitz, personal communication). This means, at the least, that there will be more widows and divorcées than in former times. (There is no certainty that the ratio of never-married women will go up: if the Hopi follow their traditional pattern of not infrequent divorce and remarriage, it may still be that almost every woman will have been married at least once.) Thus, these women will have to support themselves and their children, if they have any, and they are likely to turn to wage work to do so. Therefore, a shift to a cash economy will not necessarily entail greater economic dependence on men.

The new attitude toward fertility favors small families. One still sees families of seven or more children, but many women in their twenties are reporting the desire for two or three children as the ideal number. Birth-control methods are widely accepted. The high evaluation of fecundity is being replaced by a new emphasis on education and a higher standard of living. Even in earlier times, fecundity was valued only if the family had the means to support the children.

The changes in subsistence and domestic activities of men and women are affecting the nature of male-female interaction. The pull is away from separation and complementarity and toward similarity. The jobs available on the reservation are provided primarily by the United States government and are sex-linked in the manner typical of the Anglo world, with secretarial and clerical personnel mainly female and administrative personnel mainly male. Road work, an important source of local income, is done entirely by men. However, in the marriage in which both partners work, husband and wife are increasingly contributing equally and are providing like goods—cash—to the family, and both define themselves as much by their outside occupations as by their role in the home. In this sense, the roles of men and women are becoming more similar, and necessary interdependence is decreasing.

It is impossible to predict at this point whether female equality will be retained by the Hopi. As I have indicated, the shift toward greater participation in the United States economic system does not necessarily entail the economic subordination of women. So far, women have participated very little in the Tribal Council or the Tribal Court, the governing bodies set up under guidance from the Bureau of Indian Affairs as a system separate from the traditional village chief and his council.[11] This is due in part, at least, to the fact that until recently men had more, and more direct, contacts with the Anglo world; and there is no cause to assume that women will not in time participate more actively in these governing bodies.

If the attitude toward women changes among the Hopi, it seems most likely that this will be due to new attitudes toward fertility. As we have seen, the high evaluation of women resulted from their important roles as the source and keepers of human life. As this concept declines in importance, it may be that women's unique importance will decline as well. However, as traditional attitudes that are no longer appropriate to the adaptive system lose their salience, others that are appropriate can be activated. If women are no longer so important as mothers, they can still be important as partners, a concept that is well recognized by the Hopi within the context of cooperation in economic and ceremonial activities. As partners in maintaining the home and the community, they can retain their positions of equality in the balance of relationships that characterizes the Hopi world.

Notes

1. For a discussion of wedding customs and the pressure on girls to marry, see Schlegel 1973.

2. One wonders why infidelity is at the same time so deplored and so common. It probably provides one of the few escapes from the tight regulation of social life, and even vicarious enjoyment of infidelity is apparent in the teasing and joking that goes on about "private wives" and "hunting for two-legged deer." Men are usually the initiators of sexual activity (although women sometimes do initiate sexual affairs), so infidelity may also be a means by which men express covert resentment against their wives for their relatively insecure position in the home. Furthermore, as there are strong sanctions against the overt expression of anger between men, the seduction of another man's wife may be a way of expressing hostility toward him.

3. Actually, there is one case in which women do enter the formal authority system: if a mongwi dies without naming an heir, it is up to the Clan Mother to name his replacement (Titiev 1972, p. 82).

Today, there is even a woman who claims chieftainship of Oraibi, on the grounds that her brother, the designated chief, has not kept to the traditional Hopi way. There is considerable controversy over this: some Hopi claim that she is not a real chief, since, never having been initiated into a ceremonial fraternity, she cannot perform the chiefly rituals (see below); while others support her on the grounds that she has stepped in to provide necessary leadership. There is an earlier case of a woman chief of Moenkopi, a daughter village to Oraibi. Her position was never one of a true *kikmongwi*, as Moenkopi was included in the Oraibi ceremonial cycle; rather, she seems to have been a liaison between Moenkopi and the Anglo authorities in the nearby town of Tuba City (Nagata 1970, pp. 39–44).

4. The term *kachina* refers both to a supernatural being whose primary role is to bring rain and to the man who impersonates him in the kachina dance. It is believed that when the dancer puts on the kachina mask, the spirit of the kachina enters his body and he becomes a kachina. There are well over 100 different kachina forms, some more popular than others.

5. Shorter ceremonies are held in winter months for the women's societies discussed here and the other societies discussed below. The major ceremony in each case is held in summer or autumn, and it is these ceremonies that are discussed in this paper.

6. Marau had its own kiva, owned by the Lizard Clan which owns Marau. In 1901 it was rebuilt and taken over by the men, who have since loaned it to the Marau Society for its ceremonies. Lakon and Oaqül use a different kiva, borrowed from the men. In addition to their ceremonial use, kivas serve as men's houses.

7. The hoop is used only for women's society initiation and the initiation of children into the Powamu and Kachina Societies, which are held in Marau Kiva at Oraibi. It is not used for initiation into other societies or the men's fraternities, even though the concept of rebirth is made explicit in the latter by treating the fraternity initiates like newborn infants.

8. Flute and Snake-Antelope ceremonies are complementary to one another in timing, and, as I indicate, in symbolic expression. According to Parsons (1940), there is archaeological and ethnohistorical evidence that the ceremonies were once the same ceremony, or at least more closely related than they are today. Momtcit, a war ceremony comprising two sets of dancers like the Snake-Antelope Ceremony, is now defunct. Perhaps Momtcit was to Snake-Antelope as Oaqül is to Lakon, a restatement of the same message (see the discussion below).

9. Warfare themes are not central to the great cycle of ceremonies, even though they appear in the little cycle of summer and fall ceremonies. The Hopi have played down the prominence of warfare, and it was not the means by which manhood was achieved or validated—initiation into a fraternity accomplished that. Prowess in warfare was respected only in that it provided defense for the village and allowed the physical and spiritual activities dedicated to the maintenance of life to be pursued.

10. Nagata (1970) presents rather a different picture for Moenkopi, where men much earlier began to regard their earnings as their own property and are today

beginning to think of them as owned jointly with their wives. Since Moenkopi men had intensive contact with Anglo society and wage labor earlier than did the villages on the Mesas, it is likely that the transformation to a new form of domestic economy occurred earlier there as well.

11. In 1975, the first woman was elected to the Tribal Council.

References

Chodorow, Nancy. 1974. "Family Structure and Feminine Personality." In M. Z. Rosaldo and L. Lamphere, eds., *Women, Culture, and Society,* pp. 43–66. Stanford: Stanford University Press.

Griaule, Marcel. 1965. *Conversations with Ogotemmêli..* London: Oxford University Press.

Forde, C. D. 1931. "Hopi Agriculture and Land Ownership." *Journal of the Royal Anthropological Institute of Great Britain and Northern Ireland* 61:357–405.

Nagata, Shuichi. 1970. *Modern Transformations of Moenkopi Pueblo.* Urbana: University of Illinois Press.

Ortiz, Alfonso. 1969. *The Tewa World.* Chicago: University of Chicago Press.

Ortner, Sherry B. 1974. "Is Male to Female as Nature Is to Culture?" In M. Z. Rosaldo and L. Lamphere, eds., *Woman, Culture, and Society,* pp. 67–88. Stanford: Stanford University Press.

Parsons, Elsie Clews. 1940. "A Pre-Spanish Record of Hopi Ceremonies." *American Anthropologist* 42:541–42.

Rivière, Peter. 1969. *Marriage among the Trio: A Principle of Social Organization.* Oxford: Clarendon.

Rosaldo, Michelle Zimbalist. 1974. "Woman, Culture, and Society: A Theoretical Overview." In M. Z. Rosaldo and L. Lamphere, eds., *Woman, Culture, and Society,* pp. 17–42. Stanford: Stanford University Press.

Schlegel, Alice. 1972. *Male Dominance and Female Autonomy: Domestic Authority in Matrilineal Societies.* New Haven: Human Relations Area Files Press.

—— 1973. "The Adolescent Socialization of the Hopi Girl." *Ethnology* 12:449–62.

Stephen, Alexander M. 1936. *Hopi Journal of Alexander M. Stephen.* Edited by E. C. Parsons. New York: Columbia University Press.

Titiev, Mischa. 1944. *Old Oraibi.* Harvard University, Papers of the Peabody Museum of American Archaeology and Ethnology, 22(1).

—— 1972. *The Hopi Indians of Old Oraibi: Change and Continuity.* Ann Arbor: University of Michigan Press.

ALBERT S. BACDAYAN

Mechanistic Cooperation and Sexual Equality

12 among the Western Bontoc

C ONSISTENT WITH THE general observation regarding women in Southeast Asia, women among the Tanulong and Fedilizan peoples,[1] two Western Bontoc Igorot subgroups in Luzon, the Philippines, enjoy high status. It is one of the contentions of this paper that they also enjoy equal status with men, and that this equality is a function of mechanistic cooperation in a social milieu where the residential and economic unit is the nuclear family. Mechanistic cooperation implies the performance of the same tasks by men and women in a pattern of work that brings the sexes together in the same working situation.

The Tanulong and Fedilizan groups inhabit contiguous territories in the northern part of the municipality of Sagada along the Mabileng River, a tributary of the Chico River to the south. Their territories extend upward on both sides of the two mountain ranges bordering the river. The Tanulong and Fedilizan terrain, like most of Mountain Province, is rugged and pine-covered where not cleared for agriculture. The elevation averages 5,000 feet above sea level.

Grateful acknowledgment is made to the University of Kentucky Research Foundation and to the University of Pittsburgh Andrew W. Mellon Postdoctoral Fellowship Program for funding the research for this paper during the spring and summer of 1974.

The Tanulong and Fedilizan peoples number 1,700 and 3,000 respectively, scattered in villages spread at different elevations on the eastern side of the western range bordering the Mabileng River. There are seven Fedilizan and four Tanulong villages. The oldest villages of each group, bearing the names Fedilizan and Tanulong respectively, are close to the riverbed. The direction of growth has been toward the top of the mountain range, so that today the villages extend from top to bottom with the newest communities toward the top. They will be referred to here as the mountaintop villages. The inhabitants of these new communities are the most acculturated. Major reasons for their settlement in these villages are their attendance of mission schools, conversion to Christianity, the desire to be closer to the outside world, or all in combination. Since 1950, a dirt road has connected the Tanulong and Fedilizan mountaintop villages to other Philippine communities.

The Tanulong and Fedilizan peoples have been under missionary influence since the establishment in 1904 of the Episcopal Church mission in Sagada, now the municipal capital, five or six kilometers to the south. A school serving both places was established in 1917 in a centrally located area, which grew as one of the mountaintop Fedilizan villages. Fedilizan responded positively to missionary influence in that a large proportion of its people converted to Christianity and many of its young people have attended missionary schools. Tanulong, on the other hand, rejected missionary influences. Thus today there are far fewer educated Tanulong than educated Fedilizan people; and whereas the native animistic religion is a vital force in Tanulong life, it is weak in Fedilizan.

The Tanulong and Fedilizan peoples subsist mainly on rice and sweet potatoes (locally called *ube* or *camote*) with rice the more prestigious food. Rice is grown on elaborate terraces while *camote* is grown in dry fields around the houses or adjacent to the rice terraces, a short distance from the villages. *Camote* is also grown on the rice terraces themselves. To prepare rice fields for *camote* planting, they are drained of water just before or immediately after the harvest in June. They are cultivated as soon as they are dry and are planted by the end of July or early August at the latest.

In addition to rice, at least four kinds of legumes, corn, taro, and a number of temperate climate vegetables like cabbage, carrots, celery, and peas are grown. Coffee, especially of the Arabica variety, grows well between houses in the villages. Most of the produce is consumed, but some, especially coffee and vegetables, is sold in the market in town or to traders who come to the villages. Chickens and pigs are also raised, each family owning a pig or two and a number of chickens. A few families also own small numbers of cows and carabaos. Chickens and pigs are generally consumed for ritual purposes and are the chief sources of what little meat is eaten by the villagers. Cows and carabaos are not used for ritual and on the whole are butchered for meat only during large community affairs, particularly weddings.

The Tanulong and Fedilizan villages, except for the newly established mountaintop communities, are compact, probably because of a background of headhunting which made defense a primary necessity. Each village is divided into groups, each with a religious and political center called *dap-ay*. The number of *dap-ay* groupings depends upon the size of the village and ranges from one to six. They cooperate closely as organic parts of one entity, coordinating their activities, performing complementary functions, or taking turns performing functions for the good of the village as a whole.

The kinship system is bilateral of the classical Eskimo type. The kindred is therefore the most important kinship group outside the family. It includes one's brothers, sisters, first, second, and third cousins, and the ascendants and descendants of all these except the descendants of third cousins. The kindred also includes the spouses of all the above-mentioned kin categories.

Marriage is ideally prohibited through second cousins, although marriages between first and second cousins have been tolerated. The residential unit is the nuclear family; although widowed old parents may eat with their children, they may maintain a house where they sleep and keep their own pigs or chickens. Siblings are obligated to help each other and may engage in joint cooperative work arrangements in rice agriculture, particularly in plowing and planting.

While marriage by parental arrangement has taken place in Tanulong and Fedilizan, it is rather rare. For the most part, marriage is by common agreement of the couple. Courting was traditionally done in the context of the women's dormitories where unmarried girls slept and where the young men of the village, who ordinarily slept in the *dap-ay,* visited and slept with the girls. At marriage, the couple withdrew from the girls' dormitory and eventually established their own home. Each partner brings property to the marriage in the form of rice fields, sweet potato fields, and such valuables as porcelain jars, jewelry, and bronze gongs. In addition, they are enjoined by their elders and their friends during the night of their wedding celebration to work hard and add to their inheritance so that they will have enough to pass on to their own children.

While Tanulong and Fedilizan are set in beautiful country and enjoy an invigorating climate owing to the relatively high elevation, the people consider their life to be difficult, a reasonable assessment. The soil is poor and there is not much wild food nearby, so that the people have to work continuously simply to stay alive on rice, sweet potatoes, some vegetables, and occasionally meat. Moreover, children are greatly desired; but given the high infant-mortality rate,[2] a person's normal lifetime is marked by the loss of one's own or relatives' children. Life is a continuous witnessing of personal loss as well as a continuous struggle to eke out a living, and men and women are true partners in this hard life.

Until the extension of modern governmental authority to the area in 1902 under the initiative of the American colonial administration, the Tanulong and Fedilizan peoples were headhunters. Although it is very likely that for the most part they were defensive headhunters, whose main warlike activities were limited to protecting themselves from attacks and avenging village mates taken or killed by other groups, recent ethnohistorical research shows them to have also ranged far and wide raiding other groups of people.[3] It is possible that during headhunting times, the men dominated the women or enjoyed a special status, given the over-riding importance of the men to the survival of the society. Today, however, it is a reasonable assertion that the sexes are equal in status.

The Signs of Sexual Equality

Sexual equality in these two groups can be seen in the following cultural conditions: the equal treatment of male and female children; the sharing of economic power between men and women in its domestic and public contexts; the full participation of women in the instrumental and expressive aspects of public life; and the freedom of women to form associations or ties with other people, so that they are neither confined to the homes nor isolated from others.

Equal Treatment of Male and Female Children

Equal treatment of male and female children manifests itself in the warm welcome given both male and female children at birth; the equal portions of meat given boys and girls during family and community meals; the equal rights of males and females to the in-heritance of property following preordained norms; and the even-handedness in the socialization of children, wherein neither boys nor girls enjoy special privileges.

It is quite likely that during headhunting times there was a slight preference for males over females in view of the need for defense. Today, however, male and female children are equally welcome: *"basta kitdi matago da ma-id ma-adyan"* or, "as long as they live none is rejected." The high infant-mortality rate alluded to earlier may be responsible for this cultural attitude. What mat-ters then is not a child's sex but whether or not he or she survives. In fact, given the tendency of males today to leave the villages to find work elsewhere, females are often viewed more favorably as being more likely to stay home and take care of their parents. Another factor that may be responsible for the lack of preference for either sex is the high rate of task interchangeability discussed below, wherein a male is able to perform many tasks that a female does and vice versa. Economically it is not a serious matter whether one has female or male children. As expressed by the people: *"lalaki dedan nan baba-i, baba-i dedan nan lalaki"* (a girl is also a boy and a boy is also a girl). The rationale behind this is that when young people marry, each family gains another child of the opposite sex whose services are fully available to them as son-in-law or daughter-in-law.

Meat is a scarce and highly desirable food in the area under consideration. It is normally available during meals as part of family and communal religious rituals and of significant social events such as wedding celebrations. Whereas the other food items such as rice, vegetables, soups, and boiled sweet potatoes are normally served in common plates and bowls in front of the partakers, who squat around them in circular groups to eat, meat is invariably cut up into cubes and distributed individually. Boys and girls are given a piece of fat and a piece of lean meat each without discrimination. This holds true for older men and women as well. The only criterion for discrimination in meat distribution is age, in that the older people receive larger portions than the young.

In the inheritance of property the discriminating variable is age, not sex. The firstborn, whether boy or girl, is given the best rice fields owned by the family. Normally a boy is given the best rice fields of his father and a girl those of her mother. But if there is any dissatisfaction with this arrangement, either child may choose from his mother's fields or her father's fields as the case may be. The remainder is carefully distributed irrespective of sex to the remaining siblings, with a tendency to favor the youngest.

Unlike male-oriented societies, such as Japan, which give special latitude to boys, socialization in Tanulong and Fedilizan is evenhanded. Boys and girls are not given any special or differential treatment, but are subject to the same regimen as far as care and maintenance are concerned and to the same obedience and responsibility training. Moreover, care and socialization are the equal responsibility of both sexes, so it may be said that the young grow up in an actively bisexual context, a critical model for the child as an adult member of the society. Mutuality and equality are important themes in the socialization process, and one is likely to hear a parent or an older person advising children to share objects and chores equally because *"ay waday baken?,"* literally, "is there somebody who is not?," meaning that all are equally deserving and responsible.

The Sharing of Economic Power

Illustrative of the sharing of economic decisions and public display of economic power is the fact that any decision by either a married man or woman regarding the disposal of property by sale, inheritance, or other means and the acquisition of new property must be concurred in by the partner. This even covers inherited property, which theoretically is under the sole control of the person who inherited and contributed it to the family. Furthermore, the giving of gifts, a most public act particularly during such heavily and widely attended occasions as marriage celebrations, may be done by either the men or the women of the family. A public celebration during which property in the form of food—especially meat from hogs, chickens, carabaoes, and cows—is distributed is further understood to be a joint undertaking of husband and wife. Husband and wife are therefore both given credit that is verbalized in songs and discussions during the occasion, and prestige that may accrue therefrom is fully shared between them.

Women in Public Affairs

The participation of women in public affairs is both instrumental and expressive. (*Instrumental* refers to the decision-making processes of village politics, and *expressive* refers to those aspects of community life related primarily to entertainment or recreation, including ritual affairs.) In Tanulong and Fedilizan in earlier times, women's participation in government was less obvious and less direct, because the men's houses, which were off limits to women and which were theoretically the political and religious centers of village life, were until about 25 years ago much more influential than today. Even during those times, though, the women were able indirectly to affect public affairs significantly, since the discussions of public issues and decisions about them were made in the homes or in other public places where women were present.[4] It is recognized that public questions are women's concerns, because of the pattern of frank and direct relations between the sexes; and women may be asked what they think about any issue at hand. Thus, the women indeed had these effective avenues of contributing to and influencing the course of public affairs. Given the close relationship between husbands and wives, which will be illustrated in the discussion of the nuclear family, it is known that men often spoke in the men's house echoing their wives' positions on issues.

Today women's participation in political activity is direct. This is partly due to the weakened influence of the men's house and the growing influence of Christianity, especially in Fedilizan, but it is mostly the effect of new structures of participation such as local, provincial, and national elections and the availability of elected offices, especially in barrio and municipal administrative structures. Women campaign openly for candidates of their choice and have equal speaking opportunities with men, run for offices, and attend political meetings, even in the men's houses that formerly were closed to them. During the municipal and provincial elections of November 1971 there were as many women as men campaigners and there were two women from Fedilizan who ran for municipal councilor's office. This was also the case in the January 1972 election for barrio or village government officials; women campaigned and two ran for Barrio Captain[5] in two of the Fedilizan barrios. One woman wanted to run for Barrio Captain in one Tanulong barrio but decided not to finally for health reasons.

These developments have not upset or offended the men and

there were no objections to women's involvement in these new political activities. The only comments that may be interpreted as expressing reservations regarded not their being women per se but rather their being mothers who still had children at home needing close attention. Nothing was said at all about the women individually or generally being unfit or unsuitable for leadership roles. Their open and active participation was a natural outgrowth of the indirect participation noted above which the cultural ethos of sexual equality fully supported.

If women's participation in village politics was not very obvious previously, they have always been prominent in the expressive—the ritual and recreational—sphere of public life. A woman must do the first rice planting, watched over by the people, especially the old men, to observe omens. A woman must plant two or three taro roots to begin the new agricultural and ritual season. Women also may and do perform the ritual sacrifices in the rice terraces for a better crop. These are highly visible acts of profound significance to the group as a whole, as they have a direct bearing on the health of the one most important agricultural crop, rice, and on the order of the ensuing agricultural and ritual activities.

Participation in the recreational or social aspect of community affairs is probably the most pervasive and prominent of women's involvements in public life. Such involvement takes place in a multiplicity of contexts. The most prominent of these are the three wedding festivals occurring in September, December, and May, and the five community-wide feasts called *begnas* that center in the men's houses, which mark off significant aspects of the agricultural calendar such as sowing the seeds, planting, and harvesting. In addition, there are kinship rituals such as commemorations of the anniversary of the death of family members or ritual curing sacrifices for the ill. These normally feature eating, singing, telling stories, and serious discussions in which both sexes are equally involved. Any observer cannot but notice the free and open interaction of the sexes on these occasions. Of particular significance here are the public debates between the men and the women during public and social affairs. The content is free, spontaneous, and current. Some are informal, consisting of open conversation between the sexes discussing issues at hand. This takes place almost every time there is a gathering and there are significant topics needing discussion. Others are formal, almost always involving individual singing during which a point is articulated, followed by a chorus sung by all in the group. The most formal format is the *da-ing,* wherein the men and women each form a line sideways with the men putting their arms on each other's shoulders and the women holding each other's hands. The women's line is usually behind that of the men. There is generally a lead person of each sex articulating a point, after which everyone joins in the chorus as they sway back and forth sideways, the men punctuating their rhythm with stomping.

Women Outside the Home

Finally, we look into the freedom of women to form associations with people of their choice. The most obvious indication of this is that while it is expected that the woman is primarily in charge of the home, she is free to visit or be visited by other women in the community. She may also join mutual-labor groups or mutual-help groups in the name of the family.

The mutual-labor groups are called *ob-obbo* while the mutual-help groups are called *sosidad,* a term of unmistakable Spanish and therefore lowland Filipino origin. The former are normally of short duration during the planting, weeding, and padi cultivation stages of the rice-agricultural cycle or that of the sweet potato. Those participating take turns having the group at their fields until the round is completed, at which time a new round is begun if there is need. Sometimes some drop out after one round to be replaced by newcomers. Some *ob-obbo* are confined to kin groups, while others are not.

The *sosidad* are long-term in duration. It may take an entire lifetime for the benefit to accrue, and sometimes one's children succeed as the beneficiaries. Reciprocal help in kind or money is given according to need, and it may be that the need for one to collect may take years to arrive; one may postpone taking his turn in order to accumulate benefits for a time when a truly unmanageable need presents itself, such as the marriage of a child. As acculturation intensifies and new cash needs multiply, such as high school and college tuition for children or hardware for a contemporary frame house, the collection of dues is becoming more and more regular. This presents problems in trying to raise sufficient cash funds in time for the next collection.

During rest days, women also group together in centrally located and usually elevated spots of the village called *obob-onan* or sitting-gathering place. Here they talk as they pick each other's lice, sew or mend clothes, tend their children, or relax. Men are welcome at these places and are invariably found there. Neighborhood groups of men and women also gather in these *obob-onan* early in the evening for a bonfire and a good visit before retiring for the night. The Tanulong and Fedilizan woman is obviously not confined to the home premises.

The foregoing examples demonstrate the pervasive value in these two groups that men and women are equal human beings. To be sure, their differences are recognized, but neither is valued above the other. Nor is one defined as inherently subordinate or superordinate to the other because of sex. In only one respect, the role of women in village politics, was there a hint at male control, and that only in the final stage of political decision making. But new political opportunities have emerged in which women today openly and directly participate with no transition period, as though it were a natural thing to do. Even before the onset of new political opportunities, male prominence in this regard was in form only, not in substance.

The Importance of Mechanistic Cooperation

Sexual equality or equal status for men and women in Tanulong and Fedilizan manifests itself in the many ways described above.

It is contended here that the explanatory variable for this sexual equality is the high degree of mechanistic cooperation of males and females as defined by the high rate of interchangeability of tasks in their division of labor and the high rate of tasks done together. Our hypothesis more formally stated would be: the higher the degree of mechanistic cooperation between the sexes, the greater the likelihood of sexual equality. Let us examine mechanistic cooperation and the division of labor in Tanulong and Fedilizan.

An analysis of the division in the two communities was undertaken in summer 1975. A list of specific functions covering a wide range of important activities was made based on an intimate knowledge of the area and in consultation with key informants. Information was gathered by interview and observation on each function and coded as performed by males only (M), performed by females only (F), performed equally by males or females (B), performed usually by males (MF), and performed usually by females (FM). In all, 87 tasks covering the whole range of activities, as shown in Table 12.1 below, were surveyed and rated by their sexual assignment.

Inspection of the table indicates that of the 87 tasks included in the survey, 38 or 44 percent are equally male and female tasks, and 13 or 15 percent and 19 or 22 percent of the tasks are performed mostly by males and mostly by females respectively. On the exclusive side, 14 or 16 percent and 3 or 3 percent of the tasks are male and female respectively. Adding all the percentages, it may be said that 81 percent of the total tasks in the survey may be done by either males or females and 19 percent may be done by males or females only. Viewed in terms of the categories of the tasks surveyed it will be seen that of thirty-six expressly agricultural or subsistence tasks, eighteen are equally male and female, two are male only, one female only, seven mostly male, and eight mostly female; of twenty-nine domestic chores, twelve are equally both, one male only, one female only, ten mostly female, and five mostly male. The eight religious functions break down to four both male and female, three male only, and one

Table 12.1 Tasks and Their Performers in Tanulong and Fedilizan

Task	Performer
Agricultural or Subsistence Tasks	
Preparation of the soil	B
Planting	B
Weeding the banks of the fields	B
Plowing with animals (usually carabao)	M
Weeding in between the rice plants	FM
Watering	B
Erecting scarecrows	MF
Guarding against rice birds	B
Trapping rats and mice	M
Installing magical objects to scare rats	B
Checking to see if rice is ready for harvest	B
Harvesting	B
Sowing seeds	F
Removing seedlings from seedbeds	B
Clearing upland fields	MF
Planting vegetables	B
Clearing the padi dikes	FM
Fertilizing with organic matter, usually cut grass	B
Planting beans	FM
Installing bean poles	FM
Gathering beans	FM
Weeding upland sweet potato fields	FM
Fencing	B
Building stone/earth walls	MF
Fixing dikes	B
Fertilizing with mineral soil	B
Planting sweet-potato vines	FM
Digging up sweet potatoes	FM
Preparing upland fields	B
Taking care of animals in the pasture	MF
Cutting grass for animals	MF
Cutting sticks for fencing and poles	B
Preparing bamboo for binding rice bundles	MF
Milling sugar cane	B
Hauling rice from the fields	MF
Digging up new upland fields	B
House-Building Tasks	
Gathering thatch roofing	B
Roofing	M
Gathering vines for binding	M
Preparing wood	M
Preparing the ground for building	B
Hauling the material to building site	B

Task	Performer
Religious Functions	
Saying prayer	B
Performing sacrifices	B
Calling for souls and spirits	B
Being mediums	B
Performing sacrifices to the sacred tree	M
Ritual first planting	F
Ritual observing of omen birds outside the village in a mock headhunting expedition	M
Ritual counteraction of bad spirits	M
Domestic Household Chores	
Cooking	B
Washing dishes	B
Feeding animals	B
Skinning sweet potatoes	FM
Pounding rice	B
Keeping floors clean	FM
Gathering sweet potato leaves for pigs	FM
Waking up to cook in the morning	B
Splitting wood	MF
Cutting wood from the forest	MF
Preparing pig's food for cooking	B
Preparing cotton thread for weaving	FM
Weaving cloth	F
Washing clothes	FM
Sewing/mending clothes	FM
Washing dishes and pans	FM
Dressing and sacrificing chickens	B
Killing pigs	M
Distributing meat	MF
Cutting up meat for meals	MF
Fetching water	B
Babysitting	B
Keeping the child clean	FM
Feeding the child	B
Washing the child	FM
Cutting child's hair	MF
Seeing the medium when child is sick	B
Taking care of sick child	FM
Counseling children	B
Search for Food	
Fishing in the river	MF
Trapping birds	M
Gathering mushrooms	M
Snaring rice birds	M

Table 12.1 Tasks and Their Performers in Tanulong and Fedilizan (*Cont.*)

Task	Performer
Trapping fish in the rice fields	MF
Gathering edible snails	FM
Gathering beetles	B
Hunting	M

Note: B tasks performed equally by males or females; F tasks performed by females only; M tasks performed by males only; FM tasks performed usually by women; MF tasks performed usually by men.

female only. Of the eight search-for-food tasks, one is equally both male and female, four are male only, two are mostly male, and one is mostly female. The house-building tasks show three as equally male and female and three as male only. In gross percentages, shared tasks account for 93 percent of the domestic tasks, for 87 percent of the subsistence production, for 50 percent of the religious functions, for 50 percent of the search-for-food, and for 50 percent of the house-building tasks.

Careful consideration of the figures regarding sexual assignment and the types of tasks reveals two very important characteristics of the division of labor in Tanulong and Fedilizan that help us understand the relationship between mechanistic cooperation and egalitarian relations between men and women: there is a high frequency of task interchangeability between males and females, and there is wide distribution of the shared functions across the different task categories.

The High Frequency
of Task Interchangeability

The fact that 44 percent of the tasks surveyed are commonly done by both sexes and that 81 percent of all the tasks may be done by either men or women is impressive by itself. The former is shown to be a very high rate of interchangeability (although the data are not exactly comparable) when viewed against the study of Murdock and Provost (1973), which shows that the world equal-interchangeability rate is 16 percent.[6] There are several reasons why the significance of the 81 percent figure is even more important than the magnitude of the figure communicates. First is the non-essential and marginal nature of the tasks not shared or the low cultural value placed on them; another is the importance of the tasks included in the 81 percent shared; and a third is the fact that the societies under study are organized around the nuclear family as the basic economic and residential unit. As regards the first two reasons, those tasks included in the 81 percent of shared tasks are the most crucial and most frequently performed tasks necessary for the operation and survival of the society. They are for the most part agricultural tasks by which food is produced or domestic tasks by which the family or household is maintained. In contradistinction, the 19 percent of the tasks assigned to men or women alone are seasonal tasks that are peripheral to the society and really inconsequential. They are also engaged in by very few men and women. For instance, hunting is engaged in by no more than a total of ten men in both Fedilizan and Tanulong and weaving by perhaps no more than twenty women. The absence of expressed religious or secular sanction against the performance of any of these sexually exclusive tasks by the other sex indicates that they are ultimately interchangeable, with the exception perhaps of planting of the tarro, which is assigned to women only, and rendering the sacrifice to the sacred tree and the mock head-hunting ritual, which are assigned to men only.

Moreover, the nuclear family as the basic economic and residential unit creates beyond any question an atmosphere conducive to frequent role interchange, especially given a socially established division of labor favoring nondichotomized roles. In such a case, the husband and wife and to a certain extent the grown children make up the economic team that must keep the family in food and shelter. In the absence of other men and women for each sex to fall back on in the event of illness and absence of one or the other, and because of the need for cooperation between the two partners if the economic and emotional security of the family is not to be endangered, husband and wife or man and woman must assume each other's varying tasks at one time or another.

Viewed in proper perspective, the 81 percent figure of interchangeability looms as truly significant because it is in actual effect almost 100 percent. In Tanulong and Fedilizan this phenomenon is seen in the pervasiveness of mechanistic cooperation as we have earlier defined this concept. The ethnographer there cannot miss the predominantly bisexual nature of most work and activity groups in the fields and the village. In subsistence production, for instance, one is likely to see men, women, and children of both sexes engaged in the same tasks, harvesting, preparing the soil for planting, bundling seedlings, and planting. In cases where they are seen performing different tasks they are still working together: if men are repairing broken terraces, using a carabao to plow, or hauling the harvested rice home to the village, the women are likely to be close by smoothing the soil, cutting the grass around the field, or harvesting the rice to be hauled away.

This pattern of working together is observable in the domestic scene too. During the harvest season, one is likely to find the entire family bent over a huge basket outside their home removing the beans from their pods, spreading bundles of rice to dry, or carrying the rice inside to store in the granaries. At other times they may be pounding rice or cooking together. Even childbirth is a bisexual affair. The husband is likely to deliver his wife, attended or helped by older children and maybe an older female relative such as his own mother or the wife's mother. Many of the relatives of both sexes gather around for the birth process.

The cooperative life-style is of fundamental significance to egalitarianism for several reasons. First, it brings males and females constantly in contact with each other at work and at play. In the process they come truly to understand each other, first as persons and second as equally necessary contributors to their common endeavor, the support and perpetuation of the nuclear family. They also face a multitude of common problems to solve for their common good. This leads them to consult each other, to take direction and suggestions from each other on their merits. In this atmosphere of close and open relationships, it is hardly likely that any one sex would develop the notion that it is superior to the other. Neither is it likely that one would exclude the other from activities, because the concern of one is equally the concern of the other. Instead, a genuine appreciation of the interdependence of the two as equal partners is most likely to develop.

Second, the exchange of functions in this cooperative life-style does not permit either men or women to think that they are doing the better or worse task, and thus be led to the notion that one is undertaking more of the burden of life than the other and must therefore be given more credit. What is likely to result is that each sex understands and appreciates what each task requires to perform. The men are not thought to have it easier than the women, nor the women than the men. Rather the culture recognizes each as an equally crucial contributor to life and credits them equally for this contribution in the status they share.

Third, the cooperative life-style does not result in a system where males and females engage in specialized production. This is of great importance insofar as the issue of female status is involved, because it has been observed elsewhere that males tend to be in charge of prestigious plants or animals. In Tanulong and Fedilizan, both sexes take care of all the animals valued in the culture. Pigs and chickens, the most important and most frequently needed animals for religious and social occasions, are cared for by both men and women, as are carabaos and cows, prestige animals that relatively few people can afford to have. Rice, the most prestigious food and the most valued agricultural product, is jointly cultivated, as are sweet potatoes (see Table 12.1).

The Wide Distribution
of Task Interchangeability

The pattern of performance interchangeability cutting across different spheres of activity is easily discernible in the table. It may be worth noting again, in order of magnitude, that 93 percent of the domestic tasks, 87 percent of the subsistence production tasks, 50 percent of the religious tasks, and 50 percent of even such "universally male tasks as housebuilding,"[7] are interchangeably performed by males and females.

This crosscutting pattern signifies that the Tanulong and Fedilizan worlds are not partitioned into strict domains controlled by one or the other sex. Rather, males and females interpenetrate what may be strictly men's or women's domains in other societies. In effect their worlds are so intertwined as to be one and the same. Thus, there exist no dark unknowns in the society that either sex would or does utilize to control or check the other. For example, the men cannot really control the economic affairs of the society because economy is a shared activity; nor can women control the affairs of the household because again it is shared with the men. For much the same reason, the men cannot use religion to control women's economic and thereby political power, as Sanday (1973) has suggested for Tikopia. For this reason, the expressly male institution, the men's house or *dap-ay,* could not be used and is not used by the men for their own narrow political ends to control the women per se.

Conclusion

The inevitable conclusion from the data analyzed in this study is that where there is mechanistic cooperation, as in Fedilizan and Tanulong, there is equality of the sexes. This conclusion finds support in the recent writings in anthropology concerning the differential status of men and women. For instance, Sanday (1973, pp. 1695 ff; 1974, p. 198) found that when men and women contribute equally to subsistence production, women's status is high, and yet where women contribute most or all to subsistence production, their status is low as men still have religious means of imposing control or else are in control of the most prestigious goods. Rosaldo (1974, p. 41) suggests that where men participate in the domestic chores, as among the Ilongot of the Philippines, women's status is also high. Finally, Sacks observes: "For full social equality, men's and women's work must be of the same kind: the production of social use values" (1974, p. 222). In other words, where the sexes engage in productive activities with different ends such that women engage only in production for private use while men engage in production for exchange or social use values, then women have low status.

The data analyzed regarding mechanical cooperation unmistakably show the foregoing hypothesized relationships to obtain in Tanulong and Fedilizan. From our analysis of the data undergirding the mechanistic cooperative life-style there, it is directly evident that male-female contribution to subsistence production is equal and that males are deeply involved in domestic chores, the rate of task interchangeability being 87 percent and 93 percent respectively. Since this does not allow sexually specialized production or activity, especially in the economic sphere, it also follows that women are involved in exchange production. Put another way, the nature of the division of labor does not confine women to a particular line of economic production; instead, it makes production for whatever use, private or exchange, an endeavor of both sexes. Childrearing, agriculture, and economic decision making are jointly undertaken by men and women. If this is the required climate for "full social equality" that Sacks talks about, then Tanulong and Fedilizan have it.

The present study is of special relevance to the current concern in American society for sexual equality. It suggests that advocates of more interchangeability of sex roles and the opening up of all jobs to women as a way to achieve this sexual equality are on the right track, provided there is a context of mechanistic cooperation as here conceived.

Notes

1. Tanulong and Fedilizan refer to the same groups named in my earlier papers (A. Bacdayan 1970, 1974) as Tanowong and Pedlisan. The latter designations

reflect locally current usage while the former are designations normally used in written documents and in missionary accounts.

2. A survey done by the author and his wife in 1966 shows infant mortality to be very high in these two areas. It was found as of that time that for every eight births, three lived and five died. (See Bacdayan 1967). Recent observations indicate the infant mortality to be decreasing owing to improved medical care.

3. See Scott (1974).

4. While deliberating important issues in the men's house, the men have a pattern of interrupting the proceedings to go from house to house drinking rice wine or fermented sugar-cane juice. In the homes they continue their deliberations in the presence of the women who may then participate as seems appropriate.

5. The barrio government is the lowest local-level government unit in the Philippines. A barrio may be one or more villages and according to law must have a total population of 400 people or more. The barrio captain is the elected head of the barrio government for a term of four years.

6. This figure is obtained from Table 1 of the Murdock and Provost (1973) study based on 185 societies by counting the number of tasks (eight in all) bearing an index of male participation of 40 to 60 of a possible 100 points, and dividing it by the number of tasks surveyed, which is 50. The rationale here is that at this level female and male participation in the tasks involved is more or less equal.

7. Murdock and Provost (1973; pp. 207, 209) categorize house building as "quasi-masculine activity" (see their Table 3) with an index of male participation of 77.4 on the basis of a sample of 185 societies (see their Table 1). This indicates that on a worldwide basis, housebuilding is predominantly a male task.

References

Bacdayan, Albert S. 1970. "Religious Conversion and Social Change: A Northern Luzon Case." *Practical Anthropology* 17:119–27.
—— 1974. "Securing Water for Drying Rice Terraces: Irrigation, Community Organization and Expanding Social Relationships in a Western Bontoc Group, Philippines." *Enthnology* 13:247–60.
Bacdayan, Carolyn B. 1967. "An Analysis of Cultural Resistance to Family Planning." *Saint Louis Quarterly* (Philippines) 5:187–88.
Murdock, George P. and Caterina Provost. 1973. "Factors in the Division of Labor by Sex: A Cross-Cultural Analysis." *Ethnology* 12:203–25.
Rosaldo, Michelle Z. and Louise Lamphere, eds. 1974. *Woman, Culture, and Society*. Stanford: Stanford University Press.
Sacks, Karen. 1974. "Engels Revisited: Women, The Organization of Production, and Private Property." In M. Z. Rosaldo and L. Lamphere, eds.,

Woman, Culture, and Society, pp. 207–22. Stanford: Stanford University Press.

Sandy, Peggy. 1973. "Toward a Theory of the Status of Women." *American Anthropologist* 75:1682–1700.

—— 1974. "Female Status in the Public Domain." In M. Z. Rosaldo and L. Lamphere, eds., *Woman, Culture, and Society,* pp. 189–206. Stanford: Stanford University Press.

Scott, William Henry. 1974. *Cordillera Chronology.* Baguio, Philippines: Baguio Printing Press.

CONSTANCE SUTTON AND
SUSAN MAKIESKY-BARROW

13
Social Inequality and Sexual Status in Barbados

WE ARE ONLY beginning to develop an adequate theoretical paradigm for understanding sexual stratification. But recent studies directed at the issue of sexual equality and inequality have begun to shift the focus of analysis away from the search for universals in the nature of sex roles and tasks and toward an examination of how the structuring of sex-role differences is related to other structures of inequality. In the light of the growing documentation of the relation between an increase in inequalities among social groups and an increase in sexual inequality, the Afro-Creole societies of the Caribbean raise an intriguing set of issues and paradoxes. These societies have experienced two of the most extreme forms of exploitation and inequality known in human societies—slavery and colonialism; yet the Afro-Caribbean

Constance Sutton did research in Barbados during the summer of 1956 and from October 1957 through October 1958, supported by grants from the Research Institute for the Study of Man and from Population Council. She returned in the summers of 1968 and 1969, supported by grants from New York University Arts and Science Research Fund, the Research Institute for the Study of Man, and the Wenner-Gren Foundation for Anthropological Research. Susan Makiesky-Barrow carried out research in Barbados during the summer of 1969 and for 24 months during 1970–72. She was supported during the latter period by a grant from the Foreign Area Fellowship Program.

is notable for the absence of marked sexual inequalities. In this paper we shall relate our own observations of the positions, roles, and interactions of women and men in one Afro-Caribbean community to some more general considerations about the relationship between sexual stratification and societal inequality.

In considering the structure of sex roles in an Afro-Caribbean society, we are dealing with a colonial capitalist system that has had very different consequences for sexual stratification than was the case in Europe, where capitalism first developed, or in other colonial societies of the Third World, where capitalism was imposed on very different cultural and socioeconomic systems. In the Caribbean, the baseline for capitalist development was the slave plantation. Not only was the slave plantation one of the starkest systems of exploitation for profit ever devised, but it was a prototype of industrial economic regimentation, separating productive activity from other aspects of social life, even before such economic practices were fully established in Europe. However, in its impact on the structuring of sex roles, the slave plantation differed from other forms of capitalist economic organization (Fogel and Engerman 1974). It was perhaps the only such system that did not for the mass of the population strongly favor male economic participation at the expense of women, who elsewhere were relegated to a domestic sphere of activity and became increasingly dependent on men to support them economically and to "represent" them within the larger system. On the slave plantation, both sexes were equally involved in the "public" world of work, and both were equally exploited. Moreover, slavery and colonialism combined to divide the slave population so sharply from the dominant social groups that they were prevented from an easy identification with or adoption of the dominant group's structure and ideology of male dominance and control. In fact, their exclusion from the dominant cultural tradition fostered, in the "shadow of the plantation," the development of a distinct though not easily visible set of counterstructures and counterconcepts.

The society we examine is Barbados, a small sugar-producing island in the English-speaking West Indies. We focus on one rural community as we observed it during two different periods of fieldwork, in the late 1950s and the early 1970s. In the account that follows, we discuss both the historical background and the contemporary community in terms of the following issues: (1) participation of the sexes in familial and nondomestic realms of activity; (2) the relative autonomy of women and men and the bases by which they acquire status and prestige; (3) the significance attached to motherhood and its influence on women's economic dependence and independence; (4) the cultural conceptions of sex roles and identities; (5) the effects of recent changes on the balance of power between the sexes.

Historical Background

Of the 250,000 people living in Barbados today, 95 percent are the descendants of Africans brought as slaves to work on the island's sugar plantations during the first 200 years of its history as a British colony. Emancipation in 1838 interfered with neither sugar production nor colonial rule; not until 1966 did political independence and a measure of economic diversification produce significant departures from the patterns established by 350 years of sugar and colonialism. These recent changes have expanded the opportunities available to the large mass of black Barbadians and have permitted increased socioeconomic mobility. But despite a softening of the sharp divisions between classes and races, and despite the decline of the sugar estate as the key institution of the society, contemporary life on the island continues to reflect its history as a sugar-producing colonial plantation society, one in which the power of the white planter-merchant class was exercised by men, the primary status of the women of this class being that of wife and mother.

This tradition of male dominance among the Barbadian planter-merchant class was an extension of the tradition of patriarchy brought from Britain. However, a very different set of sex-role definitions was imposed on the slave population. The slave woman was not a ward of her father, husband, or brother and did not derive her status from her position as wife and mother; nor were her activities centered primarily on domestic and family life. Instead, her status, like that of the slave man, was determined in the first instance by her position within the plantation community. Differences in the rights and privileges of slaves were based on differences in occupational status within the plantation, and the slave woman's position was not mediated by the men of her group. She was her own economic provider and was not shielded from the harsh realities that existed in the public world of work. Moreover, laboring in the fields alongside the men, slave women were forced to deal with organizational structures of power and authority, and thus they acquired a knowledge of how the system worked and a consciousness of their oppressed and victimized position within it.

Recent work (Genovese 1976; Gutman 1976; Mathurin 1974) has begun to examine the sexual division of labor on the slave plantation and to consider its implications. While the studies are of slave communities elsewhere in the West Indies and the United States, some of their general findings can be applied to Barbados, where the slave plantations were similarly organized. One important finding of this recent research is that neither sex was particularly favored. Although it is premature to make definitive statements about the particulars of male and female activities and hardships, certain facts have begun to emerge: women and men were both distributed between house tasks and field labor; women, like men, operated in positions of authority, such as "drivers," and in such a capacity served as articulators with the dominant group, and, to some extent, as protectors of the slave community; severe punishments, including flogging and death, were equally imposed on women and men, though for a pregnant woman, the death sentence would be postponed until after she had given birth. While male and female tasks may have differed somewhat on the plantation, considerations of age and health were more important than sex in assigning work (Mathurin 1975, p. 5). And the hardships faced by the masses of women who labored in the fields and bore and reared children were certainly no less than those experienced by men.

Slave women, like men, surely used whatever weapons were available, including sex, in the struggle to resist degradation and to make a better life for themselves. Occasionally sexual liaisons between masters and slave women developed into enduring close relationships, but more often a woman's sexuality was a source of particular exploitation and vulnerability, as the accounts of sexual assaults on slave women by white men attest (Davis 1971). Others have seen the sexual relations between masters and slaves as a source of privilege for slave women. According to Wilson, "from early on, black women were treated differently from black men and were more readily and firmly attached to the alien society of the whites" (1973, p. 193). But recent research gives little support to theories of differential treatment of women and men or of women's greater attachment to or collaboration with the power structure. Instead, there is increasing documentation that women were as active as men in resisting oppression, and they played an important role in acts of rebellion (Davis 1971; Mathurin 1975).

Slavery then was a leveler of sex differences, promoting, in Angela Davis's words, a "deformed equality." Aspects of the sexual equality imposed on slaves, however, were not incongruent with patterns of sexual autonomy that had been part of their African cultural roots. Slaves brought with them traditions and cultural orientations, derived from their West African background, which defined sex roles in complementary and relatively equal terms and gave women considerable public respect and independence. Nor were the women who worked on the slave plantations unaccustomed to agricultural work or to providing for themselves and their children. For in contrast to the European pattern of conjugal pooling of economic resources with the husband as the organizer and manager of productive activities, the sexual division of labor in many West African societies involved a separation of the economic resources of husbands and wives and a greater sharing with consanguineal kin. Women and men carried on their own economic activities, and a woman was frequently the chief provider for herself and her children, though the husband contributed. Analyses emphasizing the inability of the black man to fill his role as the chief source of economic support for his family have missed the significant fact that the West African man was not viewed as the primary economic provider. Nor was the exercise of authority by women in the slave community without precedent; for in West Africa, where public life was not identified as a male domain, women occupied formal political and ritual positions in their societies.

This is to say that the slaves did not create *de novo* a set of responses to their loss of freedom. And as recent historical research on slave social life indicates (Genovese 1976; Gutman 1976), West African patterns of family, kinship, and friendship ties, once believed to have been destroyed by slavery, in fact provided cultural models that shaped the development of those aspects of slave culture outside the control of the plantation. We will mention only a few significant examples: the forging of strong extended family ties; the centrality of the mother-child and sibling bonds; the importance ascribed to the role of mother in contrast to the role of wife; a positive view of sexuality and its identification with creativity and potency rather than with temptation and sinfulness; exogamous tendencies in the selection of conjugal partners; the forging of strong and extended kin ties; respect for the powers of the elderly.

It was in the slave quarters that family and community life developed. Although the slave quarters did not fully escape the control of the plantation system, this more private "domestic" domain[1] was the one realm of plantation life that afforded slaves a measure of autonomy. Here slaves worked long hours on their own plots of land and developed a social life separate from the regimentation of the plantation. Here they garnered resources for resisting planter power and ideology and struggled to protect and expand their sphere of autonomous activities. While much of the literature on sex roles views the domestic sphere as an area of confinement that is associated with women and their dependent status, for the slave population, the domestic arena was the one

area of life that for both sexes was associated with human freedom and autonomy. Under the extreme conditions of slavery, it
acquired a very special meaning.

The slave plantation, then, provides a baseline for examining
sex roles in contemporary Barbadian society. It established the
sharp, racially based distinction between slave and free, separated the central public institutions of economy and polity from the
arena of slave and family life, and determined the relative position
of the sexes within the two domains.

Emancipation, which occurred in 1838, produced no dramatic
changes in Barbados' socioeconomic structure. Most of the freed
population was compelled to remain on the sugar estates, as land
was too scarce to permit the growth of a significant class of peasant proprietors. Working for wages, the ex-slaves became, instead, one of the earliest agricultural proletariats known. The occupational stratification established during slavery continued with
only some expansion of nonplantation employment. Skilled trades
provided opportunities primarily to men, while jobs as midwives
and seamstresses, though few in number, offered some parallel
positions for women. Both sexes moved into such nonplantation
jobs as hawking, shopkeeping, and schoolteaching. Though undoubtedly women, like men, sought to move away from plantation
employment whenever circumstances allowed, there is little evidence that they withdrew in any substantial numbers from the
wage economy, as occurred elsewhere in the West Indies after
emancipation.

Contemporary Barbados

The island, then, has had a long history of female participation in
the labor force, and in contemporary cross-cultural comparisons it
ranks, along with other Afro-Caribbean societies, as one of the
countries with the highest rates of female employment. In 1966 in
Barbados, 49 percent of the adult female population was employed. And in contrast to industrial societies, this figure rises to

63 percent for women in the childbearing years of nineteen to thirty-nine (Census Research Program 1973, pp. 194–97). (Eighty-six percent of adult males in Barbados are in the labor force.) Of the 93,200 persons in the total island labor force, 43 percent are women (Barbados Statistical Service 1966). As these figures indicate, female employment is unusually high; moreover, the systematic channeling of women into low-income "female" occupations which occurs in industrial labor markets is not so marked in Barbados, where there is a rather similar distribution of women and men in occupational categories (see Table 13.1).

The educational system also shows an absence of marked sex differentials—roughly equal proportions of males and females achieve different levels of education. The 1970 census indicates that approximately 15 percent of each sex has acquired secondary-school certificates that permit entry into white-collar occupations (Barbados Statistical Service 1974). This contrasts sharply with the sex differentials in educational achievements found in

Table 13.1 Occupational Distribution of Barbadian Women and Men in 1970 (in percent)

Major Occupational Group	Male	Female	Total
Professional and technical workers	9.0	9.0	9.0
Administrative, executive, and managerial workers	2.0	.3	1.3
Clerical and related workers	6.0	13.0	9.0
Workers in transport and communication	2.0	.3	1.3
Sales workers (including shop proprietors and assistants, hawkers)	6.0	13.0	9.0
Service workers (including domestic, hotel, protective services)	11.0	32.0	19.0
Farm managers, supervisors, and farmers	1.2	.2	.7
Other agricultural workers	14.0	14.0	14.0
Production and related workers (including artisans, seamstresses, manufacturing workers)	38.0	12.0	28.0
Laborers not elsewhere classified	6.0	2.0	4.4
Other	4.8	4.2	4.3
Total	100.0	100.0	100.0

Source: Based on Barbados Statistical Service (1974), pp. 8–11, Tables 4 and 5.

other developing countries. Barbados' literacy rate has been estimated at 98 percent, one of the highest in the world, and education has been highly valued as the main route to socioeconomic mobility. Moreover, it is valued as much for women as it is for men.

However, despite these similarities, there are some important structural inequalities in the occupational position and earnings of the sexes. We do not have figures that compare male and female incomes throughout Barbados, but smaller samples indicate a gap between their earnings. Those who control the Barbadian economy have operated with the western assumption that women have fewer economic responsibilities as providers. This bias, which has not been challenged by the (male) trade-union leaders, has been noted in a study of workers in manufacturing industries introduced into Barbados as part of a ten-year-old program of industrial development (Stoffle 1972). The management of these industries, which are primarily foreign-owned, have justified a low wage structure in terms of the preponderance of female employees. Although hiring policies favor women workers, the wage structure effectively discriminates against them. These differences may not be sufficient to erode women's interest in economic independence or to promote the kind of economic dependency that has characterized women in the West, but it fosters economic inequalities between the sexes.

Women's access to resources is further limited by the direction of recent economic developments. Although low-status agricultural jobs have been equally available to women and men, women for the most part have been excluded from the middle-level categories of skilled laborers, including artisans of various sorts. With economic diversification, these jobs have grown increasingly important as a way out of plantation labor, thus giving women fewer opportunities than men to improve their socioeconomic status. Differentials in the economic position and income of the sexes exist at various class levels, but they are most pronounced at the highest levels of the occupational pyramid, particularly at the level of management, an arena still dominated by whites.

Black Barbadian women thus face greater economic discrimination than the men of their group; but it is in politics that sexual inequality is most marked. Until recently, the political arena was totally under the control of men of the planter-merchant class. The majority of black Barbadians were excluded from any form of political participation until property qualifications were lowered in the 1940s and universal suffrage was introduced in 1950.[2] While both sexes now participate as voters, the centers of governmental decision making continue to be controlled by men. A very recent increase in the number of women seeking positions of political leadership at the national level suggests that the black Barbadians who have replaced the white political elites may not have fully adopted their assumption that political leadership should be reserved for men. At present, however, it constitutes an area in which women have lagged behind.

This overall national picture indicates a number of areas of sexual inequality. Now let us look at the organization and conceptualization of sex roles at the community level and how this relates to these national patterns and structures.

The Status of Women and Men at the Community Level

Access to Resources

Endeavor, a pseudonym for the community we studied, was originally a slave settlement. With time it encompassed a growing number of individuals who found the means to purchase small plots of land and a way to earn a livelihood outside the confines of the plantation; and today, less than one-third of Endeavor's adult population continues to work on the sugar estates that surround the community or for the nearby factory where cane is processed.

Recent changes have reduced ties to the plantation and caused its influence on community life to recede into the background. People in Endeavor now participate directly in the economic and political institutions of the island, though most occupy a subordinate position in these structures.

While they may refer to Endeavor as a place of "poor black people," Endeavor's residents are not unmindful of differences in wealth and status that exist within the community. Nor are they unaware that over the past two decades expanded educational opportunities, shifts in employment patterns, and an increase in emigration and in remittances from relatives abroad have provided greater possibilities for socioeconomic mobility. This has altered the occupational structure and social hierarchy of the community, though not its basic contours (see Makiesky-Barrow 1976). Status differences are important in structuring social interaction in Endeavor, despite the fact that in certain contexts people regard themselves as a community of social equals.

These differences are based, in part, on the criteria that are used to determine stratification at the national level—occupation, income, and education. Both women and men are ranked in these terms and both occupy varied positions in the community social hierarchy. The position a woman acquires often results from her own achievements rather than from those of her spouse, and women tend to be individually ranked even if they are married. Although both sexes speak critically of status ranking and its negative role in the social life of the community, status mobility is in fact of major concern. Women as well as men are preoccupied with finding a way of "rising a notch above" within the social hierarchy, and both look to the occupational system as the means of doing so.

We begin our examination of the status of the sexes with a look at their participation in the economy, their roles in the occupational structure, and their independent access to economic and social resources valued by the community. During the two periods of our fieldwork, between 40 and 50 percent of the women in the community were gainfully employed outside the household, and this figure rose to 59 percent for women between the ages of twenty and forty.[3] These levels of participation, which are similar to those at the parish and national levels, indicate both the economic importance of women in the work force and the fact that they, like men, work during the prime years of their adult lives. The distribution of the sexes in specific occupational categories during the two time periods is similar to that at the parish level, as shown in Table 13.2. Agricultural labor on the sugar estates remains the largest single occupation for both sexes, though the proportion of the population employed in agriculture has declined from one-third to one-quarter in the past decade. Even more dramatic is the withdrawal of women from this type of labor: in ten

Table 13.2 Occupational Distribution of Women and Men in Parish Labor Force, 1960 and 1970 (in percent)

	1960			1970		
Occupational Category	Male	Female	Total	Male	Female	Total
Professional and clerical workers	4.0	6.5	5.0	7.5	17.0	11.0
Workers in transport and communication	2.0	.5	1.0	2.0	.5	1.0
Sales workers (including shop proprietors and assistants, hawkers)	3.5	14.0	7.5	2.5	10.0	5.5
Service workers (including domestic, hotel, and protective services)	3.0	22.0	10.5	4.0	25.0	12.0
Agricultural workers	33.0	46.5	38.0	22.0	28.0	24.0
Production and related workers (including artisans, seamstresses, manufacturing workers)	43.0	10.0	30.5	52.0	14.0	38.0
Laborers not elsewhere classified	4.5	.5	2.5	6.0	3.0	5.5
Other workers	7.0	—	5.0	4.0	2.5	3.0
Total	100.0	100.0	100.0	100.0	100.0	100.0

Source: Based on Makiesky-Barrow (1976), pp. 108–9, Table 3.

years, the percentage of women who are agricultural laborers dropped from 46.5 to 28. This decline has been facilitated by the availability of other forms of employment, including low-paying unskilled jobs in the new industrial parks, and, for younger women entering the labor force with secondary education, white-collar jobs. The magnitude of the withdrawal should not come as a surprise, for agricultural labor retains the stigma of slavery and women plantation workers are even further discriminated against by male-female differentials in wages and task assignments. Thus, while plantation labor has been a source of independent income for a large number of women, it has not served to equalize access to economic resources. But neither have the sex differentials in wages and tasks been sufficient to undermine the sense of common status and common cause that exists between women and men who are agricultural laborers.

Other occupations pertinent to community members are somewhat more differentiated by sex: artisans and skilled sugar factory workers are mainly men; domestic servants are nearly all female; and market vendors, called hawkers in Barbados, are predominantely female. Neither in terms of income earned nor related social status do the latter two occupations match those of skilled production workers. But at the top of the community occupational hierarchy, sex typing is virtually absent. Both women and men are engaged in shopkeeping, one of the most remunerative occupations in Endeavor, and both women and men are found in the high-status white-collar and professional jobs, mainly as teachers, nurses, clerk-accountants, medical assistants, and other positions in the civil service. In fact, women exceed men in this category. Together with successful shopkeepers, these women and men are sometimes referred to as the community's "poor greats"—that is, the "greats" among the poor; and it is worth noting that in the late 1950s two of the four reputedly wealthiest community members were women shopkeepers, while eight women and five men were schoolteachers. In the recent past, the community's "poor greats" played an important role as cultural brokers between community members and the wider society. Although social change has reduced the significance of this brokerage role, the women and men in the top positions of the community hierarchy are still highly regarded and often turned to for advice and assistance by other members of the community.

Thus not only do both sexes occupy prestigious occupational statuses, but women, as well as men, aspire to and acquire other socially valued resources: land, houses, and education. Owning land is for Barbadians a primary goal in life, partly because of the security and potential income it provides, but also because it remains a primary symbol of independence from plantation control. No customary or legal principles bar women from inheriting or purchasing land, and many women own plots of land of varying size. Of the household heads who own land, 43 percent are women, 57 percent men. More men than women acquire their own plots of land through purchase, while women landowners more often acquire their land through inheritance. Perhaps more to the point, in the late 1950s only one-third of the adults in Endeavor had managed to acquire land. This, however, was not the case with respect to house ownership, also an important goal in establishing adult status in the community and one that in most cases precedes acquiring land. House ownership is furthermore associated with a complex concept of household headship, which is identified with ideas about personal independence and the right to impose one's will. Houseowners assert their freedom from outside control in phrases such as "I don't bow down before any person," and "Nobody can tell me what to do!" Although household heads often claim "I boss here," the aspect of authority associated with the concept of headship is more subtle and indirect. It resides in the assumption that the head of a house has a right to know about and take part in decisions affecting other members of the household, as well as to receive special consideration for his or her needs and desires. Household headship is not strongly linked with sex differences: both in the late 1950s and the early 1970s, 43 percent of the households in Endeavor were owned and headed by women (Sutton 1969; Makiesky-Barrow 1976).

While land and house ownership are associated with the important value of personal autonomy, education is viewed as the prime means of acquiring social prestige. Here sexual equality is most evident, for both sexes are actively encouraged to achieve. While parents often find it a struggle to pay the costs of keeping several children in school, their decision to give one child more schooling than another is based on the academic promise of the child, not its sex. Nor do they hesitate to express an equal pride in the educational attainments of their female and male children. Moreover, parents actively encourage young girls as well as boys to prepare themselves to earn a good living. A job or career for a woman is never spoken of as an alternative to marriage or maternity. Although it is realized that a woman's household and child-care responsibilities might necessitate her withdrawal from work for short periods, the "dual career" conflict experienced by women in industrial societies is not marked. This reflects not only different expectations and assumptions about a woman's economic and social roles but also the presence of a family and kinship system that acts as a support for women of all ages. It is a system in which strong ties between consanguineally related kin serve to distribute the chores and responsibilities of rearing children. Moreover, child fostering, whether for shorter or longer periods, is an approved practice and may in fact serve to strengthen ties of kinship and friendship. To the extent that these supports are available to employed mothers, they constitute a most valuable resource for reducing role conflict.

What then can be said in summary about the position of women in the occupational hierarchy and their available economic resources? First, it is clear that the tradition of women's active involvement in the economy has persisted through time. Second, in Endeavor women have access to those occupations that carry prestige and rank high in the community's social hierarchy. Moreover, the nature of women's distribution within the occupational categories precludes the development of any systematic link between gender differences and social status. Third, while women's economic activities and patterns of land and house acquisition indicate that they have somewhat less control over resources than men, these differences are not sufficient to give men any decisive control over the distribution of resources to women and children.

In addition, the economic imbalance between the sexes tends to be somewhat reduced by women's greater access to resources beyond those they derive from employment. Most women are likely to receive varying amounts of economic support over the course of their lives from men related to them as spouse, lover, or father of their children. Moreover, women tend to be the main re-cipients of the economic assistance that adult children, especially sons, are expected to and do give to parents. Women expressed the expectation of such support from children in comments like, "Never mind they humbug you in the early, they crown you in the late." And, as the figures on labor-force participation indicate, the rates of female employment are highest for the age groups bear-ing and rearing children and begin to decline for women over forty, who usually have adult children. (This pattern is an interest-ing reversal of a phenomenon in the United States which has received recent attention, namely, the entry of women into the labor market as a response to the "empty-nest syndrome.")

Household and Kinship Relations

While the above considerations do not imply that there is eco-nomic parity between the sexes, they do indicate the absence of female economic dependency. The significance of this point requires further comment. In previous studies of family life in Bar-bados as well as other Afro-Caribbean societies, the relatively high proportion of women in the economy has been attributed ei-ther to the absence of a male provider or to his inability to fulfill his role (Greenfield 1966). This interpretation is predicated on the western assumption that women take on major economic roles only when circumstances prevent men from doing so. But in En-deavor, the economic roles of women and men are concep-tualized differently. Providing for children and household is regarded as a joint, though not necessarily equally shared, responsibility of men and women. Women, like men, take pride in and are applauded for successfully providing for their children.[4] Women are expected not only to contribute to their own and their children's support but also to acquire and build separate economic resources, control their own earnings, and use them as they see fit. Men readily accept the idea of their wives working; in fact, a man might boast about his wife's position and earnings. A woman, like a man, is not expected to disclose her assets to her spouse, though some may do so. These cultural expectations and assumptions about women's and men's economic activities qualify analyses of sex roles that are based on a notion that providing economic support is a predominantly male activity.

As other studies of Afro-American and Afro-Caribbean peoples have shown, family and kinship relations are important dimensions of the social world of both women and men. In Endeavor, people use kinship idioms to express close social relationships, as in the claim that in the community, "all o' we family." But more significant is the density of actual kinship connections among community residents. In 1958, 66 percent of 883 senior household members had close family relatives living in the community, often in an adjacent or nearby household, along with a large number of more distantly related kin. These ties serve to reinforce the social relations based on contiguity, providing what people refer to as a "backprop"—a source of assistance and support. Women are active in maintaining these extended kinship networks; and although the system is in principle bilateral, kinship connections through women figure more prominently in defining the sets of people considered to be "family" to each other. The strong sense of family based on these connections counterbalances the relative instability of conjugal unions. Moreover, these family ties, in addition to women's economic activities, account for the relative independence women maintain within their conjugal relationships.

A large part of the literature on the West Indian family is devoted to the variability of conjugal relationships and the related complexity in the composition of domestic groups. The several accepted forms of conjugality are referred to, in this literature, as visiting relationships, consensual or common-law unions, and legal marriage. In Endeavor, children are the expected outcome of each type of union, but children may serve either to bring a man and woman closer together or to "race a man away," and are not considered by a man or woman as sufficient reason for staying together. The concept of biological parenthood is nevertheless emphasized and the principle of bilateral affiliation recognized. Parental responsibility, however, tends to be shared among a number of relatives, more often on the mother's side, though there is nothing to prevent the family members of a biological father from taking on responsibility for children he has sired, and in many cases they do. There is then wide latitude in the roles biological parents may adopt and an accepted interchangeability of persons who assume responsibility for childrearing. Most variable, though, is the role a biological father plays in relation to his own children, which ranges from no contact and no support to extensive economic support and an affectionate and enduring relationship.

The variability in the social roles assumed by biological fathers is related to the variation in types of conjugal relationships, each of which entails different definitions of conjugal and parental rights and responsibilities. Consensual unions and legal marriage involve coresidence and joint responsibility for the children produced in the union, but separate responsibility for the children a man or woman may have had from previous unions. By contrast, a man has limited rights over the children produced in a visiting relationship. In this least stable form of conjugality, the couple live separately, refer to each other as girlfriend and boyfriend, and have limited obligations to or rights over each other.

While legal marriage carries prestige, it is not necessarily seen, by either women or men, as a preferred form of living together. People in Endeavor frequently commented that "good living is better than bad marriage," a view also expressed in one woman's assertion that "plenty people living a sweet life and from the moment they get married is a different thing." Most men and women spend some part of their lives in a coresidential relationship, either with one or a series of different partners. And while some relationships develop into lifelong unions, permanence is not a strongly held expectation in entering any of the three forms of conjugality. The tendency is to move through the three types of unions sequentially, but beyond the visiting relationship, the order is not fixed. In Endeavor in the late 1950s, 20 percent of women between the ages of fifteen and twenty-four were living in visiting unions, 15 percent were living in consensual unions, and 15 percent were legally married. Forty-two percent of Endeavor women in this age category were already mothers. Between the ages of twenty-five and thirty-nine, consensual unions among women rose to 20 percent and legal marriages to 50 percent; 90 percent of the women had borne children. After forty, 70 percent of women in Endeavor were or had been married and only 2 percent were living in consensual unions, while a larger but hard to determine number of women who had been in legal or consensual unions were maintaining a visiting relationship with a different partner.

Conjugal instability and a relatively frequent changing of sexual partners are features of West Indian family life that have been attributed to a number of different factors—poverty, selective male migration, the legacy of slavery. But in Endeavor, the formation and breakup of unions is more related to the fact that a conjugal union is not the only or essential context for either economic support or childrearing. Consequently, compatibility emerges as a much more important criterion in forming and maintaining conjugal relationships.

People in Endeavor believe compatibility can only be assessed after a couple have had sufficient opportunity to observe each other's character and test each other's responses to situations that arise in an ongoing relationship. Time is needed to determine whether "minds and spirits meet"—time to know whether a couple can "live lovin'." Compatibility cannot be deduced from the qualities that attract a couple initially and lead them to form a visiting relationship. The guarded attitude that women and men express about the outcomes of their sexual and coresidential unions is reflected in descriptions of the formation of relationships as a process of "trying one's luck." As one woman stated: "I feel a certain amount of 'outdoor livin' is a good thing. I feel I could now get married because I know what would make me happy. But you first got to check a man out and got to know what you lookin' for."

The behavior of women and men in conjugal relationships is guided by cultural assumptions about such unions and the roles appropriate to each sex. We have already noted that a couple's economic resources and social interests are only partially merged. Nor is the conjugal tie expected to take priority over all other social ties or become the most intimate and emotionally intense of all social relationships, as is the case where the nuclear family forms the key unit for procreation, economic support, childrearing, and status placement. Instead, women and men assume that conjugality implies some joint responsibility for economic and childrearing responsibilities, a continued sexual interest in each other, and a mutual willingness to keep affairs between them a private matter rather than the subject of community gossip.

Women are expected to take the major responsibility for childrearing, cooking, and keeping the household clean.[5] Men cook and perform other domestic tasks when their spouses are not available to do so, but generally the sexual division of tasks allocates to men the responsibility for house building and maintaining physical structures. Men express their expectations of their conjugal partners in the following terms: a woman should not criticize her man in public (though she may do so in moderation privately); she should be a good manager of household finances and of economic resources generally, and, by extension, should try to see that her man does not spend his money foolishly (though it is recognized that meeting this expectation too zealously may create tension and conflict between a couple); she should not desert her man when he faces periods of hardship; she should cook for him, launder his clothes, and look after his general physical needs; she should treat her spouse's friends cordially and adhere to the norms of sociality that operate within the community. Finally, she should not shame her man by getting into roadside arguments, appearing unkempt or untidy, or "running around" with other men.

Women express a complementary set of expectations: a man should help with household finances and childrearing expenses; he should not divert an unreasonable amount of his income to other social obligations, to other women, or for drinking with his male friends; he should treat the children of a woman's previous unions well; he should be considerate, affectionate, and remain sexually interested in his spouse and be willing to assist her if she faces physical or verbal assault. A husband or male partner is not cast in the role of special protector and guardian of his spouse. Women are regarded neither as jural minors nor as wards of male partners who represent their interests in the wider society. Rather a woman is expected, in most situations, to represent herself, and men speak with admiration of a woman who "knows how to look out for herself."

While these are generally stated cultural expectations regarding conjugal relationships, they are not taken for granted. Each couple has to work out for themselves what they imply concretely, and each of these expectations thus becomes the subject of individually negotiated agreements on what constitute satisfactory terms for maintaining a conjugal relationship. In one woman's words: "From the start we set it clear: You mustn't hold back me and I mustn't hold back you. No man going to do me that. You lay down your terms and he lay down his, and if you don't agree, shift! Pull out!" Separation occurs when a couple "can't agree."

A particularly pervasive source of male-female conflicts is the issue of sexual fidelity. The cultural expectation that both sexes will remain sexually interesting and active makes both men and women jealously watchful for any sign of their partner's interest in outside affairs, and the issue of sexual infidelity generates a level of distrust and sex antagonism that is absent from other areas of male-female interaction. It is an area not only of conflict but of sexual inequality. For while sexual activity is viewed as equally pleasurable to women and men, women have fewer opportunities for initiating and maintaining outside affairs and are more likely than men to tolerate their spouse's infidelities. This double standard reflects the fact that a man's ability to control his partner's sexual life is an essential part of his masculine identity, whereas for a woman learning to live with a man's outside affairs does not pose a comparable threat to her feminine identity. This asymmetry favoring men produces tensions in the relations between the sexes and can lead to the dissolution of a relationship.

The relatively frequent shifting of conjugal partners creates complexities in the organization of domestic groups. While conjugal couples are the usual nucleus of household units, women who are not coresiding with a man are frequently household heads. Moreover, domestic units generally incorporate a variety of kin other than nuclear family members. These aspects of domestic and kinship organization have been cited as indices of "matrifocality," defined in terms of the prominence of women as the focus of consanguineal kin groups and the priority of consanguineal over conjugal ties. The importance of consanguineal kin has been seen as a source of conflicting loyalties, which produces marital conflicts and conjugal instability. In our view, however, conjugal instability is related to the autonomy of the sexes more generally. For in Afro-Caribbean societies, women are not enclosed in discrete, bounded domestic units that are linked to the wider system through male economic and status-defining roles; nor are they submerged within kin groups. Rather, there is an overlap in the spheres of domestic, family, and community life that makes setting off the domestic from nondomestic domains inappropriate and particularly misleading for understanding sex roles and ideologies. In Endeavor, women's important roles in the family and kinship system are neither fully distinct from nor at odds with their participation in community life.

Community Relations

Now as under slavery, the community constitutes a major arena of social life for rural residents—one in which they receive recognition and reputations that are only partially dependent on their larger societal roles. It is here that the structures and cultural val-ucs of the dominant system intersect with the Afro-Creole patterns. To the extent that the national economic and political structures favor men, this is reflected in locally based branches of national economic and political institutions. Thus, the local political and trade-union activists in Endeavor are disproportionately male, as are the officers of the local branch of the national credit union system. But there are no community-wide administrative institutions that permit the imposition of male leadership on the community as a whole, and in the locally generated social patterns, a different set of assumptions about male and female roles operates.

The community provides a context for an active life of economic cooperation, entertainments, religious activity, and socializing. In these areas, both women and men are active participants—sometimes jointly, sometimes separately, but virtually always as individuals rather than as conjugal pairs.

There are a number of locally based economic institutions for saving or raising funds, and women and men are equally involved in them. Both sexes organize and participate in rotating credit associations, known as "meeting turns," and both act as "bankers" in such associations, with responsibility for collecting and distributing monies. Husbands and wives often participate in different "meetings," with each individual maintaining full claim to the savings he or she thus amasses.

Both sexes, separately or together, also organize as money-making events dances, known as "brams," and picnic excursions. Brams are usually sponsored by one or two individuals who seek to make a profit on entrance fees and the sale of food and liquor. Both sexes attend in approximately equal numbers; couples may arrive together, but more commonly they come alone or in same-sex groups. Like brams and excursions, social clubs provide a context in which women and men socialize together. Positions of leadership in these clubs tend to be given to better-educated, high-status people, with no discernible preponderance of one or the other sex.

As in other Afro-Caribbean communities, religion is an important focus of activity in Endeavor. Most of the community's residents are Anglican, and baptism, marriage, and funeral ceremonies are usually performed at one of the parish's several Anglican churches. But more important in local social life are the dozen or so "meeting halls" that house a range of Protestant fundamentalist groups. While the largest hall in Endeavor has an active membership numbering around 100, and the smaller ones have only a dozen or so "brothers" and "sisters" in their congregations, the halls are more important in community life than the numbers of active members indicate, and nonmembers sometimes attend meetings and participate in hall activities.

In most halls women participate more actively and in greater numbers than men, but both women and men attend and offer "testimony" at hall meetings; both also take on leadership roles as singing leaders and preachers. While men more often establish a new hall and install themselves as pastors, this is not an exclusively male prerogative. Coresidential couples may be active members of different halls; for in this as in other areas of activity, both sexes are expected to behave autonomously.

Despite the numerous areas of overlapping activity, the social lives of women and men are markedly independent of each other. In activities involving both sexes, they participate as individuals, and the presence of a spouse is often merely coincidental. Other aspects of community activity involve greater separation of women and men. This is particularly pronounced in patterns of informal socializing, which are focused on same-sex friendships. There are small groups of five to ten men, similar in age and socioeconomic status, who meet in the rumshops and on the streetcorners to talk and drink rum or tour together to dances or other social events. In addition to socializing together, clique members provide for each other reciprocal assistance and support. Studies of male cliques have added an important dimension to understanding Afro-Caribbean social life and values and have served to counteract the stereotype of male powerlessness and peripherality created by the emphasis in many earlier studies on domestic units. But less attention has been given to women's patterns of informal socializing outside the household.

In Endeavor, women are both highly mobile and highly sociable, though after late adolescence their social lives tend to be less group-centered than those of men. Working women have a range of contacts and experiences similar to men's, and a recent study of women factory workers notes that female cliques similar to the all-male peer groups have emerged among coworkers (Stoffle 1972, p. 190). Women who are not employed make frequent daytime visits to neighbors, to one of the general shops, or to friends elsewhere in the district, and thus maintain a flow of information and contact among women. Most women have one or two close friends with whom they exchange confidences, and maintain relations characterized by the exchange of favors, gossip, and goods and services with a broader circle of women. These social networks are often wide-ranging and may include friends in other districts. They rarely constitute relatively bounded groups like men's cliques, and they appear to be less homogeneous in terms of social status. Women's social networks have tended to be ignored in discussions of sex roles in the West Indies, partly because they are more dispersed and therefore less visible than men's groups, but also because assumptions that women's social lives revolve around family and kinship have diverted investigators from studying these networks.

In addition to these contexts for same-sex socializing, there is considerable informal cross-sex contact among community members. Although friendship between a woman and a man may raise the suspicion of a sexual relationship, there are nevertheless many such friendships. And the "public" nature of community life—in the yards, roads, and shops of the district—means that women and men frequently encounter one another in a range of contexts and are familiar with one another's activities through elaborate networks of community gossip which include both sexes. While community social life is characterized by considerable autonomy of the sexes and a separation of some activities, this does not preclude either extensive cross-sex interaction or their joint knowledge of spheres of life that in other societies are often segregated into separate male and female domains.

Thus, we see that the importance of women in the domains of kinship and domestic life does not conflict with either economic participation or active involvement in nondomestic realms of community social life. The structure of kin relations not only provides a woman with important social ties beyond her own household, but also distributes domestic tasks and responsibilities so as to permit women to be active in a range of nondomestic contexts. The woman who confines her activities to the household is, in Endeavor, ridiculed for "always drawing up in the house" by women and men alike.

In sum, the relatively independent access women and men have to resources in the kinship system and in the economy provides a basis for considerable autonomy and promotes their relatively independent achievement of status and prestige within the community. While the status of a spouse is not irrelevant to the position of either women or men in the socioeconomic hierarchy, it is not often the sole or even the primary determinant. Moreover, men do not "represent" the domestic group in the wider society or link domestic and juropolitical domains. While there are some spheres in the community that favor male participation and leadership, there are no community-wide administrative institutions that either permit the imposition of the dominant culture's forms of male leadership and authority on the community as a whole, or through which men (or women) "represent" the community to the wider system.

Cultural Concepts
of Sex Roles and Identities

We earlier suggested that there was a congruity between aspects of the allocation of sex roles that emerged in the plantation context and aspects of West African sex-role traditions. The Afro-Creole culture of lower-class black West Indians involves a complex interaction of European-derived norms and values, and the assumptions and ideologies that emerged from the experience of

Africans on the slave plantations. While people in Endeavor share the general dualism of this cultural orientation, their attitudes and concepts expressed about appropriate sex-role behavior, sexuality, and the characteristics and abilities of women and men depart significantly, though not uniformly, from the assumptions prevalent in western societies.

This is particularly evident in attitudes toward sex and sexuality. Both men and women regard sex as pleasurable, desirable, and necessary for health and general well-being, and they discuss, separately and together, how to improve sexual performance and pleasure. Stylized sexual banter between women and men occurs in public and private settings and is enjoyed by both sexes.

Some observers of male peer groups have emphasized the importance men give to sexual prowess and the conquest of women (Freilich 1968). However, such descriptions omit the important fact that the West Indian men's preoccupation with sexual activities is, unlike machismo, very profemale. A man's reputation as a lover is not based on "conquest" of the "inaccessible" woman but on his success in sexual performance, in knowing the techniques that give a woman sexual pleasure. The West Indian notion of masculinity has built into it, then, the concept of satisfying the woman, and this performance-oriented approach to sex and sexuality is supported by the active interest and expectations of women.

Both sexes are aware of and sometimes voice the dominant culture's traditional European concepts of male and female characteristics and abilities. However, rather different definitions of masculinity and femininity guide interpersonal behavior within the community. Unlike the dominant ideology in which gender is the basis for an opposition of roles, values, and personal traits, this system of rules and meanings makes few distinctions between male and female abilities and attributes. Sex and sensuality, which symbolize creativity and "power" (in the sense of effectiveness, not dominance), are equally valued in men and women. Nor is sensuality thought to interfere with effectiveness in public roles; for both sexes, it is believed to enhance abilities to think and act decisively.

A woman's procreative powers, rather than disqualifying her from societal prestige and esteem, command considerable respect,[6] and motherhood is a basis of support in later years. But motherhood also has important symbolic meanings: bearing a child is the major *rite de passage* from girlhood to womanhood, and it constitutes the more salient element of adult female identity. Marriage, if it occurs at all, often comes later and marks a transition from one stage of adult relationships and responsibilities to another; it does not play an essential role in defining womanhood. A childless woman is pitied and occasionally derided with such epithets as "mule." Female sterility is attributed to insufficient "nature"—i.e., vaginal secretions—and thus implicitly linked to frigidity. Sexuality and procreative power are perceived to be positively associated.

Childbirth itself is viewed as a cleansing process, and while a woman's children from previous unions may occasionally be a source of conflict with a man, they constitute evidence of a womanly "cleanliness" that more often enhances than diminishes her attractiveness as a mate. The act of childbirth not only cleanses the body; it also demonstrates a woman's capacity to endure pain. Women discuss their own and other's performances during delivery, and special prestige attaches to the woman who can "stand up, hands on hips, and drop her child like so." Children express the specialness of the mother-child tie in terms that acknowledge the strength required of women in childbirth, as in the frequently heard comment, "After all, she is the one who bear the pain to have me."

Despite the cultural elaboration of motherhood, and the fact that women are the ones who speak about "making a baby," men's roles in procreation are not ignored. While they are not conceptualized as the major agents of procreation, they are believed to partake of the experience of pregnancy: when conception has occurred, it is believed that they will physically experience some of the early symptoms of pregnancy. A number of women and men told us that frequently a man knew of his woman's pregnancy before being told because he experienced the symptoms. We also heard men dispute allegations of paternity on the grounds that they did not experience the pregnancy symptoms.

Thus the distinct qualities of masculine and feminine sexual and reproductive abilities are not viewed by either sex as a basis for different male and female social capacities. And unlike the self-limiting, negative sexual identities that Euro-American women have had to struggle with, female identity in Endeavor is associated with highly valued cultural attributes. Because women are assumed to be bright, strong, and competent, nothing in the definitions of appropriate sex-role behavior systematically excludes them from areas of economic and social achievement open to men.

Changing Conditions

Historically, the sharp division in Barbados between dominant and subordinate groups not only excluded black men and women from participating in the island's political institutions but also prevented a fuller imposition and assimilation of the ideologies and norms of the dominant group. From the beginning, then, family and community life among the majority black population have operated in accordance with principles that have remained distinct from, though not unaffected by, those of the colonial elite. With recent changes in island political and economic structures, however—particularly the enfranchisement of the working class and the ascendance of middle-class blacks—the socially inherited cleavage between those in control and those controlled is no longer so marked.

Politics is one of the newer areas of achievement open to the black population of Barbados. The absence of local political institutions and the colonial tradition of island politics have precluded the development of definitions of appropriate behavior for women and men in this sphere. In 1971 and again in 1975, only one woman was among the 24 members elected to the Barbados

House of Assembly, and women seeking public office were at a disadvantage in the campaigning techniques of canvassing and buying drinks in the rumshops. However, female candidates and speakers at political rallies were well received; and many women in Endeavor are knowledgeable and interested in island politics, following closely the issues of general concern in the community, discussing with one another and with men the pros and cons of governmental policy, and often expressing enthusiastic partisanship in their political allegiances.

Emigration is another phenomenon that has expanded considerably in recent years. Both women and men seek to go abroad to England, Canada, or the United States, and for the same reasons—primarily financial but also for the "experience." The relative proportions of male to female emigrants have been determined more by the nature of job opportunities in these countries than by women's marital status or domestic roles. A woman with children may leave them with relatives until she can send for them to join her abroad. Like male emigrants, she has obligations and responsibilities to support or assist relatives at home through remittances.

The ultimate impact of this expansion of economic and political options for black women and men in Barbados is not yet clear. Whether present political and economic changes will contribute to a decline in women's autonomy and status, or whether Barbadian women will respond to the new situation in the light of their historical experience and cultural assumptions, remains an open question. To the extent that a different set of cultural assumptions influences societal arrangements, there is reason to believe that women and men in Barbados will avoid the development of the sexual stratification that has accompanied capitalist economic and political development in the West.

Conclusion

In this paper we have focused on an Afro-Caribbean society in which women are both more autonomous and more highly regarded than in western industrial societies. This is particularly interesting because Barbados shares with western industrial nations a capitalist economy with a well-developed labor market and a pronounced division between "domestic" and "public" spheres of activity. These conditions have been identified as the source of women's loss of autonomy and public esteem and of their dependent roles within the family. We have sought to identify the conditions that have prevented West Indian societies from replicating the western pattern of sexual stratification.

Two factors emerge as critical in accounting for the relative equality and autonomy of the sexes. First, the sexual division of labor on the slave plantation produced few differences in the "public" economic participation of women and men; and second, the social cleavage between free whites and enslaved blacks minimized the imposition of the dominant class ideologies and permitted the slaves a degree of autonomy in retaining and developing distinct cultural patterns and concepts about sex roles and attributes. We have examined the contemporary legacy of these differences in the sexual division of labor and cultural ideologies. We found that women's independent income-producing activities, combined with their positions within the kinship system, provide a basis for their autonomy and self-esteem and for maintaining a relatively equal balance of power between the sexes. Moreover, they operate with a cultural ideology that attributes to women and men a similar set of positively valued characteristics and abilities and that identifies parenthood and sex as two highly valued experiences.

At a more general level, our analysis suggests that for women as well as men a wide network of social relations and supports provides an important basis for independence and autonomy. In contrast to the western concept of individual autonomy and equality, which implies a shedding of social attachments, the Afro-Caribbean and black American concept of autonomy is linked to a strong sense of interpersonal connectedness—an involvement in the lives of others. The status of the sexes in Barbados, therefore, rests on their relatively independent access to the resources of the

kinship system and the economy and on an ideology that mini-
mizes sexual differences and emphasizes the effectiveness of the
individual regardless of gender.

Notes

1. The distinction between "domestic" (private, familial, informal system) and
"public" (juropolitical, formal, external system) has been applied both to roles and
to spheres of activity. The terms have been widely used and variously defined in
recent studies of sex roles, sometimes as an analytic distinction and sometimes as
a presumed difference "out there" in society. "Domestic domain" typically refers to
the internal affairs of a small social unit, usually the household or extended family,
and has been regarded as the locus of female activity. The "public domain" is the
term used most frequently in referring to all aspects of social life occurring outside
the "domestic domain," especially those activities and networks of social ties that
link one domestic unit to another. The public domain is allegedly where men and
societal power are located. Although we do not accept its universal applicability or
its universal identification with a sex dichotomy, it is a useful distinction in the
analysis of particular societies. On the slave plantation it was, rather, the sharp
cleavage between the slave community and the wider society that formed the
boundary between internally and externally oriented spheres of activity. We have
therefore treated the community and family together as constituting a more relevant
domain of "internal relations" than the more narrowly defined domestic sphere.

2. This pattern was evidently established early. Handler (1974; p. 215) indicates
that among both the white elite class and the free colored population prior to
emancipation, the absence of women from political activity was notably similar.

3. These and subsequent statistics are based on a personal census of Endeavor
taken in 1958 by C. Sutton and on material drawn from the 1960 and 1970 Commonwealth Caribbean Population Censuses.

4. A similar phenomenon was reported in a study on self-esteem among black
American women: "76 per cent of the employed women referred to themselves as
successful mothers based on being 'a good provider' " (Myers 1975; p. 247).

5. Cooking is an especially important aspect of a woman's relationship to a man.
In male-female exchanges, there is a symbolic association between the giving and
receiving of sex and food.

6. The cultural meanings assigned to pregnancy and childbirth, and the social
power thought to reside in the role of mother, throw an interesting sidelight on the
argument that these activities and roles are responsible for an alleged universal
cultural devaluation of women (Ortner 1974). This devaluation is attributed to a universal identification of women with nature and men with culture. In this culture/
nature dichotomy, "cultural" activities are more highly regarded than those defined
as "natural" and are thus the source of male ideological dominance. Not only were

we unable to find such a linkage at either the conscious or unconscious symbolic level, but people in Endeavor explicitly and consistently reverse the allegedly universal superiority of culture over nature. What is identified as "natural" is more highly regarded, while "culture" is linked to artifice, hypocrisy, and the exploitation of the dominant group. Moreover, the nature/culture dichotomy was not symbolically coded in sex-linked terms.

References

Barbados, Statistical Service. 1966. *Labour Force Survey, April*. St. Michael, Barbados.

—— 1974. *Commonwealth Caribbean Population Census, 1970. Barbados Preliminary Bulletin, Education*. St. Michael, Barbados.

Census Research Program. 1973. *Commonwealth Caribbean Population Census*, 4 (4): *Economic Activity, Barbados, 1970*. Jamaica: University of the West Indies.

Davis, Angela. 1971. "Reflections on the Black Woman's Role in the Community of Slaves." *Black Scholar* 3:3–15.

Fogel, Robert and Stanley L. Engerman. 1974. *Time on the Cross: The Economics of American Negro Slavery*. Boston: Little, Brown.

Freilich, Morris. 1968. "Sex, Secrets, and Systems. "In S. Gerber, ed., *The Family in the Caribbean*, pp. 47–62. Rio Piedras, Puerto Rico: Institute of Caribbean Studies.

Genovese, Eugene. 1976. *Roll Jordan Roll: The World the Slaves Made*. New York: Vintage.

Greenfield, Sidney. 1966. *English Rustics in Black Skin*. New Haven: College and University Press.

Gutman, Herbert. 1976. *The Black Family in Slavery and Freedom, 1750–1925*. New York: Pantheon.

Handler, Jerome. 1974. *The Unappropriated People: Freedmen in the Slave Society of Barbados*. Baltimore: Johns Hopkins Press.

Makiesky-Barrow, Susan. 1976. "Class, Culture, and Politics in a Barbadian Community." Ph.D. dissertation, Brandeis University.

Mathurin, Lucille. 1974. "A Historical Study of Women in Jamaica from 1655 to 1844." Ph.D. dissertation, University of the West Indies (Mona, Jamaica).

—— 1975. *The Rebel Woman in the British West Indies*. Kingston, Jamaica: The Institute of Jamaica.

Myers, Lena W. 1975. "Black Women and Self-Esteem." In M. Millman and R. M. Kanter, eds., *Another Voice: Feminist Perspectives on Social Life and Social Science*, pp. 240–50. New York: Doubleday Anchor.

Ortner, Sherry B. 1974. "Is Female to Male as Nature Is to Culture?" In M. Z. Rosaldo and L. Lamphere, eds., *Woman, Culture, and Society,* pp. 67–88. Stanford: Stanford University Press.

Stoffle, Richard W. 1972. "Industrial Employment and Inter-Spouse Conflict: Barbados, West Indies." Ph.D. dissertation, University of Kentucky.

Sutton, Constance. 1969. "The Scene of the Action: A Wildcat Strike in Barbados." Ph.D. dissertation, Columbia University.

Wilson, Peter J. 1971. "Caribbean Crews: Peer Groups and Male Society." *Caribbean Studies* 10: 18–34.

—— 1973. *Crab Antics: The Social Anthropology of English-Speaking Negro Societies of the Caribbean.* New Haven: Yale University Press.

NANCY DATAN

Ecological Antecedents and Sex-Role Consequences

14

in Traditional and Modern
Israeli Subcultures

T HE ROLE OF the human female, which has recently become a cause for protest if not revolution, had its origin in necessity and evolved to meet the exigencies of bearing and rearing an animal that required years to reach adulthood, in a world where childbearing was of paramount importance. Present protesters often ignore the natural, functional origins of male and female roles when focusing on the dysfunctional aspects of these roles as they persist, sometimes anachronistically, in a world where reproduction of the species is not perceived by humanity as its principal goal.

In the present paper subcultural variation in certain aspects of sex-role differentiation will be discussed within the framework of two social settings within a single nation, Israel: the traditional Arab village of Kafr Ibrahim and the modern kibbutz of Ein Haeyal. It is possible to see in the traditional village shadows of an earlier,

The study of women in middle age was carried out at the Israel Institute of Applied Social Research, Jerusalem. It was directed by Aaron Antonovsky, and Benjamin Maoz was project co-director. The study was supported by a grant from the U.S. National Institute of Mental Health (P.L. 480 Agreement No. 06-276-2).

The places named in the ecological descriptions in this paper are: a pseudonym for an Arab village in the Judaean mountains, and a composite picture of kibbutzim in the Judaean foothills, the Beit-Shean Valley, and the upper Galilee.

preliterate way of life (Patai 1959), while certain transformations in sex roles brought about by modernization—notably a constriction of the childbearing and childrearing functions in the female life-span (Myrdal and Klein 1956)—have evolved dramatically to meet the demands of a seemingly similar ecological niche, the kibbutz. These two social environments, and the role models characteristic of them, will be described; and these role models will be used in a discussion of findings from a cross-cultural study of women in five Israeli subcultures.

The Arab Village

One day a man was out walking and saw an old man planting an olive tree. He stopped and asked him: "Why do you plant an olive tree and not some other fruit? For you are an old man, and will not live until this tree gives fruit."
The old man answered him: "Listen, my son! They (of the past) planted and we have eaten; and now we plant for them (of the future) so they will eat."

—Tale from the Muslim and Jewish traditions

Interviewer: Have you ever listened to a radio?
Bedouin: Oh, my God. Why do you ask me such a question? Look at the Palestinians. They listened to the radio and God destroyed them! We don't want that trouble here.
            —from *The Passing of Traditional Society* (Lerner, 1968)

Throughout the Arab world, the village is a place of ancient traditions. Modernization can be seen in the cities, but it is imported from the outside and artificial in many respects: the revolution in communication often precedes the technological revolution and the social transformations it brings in its wake. Thus Lerner (1958) describes a grocer in Turkey whose dream is to manage an American supermarket, with shelves of shining tinned goods; while in 1973, in the mountain villages of Judaea and Samaria, it was still possible to see *fellahin* using a wooden plough for fear that steel would poison the earth.

Stone is plentiful in the Judaean hills, although very little else is; thus Kafr Ibrahim consists of a cluster of one- or two-room houses, built of fairly well-cut stones cemented together into low, domed structures with thick walls and tiny, unglazed windows. The pale Jerusalem limestone is hardly different in color from the light brown of the soil, and at a distance the village seems to have sprung quite naturally out of the hillside and is hard to distinguish from it. Jerusalem is recorded in biblical history as built at the tops of the mountains, and this practical habit has not altered over the centuries.

The homes of the villagers, then, form a tightly knit, and if necessary, readily defensible unit, on the hilltop. Between the houses and around them are vineyards. The relationship of the village to its land is an intimate and precarious one, for farming is difficult: the soil is poor and sparse, and there are few crops that can be grown on a mountainside. The antiquity of this problem can be seen in the ancient stone terraces that ring the mountains and are carefully maintained to this day. The terraces create narrow, shallow plateaus of soil round the sides of the mountain, and dew condenses on the chilled stones in the early morning and trickles into the earth. Grapevines can be cultivated laboriously on these ridges, rather like farming on an endless descent of narrow stairs; and on the broader terraces, fruit trees will survive. Where the hillsides are too steep for terraces, or too barren for crops, olive trees can still live: short, gnarled, silvery leaved, they blend like the houses into the hillside, and survive for centuries. On neighboring hillsides, which are not farmed, flocks of goats or sheep may be kept. They are sheared for wool, bred to increase or maintain their numbers, milked for both milk and the sharp, salty sheep's and goat's cheeses, slaughtered for meat, and skinned for hides. Thus the single village on a bare hillside yet manages to supply a large proportion of its own needs—if by "needs" is meant merely something to eat, something to wear, and somewhere to live. But there were, until very recently, no other meanings.

The inhabitants of Kafr Ibrahim are members of a single *ha-*

moula, or clan. Even large cities such as Hebron or Shehem are made up, at the upper social strata, of a few *hamoulot,* and generally the mayor is the most powerful member of the strongest one. A single, small village is hardly enough for a small *hamoula.*

It would be difficult to say which is more vital to village life, the obtaining of food or the bearing of children. The land cannot be made to yield much, and one must prepare the soil, mend the terraces, prune the vines, prevent the sheep and goats from grazing the crops, or harvest. A full day's work is barely enough. The land admits of no flexibility in sex-role differentation: if there is to be a crop for this season and children for the next generation, men must spend the day on the hillsides and women must spend the day at home.

Like the raising of crops, the rearing of children is a full-time occupation. Women commence childbearing as soon as they are able, nurse each baby about a year and a half, and bear children approximately every two years. Large families are not merely a result of lack of planning, but an actively desired goal. The hard work required to run a household strains the health of women, and a large proportion of pregnancies never come to term. In the absence of modern medical facilities, babies often die at birth. Of those babies that survive pregnancy and birth, many die in early childhood. Thus, if a family's goal were only the modest hope of keeping its numbers constant, it would nevertheless claim a large portion of a woman's life merely to produce three or four children to ensure replacement.

However, families want as many children as possible. Perhaps this now traditional cultural value had its origins in the need for helpers, which children quickly become. Present cultural patterns suggest that another consequence and another value are closely linked: the family with many children becomes, relatively, more well-to-do, and therefore more powerful. If a conflict between two *hamoulot* arises, the larger has an advantage. Out of this elemental fact the marked preference for sons may have grown, for they could both till the land and defend it.

Women of Kafr Ibrahim

A woman's primary function in the traditional Arab world might be summed up very briefly: to bear sons. However, of necessity this entails many other difficult and essential tasks of household management: the traditional "woman of valor" of Proverbs does not resemble our contemporary stereotype of so-called traditional women, for she is not "confined" to the household; rather she is exercising a broad range of talents in a variety of roles both domestic and economic (Datan 1972), and it is likely that her energies and abilities are stretched as far as they can go. Furthermore, despite unequivocal status differentiations, the vital functions in the traditional woman's role may secure her position more effectively than a verbal affirmation of equal rights. No status differentials favoring men can possibly blur the more elemental primacy of the woman's contribution: she bears and rears the next generation, and in this harsh ecology, where her role appears to the western observer to be so completely subservient, within the family and within the *hamoula* her position is secure.

It is more than probable, as speculation in the preceding section has suggested, that the sharp sex-role differentiation and even the favoring of sons had their origins as a response to a harsh environment. Regardless of its origin, however, it is possible to see the entire complex of role expectations for women as a way of ensuring a supply of strong and loyal sons; paradoxically, this ensures the woman a pivotal role in the family and in the *hamoula,* perhaps more obvious to the husband and sons who depend upon her contribution to the family and village ecology than it is to one viewing the village from outside.

Girls enter the world as a disappointment to their parents, who were hoping for, and had probably practiced rituals designed to ensure, a son's birth. Even among the youngest and most modern women, the ideal family is not seen as "a boy for you and a girl for me," but two boys, to ensure that the male line is carried on, and then—only then, after the woman has proven she can bear sons—a girl, to help around the house (Zenner 1968). In Kafr

Ibrahim, despite the fact that the girl's birth was not a cause for rejoicing, her help around the house becomes essential as the family grows, and she takes on household tasks as soon as she is able. Girls of four or five may already be trying out their destiny by minding a baby brother.

By eight or nine, the girl is probably betrothed and has become a source of concern, for she is still young and yet she must maintain the family honor by learning to be an obedient and competent daughter-in-law and by remaining a virgin. A girl who betrays this latter trust may be stabbed to death by her brothers to redeem the family honor; and at the very least, her parents will have to return the *mohar* (bride price) to the disappointed groom (Peters 1965).

The word in Arabic and in Hebrew for husband is *ba'al,* in antiquity a name for a Canaanite deity, and even at present it is used in many contexts with a connotation of divinity. In ordinary usage, its two most common meanings are "husband" and "owner," since in fact with regard to a married woman there was not historically much difference. For traditional Arabs this dual meaning remains congruent with cultural values; the incongruity, and the steps taken to deal with it in the kibbutz, will be discussed later.

Urban women from traditional Arab families go veiled, and great precautions are taken to ensure sexual seclusion. In the villages, however, the small and intimate community and the exhausting daily life permit little opportunity or leisure for sexual adventures; women go unveiled, and older women whose children are grown help their husbands in the fields. In the home, males and females eat separately, and when the men are visiting the wife may not even serve them unless they are members of the same *hamoula*. These restrictions are lifted only after the woman has reached middle age, when, as the mother of grown, married sons, she acquires the status of matriarch.

Arab dress looks extremely modest to a western outsider. Both men and women wear loosely draped full-length clothing, baggy pants for men and gowns—white in the country, black in the city—for women. It is again possible to see, however, how an originally adaptive and protective custom came to have secondary significance that was bound to cultural values. The best protection against sun and sandstorms even today is the traditional costume. However, in town or in the mountain fields, kibbutzniks have found equally comfortable alternatives, and their clothing— shorts and a short-sleeved shirt or none at all—was accepted by the Arabs for young boys. A *sabra* Arab boy is indistinguishable from a *sabra* Jew, yet Arab girls continue to wear long dresses and long trousers under their dresses.

The Arab woman who has borne a son seems to lose her identity once and for all, for it is a custom to call her by the name of her firstborn son. Although our fieldwork was carried out in relatively modern villages, there were nevertheless some middle-aged women whose identification might read as follows: F015 (subject number); Maswadeh (name of hamoula); Mahmoud (name of father); Ahmed (name of grandfather); Um Salim (mother of Salim—subject's name). There were cases of women in our study who could not remember what their own names had been.

This study focused on the relationship between overall adjustment and degree of modernity among women of five Israeli subcultures which ranged along a continuum from modernity to traditionalism. The study yielded a surprising curvilinear relationship between the degree of modernity and overall measures of adjustment: the European women in our study were best adjusted, closely followed by the Muslim Arab villagers (Datan 1972). This finding forced us to reconsider the significance of tradition, and led us to the conclusion aleady noted above: that despite the "confines" of tradition, the vital functions performed by women in traditional settings may be a more meaningful source of satisfaction than the symbolic equality—where it does not rest on a functional basis—available to women in more modern cultures. If they have forgotten their names, the Arab women of this study know and are secure in their place in the world.

Men of Kafr Ibrahim

The subordination of women, the high price of virginity, and the drastic consequences of a breach of fidelity, it is here suggested, are part of a culture-complex intended to result in a powerful family of loyal sons. Some of the social and cultural consequences, as described elsewhere, will be discussed here.

The overvaluation of the male in Arab society has created what Lerner (1968) calls a "male vanity culture." Far from creating strong family bonds, this appears to lead to intense intrafamily hostilities and jealousies, for every man views his brothers and cousins as potential sexual rivals. The only loyalty is to the *hamoula,* but it is an intensely ambivalent and mistrustful loyalty. Sociologists in a number of contexts have expressed this in various ways: Berger (1964) cites several studies of Arab society that indicate the weakness of the social bonds, and a high degree of hostility and distrust between men. (This view of Arab society is very much an outsider's view, however; most Arab writers, speaking of a lack of unity in Arab society, point to their status as a developing people, lacking technology and the mass communication that facilitates the growth of a sense of peoplehood beyond the boundaries of the *hamoula* and the village.)

The initial function of the family, here suggested as self-maintenance and self-defense, may become inadequate when the unit of self-defense is broadened beyond village boundaries. These problems have been discussed by Israeli strategists, for whom the extent of unity among Arab nations has practical significance. A former head of Military Intelligence, Col. Y. Harkabi (1967), is of the opinion that the total collapse of Arab military forces in 1967 could not have resulted solely from battlefield failures, and must be assumed to have its causes in the national fabric. This fabric he has elsewhere characterized as atomized (Harkabi 1969), with fragile social links and a marked lack of mutual trust. It might be suggested that traditional ways of life are becoming dysfunctional more rapidly for men, whom they favor, than for women, who are still living within the traditional framework and its protection—a protection often ignored by critics of traditional society, who view tradition (correctly) as outmoded, but fail to see the origins of tradition as the struggle for adaptation.

Israelites and Israelis: Tradition and Innovation

And God said, Let us make man in our own image, after our likeness: and let him have dominion over the fish of the sea, and over the fowl of the air, and over the cattle, and over all the earth, and over every creeping thing that creepeth upon the earth.

So God made man in his own image, in the image of God created he him; male and female created he them . . . and the rib, which the Lord God had taken from man, made he a woman, and brought her unto the man. . . . And the man said, The woman whom thou gavest to be with me, she gave me of the tree, and I did eat. . . .

Unto the woman the Lord said, I will greatly multiply thy sorrow and thy conception; in sorrow thou shalt bring forth children; and thy desire shall be to thy husband, and he shall rule over thee.

Genesis 1:26-3:16

And the Lord spake unto Moses, saying, Speak unto the children of Israel, saying, If a woman have conceived seed and born a man child: then she shall be unclean seven days. . . . But if she bear a female child, then she shall be unclean two weeks. . . .

Leviticus 7:25

The State of Israel . . . will maintain complete equality of social and political rights for all its citizens, without distinction of creed, race, or sex.

Proclamation of Independence, 1948

Tribal life in ancient Israel was probably not unlike life in a small traditional village in present-day Arab countries (Patai 1959). Judaic law prescribed rigid sex-role differentiation, large families, and a subordinate role for the woman. At the time of the proclamation of the State of Israel in 1948, however, new traditions had grown up with the resettling of the land. It may have been awareness of the force with which innovation had superseded tradition, or perhaps it was merely a consciousness of the extent of contradiction between the ancient laws—still followed among the ultraorthodox minorities in Israel today—and the customs of the majority; in either case the Proclamation of Independence rescinded the earlier proclamation in Genesis.

Innovation sprang from the soil as certainly as earlier traditions had done. The forces that brought about an attempt to eliminate sex-role differentiation can be seen most clearly at their source, in the early pioneering kibbutzim. The kibbutzim were the first homes of many of Israel's most powerful political figures; social changes originating in the kibbutzim spread, because they were adapted to the rigors of life in Israel, to the cities; and today, although they account for less than 4 percent of the population, the kibbutzim have a disproportionately strong influence on the ideological and social climate of Israel.

The land on which Ein Haeyal was born was no more promising than the poorest hill village. Characteristically, a *gar'in* or nucleus of 30 or 40 people set up tents in a rocky but potentially arable region near the border, strategically placed on a hillside so as to be maximally defensible. Food came from neighbors until the first crops were harvested. Ideology dictated that the kibbutz sustain itself as soon as possible, and in the early years of settlement in Palestine, the self-supporting kibbutz was also safer if attacked.

It is worth recalling the small Arab village at this point, for it is similar in many ways to the young kibbutz: between 50 and 200 people make up the populace, their livelihood is to be taken from the ungenerous earth, and they must defend themselves. In this the two communities are alike, but the ways in which community behavior has evolved to meet the demands of the inhospitable environment are entirely different in village and kibbutz.

Housing in Ein Haeyal, when it replaced tents, was no more than a few rows of prefabricated barracks-like structures, except in areas under fire, where buildings of reinforced concrete, trenches, and shelters were constructed. As in the village, homes were in a small central area, the *mesheq,* and fields surrounded them. The family did not, however, occupy a common residence.

A husband and wife would have a room together; but children, as they were born, were put into a common nursery, and the children of many families were under the care of one woman. This radical restructuring of childrearing practices had two aims: the abolition of intense nuclear family ties in favor of loyalty to the community as a whole, and the emancipation of women from their traditional roles as homemakers and mothers (Spiro 1970).

It is difficult to differentiate between ideology and ecology as determinants of the transformation of the female sex role. The first settlers brought with them an egalitarian, collective ideology which, most probably, thrived because it was suited to the land. A group of 50 settlers would be halved if all the women were to mind their homes and babies, and there simply were not enough people to be spared. Ideology led to women's operating heavy farm machinery, but necessity led to collective dining halls, collective childrearing, collective laundry, and the freeing of women for productive labor.

Women of Ein Haeyal

The removal of patriarchical discriminations begins at birth. No ceremonies distinguish boys from their sisters, for the rite of circumcision on the eighth day has been transformed into a casual visit by the local surgeon, who circumcises the latest crop of baby boys. Thus, the Covenant of Abraham is kept only minimally. All babies are welcome, but there were not, in the early days of the kibbutzim, very many. Even the most emancipated woman was not able to take a full workload in the last months of pregnancy or while nursing her baby; and the kibbutzim could not afford the cost of rearing large families. Contraception or abortion (the latter formally banned by religious proscription but easily and safely obtainable) were used to limit family size to one or two children. At present, although the government uses a variety of incentives to encourage large families, it is noteworthy that large families are only seen among the traditional Jews and on kibbutzim.

In the rearing of children, no differentiation is made by sex.

Boys and girls sleep together in children's houses which are divided by age. A second-generation kibbutz has a nursery, a toddler's house, a kindergarten, a primary school, and until recently had a high-school-age residence. Following high school, everyone is inducted into the army, and upon returning they live in housing for unmarried adults, which does separate men and women. More recently, the separation of boys and girls has begun at adolescence, at least to the extent that they no longer take common showers, chiefly because the early-maturing girls protested at the boys' teasing.

Some sex differentiation can be seen in the occupations held by men and women. Heavy labor is predominantly men's, although this is sometimes protested, while jobs in the kitchen, laundry, and nurseries are held by women. Kitchen and laundry work are considered to be low status and rotated frequently; however, the role of *metapelet,* "child caretaker," is a high-status position and either requires training or is conferred on the most able women in the *mesheq,* women who are not necessarily themselves married or mothers. Indeed, it is thought undesirable for a woman to be caretaker in a house where her own child lives, because she could not be expected to treat the child with the rigorous fairness that is the ideal. Parents are expected only to adore and indulge their children for two or three leisure hours in the afternoon, leaving the rearing to the *metapelet.* Paradoxically, the traditional, ascribed role of mother from which kibbutz social structure sought to liberate women has been transformed into a high-status, achieved role, for which women compete eagerly (Datan 1973).

All the traditional marriage customs were abolished, and in the early years of kibbutzim there were strong attempts to abolish marriage itself. The ideal kibbutz marriage is contracted by going to the kibbutz secretary and applying for a common room. If the relationship fails, the partners return to their former rooms. A child of such a union would not, within the kibbutz itself, suffer the economic or social deprivations usually consequent upon urban divorce, since he lives in any case in the children's house, and all adults refer to all kibbutz children not as "boys and girls" but as *banim u'vanot,* "sons and daughters," an idiom that has spread to the cities. However, Judaic law deprives a bastard of civil rights, and family law in Israel is still administered as it was in the Ottoman Empire, by and for each religious community separately. Thus, couples who were living together and wanted a child would marry, sometimes when the pregnancy was near its conclusion; and it was not uncommon to see a rather incongruous combination of long sleeves—for modesty's sake—and an eight-month pregnancy on a bride. The insistence on virginity is still to be found in the traditional code, and in accordance with it rabbis might enquire whether the girl is a virgin, with the reply that she is. No marriages were ever obstructed by the rabbinate despite the flagrant violation of the custom.

The word *ba'al* is not used for *husband* in Ein Haeyal even today. Instead the word "comrade" (*haver*), which has an array of meanings including "kibbutz member," "friend," "coworker," is used; similarly, the word for wife—*ishah,* meaning "woman"—was discarded for the feminine form of *haver, haverah.* Thus, the original words for *husband* and *wife,* meaning literally "owner" and "woman," were discarded for the expression *comrades,* symbolizing the dissolution of traditional sex roles for a more fluid and egalitarian relationship with almost no sex-role differentiation.

Men of Ein Haeyal

The dissolution of family ties in favor of community bonds appears to have had an impact on the role of the male as a defender. It was suggested earlier that sexual rivalry even within the *hamoula* impairs its unity, that a persistent mistrust weakens social bonds throughout the Arab world, and that this has been a major factor in the collapse of the Arab armies. The question may be raised, then, whether the effect of kibbutz living is to improve the effectiveness of a combat unit, or to dissolve the spirit of competitiveness and aggression entirely.

Both these consequences can be seen in Ein Haeyal, but in different spheres of activity. Kibbutz men are recognized as more effective officers and are more frequently cited for heroism under circumstances where group survival is at stake; a comparison of kibbutz and urban officer candidates would suggest that kibbutz men are more group-oriented and tend more often to base decisions on group welfare.

These tendencies have some curious consequences in academic life. Ein Haeyal students who go on to university often organize study groups that prepare and publish summaries of lecture series, making class attendance unnecessary for students in later years so long as lectures remain unchanged. These publications, while frowned on by university officials, are purchased by the students, who do not value highly the standards of individualistic learning and competition that are being challenged. Similarly, they may write examinations cooperatively and do not perceive this as cheating but rather as the most efficient way to obtain a maximum performance. Urban-reared students who attempt this express guilt upon discovery, but kibbutznikim do not.

Conclusion

In two very similar ecological niches, two strikingly different forms of cultural adaption have been described. The traditional Arab villagers respond to a harsh environment by attempting to increase their strength through large families, which entails a strict differentiation of sex roles and the confinement of women to a life of childbearing and childrearing. It has been suggested that the need for self-defense in the village led gradually to an overvaluation of males and the subordination of females; the male vanity culture that evolved has proved dysfunctional for unity and defense and is disappearing slowly among Arabs who are exposed to more modern environments.

Under very similar environmental conditions, kibbutz settlers increased their strength by reducing the burdens of childrearing through collectivization and communal living, and thus freed women to participate in productive labor. Ideology and technology combined to produce a culture that attempted to erase sex-role differentiation entirely, and that succeeded in drastically modifying traditional roles. Need alone, then, has not shaped adaptive responses, for the needs of the two communities are remarkably similar. Modern medicine has made it possible for the kibbutzim to resolve the problem of reproduction with fewer births, and this is the fundamental difference permitting the kibbutz to give over a higher proportion of the energies of both women and men to the other needs common to the village and the kibbutz: production and defense.

The remarkable differences in sex-role differentiation seen in kibbutz and village, which seem almost to be a caricature of differences between "traditional" and "modern" families in modern society, may obscure a more fundamental similarity, one which can be seen in modern modifications of sex-role differentiation as well. While Kafr Ibrahim glorified its males, Ein Haeyal, at least at first, masculinized everyone in the service of equality, as I have remarked elsewhere (Datan 1973). That is to say, the values of the kibbutz were a modified version of the cult of the warrior. But the warrior was not primarily a conquerer; rather, he was some combination of the Renaissance Man and the peasant—highly educated, dedicated to an egalitarian ideology, and committed to working with his hands. If the best soldiers were kibbutz men, the most articulate and painful soul-searching in the wake of war was to be found in the writings of kibbutz children (*Yaldut Ba'a b'Esh* 1968) and in the dialogues among kibbutz-born soldiers (Shapira 1968). Nevertheless, the dominant values of courage, resilience, a willingness to labor, were masculine: the significant difference between the kibbutz and the village was that the roles expressing these values were available to kibbutz women as well.

The radical abolition of sex roles stimulated in Ein Haeyal by early kibbutz ideology was to provide, surprisingly, support for the strength of traditional family roles for women, as kibbutz women themselves sought to reestablish some of the components of tradition: individuality and femininity in dress; a restoration of some of the prerogatives of maternity by having children sleep in the parental home. Perhaps the ebb and flow of feminist movements, the seeming "regression" to somewhat more traditional roles after the initial impetus of feminism has subsided—seen in the European feminism movement a century ago and in the United States at the start of this century as well as in the roles of kibbutz women—suggests a possible appeal in traditional female roles for women themselves.

The appeal of the traditional female role is easier to infer than to establish, however, for it has seldom been studied seriously. The appeal of masculinity seems obvious: status, power, and freedom in the extrafamilial arena. Feminist movements generally corroborate this appeal through efforts to secure these prerogatives for women as well, and only by default—that is, in such phenomena as the "backlash" response supporting the family-centered role for women—can any relatively direct evidence for the appeal of tradition be seen.

Perhaps some steps toward clarification of this question can be taken through a reconsideration of tradition and of egalitarianism. The traditional female role is family-centered; traditionally women have therefore been vulnerable to the vicissitudes of the reproductive cycle. Feminist movements recognize and often attempt to reject this vulnerability. This can be seen in the efforts of early kibbutz settlers to emancipate women from what was sometimes called "the biological tragedy of femininity," that is to say, to free them to follow the modified warrior-peasant male ideal.

The kibbutzim as a whole absorbed a major component of the female role, bureaucratizing motherhood with designated child caretakers and fostering freer expression of nurturance among men and women alike. Yet there has been no rejection of the soldier-protector male—nor, in the current Middle Eastern political arena, does such a rejection seem likely—and the role modifications on the kibbutz, as in other feminist movements, are conceived as efforts to free women, not men. Why has there been no corresponding role transformation among men?

A reconsideration of the traditional western roles of women

and men suggests some tentative answers. Put simplistically, women bear and rear children, while men obtain sustenance for the family. With modernization has come the possibility of widespread participation in the extrafamilial labor force for women, and increased participation in childrearing for men; but the pivotal position of the traditional woman, who bears the children, and upon whom the succession of generations is dependent, is unchanged. That is to say: feminism leads to a significant increase in options for women, but no corresponding increase in options is available for men.

Thus feminists have indeed achieved a more equitable share in what was traditionally men's extrafamilial status, power, and freedom; but men cannot, finally, obtain a more equitable share in the process of procreation. Perhaps the psychological well-being of the traditional women in our Israeli study and the seeming "regression" to tradition that has followed feminist movements in Europe and America have a common origin in the appeal of childbearing and childrearing. If that is so, then future patterns of sex-role differentiation may, as in the past, continue to reflect an ongoing tension between the benefits of egalitarianism and the appeal of tradition.

References

Berger, Morroe. 1964. *The Arab World Today.* New York: Doubleday Anchor Books.

Bettelheim, Bruno. 1962. *Symbolic Wounds.* Rev. ed. Glencoe, Ill.: Free Press.

Datan, Nancy. 1972. "To Be a Woman in Israel." *School Review* 80: 319–32.

——. 1973. "Your Daughters Shall Prophesy: Ancient and Contemporary Perspectives on the Women of Israel." In M. Curtis and M. Kaplan, eds., *Israel: Social Structure and Change,* pp. 379–88. New Brunswick, N.J.: Transaction Books.

Harkabi, Yehosephat. 1967. "Basic Factors in the Arab Collapse during the Six-Day War." *Orbis* 11: 677–91.

——. 1969. "The Arab-Israeli Confronation." Report submitted to the Ministry of Defense, Jerusalem.

Lerner, Daniel. 1968. *The Passing of Traditional Society: Modernizing the Middle East.* Glencoe, Ill.: Free Press.

Myrdal, Alva and Viola Klein. 1956. *Women's Two Roles: Home and Work.* London: Routledge and Kegan Paul.

Patai, Raphael. 1959. *Sex and Family in the Bible and the Middle East.* New York: Doubleday.

Peters, E. L. 1965. "Aspects of the Family among the Bedouin of Cyrenaica." In M. F. Nimkoff, ed., *Comparative Family Systems,* pp. 121–46. Boston: Houghton Mifflin.

Shapira, Avraham, ed. 1968. *The Seventh Day.* New York: Scribner's.

Spiro, Melford. 1970. *Kibbutz: Venture in Utopia.* New York: Schocken.

Yaldut Ba'a b'Esh (Childhood Come under Fire). 1968. Tel Aviv: Hakibbutz Hameuchad.

Zenner, Walter. 1968. Unpublished anthropological field report prepared for the Israel Institute of Applied Social Research, Jerusalem.

ALICE SCHLEGEL

15

An Overview

THE PAPERS IN this collection have demonstrated the variability of sexual status across societies. We have seen that even
in the most extreme cases, dominance over women is not complete but is mitigated by social conditions or by strategies of autonomy, and that equality of the sexes does not necessarily imply
identity of social roles.

From Stratification to Equality

Our overview begins with the most striking example of male dominance in these case studies, Morocco. Dwyer shows how the
world of women is separated from the world of men, necessitating
the role of "broker" between the sexes under some conditions.
She makes it clear that a climate of male superiority does not,
however, deny gratification to women, a point also made by Datan
for Israeli Arabs; rather, women derive their social and emotional
satisfaction from operating within the female domain. (Relevant
to this is the finding of Gladwin and Sarason [1953, pp. 224–25,
245] that Trukese women, who are subordinate to men, show
up on psychological tests to be less anxious and inhibited than
men.)

   The ideal of male dominance is also a powerful value in Sicily, as discussed by Cronin. There, however, the organization of

men's labor makes it impossible for men to have the time to deal with local bureaucracies: thus they leave this task to women. This division of labor, while not publicly recognized, makes the woman an important contributing member of the household, held in esteem by her husband. By means of wit and mockery, women can be a threat to masculine prestige; indeed, the cultural ideal of male infallibility makes men particularly vulnerable to this threat. Through humor and their social contribution to the household, then, women have some check on male dominance.

While the superiority of men is an unquestioned feature of the Indian value system, Ullrich shows how this is subverted to some degree by lower-caste women. First, it is not so important that lower-caste people maintain the cultural ideal; and second, women's economic contribution to production makes them valued members of the family and gives them autonomy and community recognition that the high-caste women lack.

The distinction between the social categories of female and male is strong among the Southern Bantu peoples. O'Brien points out that women who move into extradomestic statuses of high prestige also move into the social category "male." The subordinate role of wife would be incompatible with a position of high status, so the possibility of this anomaly is removed by restricting these women from conventional marriage. In fact, they take on the male social role by becoming husbands and heads of households. In these societies, women who move up, move out.

The presence of an active, male-supported women's movement in Sudan, with its male-dominant Muslim tradition similar to that of Morocco, takes us rather by surprise. This movement, as described by Fluehr-Lobban, has been cautious about introducing many changes rapidly. Those with some chance of success, such as equal pay for equal work, have been the most readily implemented; those that would encounter strong resistance, such as changes in divorce laws, have been approached less vigorously. Whatever success these women have had can be attributed to their organizing for political action; with the aid of sympathetic men, they created a political and social force that had to be reckoned with by the government and the populace.

For traditional Yoruba society, and to some degree today in spite of the negative effects of colonial domination on the power of women, the office of the Iyalode is indicative of the inclusion of women in the political process. The Iyalode, as Awe points out, was more than merely a nominal representative of the women; rather, she was the channel through which Yoruba women participated in political activity. While women had not the same access to resources or to decision-making positions as men, their important roles in the economic and religious systems made them a force to contend with, particularly as they allied together into a female interest group. The Iyalode stood at the apex of this interest group and operated as an equal in the male council of chiefs.

Lewis' paper on urban Ivory Coast women looks at present-day conditions of these West African women. While education and a modernizing economy have provided new opportunities to women, their economic position is still inferior to that of men. This paper emphasizes not positions of authority that women hold but rather the autonomy they seek and achieve for themselves through work and their own incomes. There are great social and emotional satisfactions to be gained by being active members in the kin network and in female associations, and these roles are enhanced if they can make economic contributions. It is not so much that women are in competition with men as that they are maximizing their ability to move within a system that still places a high value on the traditions of kinship ties and single-sex social groups. An investment in an exclusive marital bond at the expense of other social bonds would jeopardize this ability. This is not to say that women do not strive for good marriages; in fact, their economic contribution and prestige as wage earners make them desirable wives, and as such their position in the marital relation is enhanced. The strategy for these women is to maximize all of their social relationships—with spouses, kin, and associates—through their occupational positions.

Smock also discusses West African women, of Ghana. She emphasizes the decline of female status and autonomy during the colonial period, since the beginning of the twentieth century.

Owing to the patterns imposed by colonial economic and political policies and by the missionaries backed by colonial power, women's access to economic resources and to political or religious offices has markedly declined. It is one of the ironies of history that at the same time the suffragettes were championing feminist causes in England and increasing support for female participation in government, colonial development was guided by Victorian principles that were losing credibility at home. This suggests that when we look at the colonial impact on sex roles and sex status, we pay attention to who is recruited or self-recruited to service in the colonies: it may be that the actions and ideologies of the colonial class itself has as great an impact as the policies initiated by the home government.

The picture is brighter for Yugoslavia, as discussed by Denich, where modernization is bringing greater autonomy to women. The disruptions of World War II altered the immediate position of women drastically, for they fought as partisans alongside men and were not excluded from decision-making positions. The political and economic development of that nation since the War has made it both possible and necessary for women to enter the urban occupational force. The ideal of male dominance, which characterized the earlier peasant economy, is undergoing rapid change, in large part because of the acceptance of the socialist ideology of the equality of all. The pace of change in women's traditional domestic responsibilities has not kept up with changes in female labor, however; thus women, whose time and energy are restricted, are at a disadvantage in achieving high-prestige economic and political positions.

The egalitarian societies in this collection are those in which an ideology of male superiority is absent or at least very weak, and women have the means to gain access to resources and to decision-making roles and positions.

Complementarity of sex role and societal function characterizes the Hopi, discussed by Schlegel. The strength of the matrilocal household and the matrilineal clan and the relative weakness of male-controlled community organization are important factors leading to sexual equality in this society. Another is female ownership of houses and control of land, which, although usually allocated by men, is held in usufruct right by women. Women also control the allocation and exchange of agricultural produce, which is not only the staple food but also a major product for trade with other tribes. These factors provide the material and structural bases for female equality, which is reinforced by the cosmic principle of the female as the source of life.

A rather different relation between the sexes forms the basis for sexual equality among the Bontoc, as discussed by Bacdayan. Here similarity rather than complementarity of sex roles prevents any invidious distinctions from being made. Both sexes participate in most tasks, and the participation of both sexes is equally regarded and valued. This equality apparently characterized earlier times as well, even though the presence of men's houses in which political decisions were ratified would lead us to assume that males were dominant. This may not have been the case: it is likely that men were as much the representatives of the women—conveying women's wishes and opinions to the council—as decision makers for them.

Sex roles among Barbadian blacks are also flexible, as Sutton and Makiesky-Barrow indicate. The social organization of the Barbados plantation around production for trade, with its division into owners and workers—at first slaves, later a rural proletariat—has had profound effects on the position of black women. From its beginning, there was no division between working men and "domestic" women: all worked and derived their status from their labors. Furthermore, neither men nor women of the working class have had much access to positions of political power or social prestige in the larger island system, although both sexes do within the community; so there has been little basis for sexual inequality in these black working-class communities. Both men and women achieve independence through work, and men are able to, and in fact do, take on domestic responsibilities when there is no woman to do so. While there is competition for desired resources such as education, white-collar jobs, and land ownership, such competition is not along sex lines. The colonial model of female subordination was not internalized, and neither their traditions nor their experiences provided a basis for adopting such a view.

Datan compares the role of Israeli women in the kibbutz to the role of women in the Israeli Arab community. Both communities have the same goal of subsistence, and both are adapted to the same environment. The difference, however, is striking: the kibbutz holds an ideal of social and sexual equality, and it utilizes modern techniques of production that have mitigated the necessity for a rigid division of labor between the sexes. In addition, female access to prestigious occupational and administrative positions has been made possible by freeing women from the responsibilities of childcare. Those women who do assume this responsibility for the community are honored. Women, like men, can achieve prestige, authority, and power, positions held in traditional Judaism by men. But there has been a tendency on the part of women to push for a reestablishment of more traditional female roles, through femininity in dress and assumption of responsibility in childcare. This raises a critical question: is this a falling back on traditional roles for status because female success in kibbutz power roles has been less than satisfactory? As Datan points out, the honored role in the kibbutz is heavily masculine, emphasizing physical strength in warfare and production. Thus, the alleged equality of opportunity for women must be seen as a qualified one, as recruitment to positions of authority partially depends upon characteristics disproportionately found among men.

Issues in the Study
of Sexual Stratification

An issue that crops up again and again in these papers is the relation of women to the manner of production and distribution of goods. The organization of production or exchange as a factor or set of factors in conditioning female roles and behavior is examined in Sicily, India, Israel, Barbados, Ghana, and among the Bontoc. The opening of new, generally favorable occupations for women through urbanization and modernization is examined in Yugoslavia and Ivory Coast.

It does not surprise us that women, like men, are affected by the richness and distribution of resources, the manner of production and exchange, and the expansion of opportunities through economic growth. In economic systems in which the domestic group is the unit of production, women may use older children or kin as childminders or resort to such practices as early supplementary feeding (Nerlove 1974) to free themselves for other tasks. Ullrich contrasts the Havik Brahmin women, who do not use other persons for childcare and are very much restricted as a result, with the Divaru women, who do, and thereby are free to take an active role in production. In economic systems where the domestic group is not the unit of production, or where economic avenues to prestige lead away from the home, women are restricted from extradomestic activities unless there are alternate methods of childcare. Again, older children are often utilized, as in Barbados. But where the majority of older children are in school or otherwise occupied, childminders are not always easy to find: Denich speaks of this problem for Yugoslav women. Elite Ivoirian women are enabled to take salaried jobs only because there is a large uneducated class providing a pool of women who cannot take more prestigious jobs; if the economy expands and these women are enabled to go into other occupations, it is likely that childcare will become more of a problem for the elite. It is in societies that are modernizing, rather than fully industrialized, that educated women have the best chance for finding paid child tenders; in this respect, European and American middle-class women are at a disadvantage. The most efficient system for childcare in modern societies may be that of the Israeli kibbutz, where parental responsibilities have been taken over by the community. Thus, economic expansion and the growth of opportunity are not sufficient: also required are social mechanisms, such as freedom from childcare responsibilities, by which women can gain access to these opportunities.

   Another issue of primary importance is the nature and structure of institutions central to societal organization, and the effects
these have on relations between the sexes. Where the household
is a central institution and suprahousehold organization is weak or
decentralized, women are likely to have a strong or equal voice in
decision making.[1] We see this at work among the Hopi and the
Bontoc: although in both societies jural decisions are announced
and ratified by men, the wishes of women expressed informally
are given as much weight as the wishes of men. (In fact, even to
pose the problem in this fashion, as if men constituted one interest
group in opposition to women, is misleading.) Even clan organization among the Hopi does not override the importance of the
household, for the clan is centered on a female-governed household and divides authority between the sexes. In contrast, the
centrality of the Israeli Arab patrilineal clan has the opposite effect: as a male-centered unit for production and defense, it rele-
gates women to a secondary role.
   We find the household central in those societies in which
production is for subsistence or small-scale exchange, defense or
expansion needs do not foster male-centered military organization, and civil or religious bureaucracies are absent. In contrast to
such societies, we see traditional states like Morocco and the
Yoruba polities, where other institutions override the household as
a societal decision-making unit. Even here, it is difficult to make
generalizations about the status of women in such societies; in
both of these examples the primary decision makers are men, but
the opportunities given to women to participate in this process are
considerably different. This is clear from a contrast between the
two civil offices that represent women to the jural domain: the Moroccan 'arifa and the Yoruban Iyalode. The 'arifa is simply a go-
between who does the best she can for the women under her
charge. The Iyalode, on the other hand, speaks for women's interests. Unlike the 'arifa, she speaks from the power of women, not
from the power of men. The importance of women in Yoruba society beyond the household, and the basis for the power of the
Iyalode, is the prominent role women play in economic and religious institutions, particularly in the market. Moroccan women,

who do not participate in central institutions, have no such basis for power.

A discussion of the position of women in complex societies must take into account the differential locations, and the structural contexts of these locations, of women in different status groupings. It is often the case that only the highest status groups have the resources that enable them to fulfill the roles prescribed by societal ideals. Thus, it is Mafioso families in Sicily and the Havik Brahmin families in southern India that can afford to keep women secluded in the home away from the public eye. The differential in allocation of resources between social classes in Ivory Coast has marked effects upon the strategies that women can employ toward financial independence, personal autonomy, and social support outside the home. This is also true in Ghana, where elite women have actually lost power vis-à-vis men as a result of colonial and current developmental policies.

Relevant to this question of status location is the somewhat surprising success the women's movement has had in Sudan. It is quite likely that this is due in part to this movement's originating within the educated elite, rather than from within a subordinate class; it has been but one part of a general liberalization movement among the elite.

Like the Divaru women in southern India, lower-class women in Barbados had greater opportunity to achieve sexual equality than did women of the higher-status colonial class. The Barbadian plantation was and is a productive institution in which both sexes work, and neither sex has greater decision-making power than the other—in fact, neither sex in the working class has much power at all. The result for Barbados blacks has been the absence of any material basis for sexual stratification under the traditional economic system.

Interwoven with economic forces and social structure, the ideology of sex roles provides a model for behavior that can be activated to greater or lesser degrees. We have already looked at the contrast between Mafioso and non-Mafioso families in Sicily, and the Havik and Divaru castes in India, in implementing a cultural ideal of male dominance and female seclusion.

An ideology of female equality among the Hopi and the Bontoc provides a strong motive and justification for expressions of female authority and autonomy, behavior that encounters resistance in societies that perceive men as superior, even when these societies are moving toward the liberalization of women, as in Sudan. Those male-dominant societies that do allow women to move into high-status roles may do so by socially masculinizing women: female husbands among the Bantu are not wives, as this subordinate role is incompatible with the superordinate role of husband, with the result that these women are regarded not so much the equals of men as socially male.

Denich's paper is of considerable interest in reference to sex-role ideology, for the Yugoslav society she describes is moving toward a new set of values regarding female behavior, one that is consonant with the need in an industrializing society for female participation in the urban labor force. Unfortunately, there is a lag between approved female role behavior outside and within the home, so that these women carry the double burden of new occupational participation and traditional domestic responsibilities. It would seem that Yugoslav men welcome the addition of women to the work force where they are needed but resist liberalization in the home, which would cut down on their own free time and energy.

Conclusion

What have we learned from this collection? What sorts of regularities and variability do we observe from this cross-cultural look at sex roles and sexual stratification?

The broadest generalization we can make is that the emergence of sexual stratification in any society is multidimensional, and the forms it acquires are the unfolding consequences of many different kinds of forces intermingling over time. In this respect, stratification or equality are responses to economic, political, social, and ideological conditions internal to the society or impinging on it from its relations with other societies. Of these external relations, we can regard three as critical: relations of exchange, relations of power, and relations of goal direction.

All of the societies we have looked at engage in relations of exchange with other societies—all are involved to some degree in an intersocietal trade network. This effects the relations of production and exchange within the society, and in turn the position of the sexes in the economic system.

Relations of power encompass political alliances or warfare between polities where power is balanced or in question, and relations of dominance and submission between unequal polities. Relations of power also are important causal factors in the social organization of subordinate groups, such as exploited classes or social groups within a society. The effects of political subordination emerge most clearly in Smock's paper on colonial domination in Ghana, whose internal organization was until recently more responsive to imposed conditions than to indigenous developments.

Relations of goal direction involve the assumption by one society of' the goals developed in another, which bring in train changes in ideology to support these goals and changes in internal organization to implement them. This situation is emerging in Yugoslavia and Sudan, and it has reached its most developed form in the Israeli kibbutz. This last case is very instructive, for the goals of European social egalitarianism were implemented with full accord by all involved in the construction of a new social system.

It is of the utmost importance, therefore, in assessing the forces leading to stratification or equality, to consider sex roles as responsive both to the internal dynamic of the society and to the external conditions to which the society itself must respond. It is critical to examine central institutions in the society and the degree to which they favor one sex or the other. Where the household or lineage is central, as it is among the Hopi and the Bontoc, or where the economic system involves more or less equal tasks and decision-making roles, as on the Barbadian plantation or in the Israeli kibbutz, the relation between the sexes tends to be balanced and complementary. Where economic production favors male control, as in colonial Ghana, or where male-controlled military activities are central, as in the feuding pattern among Israeli Arab clans, male activities become predominant and men come to be the primary decision makers in almost all aspects of social life.

Inequality between the sexes is not unidimensional; rather, each sex in any society has primary control over certain activities, and the rewards and power accruing to each sex depend upon the centrality of these activities to the society as a whole. Even in the most male-dominant society, Morocco, women have clear areas of control within the household, and male interference in these areas is censured by both sexes. It may be that the increasing pull toward domesticity that Datan finds in the Israeli kibbutz represents a desire on the part of women to gain control over an area, that of childrearing, which they feel they have lost. There may, of course, be more fundamental reasons for women's desire to reestablish primacy in childrearing, as I have discussed in the first paper.

It is important to recognize that even in sexually stratified societies, there are mitigating circumstances that check male dominance and permit women to gain some measure of autonomy. Surely one of the most important is the solidarity within the family and kin group that flows from intimacy, common needs and goals, and joint concern for the well-being of children. No matter how much interests and access to resources of the sexes may diverge, there are still those ties of affection and loyalty that bind father to daughter, mother to son, brother to sister, and husband to wife. The family and kin group may be the arena within which relations of sexual inequality are played out, but it is also an arena within which bonds of solidarity operate. It is no accident that the role of mother receives so much prominence in many male-dominant societies, for women are the channel through which men become fathers. Thus, males enter the system through the reproductive and nurturant activities of women, and this critical social function cannot be denied. Kinship roles, and the necessary dependency of one sex upon the other, provide the basis for relationships of solidarity that mitigate the free play of sexual dominance.

We have observed more specific examples of mitigation of male dominance, cases where women employ strategies as a check to loss of autonomy. The prominence of humor and mockery as practiced by Sicilian women is one such mitigating strategy, as is the use Moroccan women make of the 'arifa for deceiving men or making them amenable. Such strategies vary from society to society.

It is clear that in all known human societies, gender provides the basis for a fundamental division in social function. In no society to date do men take primary responsibility for the care of young children, nor do women take a principal role in organizing and implementing activities of offense or defense, although the degree to which the opposite sex is involved in these activities varies greatly from society to society. Even where division of labor by sex is minimal or nonexistent, as it seems to have been for the Tasaday before contact with the outside world (Nance 1975), this division of function occurs.[2] Division of function, however, does not necessarily lead to stratification; rather, it can lead to balanced complementarity. Sexual stratification, then, is not panhuman but rather poses a problem that must be explained, for each society in terms of the forces to which it is responsive, and cross-culturally in terms of variables that exist across societies. It is an enormously complex problem, and a challenging one.

Notes

1. Friedl (1975) claims that sexual stratification exists even among some loosely organized foraging societies where the household is a central institution. She relates this to control by men over the meat supply, a scarce and valued resource that, in her view, can be utilized in extradomestic exchange by men as a basis for prestige and power. In the cases she describes, however, a central economic institution is the hunting party made up of men of different households under the leadership of one man. Among the inland Eskimo, a successful and generous hunter is accepted as the leader of caribou drives; among the maritime Eskimo, the owner of

a boat leads the whaling crew. In neither case is economic decision making equally or randomly distributed among men.

2. Nance relates that when visitors from the outside world first approached the Tasaday, they were met by men while women and children remained back in the caves where the visitors were conducted, so that protection would appear to be a part of the male role. In this society without formal centralized authority, there is some evidence that the individual with greatest influence and who received the most deference was a woman.

References

Friedl, Ernestine. 1975. *Women and Men: An Anthropologist's View*. New York: Holt, Rinehart and Winston.

Gladwin, Thomas and Seymour B. Sarason. 1953. *Truk: Man in Paradise*. Viking Fund Publications in Anthropology, Number 20. New York: Wenner-Gren Foundation for Anthropological Research.

Nance, John. 1975. *The Gentle Tasaday*. New York: Harcourt Brace Jovanovich.

Nerlove, Sara B. 1974. "Women's Workload and Infant Feeding Practices: A Relationship with Demographic Implications." *Ethnology* 13: 207–14.

Index of Names

Abiola, J. D. E., 144, 154
Abu-Lughod, Janet, 129
Addo, Nelson, 203
Adizes, Ichak, 243
Alland, Alexander, Jr., 22
Aryee, A. F., 205
Ashton, Hugh, 115
Awe, Bolanle, 144, 346

Babayemi, S. O., 150
Bacdayan, Albert S., 31, 270, 289, 348
Bacdayan, Carolyn B., 290
Bailey, F. G., 61
Banfield, Edward, 69, 71
Barnes, J. A., 111
Barnes, Sandra, 122
Barth, Fredrick, 61
Barton, J., 110
Barzini, Luigi, 69
Beattie, J. H. M., 121
Berger, Morroe, 333

Biobaku, S. O., 154, 159
Blacking, J., 115
Boserup, Ester, 31, 192, 203, 242
Brokensha, David W., 210
Brown, Judith K., 23
Brunot, Louis, 47, 55, 62
Buric, Olivera, 225, 228, 231, 232, 233, 234, 236, 242
Busia, K. A., 147, 197

Caldwell, John C., 207, 209, 210
Chapman, Charlotte Gower, 69, 72
Chagnon, Napoleon, 30
Choderow, Nancy, 15, 245
Colecraft, E. A., 206, 210
Collins, Randall, 14
Covello, Leonard, 71
Cronin, Constance, 67, 69, 344

Datan, Nancy, 35, 326, 330, 337, 340, 344, 349

Davis, Angela, 296
Degraft-Johnson, K. T., 206, 210
Denich, Bette, 215, 217, 221, 223, 230, 232, 241, 350, 353
Denitch, Bogdan, 227
Durkheim, Emile, 31
Dwyer, Daisy Hilse, 41, 45, 135, 344
Dzhanashvili, M. G., 4

Ellenberger, D. F., 114
Engels, Freidrich, 2, 10, 11, 12
Engerman, Stanley, 293
Erlich, Vera, 217
Evans-Pritchard, E. E., 110, 113, 148

Fadipe, N. A., 145, 151
Fallers, Lloyd, 92
Fallers, Margaret, 92
Farran, Charles, 120, 121
Feibleman, James K., 19, 31
Field, M. J., 197, 198, 209
First-Delić, Ruža, 232
Fluehr-Lobban, Carolyn, 127, 345
Fogel, Robert, 293
Folson, B. D. G., 198
Forde, C. D., 250
Fortes, Meyer, 196, 199, 200
Foster, Philip, 194
Fox, Robin, 29
Freilich, Morris, 318
Friedl, Ernestine, 13, 21, 26, 37, 111

Genovese, Eugene, 295, 297
Ghansah, D. K., 205
Gil, B., 205, 206, 210
Gladwin, Thomas, 344
Gluckman, M., 112, 115, 120
Goldschmidt, Walter, 217
Goode, William J., 27
Gough, E. K., 111
Graham, C. K., 202
Greenfield, Sidney, 307
Griaule, Marcel, 246
Griffiths, John, 202
Gutman, Herbert, 295, 297

Handler, Jerome, 323
Harkabi, Yehosephat, 333
Harper, Edward B., 8, 95, 107, 108
Harper, Judy Wiltse, 102
Harries, C. L., 114
Harris, Marvin, 30
Herskovits, Melville J., 19, 111, 123
Hill, Polly, 203
Hinderer, Anna, 147, 152
Hong, Lawrence K., 200
Huber, H., 111, 112
Huffman, Ray, 111
Hunnius, Gerry, 243
Hutchinson, Ira W., 200

Ibrahim, Fatma Ahmed, 138

Jacobs, Sue-Ellen, 4
Johnson, S., 153
Jones, David E., 20

Kaberry, Phyllis M., 2
Kanter, Rosabeth M., 6
Keesing, Roger M., 32
Kimble, David, 204
Klein, Vida, 327
Krige, E. J., 111, 112, 113, 115, 117, 119, 120, 121, 122, 123
Krige, J. D., 111, 112, 113
Kunitz, Stephen J., 265
Kunkel, Evalyn J., 217

Lamphere, Louise, 111
Landes, Ruth, 2
Langness, L. L., 30
Law, R. C. C., 149
Laydevant, le R. P. J., 114
Leach, E. R., 120
Leacock, Eleanor B., 11, 12, 215
Lebeuf, Annie M. D., 145
Lerner, Daniel, 327, 333
Lestrade, G. P., 113, 115
Lévi-Strauss, Claude, 7
LeVine, Robert A., 113
Levy, Marion J., Jr., 18
Levy, Reuben, 4
Lewis, Barbara C., 7, 160, 190, 203, 346
Lewis, Oscar, 4
Little, Kenneth, 209
Liu, William T., 200
Lloyd, P. C., 149, 207, 209
Lobban, Richard, 130

Mabogunje, A. L., 145
Makiesky-Barrow, Susan, 292, 302, 305, 348

Manoukian, Madeline, 196, 197, 198
Marx, Karl, 10, 31
Mason, Otis T., 2
Mathurin, Lucille, 295, 296
Mayer, P., 113
McCall, D., 196, 203
Mead, Margaret, 2
Meek, C. K., 113
Mercier, L., 47, 55
Michaux-Bellaire, E., 47, 55
Mitchell, Juliet, 242
Mönnig, H. O., 114
Moss, Leonard, 69
Murdock, George Peter, 23, 110, 111, 114, 284, 290
Murphy, Robert F., 8, 20
Murphy, Yolanda, 8, 20
Myers, Lena, 323
Myrdal, Alva, 327

Nadel, S. F., 147, 166, 191
Nagata, Shuichi, 251, 268
Nance, John, 356, 357
Nerlove, Sara B., 24, 350
Nicolaison, Johannes, 6
Norbeck, Edward, 28
Nukunya, G. K., 196, 200

O'Brien, Denise, 109, 345
Oluwo Folasade Labosinde, 159
Onwuejeogwu, Michael, 159
Oppong, Christine, 182, 198, 207, 208
Ortiz, Alfonso, 246

Ortner, Sherry B., 15, 16, 245, 323
O'Sullivan, H., 110
Otto, Barbara, 226, 227, 230, 233

Parsons, Elsie Clews, 2, 268
Patai, Raphael, 327, 334
Paulme, Denise, 198
Peristiany, J. G., 132
Peters, E. L., 331
Pitkin, Donald, 72
Provost, Catarina, 284, 290

Rattray, R. S., 197
Rawles, John, 19
Rivière, Peter G., 33, 120, 246
Rosaldo, Michelle Zimbalist, 111, 215, 245, 288
Roscoe, John, 121
Rowbotham, Sheila, 241

Sacks, Karen, 12, 289
Sahlins, Marshall, 23, 32, 33
Salmon, G., 55
Sanday, Peggy R., 12, 13, 195, 288
Sarason, Seymour B., 344
Schlegel, Alice, 5, 90, 200, 245, 250, 267, 347
Schwellnus, P. E., 115
Scott, William Henry, 289
Seligman, B., 111, 121, 123
Seligman, C. G., 111, 121, 123
Shapira, Avraham, 340
Shepher, Joseph, 25
Sidel, Ruth, 241

Simic, Andrei, 241
Smock, Audry Chapman, 31, 192, 346
Snell, G. S., 114, 115, 120
Spiro, Melford, 336
Stayt, H. A., 114, 115
Stephen, Alexander M., 260
Stoffle, Richard W., 300
Sudarkasa, Niara, 166
Sutton, Constance, 292, 305, 323, 348
Swanson, Guy, 33

Tait, David, 196
Talbot, P. A., 113
Taylor, Maida, 226, 227, 230, 233
Tettah, P. A., 198, 204, 211
Thomas, Northcote, 110
Thompson, Walter H., 69
Tiger, Lionel, 14, 25, 35
Tillion, Germaine, 131
Titiev, Mischa, 253, 259, 267
Tooker, Elizabeth, 33
Turner, Jonathan H., 19

Uchendu, Victor, 122
Ullrich, Helen E., 94, 95, 345, 350

Van Warmelo, N. J., 115, 116, 117, 118, 119, 121
Vallenga, Dorothy Dee, 198, 204, 210
Vilakazi, Absolam, 114

Wallace, Anthony F. C., 30
Whitfield, G. M. B., 112, 114
Whyte, Martin, 17, 26, 27, 37
Wilson, Peter J., 296
Wolf, Eric, 242

Yang, C. K., 242

Zečevic, Andjelka, 231, 232, 233, 242
Zenner, Walter, 331

Subject Index

Abidjan, 163–64

Acculturation, 122, 280

Africa: traditions in New World, 296 ff.; *see also* Bantu; Ivory Coast; Yoruba; Sudan; East Africa; South Africa; West Africa

Afro-Americans, 308

Age: and female status, 20, 197, 211, 251, 297; and economic activity, 168 ff.

Agriculture, female participation in, 97–98, 106, 196, 203, 303–4, 331

Akan, *see* Ghana

Alimony (Sudan), 140

Arab village in Israel, 327 ff., 349

'*Arifa,* 42, 45, 47 ff., 351

Asia, Southeast, *see* Southeast Asia

Associations: men's, 255, 257; mutual help, 279; rotating credit, 314; *see also* Women's associations

Authority, 8, 9, 89–90, 98 ff., 148, 157; *see also* Households; Power

Autonomy, 9, 198, 240

Autonomy, female: in India, 98 ff.; in Ghana, 198–99; in Yugoslavia, 240; among Hopi, 250; in Barbados, 294, 317

Bantu, female husbands among: Southern, 109 ff.; Interlacustrine, 111

Barbados, 293 ff., 348, 352

Berdache, 4

Birth control, 68, 266, 333

Bonds, bonding: male, 14, 37, 333; female, 29; mother-child, 35, 201, 207, 297, 319; with kin, 163, 200; to community, 336, 338; *see also* Associations; Women's associations; Women's social groups; Kin

Bontoc, 31, 270 ff., 348

Brahmin, Havik, 94 ff., 104 ff., 352

Bride price, 331

Caribbean, see Barbados

Castes (India), see Brahmin; Divaru

Central institution, 9, 18 ff., 25, 26, 29, 30, 31, 34, 36, 351; warfare as, 262; household as, 351, 356; market as, 351

Ceremonies: Hopi, 255 ff.; see also Religion; Ritual(s)

Child bearing: effects on women, 15, 23, 35, 36, 329, 339; importance to women, 166, 188, 319, 326, 330, 342; see also Motherhood; Reproduction

Child care, 23, 35, 36, 350; in India, 97; in Sudan, 132; in Yugoslavia, 229; in kibbutzim, 336

Children: career expectations for (Yugoslavia), 224 ff.; male and female, treatment of, 224, 274 ff., 336–37

Child socialization practices, 15, 36, 250, 275–76, 336; Sicilian, 80–81; Israeli, 336

China, Chinese, 241, 242, 246

Christianity, 135, 146, 271; see also Missionary influence

Circumcision, female, 132–33, 137, 142

Clan: matrilineal (Hopi), 252–53; patrilineal (Israeli Arab), 330 ff.

Class, social, see Social stratification

Collectivization, see Kibbutz

Colonialism: and status of women, 11, 27, 30–31, 346–47, 145–46, 158, 193, 202 ff., 293; in Sudan, 128–29; and Yoruba, 145 ff.; in Ghana, 201 ff.; and Bontoc, 273; in Barbados, 294 ff.

Communist Party: in Sudan, 136, 139, 141; in Yugoslavia, 218

Conflicts over career, women's, 306

Cooperation: between men and women, 267; mechanistic, 270 ff.; see also Associations

Cosmic dualism, see Sexual dualism

Decision-making roles, see Authority; Households; Political systems

Defense, effects on social organization, 328–29, 333, 338, 340; see also Protection

Divaru, 94 ff., 102 ff., 352

Division of labor, sexual, 5–6, 12, 25 ff., 35, 205, 295, 348, 356; in Ghana, 194, 209; among Bontoc, 281 ff.; see

Division of labor (*Continued*) *also* Occupational sex-typing; Occupations; Task interchangeability

Divorce: in Morocco, 46, 53, 58; in Sudan, 130; in Ivory Coast, 177; in Ghana, 210; in Yugoslavia, 217; Hopi, 265–66; *see also* Marital instability

Domains, public and domestic, 17, 123, 131

East Africa, female husbands in, 110 ff.

Ecology, responses to affecting women, 326 ff.

Economic contributions of women: and power, 94, 276; in India, 94, 98; in Sudan, 131; *see also* Division of labor; Labor-force participation; Occupations

Economic development, *see* Modernization

Education: in Sicily, 76; and position of women, 162; and social stratification, 162; as an economic resource, 165 ff., 182–83, 300; in Ghana, 194; in Barbados, 299 ff.

Emigration, 68, 321

Eskimo, 26, 37, 356–57

Evaluation, 7–8; of women, 245, 251, 263, 320; of men, 330, 340

Ewe, *see* Ghana

Exchange, relations of, 12, 13, 354

Family, 18; nuclear, 72, 78, 270, 285; in Sicily, 72 ff.; extended, 178; in Ghana, 205 ff.; in Yugoslavia, 217, 241; Israeli Arab, 327

Fatherhood, 111, 201, 253

Female chiefs, 115 ff., 144, 145, 197, 268

Female husbands, 109 ff., 345

Fertility, evaluation of, 26, 222, 262 ff., 267, 329; *see also* Birth control; Motherhood

Financial autonomy of women, 178 ff., 196

Foragers, 26, 37

Friendship: in Sicily, 83; in Yugoslavia, 221

Ga, *see* Ghana

Ghana, 192 ff., 346

Goal-direction, relations of, 354

Government, *see* Political systems

Groom service, 248

Homosexuality, 4, 109, 123, 134

Honor and shame complex (Sicilian), 68, 74

Hopi, 9, 19, 25, 28, 32, 245 ff., 347

Households: domestic unit of production, 24, 350; female heads of, 102, 206, 246, 305;

Ghanaian, 199, 208; Yugoslav, 232 ff.; Hopi, 246 ff., Barbadian, 305
Housework: in India, 96–97; in Yugoslavia, 228 ff.; in Barbados, 311
Humor, as social control, 86
Husbands, roles of: in Sicily, 72, 78–79; in Ghana, 199; among Hopi, 247 ff., 262; in Barbados, 312; in the kibbutz, 338

Ideology, 14, 16, 31 ff.; of Hopi, 260 ff., 353; of female equality, 323, 353
Ijesa kingdom, 154 ff.
India, 94 ff., 345
Industrial mode of production, 26 ff.
Industrialization, 219 ff.; and status of women, 27; see also Modernization
Inheritance, 6, 29; in Sicily, 70; in India, 107; among Hopi, 247; among Bontoc, 275
Iroquois, 20, 30, 33
Islam, Islamic culture, 4, 41 ff., 129 ff.
Israel, 6, 326 ff., 349
Italy, see Sicily
Ivoirian Civil Code, 178 ff.
Ivory Coast, 161 ff., 346
Iyalode, 144 ff., 346, 351

Japan, 28
Judicial domain, see Law

Karnataka State, 94
Kibbutz, 25, 35, 335 ff., 354
Kin, as source of support, 29, 346; in Ivory Coast, 185, 187–88; in Ghana, 200, 206; in Yugoslavia, 221; in Barbados, 307–8
Kinship: matrilineal, 19, 197, 201, 246, 250; patrilineal, 19, 145; and sexual status, 29; bilateral, 72, 272
Khartoum, 129
Kwaio, 32

Labor, division of, see Division of Labor
Labor force participation, women's: in India, 97–98; and status of women, 106, 163 ff., 173 ff.; in Ivory Coast, 163 ff., 193; in Yugoslavia, 219 ff.; in Barbados, 293, 298 ff.; in the kibbutz, 339
Law: Moroccan, 45 ff.; Italian, 70; Islamic (Sudan), 130, 132; Judaic, 334, 338
Love: hunger for in Sicily, 81, 87 ff.; as basis for marriage, 187, 205–6, 273, 310

Mafia, mafioso, 80, 352
Male dominance, 8, 14, 20, 123, 334, 344; effects of on women, 44; mitigating strategies, 62, 86, 90–91, 101, 162–63; effect of on men, 65, 333; mitigating

Male dominance (*Continued*) circumstances, 65, 345, 355–56; and role of mother, 355

Markets: Iyalode's authority over, 145–46; *see also* Trading and marketing

Marriage: as alliance, 29; and political authority, 119 ff.; in Ivory Coast, 161 ff.; importance of to women, 166, 188 ff., 248, 309–10; in the kibbutz, 337–38

Marriage types: first cousin, 130, 133; polygynous, 138, 142, 204; monogamous, 182, 204; arranged, 217, 219, 273; *see also* Love

Marital conflict, 58, 182, 188, 210, 231, 250

Marital instability, 205, 209, 310; *see also* Divorce

Marital relationships, 207; and wives' employment, 162

Marital rights and duties, *see* Husbands; Wives

Matrifocality, 313

Mechanistic cooperation, 270; *see also* Sexual similarity

Mediators, women as, 65, 85

Men, *see* Fatherhood; Husbands; Male Dominance

Men's houses, 268, 277, 288

Menopause, female status after, 20; *see also* Age

Menstrual taboos, 104–5

Missionary influence: in Ghana, 193, 202, 204; among Bontoc, 271

Moala, 32

Modernization, effects on women, 158, 192 ff., 219 ff., 265 ff., 300, 327, 342

Morocco, 41 ff., 344

Motherhood, 7, 35, 294, 319, 341, 355; and female status, 15, 245–46, 249, 262; *see also* Child bearing

Muslim cultures, *see* Islam

Nature/culture and gender, 15–16, 33

Occupational sex-typing, 226, 266, 337

Occupations open to women, 36, 194, 220 ff., 226 ff., 298, 304, 349

October Revolution, Sudanese, 139

Ondo kingdom, 154 ff.

Owu-Ijebu kingdom, 153–54

Oyo kingdom, 150 ff.

Peasants, peasantry: Latin American, 6; Sicilian, 69 ff.; Yugoslav, 216 ff., 220–21, 347

Philippines, *see* Bontoc, Tasaday

Political systems: women as leaders in, 113, 115 ff., 267, 268, 269, 277; women's par-

ticipation in, 136 ff., 144, 150, 186, 197, 233 ff., 253 ff., 277 ff., 290, 301, 326, 346, 348; see also Female chiefs, Iyalode
Power: and female status, 8, 9, 89–90, 157, 215; relations of, 354
Prestige and sexual status, 7 ff.; see also Evaluation
Priestesses, 150, 157, 256
Procreation; and unit of production, 24 ff.; see also Child bearing
Production: and sexual status, 10 ff., 28, 196; relations of, 11, 24; modes of, 23 ff.; unit of, 24 ff., 350; and procreation, see Procreation; female contributions to, see Agriculture; Occupations
Property, control over, 6, 10, 12, 196
Protection, of women by men, 262, 357
Protest movements, women's, 156

Rape, 96–97
Religion: in Sudan, 130; female participation in, 130, 150, 157; in Barbados, 314–15; see also Ceremonies; Christianity; Islam; Missionary influence; Priestesses

Reproduction and female status, 15, 245, 319
Residence: matrilocal, 29, 246 ff.; patrilocal, 29; neolocal, 68, 272; mother-child household, 199
Rewards and sexual status, 5 ff.
Ritual(s): Indian women and, 100, 104 ff., 278; Iyalode and, 155; Hopi women's, 247, 256 ff.

Satire, 85–86
Serbia, see Yugoslavia
Sex role change: in India, 107–8; in Sudan, 136 ff.; in Ghana, 201 ff.; in Yugoslavia, 218 ff.; among Hopi, 265 ff.; in Barbados, 320–21
Sex roles, 2, 67, 354 ff.; in Sicily, 73 ff.; among Hopi, 246 ff., 252 ff., 262–63; in Barbados, 317 ff.; among Israeli Arabs, 329 ff.; in kibbutz, 336 ff.
Sexual activity: extramarital, 171, 182, 198, 211, 250, 259, 267, 312; premarital, 198; positive attitude toward, 297, 318–19; see also Homosexuality; Virginity
Sexual complementarity, 264, 266; see also Sexual similarity
Sexual dualism, symbolic, 25, 32 ff., 246

Sexual equality, 2, 246, 251, 263, 274, 280, 334, 348; ideology of, 6, 334

Sexual inequality, 2, 3, 215, 355; theories of, 10 ff.

Sexual interdependence, 246, 260, 264 ff.

Sexual segregation, separation, 17, 67, 198, 245; in Morocco, 42 ff.; in India, 106; in Sudan, 130; in Ghana, 199; in Yugoslavia, 230

Sexual similarity, 244, 246, 340; see also Sexual complementarity

Sexual status, 1, 8; and economic relations, 10 ff.; and femaleness, 14 ff.; assessment of, 17 ff.; and social status, 20, 211, 352; and achievement, 21, 35 ff., 147, 302, 317, 337; determinants of, 22 ff.; variability of, 34; in Barbados, 301 ff.; and aging, see Age

Sexual stratification, 1, 3 ff., 14, 353; theories of, 1, 16–17; and social stratification, 5, 292 ff.; see also Sexual inequality

Sicily, 67 ff., 344

Slaves, slavery, 7; and 'arifa's position, 55 ff.; in Barbados, 294 ff.

Socialism, 241

Social mobility, 172, 302

Social networks, see Kin; Women's Associations; Women's social groups

Social status, 20, 21, 352; achieved, ascribed, 122

Social stratification: in Sicily, 76; in Barbados, 292 ff.

South Africa, female husbands in, 110 ff.

Southeast Asia, 192; see also Bontoc; Tasaday

Status of women, see Sexual status

Strategies of women, see Male dominance

Subsistence and female status, 23; see also Agriculture; Labor-force participation

Sudan, 127 ff., 345

Sudanese women's movement, 136 ff.

Sudanese Women's Union, 137

Symbols, symbolization: Hopi, 15, 252–53; in Barbados, 319; see also Sexual dualism

Tasaday, 356, 357

Task interchangeability, 284 ff.

Trade and sexual status, 30, 164–65

Trading and marketing: West African women, 113, 161, 203; Ivoirian women, 164 ff.

Transvestitism, 4

Turkey, women's groups in, 92

Urbanization, *see* Modernization

Virginity, 51–52, 63, 73, 331

Warfare: and female status, 12, 13, 19, 20, 26, 30, 274; Iyalode's role in, 145, 151–52, 154; Hopi, 255; as central institution, 262; Bontoc, 273–74; *see also* Defense; Protection

West Africa: female husbands in, 110; female participation in government, 144 ff.; female traders in, 113, 161, 203; women's roles in, 193, 296, 317

West Indies, *see* Barbados

Wives, roles of: in Sicily, 72, 78–79; in Barbados, 311; in the kibbutz, 338

Women's associations, 29, 346; Moroccan, 56; Ivoirian, 185–87, 189; Yugoslav, 218; Hopi, 256 ff.

Women's social groups: in Sicily, 77 ff.; in Turkey, 92; in Ghana, 198; among Bontoc, 280; in Barbados, 316

Worker's self-management (Yugoslavia), 235 ff.

Yoruba, 110, 122, 144 ff., 166, 246

Yugoslavia, 4, 215 ff., 347, 353